Lecture Notes in Artificial Intelligence 12311

Subseries of Lecture Notes in Computer Science

More information about this series at http://www.springer.com/series/1244

Ian Watson · Rosina Weber (Eds.)

Case-Based Reasoning Research and Development

28th International Conference, ICCBR 2020
Salamanca, Spain, June 8–12, 2020
Proceedings

Springer

Editors
Ian Watson
School of Computer Science
University of Auckland
Auckland, New Zealand

Rosina Weber
College of Computing and Informatics
Drexel University
Philadelphia, PA, USA

ISSN 0302-9743 ISSN 1611-3349 (electronic)
Lecture Notes in Artificial Intelligence
ISBN 978-3-030-58341-5 ISBN 978-3-030-58342-2 (eBook)
https://doi.org/10.1007/978-3-030-58342-2

LNCS Sublibrary: SL7 – Artificial Intelligence

This Springer imprint is published by the registered company Springer Nature Switzerland AG
The registered company address is: Gewerbestrasse 11, 6330 Cham, Switzerland

Preface

This volume contains the papers presented at the 28th International Conference on Case-Based Reasoning (ICCBR 2020), which was held June 8–12, 2020. ICCBR is the premier annual meeting of the Case-Based Reasoning (CBR) research community. The theme of ICCBR 2020 was "CBR Across Bridges," aiming to help guide future developments in CBR by encouraging members from within and outside the CBR community to discuss new ideas.

Previous ICCBRs, including the merged European Workshops and Conferences on CBR, were as follows: Otzenhausen, Germany (1993); Chantilly, France (1994); Sesimbra, Portugal (1995); Lausanne, Switzerland (1996); Providence, USA (1997); Dublin, Ireland (1998); Seeon Monastery, Germany (1999); Trento, Italy (2000); Vancouver, Canada (2001); Aberdeen, UK (2002); Trondheim, Norway (2003); Madrid, Spain (2004); Chicago, USA (2005); Fethiye, Turkey (2006); Belfast, UK (2007); Trier, Germany (2008); Seattle, USA (2009); Alessandria, Italy (2010); Greenwich, UK (2011); Lyon, France (2012); Saratoga Springs, USA (2013); Cork, Ireland (2014); Frankfurt, Germany (2015); Atlanta, USA (2016); Trondheim, Norway (2017); Stockholm, Sweden (2018); and Otzenhausen, Germany (2019).

Of course 2020 was a very unusual year. ICCBR 2020 was planned to be held in Salamanca, Spain, but as it became obvious that travel in June would be impossible, due to the COVID-19 pandemic, a decision was made to hold the conference virtually.

ICCBR 2020 received 64 submissions from 23 countries, spanning Europe, North America, and Asia. Three Program Committee members reviewed each submission. Papers for which the reviewers did not reach consensus were referred to members of the ICCBR Advisory Council and program chairs for meta-review. Of the 64 submissions, 22 (34%) were selected for oral presentation. There were no posters in 2020 as delivering them was deemed impractical. Instead they were given as oral presentations.

ICCBR 2020 began as the community assembled online on the afternoon of June 8, 2020. The only formal activity on that day was for the Doctoral Consortium (DC) participants, who met their mentors for the first time and prepared for their upcoming presentations. The DC provides opportunities for PhD students to share and obtain mutual feedback on their research and career objectives with senior CBR researchers and peers. After the DC session, all conference attendees gathered together for an online social event.

The first full day of the conference started with an opening session that provided information on how the online conference would be run. This session concluded with a tribute to Professor Miltos Petridis who sadly died in April from COVID-19. Miltos was a very regular attendee at ICCBR, he had been a local chair when the conference was held in Greenwich, UK, and was a long-standing member of the Program Committee. A moment's silence in Miltos' honor was followed by the presentation of the Miltos Petridis Best Paper Award. This was awarded to Mark Keane and Barry

Smyth of University College Dublin, Ireland, for their paper "Good Counterfactuals and Where to Find Them: A Case-Based Technique for Generating Counterfactuals for Explainable AI (XAI)." An honorable mention was made to Ikechukwu Nkisi-Orji1, Nirmalie Wiratunga, Chamath Palihawadana, Juan A. Recio-Garcia, and David Corsar for their paper "Clood CBR: Towards Microservices Oriented Case-Based Reasoning."

The Best Paper Award was followed by an invited keynote talk by Professor Francesco Ricci of the Free University of Bozen-Bolzano, Italy. His talk, "Computing useful recommendations: still requires knowledge," was well received. The main technical track then continued throughout most of the day ending with a social event.

The third day started with a technical session on "New Paradigms" followed by presentations from DC students on their research topics. The day ended with a social event. The following day started with an invited keynote "Learning to Compare with Few Data for Personalised Human Activity Recognition" given by Professor Nirmalie Wiratunga of the Robert Gordon University, UK. This was followed by technical sessions, and the day ending with an online gala dinner where attendees were encourage to have a meal to virtually share with others. The final day finished off the technical sessions followed by a private Program Committee meeting and an open to all CBR community meeting. It was generally felt that the technical sessions had worked very well online. The local chair, Juan Manuel Corchado of the University of Salamanca, Spain, and his support team were praised for handling all of the technical aspects involved with managing an online conference. The conference ended with a final social event.

We gratefully acknowledge the support of the following people, without whose contributions ICCBR 2020 would not have been possible. Local chair Juan Manuel Corchado and his team managed the technical aspects of the online conference and also managed the registration process. Workshop chairs, Hayley Borck and David Wilson, planned a lively workshop program, but regrettably there were not enough submissions to the workshops for whatever reason. We also extend our thanks to Stewart Massie and Michael Floyd who chaired the DC, providing invaluable support to the next generation of CBR researchers.

We extend our gratitude to the members of the ICCBR Advisory Council, Agnar Aamodt, David Aha, David Leake, Mehmet Goker, and Ramon Lopez de Mantaras, Barry Smyth, and Cindy Marling, for their advice and support. We would also like to thank the Program Committee and additional reviewers, who thoughtfully assessed the submissions and did an excellent job of providing constructive feedback to the authors.

July 2020

Ian Watson
Rosina Weber

Organization

Program Chairs

Ian Watson	The University of Auckland, New Zealand
Rosina Weber	Drexel University, USA

Local Chair

Juan Manuel Corchado	University of Salamanca, Spain

Workshop Chairs

Hayley Borck	Honeywell, USA
David Wilson	UNC Charlotte, USA

Doctoral Consortium Chairs

Stewart Massie	The Robert Gordon University, UK
Michael Floyd	Knexus Research Corporation, USA

Advisory Council

Agnar Aamodt	NTNU, Norway
David Aha	Naval Research Laboratory, USA
Mehmet H. Göker	ServiceNow, USA
David Leake	Indiana University, USA
Ramon López de Mántaras	IIIA-CSIC, Spain
Cindy Marling	Ohio University, USA
Barry Smyth	University College Dublin, Ireland

Program Committee

Klaus-Dieter Althoff	University of Hildesheim, DFKI, Germany
Ralph Bergmann	University of Trier, Germany
Isabelle Bichindaritz	State University of New York at Oswego, USA
Hayley Borck	Honeywell, USA
Derek Bridge	University College Cork, Ireland
Sutanu Chakraborti	Indian Institute of Technology Madras, India
Alexandra Coman	Capital One, USA
Sarah Jane Delany	Technological University Dublin, Ireland
Belén Díaz Agudo	Universidad Complutense de Madrid, Spain
Michael Floyd	Knexus Research, USA

Peter Funk	Mälardalen University, Sweden
Mehmet H. Göker	ServiceNow, USA
Pedro González Calero	Universidad Politécnica de Madrid, Spain
Odd Erik Gundersen	NTNU, Norway
Vahid Jalali	Indiana University Bloomington, USA
Stelios Kapetanakis	University of Brighton, UK
Mark Keane	University College Dublin, Ireland
Joseph Kendall-Morwick	Missouri Western State University, USA
Luc Lamontagne	Laval University, Canada
Jean Lieber	LORIA, Inria Lorraine, France
Mirjam Minor	Goethe University Frankfurt, Germany
Stefania Montani	Università del Piemonte Orientale, Italy
Héctor Muñoz-Avila	Lehigh University, USA
Emmanuel Nauer	LORIA, France
Santiago Ontañón	Drexel University, USA
Miltos Petridis (R.I.P.)	Middlesex University London, UK
Enric Plaza	IIIA-CSIC, Spain
Luigi Portinale	Università del Piemonte Orientale A. Avogadro, Italy
Juan Recio-Garcia	Universidad Complutense de Madrid, Spain
Jonathan Rubin	Philips Research North America, USA
Antonio Sánchez-Ruiz	Universidad Complutense de Madrid, Spain
Frode Sørmo	Verdande Technology, Norway
David Wilson	UNC Charlotte, USA
Nirmalie Wiratunga	The Robert Gordon University, UK

Local Committee

Juan M. Corchado (Local Chair)	University of Salamanca, Spain
Fernando De la Prieta Pintado	University of Salamanca, Spain
Sara Rodríguez González	University of Salamanca, Spain
Javier Prieto Tejedor	University of Salamanca, Spain
Pablo Chamoso Santos	University of Salamanca, Spain
Roberto Casado Vara	University of Salamanca, Spain
Alfonso González Briones	Universidad Complutense de Madrid
Elena Hernández Nieves	University of Salamanca, Spain
Liliana Durón Figueroa	University of Salamanca, Spain
Alberto Rivas Camacho	University of Salamanca, Spain
Marta Plaza Hernández	University of Salamanca, Spain
Yeray Mezquita Martín	University of Salamanca, Spain
Niloufar Shoeibi	University of Salamanca, Spain
Eugenia Pérez Pons	University of Salamanca, Spain

Additional Reviewers

Shideh Amiri
Christopher Bartlett
Viktor Eisenstadt
Ömer Ibrahim Erduran
Prateek Goel
Miriam Herold
Adam Johs
Guanghui Liu
Kyle Martin
Jakob Schoenborn
Anjana Wijekoon

Invited Talks

Computing Useful Recommendations: Still Requires Knowledge

Francesco Ricci

Free University of Bozen-Bolzano, Italy

Abstract. Recommender systems have been introduced as information search and filtering tools for providing suggestions for items to be of use to a user. State-of-the-art recommender systems mostly focus on the usage of data mining and information retrieval techniques to predict to what extent an item fits user needs and wants. But often they end up making uninteresting suggestions, especially in complex domains, such as tourism. In this talk, classical recommender systems ideas will be introduced and critically scrutinized in the attempt to better understand the role of observed and predicted choices and preferences. We will discuss some of the key ingredients necessary to build a useful recommender system. Hence, we will point out some limitations and open challenges for recommender systems research. We will also present a novel recommendation technique that leverages data collected from observation of tourists behavior to generate more useful individual and group recommendations.

Learning to Compare with Few Data for Personalised Human Activity Recognition

Nirmalie Wiratunga

The Robert Gordon University, UK

Abstract. Recent advances in meta-learning provides an interesting opportunity for CBR research, in similarity learning, case comparison, and personalized recommendations. Rather than learning a single model for a specific task, meta-learners adopt a generalist view of learning-to-learn, such that models are rapidly transferable to related but different new tasks. Unlike task-specific model training; a meta-learner's training instance, referred to as a meta-instance is a composite of two sets: a support set and a query set of instances. In our work, we introduce learning-to-learn personalized models from few data. We motivate our contribution through an application where personalization plays an important role, mainly that of human activity recognition for self-management of chronic diseases. We extend the meta-instance creation process where random sampling of support and query sets is carried out on a reduced sample conditioned by a domain-specific attribute; namely the person or user, in order to create meta-instances for personalized HAR. Our meta-learning for personalization is compared with several state-of-the-art meta-learning strategies: 1) matching network (MN) which learns an embedding for a metric function; 2) relation network (RN) that learns to predict similarity between paired instances; and 3) MAML, a model agnostic machine learning algorithm that optimizes the model parameters for rapid adaptation. Results confirm that personalized meta-learning significantly improves performance over non-personalized meta-learners.

Contents

Technical Session: Retrieval and Adaptation

Special Track Challenges and Promises

Invited Paper

Learning to Compare with Few Data for Personalised Human Activity Recognition

Nirmalie Wiratunga[1(✉)], Anjana Wijekoon[1], and Kay Cooper[2]

[1] School of Computing, Robert Gordon University, Aberdeen AB10 7GJ, Scotland, UK
{n.wiratunga,a.wijekoon}@rgu.ac.uk

[2] School of Health Sciences, Robert Gordon University, Aberdeen AB10 7GJ, Scotland, UK
k.cooper@rgu.ac.uk

Abstract. Recent advances in meta-learning provides interesting opportunities for CBR research, in similarity learning, case comparison and personalised recommendations. Rather than learning a single model for a specific task, meta-learners adopt a generalist view of learning-to-learn, such that models are rapidly transferable to related but different new tasks. Unlike task-specific model training; a meta-learner's training instance, referred to as a meta-instance is a composite of two sets: a support set and a query set of instances. In our work, we introduce learning-to-learn personalised models from few data. We motivate our contribution through an application where personalisation plays an important role, mainly that of human activity recognition for self-management of chronic diseases. We extend the meta-instance creation process where random sampling of support and query sets is carried out on a reduced sample conditioned by a domain-specific attribute; namely the person or user, in order to create meta-instances for personalised HAR. Our meta-learning for personalisation is compared with several state-of-the-art meta-learning strategies: 1) matching network (MN) which learns an embedding for a metric function; 2) relation network (RN) that learns to predict similarity between paired instances; and 3) MAML, a model agnostic machine learning algorithm that optimizes the model parameters for rapid adaptation. Results confirm that personalised meta-learning significantly improves performance over non personalised meta-learners.

1 Introduction

Integrated human activity recognition (HAR) and assistive technologies promise to enable people to live their life well regardless of their chronic conditions. A systematic review of interventions to promote physical activity [10] illustrated

This work was part funded by SelfBACK, a project funded by the European Union's H2020 research and innovation programme under grant agreement No. 689043. More details available at http://www.selfback.eu.

I. Watson and R. Weber (Eds.): ICCBR 2020, LNAI 12311, pp. 3–14, 2020.
https://doi.org/10.1007/978-3-030-58342-2_1

that interventions involving behaviour change strategies are more effective for sustaining longer-term physically active lifestyles than time-limited interventions involving structured exercises alone. Advances in telecommunications and Artificial Intelligence (AI) technologies paves the way for personalised virtual health companions to provide adherence monitoring along side behaviour change digital interventions. Innovative, person-centred strategies to monitor and predict physical activity and exercise behaviours, to scan and anticipate environmental barriers to activity, and to provide social and motivation support are required.

In this paper, we focus on one specific aspect of self-management; which is to reason from sensing data to monitor adherence to personalised self-management plans. A plan requires a user to follow physical activities such as walking and specific physiotherapy exercises. Pervasive and ubiquitous AI enabled devices are arguably best placed to continuously monitor a person's adherence to self-management plans, make real-time predictions about the likelihood of adherence and the impact of that. What is lacking are HAR algorithms that can adapt to differences in person-specific movements (e.g. gait, disabilities, weight, height); and to do so with few data.

The idea of meta-learning is to train exactly as we would expect to deploy the system [7]. What this means is that rather than treating a specific "activity" as a class to be recognised across all persons; we instead learn to recognise the "person-activity" pair as the class; and importantly do so with a limited number of data instances per person. This can be viewed as a few-shot classification scenario [13,15] commonly used in image classification where the aim is to train with one or few data instances. Meta-learning is arguably the state-of-the-art in few-shot classification [5,11], where a wide range of tasks abstracting their learning to a meta-model, such that, it is transferable to any unseen task. Meta-learning algorithms such as MAML [5] and Relation Networks (RN) [14] are grounded in theories of metric learning and parametric optimisation, and capable of learning generalised models. The meta-learning concept of learning-to-compare aligns well with personalisation where modelling a person can be viewed as a single task; whereby a meta-model must help learn a model that is rapidly adaptable or is applicable to a new person at deployment. Here we propose *Personalised Meta-Learning* to create personalised HAR models, with a small amount of data (about one minute worth of calibration data) extracted from a person's sensing devices. We make the following contributions:

- present personalised meta-learning in the context of matching networks (MN), relation networks (RN) and MAML;
- perform a comparative evaluation with a self-management dataset from the SELFBACK EU project to compare the utility of personalised meta-learning algorithms over conventional learning algorithms with focus on using few data; and
- provide results from an exploratory study on the transferability of meta-modals from physiotherapy experts to non-experts

2 Reasoning with Sensor Data for HAR

Previous work has demonstrated the effectiveness of applying decision support and reasoning systems to the management of a specific chronic disease. For instance Case-based reasoning (CBR), has been successfully used to incorporate evidence-base practices. For instance in managing diabetes types 1 and 2, CBR uses records that provide details about periodical visits with a physician in a case consisting of features that represent a problem (e.g. weight, blood glucose level), its solution (e.g. levels of insulin) and the outcome (e.g. hyper/hypo(glycemia)) observed after applying the solution [8,9]. More recent work [4], explored the self-management of diabetes type 1 to support monitoring of blood glucose levels before, during and after exercises. Interventions recommend carbohydrate intake based on similar cases retrieved for given HAR an exercise types.

In related work on self-management of low-back pain (LBP) [1], the SelfBACK CBR system recommends personalised care plans from similar patients. Management involves a human activity recognition (HAR) component to monitor the patient activity using sensor data that is continuously polled from a wearable device. Here a combination of patient reported monitoring, and HAR from sensor data, are used by the SelfBACK system to manage exercise adherence. Monitoring allows the system to detect periods of low activity behaviour, at which point a notification is generated to nudge the user to be more active - the intervention. An important contribution of this work is the integration of behaviour change techniques such as goal setting to focus the expected level of activity. Thereafter comparison of expected and actual behaviours to analyse goal achievement. Personalisation is important to ensure that care plans are tailored to the needs of the individual. Although there has been recent work on personalised learning using matching networks [17], more work is needed to understand them in the context of other state-of-the-art meta-learners like MAML and RN with few data.

2.1 HAR Using selfBACK Accelerometer Data

Wearables, such as smart watches or phones, are the most common form of physical activity monitoring devices and sources of delivering digital interventions. These are embedded with inertial measurement devices (e.g. accelerometers or gyroscopes) that generate time-series data which can be exploited for human activity recognition of ambulatory activities, activities of daily living, gait analysis and pose recognition [3,12,17]. In the SELFBACK project the HAR dataset has 6 ambulatory and 3 stationary activities[1]. Each activity has approximately 3 min of data with a 100 Hz sampling rate recorded with 33 participants using two accelerometers on the wrist (W) and the thigh (T).

[1] https://github.com/rgu-selfback/Datasets.

2.2 Multi-modal Exercise Recognition with MEx Data

Exercise recognition requires more sophisticated sensors such as pressure mats and depth cameras to capture complex human movements. The MEx sensor-rich dataset[2] contains data from 7 exercises, selected by physiotherapists for the self-management of LBP. Data is recorded with 30 participants, performing 7 exercises, each for 60 s (maximum). Of the 30 participants, 7 were qualified in physiotherapy exercises (i.e expert users) whilst the others were general users (i.e. non-expert users). Figure 1 shows the 4 modalities: a depth camera (DC) with a frame rate 15 Hz & frame size of 240×320; a pressure mat (PM) using a frame rate 15 Hz & frame size: 32×16; and two accelerometers 100 Hz sampling rate, on the wrist (ACW) & the thigh (ACT).

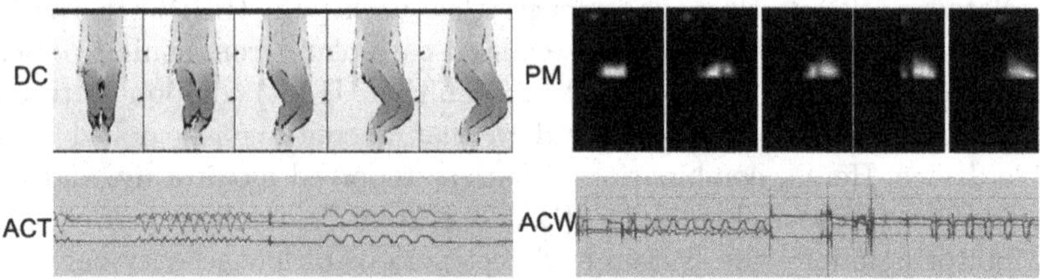

Fig. 1. Multi modal data in the MEx dataset

2.3 Personalisation with Non-iid Data

Analysis of a single person's pressure mat data, compared to data from the general population shows that their are inherent variations between persons data. For instance in Fig. 2, we have visualised 2-dimensional compressed pressure mat data (using PCA) colour coded by exercise class. The class distribution observed using all of the 30 persons data is very different from that observed with individuals (e.g. Persons 1 and 2 in the figure). We view this as a non identical and independent (non-iid) distributions problem where personalised meta-learning needs to be able to cope with such distributions at deployment. Accordingly we ensure that meta-modals are trained such that they are exposed to learning from such non-iid samples.

3 Learning to Personalise with Few Data

A meta-learner learns a meta-model, θ, trained over many tasks, where a task is equivalent to a "data instance" or "labelled example" in conventional machine learning. In few-shot classification, meta-learning can be seen as optimisation of a parametric model over many few-shot tasks (i.e. meta-train instances). Personalised meta-learning for HAR learns a meta-model θ from a population, $\mathcal{P}$,

[2] https://archive.ics.uci.edu/ml/datasets/MEx.

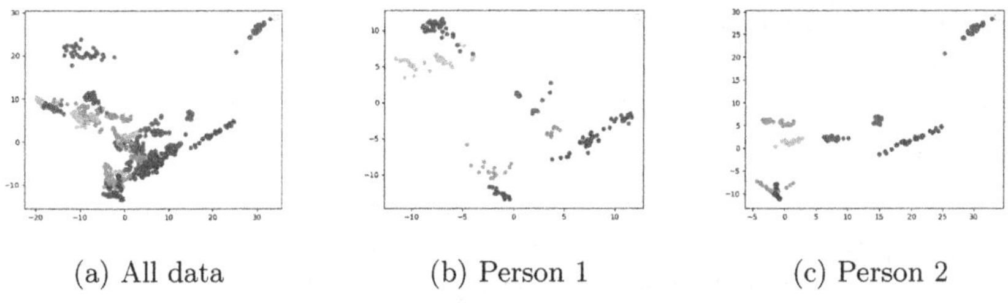

(a) All data (b) Person 1 (c) Person 2

Fig. 2. MEx data distributions visualised with MEx_{PM} data

while treating activity recognition for a person as an independent task. Figure 3 illustrates the task composition for such a setting, where a dataset, $\mathcal{D}$, is organised over a person population, $\mathcal{P}$, by creating person-centric tasks, where each "person-task", $\mathcal{P}_i$, contains data for a specific person. For example, in Fig. 3, $\mathcal{P}_1$ has a support set of distinct human activities (or activity classes) formed with data from one person. In this example we have just a single instance (i.e. $K^s = 1$) to represent each class (where $\mathcal{C} = 5$).

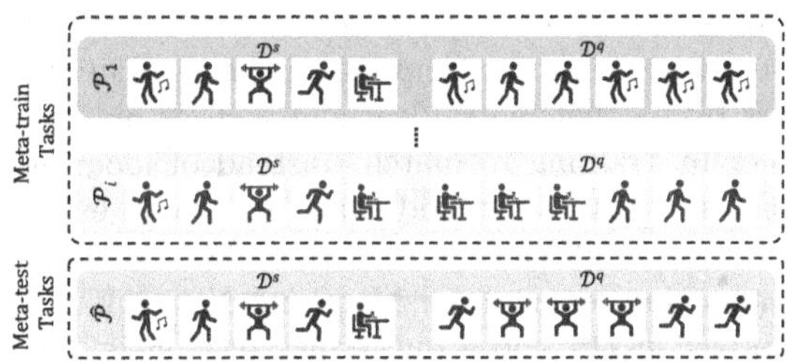

Fig. 3. Composing a meta task for training and testing a meta-learner

Meta-train and meta-test sets, are formed by randomly selection $K^s \times |\mathcal{C}|$ number of labelled data instances from a person, stratified across activity classes, $\mathcal{C}$, such that there are K^s amount of representatives for each class. We follow a similar approach when selecting a query set, $\mathcal{D}^q$, for $\mathcal{P}_i$. Each task contains an equal number of classes but not necessarily the same sub set of classes. Typically the query set, $\mathcal{D}^q$, has no overlap with the support set, $\mathcal{D}^s$ similar to a train/test split in supervised learning; and unlike the support set, composition of the query set need not be constrained to represent all $\mathcal{C}$. Once the meta-model is trained using the meta-train tasks, it is tested using the meta-test tasks. An instance of a meta-test task, $\hat{\mathcal{P}}$, has a similar composition to a meta-train task instance, in that it also has a support set, $\hat{\mathcal{D}}^s$, and a query set, $\hat{\mathcal{D}}^q$. Unlike traditional classifier testing; with meta-testing, we use the support set in conjunction with the trained meta-model to classify instances in the query sets. How the meta-test support and query sets are used change depending on the aim of the meta-learning.

3.1 Learning to Match

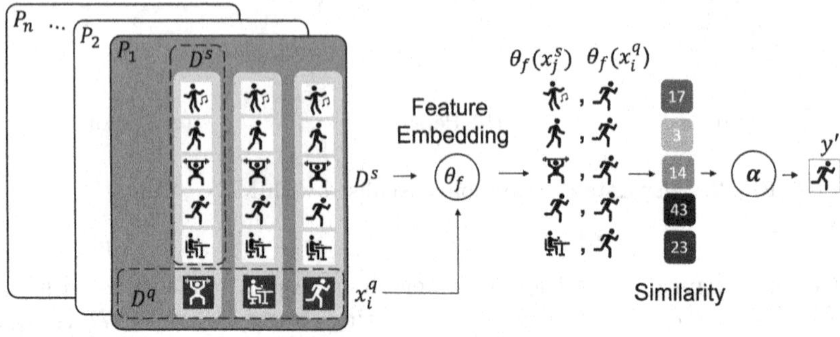

Fig. 4. Training a Matching Network

Matching Networks (MN) [15] can be viewed as an end-to-end neural implementation of the otherwise static kNN algorithm. It aims to learn a feature space by iteratively matching a query instance to a support set, which contains both positive and negative matches to the query instance. It is essentially "training to match" over representative instances from multiple classes in an iteration; which is what sets it apart from other metric learners such as Siamese [2] and triplet networks [6]. Further by training to match (instead of focusing solely on classification alone) makes it possible to add examples from new or unseen classes with no re-training of the model for transfer to related domains [17].

Figure 4 illustrates the Personalised Matching Network, MN^p, where each support set instance, x_i^s in $\mathcal{D}^s$, and a query instance, x^q in $\mathcal{D}^q$, are created for the person-specific task (i.e. using instances from $\mathcal{P}_i$). All instances in a task are transformed using the feature embedding function, θ_f (a neural network model), into feature vectors. Thereafter the process of matching is applied to every pair formed by each instance, x^q in $\mathcal{D}^q$, with every instance in $\mathcal{D}^s$. In the figure we can see that all pair-wise combinations are formed once $\mathcal{D}^s$ is duplicated thrice for a $\mathcal{D}^q$ with three query instances.

Similarity between a query instance and each of its support set instance pairs are calculated with an appropriate similarity metric (e.g. Cosine Similarity). Finally an attention mechanism, *att*, in the form of similarity weighted majority vote estimates the class, y^q (see Eqs. 1 and 2).

$$att(\theta_f(x^q), \theta_f(x_i^s)) = \frac{e^{sim(\theta_f(x^q), \theta_f(x_i^s))}}{\sum^{|s|} e^{sim(\theta_f(x^q), \theta_f(x_i^s))}} \tag{1}$$

$$y^q = \arg\max_i \sum^{|S|} att(\theta_f(x^q), \theta_f(x_i^s)) \times y_i^s \tag{2}$$

During training, the network iteratively updates weights of θ_f to maximise the similarity between the query instance and support set instance pairs from the same activity class. This is enforced by the loss function, categorical cross-entropy, which quantifies the difference between the estimated, y^q and actual class, y, distributions. One-hot encoding is used to represent classes enabling the attention kernel multiplication with the similarity value (in the range [0 .. 100]).

The concept of "learning to match" is achieved with attention where pair-wise similarity computations are used to influence the network's back propagation and consequent weight updates. This means that the embedding function that is learnt is optimised for matching which is a proxy to class prediction. At deployment, given a meta-test instance, $\hat{\mathcal{P}}$, MN predicts the label for a query instance $\hat{x^q}$ with respect to its support set $\hat{\mathcal{D}^s}$. In other words, the network learns to retrieve the best match from the support set elements, thereafter using them with similarity weighted majority voting to predict the class.

3.2 Learning to Relate

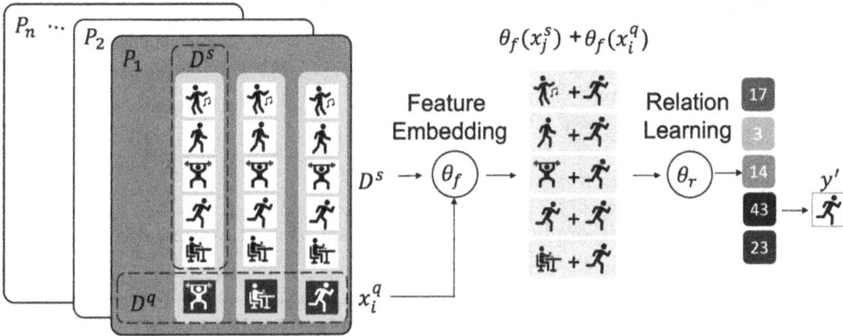

Fig. 5. Training a Relation Network

Personalised Relation Networks RN^p learns to relate by comparing query and support instance pairs using the person-tasks ($\mathcal{P}_i$) design discussed in Sect. 3. A RN^p has two parametric modules, one for feature representation learning, θ_f (like with MN^p) and a further one for relationship learning, θ_r (Fig. 5). Instead of capturing the relationship with a similarity metric (e.g. cosine) in the feature space, it is predicted as a score, $r_i^{q,s}$, by θ_r which is a Convolutional Neural Net (CNN) based on, $|\mathcal{C}|$ pair-wise relations.

$$r_i^{q,s} = \theta_r(\mathcal{C}(\theta_f(x^q), \theta_f(x_i^s))))), \; i = 1, 2, \cdots, |\mathcal{C}| \tag{3}$$

$$y^q = \arg\max_i r_i^{q,s} \tag{4}$$

Unlike MN^p, the similarity-weighted attention layer is replaced with a parameterised relation learning model, θ_r, which takes as input query and support instance (concatenated) pairs to learn similarity such that matched pairs have similarity 1 and the mismatched pair have similarity 0. Here learning similarity scores are viewed as a regression problem with mean-squared-error forming the loss function that optimises both θ_f and θ_r. At deployment, as with MN^p, given a test query instance $\hat{x^q}$ the RN^p predicts the class label, with respect to its support set $\hat{\mathcal{D}^s}$.

3.3 Learning to Adapt

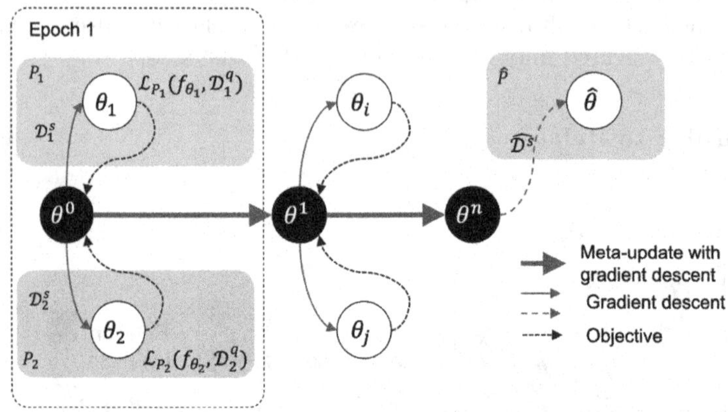

Fig. 6. Training a Personalised Model-Agnostic Meta-Learner, $MAML^p$

Unlike MN^p and RN^p, with Personalised MAML ($MAML^p$) there is less focus on similarity and instance pairing, instead the aim is to learn a generic model prototype (i.e. a meta-model), θ, such that it can be rapidly adapted to any new person encountered at test time $\hat{\mathcal{P}}$. Task design for $MAML^p$ is as described in Sect. 3. Adaptation optimised learning is illustrated in Fig. 6. At the start of each iteration (epoch), a set of person tasks are sampled, P_i to optimise their person-specific model using a generic model θ^j as the model initialisation. Thereafter each person-specific model, θ_i is locally trained by optimising over the $\mathcal{D}_i^s$ using one or few steps of gradient descents. The loss computed using $\mathcal{D}^q$ by each person-task is passed on to the meta-learner; which in turn aggregates these losses and optimises, θ^j, using its own gradient descent step forming the meta-update for the epoch. This process is repeated n epochs, to learn a generic model prototype θ that can be rapidly adapted to a new $\hat{\mathcal{P}}$.

At deployment, $\hat{\mathcal{P}}$, not seen during training, uses its support set, $\hat{\mathcal{D}^s}$ for local training of the parametric model $\hat{\theta}$, initialised by the meta-model θ. Thereafter, the adapted, $\hat{\theta}$ is used to classify instances in $\hat{\mathcal{P}}$'s query set, $\mathcal{D}^q$. Personalised MAML is model-agnostic, which is advantageous for HAR applications with heterogeneous sensor modalities or modality combinations.

4 Evaluations

The aim of the evaluations is to compare performance of the 3 personalised meta-learners discussed in Sect. 3 with several established benchmark algorithms.

DL: Best performing deep learners from benchmarks published in [16].
Meta-learners (MN, RN & MAML): The 3 meta-learners used in our comparison include; Matching Networks (MN) [15]; Relation Networks [14] (RN); and MAML (using the first-order implementation) [5] .
Personalised meta-learners (MN^p, RN^p & MAML^p): Personalised versions of meta-learners discussed in Sect. 3.

We follow the person-aware evaluation methodology Leave-One-Person-Out (LOPO) in our experiments; where data from one person is left out to create meta-test instances and the rest used to create meta-train instances. Accuracy on meta-test is presented and any significance reported is at 95% confidence level using the Wilcoxon signed ranked test. Sensor data streams are converted into instances by applying a sliding window of size 5 s, and an overlap of 3 and 2.5 for data sources MEx and SELFBACK creating 30 and 88 data instance per person-activity on average (K). We select $K^s = 5$ and $K^q = K - K^s$ to create meta-train and test instances.

MN and MN^p are trained for 20 epochs, and $MAML$, $MAML^p$, RN and RN^p for 100 epochs; all using early stopping. $MAML$ and $MAML^p$, use 5 and 10 as the number of gradients steps when training and testing respectively. MN, MN^p, $MAML$ and $MAML^p$ use a single dense layer with 1200 units as θ_f and θ. The θ_f in RN and RN^p consists of a single layer CNN (64 kernels and kernel size 3×3); θ_r is a single layer CNN (64 kernels and kernel size 3×3), followed by 2 dense layers (120 units and 1 unit); here, the last dense layer has an output of size 1 for the regression task (Sect. 3.2).

4.1 HAR Comparative Study

Results appear in Table 1 on 6 datasets derived from SELFBACK and MEx. As expected personalised meta-learning models significantly outperform conventional DL and (non-personalised) meta-learning models on all datasets. The two visual datasets; MEx$_{DC}$ and MEx$_{PM}$, recorded the best performance with $MAML^p$. Both accelerometer datasets from MEx and one dataset from SELFBACK achieved best performance with RN^p. Notably, both $MAML^p$ and RN^p fail to outperform the personalised few-shot learning algorithm MN^p on the SB$_W$ dataset which consists of sensing data obtained from the wrist having the greatest degree of freedom and therefore most prone to "noisy" movements. Interestingly, MN^p, has comparable performance against $MAML^p$ on the MEx$_{ACT}$ dataset and outperform RN^p model on the MEx$_{DC}$ dataset. When comparing conventional meta-learners (i.e. RN, $MAML$) and Personalised Few-Shot Learner, MN^p, we see that, MN^p models achieve comparable performances or significantly outperform at least one conventional meta-learner with all four

Table 1. Comparative Study: mean accuracy results, LOPO, 5-shot

Algorithm	MEx_{ACT}	MEx_{ACW}	MEx_{DC}	MEx_{PM}	SB_{T}	SB_{W}
Best DL	0.9015	0.6335	0.8720	0.7408	0.7880	0.6997
MN	0.9073	0.4620	0.5065	0.6187	0.8392	0.7669
RN	0.9327	0.7279	0.8189	0.8145	0.9334	0.8276
$MAML$	0.8673	0.6525	0.9629	0.9283	0.8398	0.7532
MN^p	0.9155	0.6663	0.9342	0.8205	0.9124	**0.8653**
RN^p	**0.9436**	**0.7719**	0.9205	0.8520	**0.9487**	0.8528
$MAML^p$	0.9106	0.6834	**0.9795**	**0.9408**	0.8625	0.8075

experiments; which further confirm the importance of personalisation. Overall, we find that optimisation based meta-learning algorithm (i.e. $MAML^p$) performs well on visual sensing modalities; whilst comparison based meta-learners (i.e. MN^p and RN^p) perform well on time-series data.

4.2 Discussion

In a real-world situation the data for meta-model training is likely to be provided by physiotherapy experts performing exercises. Thereafter learnt models can be applied to non-physio users. We can simulate this situation with the MEx dataset where the 7 physio experts can be used to train a meta-modal and observe how these transfer to the rest (23 persons).

Figure 7 plots meta-test accuracy for incrementally increasing values of meta-train epochs for RN^p for all 23 persons (in grey) against the average results plot. We can observe the elbow point at about 40-50 epochs. Local learning with no meta-learning as expected is very low (results x-axis = 0). The general trend is that most persons show improvements in transferability with increasing epochs. Even those that struggle to improve accuracy early on seem to benefit from using the meta-modal with increasing epochs. $MAML^p$ has benefited from its local training and presents a gradual increase (~5%) with increasing meta-training. For comparison results of $MAML^p$ before local training (no adaptation) is included and highlights the importance of personalised model adaptation.

Figure 8 shows the impact of meta-learning on model adaptation with $MAML^p$. The rising and falling cyclic pattern can be explained by observing that local models, $\hat{\theta}_i$, are initialised at each epoch with the meta-model, and have a low meta-test accuracy starting point. As $\hat{\theta}_i$s are refined through local training, we observe the rising trend in meta-test accuracy. We observed 3 distinct adaptation patterns among the 23 persons (bolded line graphs in Fig. 8): meta-model being easily adapted with 1 or 2 gradient steps (blue); meta-model successfully adapted over several gradient steps (orange); and failure to adapt (green). Overall it is evident that gains from personalised model transfer in most cases gradually improve with increasing meta-training.

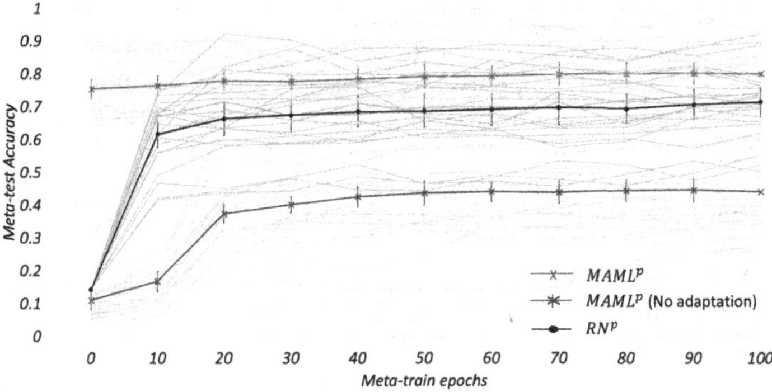

Fig. 7. Transferability of meta-modals from physiotherapy experts to non-experts

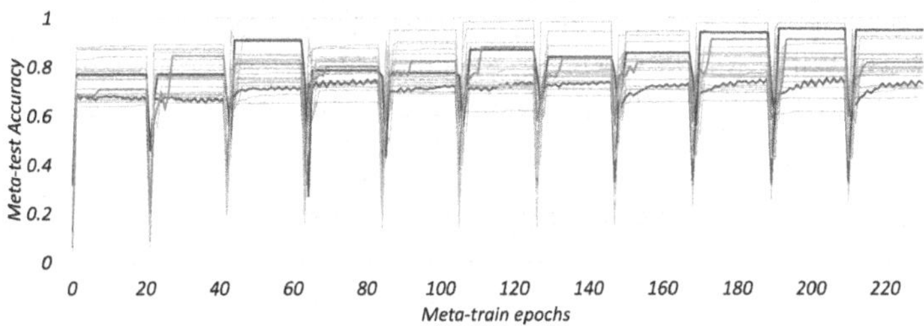

Fig. 8. Adaptation of $MAML^P$ over meta-model training (Color figure online)

5 Conclusion

Personalised meta-learning, supports model transfer to new situations in applications where there is few data. With HAR models can be transferred with a few instances of calibration data obtained from the end-user at deployment. $MAML^p$ uses calibration data to adapt through re-training; whilst MN^p and RN^p uses calibration data directly for matching (without re-training). Our results on MEx and SELFBACK datasets with personalised meta-learning show significant performance improvements over conventional and non-personalised meta-learning algorithms. Importantly we find, while RN^p outperform $MAML^p$, $MAML^p$ performs significantly faster due to the absence of paired matching. We hope that the parameterised learning-to-compare methods discussed here will help inspire new ideas relevant for CBR research.

References

1. Bach, K., Szczepanski, T., Aamodt, A., Gundersen, O.E., Mork, P.J.: Case representation and similarity assessment in the SELFBACK decision support system. In: Goel, A., Díaz-Agudo, M.B., Roth-Berghofer, T. (eds.) ICCBR 2016. LNCS (LNAI), vol. 9969, pp. 32–46. Springer, Cham (2016). https://doi.org/10.1007/978-3-319-47096-2_3

2. Bromley, J., Guyon, I., LeCun, Y.: Signature verification using a 'siamese' time delay neural network. Int. J. Pattern Recognit. Artif. Intell. **7**(4), 669–688 (1993)
3. Chavarriaga, R., et al.: The opportunity challenge: a benchmark database for on-body sensor-based har. Pattern Recogn. Lett. **34**(15), 2033–2042 (2013)
4. Chen, Y.Y., et al.: Designing a personalised case-based recommender system for mobile self-management of diabetes during exercise. In: Workshop Proceedings of the 2nd Knowledge Discovery from Health Workshop at the International Joint Conference on AI (2017)
5. Finn, C., Abbeel, P., Levine, S.: Model-agnostic meta-learning for fast adaptation of deep networks. In: Proceedings of the 34th International Conference on Machine Learning, vol. 70, pp. 1126–1135. JMLR. org (2017)
6. Hoffer, E., Ailon, N.: Deep metric learning using triplet network. In: Feragen, A., Pelillo, M., Loog, M. (eds.) Similarity-Based Pattern Recognition, pp. 84–92. Springer, Cham (2015). https://doi.org/10.1007/978-3-319-24261-3_7
7. Hospedales, T., Antoniou, A., Micaelli, P., Storkey, A.: Meta-learning in neural networks: a survey. arXiv preprint arXiv:2004.05439 (2020)
8. Marling, C., Wiley, M., Bunescu, R., Shubrook, J., Schwartz, F.: Emerging applications for intelligent diabetes management. AI Mag. **33**(2), 67–67 (2012)
9. Montani, S., Bellazzi, R., Portinale, L., d'Annunzio, G., Fiocchi, S., Stefanelli, M.: Diabetic patients management exploiting case-based reasoning techniques. Comput. Methods Programs Biomed. **62**(3), 205–218 (2000)
10. Morris, J.H., MacGillivray, S., Mcfarlane, S.: Interventions to promote long-term participation in physical activity after stroke: a systematic review of the literature. Arch. Phys. Med. Rehabil. **95**(5), 956–967 (2014)
11. Nichol, A., Achiam, J., Schulman, J.: On first-order meta-learning algorithms. arXiv preprint arXiv:1803.02999 (2018)
12. Reiss, A., Stricker, D.: Introducing a new benchmarked dataset for activity monitoring. In: 2012 16th International Symposium on Wearable Computers (ISWC), pp. 108–109. IEEE (2012)
13. Snell, J., Swersky, K., Zemel, R.: Prototypical networks for few-shot learning. In: Advances in Neural Information Processing Systems, pp. 4077–4087 (2017)
14. Sung, F., Yang, Y., Zhang, L., Xiang, T., Torr, P.H., Hospedales, T.M.: Learning to compare: relation network for few-shot learning. In: Proceedings of the IEEE Conference on Computer Vision and Pattern Recognition, pp. 1199–1208 (2018)
15. Vinyals, O., Blundell, C., Lillicrap, T., Wierstra, D., et al.: Matching networks for one shot learning. In: Advances in Neural Information Processing Systems, pp. 3630–3638 (2016)
16. Wijekoon, A., Wiratunga, N., Cooper, K., Bach, K.: Learning to recognise exercises in the self-management of low back pain. In: Florida Artificial Intelligence Research Society Conference (2020)
17. Wijekoon, A., Wiratunga, N., Sani, S., Cooper, K.: A knowledge-light approach to personalised and open-ended human activity recognition. Knowl.-Based Syst. **192**, 105651 (2020)

Technical Session: Workflows

A*-Based Similarity Assessment of Semantic Graphs

Christian Zeyen[1(✉)] and Ralph Bergmann[1,2]

[1] Business Information Systems II, University of Trier, 54286 Trier, Germany
{zeyen,bergmann}@uni-trier.de
[2] German Research Center for Artificial Intelligence (DFKI), Branch University of Trier, Behringstraße 21, 54296 Trier, Germany
ralph.bergmann@dfki.de
http://www.wi2.uni-trier.de

Abstract. The similarity assessment of graphs is a fundamental problem that is particularly challenging if efficiency is of core importance. In this paper, we focus on a similarity measure for semantically labeled graphs whose labels are composed in an object-oriented manner. The measure is based on A* search and is particularly suited for case-based reasoning as it can be combined with knowledge-intensive local similarity measures and outputs similarities and corresponding mappings usable for explanation and adaptation. However, particularly for large graphs, the search space must be pruned to improve efficiency of A* search at the cost of sacrificing global optimality. We address this issue and present complementary improvements of the measure, which we systematically evaluate for the similarity assessment of semantic workflow graphs. The experimental results demonstrate that the new measure considerably reduces the computation time and memory consumption while increasing the accuracy.

Keywords: Semantic graphs · Graph matching · Graph similarity

1 Introduction

Graph-based case representations with semantically labeled nodes and/or edges are significantly gaining importance in case-based reasoning (CBR). They allow to represent arbitrary relational structures and thus considerably increase expressiveness compared to attribute-value or pure object-oriented representations. However, the gain in expressiveness comes with the cost of increased complexity in the similarity assessment during the retrieval phase. In the literature, various similarity measures for graph-based representations have been proposed [12]. However, assessing the similarity in an efficient way is a fundamental problem due to the computational complexity of the approximate graph matching involved. It is particularly challenging for semantically enriched graphs since their similarity is affected by structure and semantics.

I. Watson and R. Weber (Eds.): ICCBR 2020, LNAI 12311, pp. 17–32, 2020.
https://doi.org/10.1007/978-3-030-58342-2_2

In this paper, we consider a specific form of semantically enriched graphs, which we refer to as semantic graphs. A semantic graph is a generic directed graph whose nodes and edges have different types and are associated with semantic descriptions, which can be composed in an object-oriented manner. Semantic graphs are particularly used as case representation in process-oriented case-based reasoning (POCBR) for representing semantic workflows [2] but also for representing arguments [4] in case-based argumentation.

To assess the similarity of such graphs, Bergmann and Gil [2] proposed a generic semantic similarity measure following the well-known local-global principle [1,6] that is based on finding the best possible mapping of similar nodes and edges between the graphs to be compared. In particular, this measure outputs the similarity values along with the corresponding mappings, which can be the basis for adaptation [5] and which can be also used for explanation purposes. The involved optimization problem can be solved in principle by applying A* search, which is theoretically able to find the optimal mapping. However, in practical applications with large graphs, the search space can become so large that it must be limited, thus trading optimality against efficiency. To overcome this performance issue during retrieval, several two-step MAC/FAC retrieval approaches [5,9,10] have been proposed, which reduce the number of expensive similarity computations by using an efficient pre-selection of cases. A recent approach by Hoffmann et al. [8] shows promising results in approximating graph similarities with siamese graph neural networks. In this paper, however, we follow a different route of research as we aim at improving the efficiency of each single similarity computation by speeding-up the A* search. We do so by reorganizing the search space and by proposing a better-informed heuristic that guides the search. In total, four complementary improvements are described and evaluated systematically.

The following Sect. 2 introduces the graph representation and briefly surveys approaches to graph similarity before we describe the A*-based similarity measure to be improved. Section 3 presents the improvements for the measure while Sect. 4 investigates the performance impact in an experimental evaluation. Finally, we summarize the paper and discuss future work.

2 Background

2.1 Semantic Graphs

Based on the definition of semantic workflow graphs [2], we consider a semantic graph as a quadruple $G = (N, E, S, T)$. The graph elements are defined by a set of nodes N and a set of edges $E \subseteq N \times N$. $S : N \cup E \rightarrow \Sigma$ associates to each graph element a semantic description from a semantic metadata language Σ while $T : N \cup E \rightarrow \Omega$ associates to each graph element a type from Ω. While types are assumed to be disjoint, semantic descriptions can be organized in a hierarchy. Figure 1 gives an example of a semantic workflow graph representing a sandwich recipe. The graph consists of three different types of nodes and edges, which can be distinguished by the different shapes and lines in the figure.

The workflow node (diamond) represents general information about the recipe, task nodes (rectangles) represent preparation steps, and data nodes (ovals) represent ingredients. Furthermore, control-flow edges (solid lines) define the execution order of preparation steps, data-flow edges (dotted lines) specify the consumption and production of ingredients, and part-of edges (dashed lines) link all nodes to the workflow node. Semantic descriptions of the nodes are written in grey boxes. In this implementation, we treat the semantic descriptions in an object-oriented fashion and use the local-global principle [1,6] for assessing sim_{Σ}.

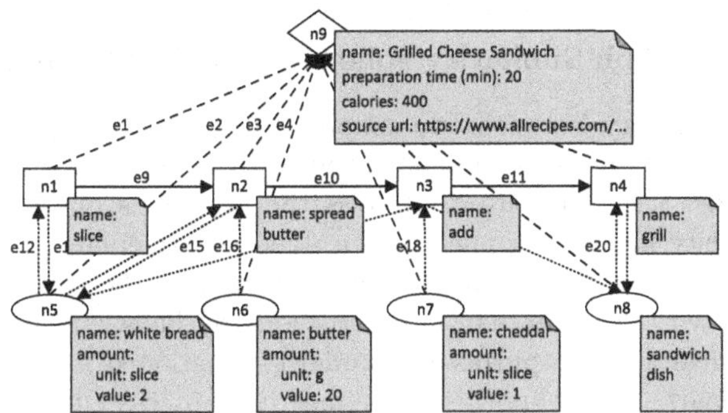

Fig. 1. Example of a semantic workflow graph

Following the CBR paradigm, the underlying retrieval problem that requires computing graph similarities is the following: For a given query graph G_q, the best-matching graph $G_c \in CB$ is being searched in a repository of graphs CB, which is referred to as case base. For this purpose, G_q is compared with each case graph G_c and rated with a similarity $sim(G_q, G_c) \in [0, 1]$.

2.2 Approaches to Similarity Assessment of Multi-labeled Graphs

In general, numerous similarity measures for graph-based representations have been proposed in the literature [12]. For semantically labeled graphs and particularly for graphs with multiple labels (also referred to as multi-attributed graphs), considerably less approaches exist. For such graphs, approaches based on greedy search [7] and Tabu search [14] have been proposed. However, due to the incomplete search only local optima are found and the similarity error can be hardly controlled. Particularly tailored for large graphs, Zhu et al. [15] presented an index-based approach combined with a greedy algorithm and Shemshadi et al. [13] presented an approach based on graph simulation. The focus is put on graphs with textual labels instead of composed semantic descriptions. More recently, Li et al. [11] proposed an embedding approach with graph neural networks, which was extended by Hoffmann et al. [8] to support composed semantic descriptions. Like any other supervised learning approach, a sufficiently large number of training data is required. To reduce the manual effort, further unsupervised approaches to graph similarity are required that allow for assessing graph similarity values in an appropriate and efficient manner.

Most approaches have in common that they restrict the semantic annotations of graph elements to attribute-value representation. More importantly, they do not allow for knowledge-intensive similarity assessments of semantic descriptions. Ontañón [12] recently identified, among others, scalability and interpretability as open research questions. While graph embeddings using neural networks is a promising research direction to address scalability, interpretability remains a major challenge.

2.3 Semantic Graph Similarity Following the Local-Global Principle

To assess the similarity between two graphs $G_q = (N_q, E_q, S_q, T_q)$ and $G_c = (N_c, E_c, S_c, T_c)$, we follow the approach proposed by Bergmann and Gil [2] which allows to consider the structure as well as the semantics of the graphs. The proposed similarity measure applies the local-global principle [1,6] to allow for assessing the similarity in a flexible manner. It enables the comparison of the graph elements w.r.t. their semantic descriptions by knowledge-intensive local similarity measures. For this purpose, a similarity function $sim_\Sigma : \Sigma \times \Sigma \rightarrow [0,1]$ is modeled as part of the knowledge-engineering process such that semantic descriptions of nodes and edges from query and case can be compared w.r.t. their similarity. Depending on the choice of Σ, this similarity can itself be assessed following the local-global principle. This is particularly useful for semantic descriptions represented in an object-oriented fashion. Thus, available similarity knowledge for the graph elements can be considered in a flexible manner and the computed similarity values are transparent and interpretable.

Following the local-global principle, the global similarity during graph comparison is obtained by an aggregation function combining the local similarities of related graph elements from G_q and G_c. Based on this principle, the node similarity $sim_N(n_q, n_c)$ for $n_q \in N_q$ and $n_c \in N_c$ is defined as follows:

$$sim_N(n_q, n_c) = \begin{cases} sim_\Sigma(S_q(n_q), S_c(n_c)) & \text{if} \quad T_q(n_q) = T_c(n_c) \\ 0 & \text{otherwise} \end{cases}$$

Edge similarity does not only consider the semantic description of the edges being compared, but also the nodes linked by the edges. We define edge similarity $sim_E(e_q, e_c)$ for $e_q \in E_q$ and $e_c \in E_c$ as follows:

$$sim_E(e_q, e_c) = \begin{cases} F_E \begin{pmatrix} sim_\Sigma(S_q(e_q), S_c(e_c)), \\ sim_N(e_q.l, e_c.l), \\ sim_N(e_q.r, e_c.r) \end{pmatrix} & \text{if} \quad T_q(e_q) = T_c(e_c) \\ 0 & \text{otherwise} \end{cases}$$

$e.l$ denotes the left node of an edge e and $e.r$ denotes its right node. The function F_E is an *aggregation function* that combines the semantic similarity between the edges and the similarities of the connected nodes to the overall similarity value. In our implementations we define F_E as follows: $F_E(s_e, s_l, s_r) = s_e \cdot (s_l + s_r)/2$.

The similarity $sim_m(G_q, G_c)$ between G_q and G_c is defined with respect to a *legal mapping* $m : N_q \cup E_q \rightarrow N_c \cup E_c$ that satisfies the following five constraints:

$$\begin{array}{lll} T_q(n_q) = T_c(m(n_q)) & T_q(e_q) = T_c(m(e_q)) & \\ m(e_q.l) = m(e_q).l & m(e_q.r) = m(e_q).r & \forall x, y\ m(x) = m(y) \rightarrow x = y \end{array}$$

Please note that such a legal mapping m is *type-preserving*, i.e., only nodes and edges of the same type can be mapped. The mapping is *injective*, which means that a case node or edge can only be the target of one query node or edge, respectively. Moreover, the mapping can be *partial*, i.e., not all nodes and edges of the query must be mapped to case elements and can be mapped to null instead. For instance, null mappings are required if more query elements exist than case elements of a certain type. An edge can only be mapped if the nodes that the edge connects are also mapped to the respective nodes that the mapped edge connects. For a given mapping m, a second aggregation function F_G is defined that combines the individual similarity values for mapped elements:

$$sim_m(G_g, G_c) = F_G \left(\begin{array}{l} (sim_N(n, m(n)) | n \in N_q \cap \mathrm{Dom}(m)), \\ (sim_E(e, m(e)) | e \in E_q \cap \mathrm{Dom}(m)), |N_q|, |E_q| \end{array} \right)$$

$\mathrm{Dom}(m)$ denotes the domain of m. The parameters $|N_q|$ and $|E_q|$ enable F_G to consider partial mappings, i.e., nodes and edges not mapped should not contribute to the similarity. In our implementation we define F_G as follows:

$$F_W((sn_1, \ldots, sn_i), (se_1, \ldots, se_j), n_N, n_E) = \frac{sn_1 + \cdots + sn_i + se_1 + \cdots + se_j}{n_N + n_E}$$

The overall similarity $sim(G_q, G_c)$ is determined by the mapping with the highest similarity:

$$sim(G_q, G_c) = \max\{sim_m(G_q, G_c) |\ m \text{ is legal mapping}\}$$

2.4 A*-Based Similarity Search

To find the best mapping m, Bergmann and Gil [2] proposed to apply an A* search. The A* algorithm maintains a priority queue Q of partial solutions for this optimization problem. In such a solution Sol, $Sol.m$ represents the current mapping and $Sol.N$ and $Sol.E$ are the not yet mapped nodes and edges of the query graph. In each step, the first (best) solution in the queue $first(Q)$ is removed. If it represents a completely expanded solution, A* terminates. Otherwise, the solution is expanded, i.e., the next query graph element x_q is selected and all legal mappings to the case graph elements are determined. For each such mapping, a new solution extended by this additional mapping is created and inserted into the priority queue. If more query elements exist than case elements of a certain type, an additional *null mapping* must be added as a new solution to allow for partial mapping. The total amount of required null mappings corresponds to the difference between the query and case elements. The order in which the solutions are inserted into the priority queue is essential for A*. Therefore, each solution *Sol* is evaluated by a function $f(Sol) = g(Sol) + h(Sol)$ and the value is stored in the solution as $Sol.f$. In the traditional formulation, A* aims at minimizing cost, hence $g(Sol)$ are the cost already occurred and $h(Sol)$ is a heuristic estimation function for the remaining cost to the solution. As we apply A* for maximizing the similarity value, $g(Sol)$ is the similarity of the current mapping $Sol.m$, while $h(Sol)$ is a heuristic estimation of the additional similarity that can be achieved through the mapping of the remaining nodes and edges. Solutions are inserted into the priority queue in decreasing order of $f(Sol)$. Consequently, the solution with the highest f-value is expanded first. To achieve an admissible heuristic estimation function, which ensures that the optimal solution is found, $h(Sol)$ must be an upper bound of the similarity.

```
A*Search(Gq = (Nq, Eq, Sq, Tq), Gc = (Nc, Ec, Sc, Tc))
  | Q = insert(initSolution(), Q);
  | while first(Q).N ≠ ∅ ∧ first(Q).E ≠ ∅ do
  |   | Q = expand(Q);
  | end
return first(Q).f;

initSolution()
  | Sol0.N = Nq;   Sol0.E = Eq;   Sol0.m = ∅;   Sol0.f = 1;
return Sol0;

expand(Q)
  | Sol = first(Q);   Q = rest(Q);   xq = select(Sol);
  | forall xc ∈ Nc ∪ Ec such that the mapping Sol.m ∪ (xq, xc) is legal do
  |   | Q = insert(newSolution(Sol, xq, xc), Q);
  | end
  | if Tq(xq) requires null mapping w.r.t. Sol.m then
  |   | Q = insert(newSolution(Sol, xq, ∅), Q);
  | end
return Q;

newSolution(Sol, xq, xc)
  | Sol'.N = Sol.N \ {xq};   Sol'.E = Sol.E \ {xq};
  | Sol'.m = Sol.m ∪ (xq, xc);
  | Sol'.f = sim_Sol'.m(Gq, Gc) + h(Sol');
return Sol';
```

The overall A* search algorithm is sketched above. The function *first*(Q) returns the first solution in the priority queue, *rest*(Q) removes the first solution and returns the rest and *select* determines the next graph element x_q to be mapped, which can be either a query node or edge. The function *insert*(Sol, Q) inserts a solution *Sol* into Q according to the f-value. During insert, the maximum size of the queue can be restricted to prune the search space for improving the performance on the risk of losing global optimality.

Bergmann and Gil [2] presented two A* variants named *A*I* and *A*II* with different estimation and select functions. In this paper, we build up upon *A*II*:

$$h_{II}(Sol) = \sum_{x \in Sol.N \cup Sol.E} \left(\max_{y \in N_c \cup E_c} \{sim_{N/E}(x, y)\} \right) \cdot \frac{1}{|N_q| + |E_q|}$$

$$select_{II}(Sol) = \begin{cases} e_q \in Sol.E & \text{if } e_q.l \notin Sol.N \wedge e_q.r \notin Sol.N \\ n_q \in Sol.N & otherwise \end{cases}$$

$sim_{N/E}(x, y)$ refers to the corresponding similarity function sim_N or sim_E. It was shown that *A*II* clearly outperforms *A*I* since it uses a more informed admissible heuristic. While h_I uses the maximum similarity of 1.0 as estimation for each not mapped query graph element, h_{II} determines the best possible similarity a mapping can achieve independent of the mapping of the other elements. This can be computed in advance and cached. The select function chooses elements randomly according to an internal id and selects edges as soon as possible. As mapping edges requires the linked nodes being mapped already, it requires only a low number of new solutions to be added to the priority queue. Only one solution is created, if between nodes there is at most one edge per type. Hence, the size of the queue does not increase while the accuracy of $f(Sol')$ increases.

3 Improving the A*-Based Similarity Search

We now present four complementary improvements for enhancing the performance of the A*-based similarity search. For illustration purposes, we refer to the simple example graphs G_q and G_c depicted in Fig. 2. The graphs consist of two different types of nodes and edges (depicted by different shapes and lines). The semantic descriptions consist of symbolic values with $\Sigma = \{a, b, c\}$ and we assume sim_Σ to be defined as a binary measure returning 1 if symbols are equal and 0 otherwise. Moreover, edges and diamond shaped nodes do not have semantic descriptions and thus match with a similarity of 1. Please note that the similarity assessment is asymmetric. Hence, $sim(G_q, G_c) = \frac{6}{9}$ although G_c is sub-graph isomorphic with G_q, i.e., $sim(G_c, G_q) = 1$.

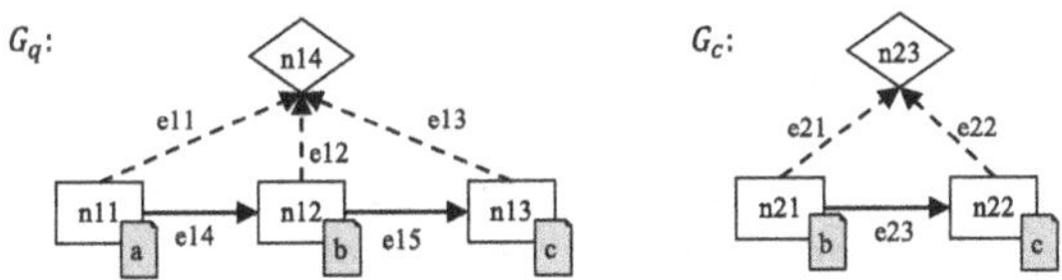

Fig. 2. Example of a query and case graph

3.1 Search Space Reduction

According to the definition of semantic graphs, a query $G_q = (N_q, E_q, S_q, T_q)$ and a case graph $G_c = (N_c, E_c, S_c, T_c)$ consist of different types $T_q \subseteq \Omega$ and $T_c \subseteq \Omega$ of nodes and edges. A legal mapping of graph elements is type-preserving. Consequently, we can add element pairs (x_q, x_c) to the initial solution for which only one legal mapping exists. By this means, the search space can be reduced prior to the A* search. Regarding the graph representation, it is advisable to assign different types to graph elements whenever their semantic descriptions are disjoint. To implement this improvement, we redefine *initSolution* as follows:

```
initSolution2()
    Sol_0 = initSolution();
    forall (x_q, x_c) ∈ N_q × N_c such that the mapping is legal ∧ (∄x'_q : x'_q ≠ x_q
     ∧ T_q(x'_q) = T_q(x_q)) ∧ (∄x'_c : x'_c ≠ x_c ∧ T_c(x'_c) = T_c(x_c)) do
    |   Sol_0 = newSolution(Sol_0, x_q, x_c);
    end
return Sol_0;
```

In the given example, types $T_q(n14) = T_c(n23)$ are equal and the mapping of the nodes is the only possible legal mapping. Consequently, it can be added to the initial solution. This improvement also comes into effect for the semantic workflow graph representation depicted in Fig. 1 since such graphs have a single workflow node linked to all other nodes via part-of edges. During the mapping process, the already mapped workflow node enables that a part-of edge can be always mapped subsequent to the mapping of another node.

3.2 Adaptive Mapping Orientation

If the query graph is larger than the case graph, we assume that the mapping process can be made more efficient by orienting the mapping towards the case elements. This is referred to as *case-oriented mapping*. Please note that the direction of the mappings and the similarity assessment is unaffected, i.e., mapping and similarity are still oriented from the query elements to the case elements. The mapping mode is selected prior to the search according to the following rule:

$$mapping\_mode = \begin{cases} \textit{case-oriented} & \text{if } |N_q \cup E_q| > |N_c \cup E_c| \\ \textit{query-oriented} & \textit{otherwise} \end{cases}$$

To implement case-oriented mapping, the algorithm is modified as follows: The collections of not mapped elements are initialized with the case graph elements $Sol_0.N = N_c$ and $Sol_0.E = E_c$ instead of the query elements. In each expansion step (invocation of *expand*), the *select*-function identifies the next case element to which all query elements are mapped:

$$select_{II_C}(Sol) = \begin{cases} e_c \in Sol.E & \text{if } e_c.l \notin Sol.N \wedge e_c.r \notin Sol.N \\ n_c \in Sol.N & \textit{otherwise} \end{cases}$$

New solutions are created for each legal mapping and the f-value is updated using the following modified heuristic estimation function:

$$h_{II_C}(Sol) = \sum_{y \in Sol.N \cup Sol.E} \left(\max_{x \in N_q \cup E_q} \{sim_{N/E}(x, y)\} \right) \cdot \tfrac{1}{|N_q| + |E_q|}$$

When creating new solutions in case-oriented mapping mode, in contrast to the query-oriented mapping mode, null mappings $(\varnothing, x_c)$ are not meaningful to the final mapping and thus are not added to the solution. Instead, it is checked whether all case elements have been considered by the search. In this event, a function *completeSolution* is invoked that adds a null mapping $(x_q, \varnothing)$ to the solution for each not mapped query element x_q. Following this approach, all required null mappings are added in a single step to the same solution. Consequently, fewer solutions are added to the priority queue and we expect that the computation time as well as the memory consumption is reduced. The effect of the adaptive mapping orientation can be demonstrated with the given example. Here, the required null mappings $(n11, \varnothing)$, $(e11, \varnothing)$, and $(e14, \varnothing)$ are postponed in case-oriented mapping mode. The modified functions are as follows:

```
initSolution_C()
| Sol_0.N = N_c;  Sol_0.E = E_c;  Sol_0.m = ∅;  Sol_0.f = 1;
return Sol_0;
```

```
expand_C(Q)
| Sol = first(Q);  Q = rest(Q);  x_c = select_C(Sol);
| forall x_q ∈ N_q ∪ E_q such that the mapping Sol.m ∪ (x_q, x_c) is legal do
| | Q = insert(newSolution_C(Sol, x_q, x_c), Q);
| end
| if T_c(x_c) requires null mapping wrt. Sol.m then
| | Q = insert(newSolution_C(Sol, ∅, x_c), Q);
| end
return Q;
```

```
newSolution_C(Sol, x_q, x_c)
| Sol'.N = Sol.N \ {x_c};  Sol'.E = Sol.E \ {x_c};
| if x_q ≠ ∅ then
| | Sol'.m = Sol.m ∪ (x_q, x_c);
| end
| if Sol'.N = ∅ ∧ Sol'.E = ∅ then
| | completeSolution(Sol');
| end
| Sol'.f = sim_{Sol'.m}(G_q, G_c) + h(Sol');
return Sol';
```

3.3 More Informed Heuristic

A well-informed admissible heuristic $h(Sol)$ is crucial for the efficiency of the A* search. Since $h(Sol)$ must be an upper bound of the estimated similarity, a more informed heuristic overestimates the similarity to a lower degree. Higher accuracy is beneficial since it decreases the possibility that less expanded solutions are ranked higher in the priority queue. Consequently, the search becomes more like a depth-first search and expanding the same element is less often required.

We propose a novel heuristic $h_{III}(Sol)$ that, in contrast to heuristic $h_{II}(Sol)$, considers the current mapping $Sol.m$ for determining the maximum possible similarity a new mapping can achieve. It excludes mappings from the estimation that do not lead to a legal mapping when added to $Sol.m$. Hence, this heuristic is computationally more expensive since all independent mappings must be computed in advance and the heuristic must be updated with respect to the current mapping $Sol.m$. However, since the heuristic is more accurate, we expect that partial solutions with non-optimal (but legal) mappings are ranked lower in the priority queue and hence the overall performance of the search is improved. We define the heuristic estimation function as follows:

$$
\begin{aligned}
h_{III}(Sol) = \tfrac{1}{|N_q|+|E_q|} (& \sum_{x \in Sol.N} \max_{y \in N_c}\{sim_N(x,y)| \; \nexists n \in Sol.N : (n,y) \in Sol.m\} \\
+ & \sum_{x \in Sol.E} \max_{y \in E_c}\{sim_E(x,y)| \; \nexists e \in Sol.E : (e,y) \in Sol.m \\
& \qquad \wedge \nexists (x.l, n) \in Sol.m : y.l \neq n \\
& \qquad \wedge \nexists (x.r, n) \in Sol.m : y.r \neq n \\
& \qquad \wedge \nexists (n, y.l) \in Sol.m : x.l \neq n \\
& \qquad \wedge \nexists (n, y.r) \in Sol.m : x.r \neq n\})
\end{aligned}
$$

An isolated mapping (x, y) between nodes/edges is invalid and thus not considered for estimating the similarity of x, if another node n/edge e was already mapped to y. With respect to isolated edge mappings, it is required that if the left/right node of the edge was already mapped to another node n, the mapping must correspond with the node mapping that is prerequisite for the edge mapping. For the given example graphs, a mapping $(n11, n21) \in Sol.m$ invalidates e.g. the isolated mappings $(n12, n21)$ and $(e15, e23)$. Regarding case-oriented mapping mode, $h_{III}(Sol)$ is slightly modified analogous to $h_{II_C}(Sol)$.

3.4 Heuristic-Based Element Selection

Besides the heuristic, the selection of the next element to be mapped is essential for the A* search and has a significant impact on the performance. If the next element is mapped with a high similarity, the expanded solution is ranked in front of the priority queue. For this reason, we propose to use the estimated similarities from the heuristic. The new select function first selects the element whose best-possible mappings are rated with the highest similarity. If several of such elements exist, the element is chosen with the smallest number of best-possible mappings. If still several elements remain, the element is chosen randomly according to an internal id analogous to $select_{II}(Sol)$. In contrast to $select_{II}(Sol)$, edges are not preferred over nodes. However, if an edge x is selected with respect to the new criteria but the linked nodes have not been mapped yet ($x.l \in Sol.N \vee x.r \in Sol.N$), such nodes are mapped first. The *select*-function is formalized as follows:

```
select_III(Sol)
    x = select_h_III(Sol.N ∪ Sol.E);
    if x ∈ Sol.E ∧ x.l ∈ Sol.N then
        return x.l;
    else if x ∈ Sol.E ∧ x.r ∈ Sol.N then
        return x.r;
    end
return x;
```

Here, $select_{h_{III}}(Sol.N \cup Sol.E)$ determines the best graph element (node or edge) to be mapped with heuristic h_{III} regarding the criteria mentioned above.

4 Experimental Evaluation

The evaluation is structured in two experiments. In the first experiment, we evaluate the performance of the A* variants without pruning the solution space.

Consequently, the measures ensure that the obtained graph similarity is the global optimum. We compare the A* variants regarding the computation time and the maximum number of solutions in the priority queue as an indicator of memory consumption. In the second experiment, we enable pruning and compare the best performing A* variant from the first experiment with the baseline approach *A*II*. We compare the computation time and the similarity error for different size limits of the priority queue.

The experiments are conducted with a set of 40 sandwich recipes represented as semantic workflow graphs[1] such as the graph depicted in Fig. 1 showing the smallest workflow graph from the case base. In both experiments, all pairwise similarities are computed between the graphs (i.e., each graph is used once as query) resulting in a total of 1600 computations. The similarity values of the graph pairs range from 0.0758 to 1.0 with an average of 0.4331. Table 1 shows the quantities of graph elements in the case base. Even though the workflow graphs have a particular structure such as a single workflow node, we note that the improvements are largely independent of specific graph characteristics.

Table 1. Workflow graph elements in the case base

	Size	Workflow nodes	Task nodes	Data nodes	Part-of edges	Control-flow edges	Data-flow edges
Min	30	1	4	4	8	3	10
Median	72	1	8	12	20	7	24
Max	148	1	20	17	37	19	54
Avg	77	1	10	10	20	9	27

We implemented all A* variants in Java for the ProCAKE framework [3]. Each similarity computation is run on a new Java Virtual Machine (JVM) instance to minimize the effects of JVM runtime optimizations. The experiments are run on a computer with a 2.1 GHz processor and each JVM may use a maximum of 80 GB of memory, which does not constitute a restriction.

4.1 Similarity Computation with Ensured Optimality

In the first experiment, we investigate the impact of each single A* improvement and their combination on the performance of the similarity computation. Performance is assessed with respect to the computation time and the maximum number of solutions in the priority queue as an indicator of memory consumption. We test the following hypotheses:

H1a *Search Space Reduction* improves the avg. performance of A* variants.
H1b *Adaptive Mapping Orient.* improves the avg. performance of A* variants.

[1] For implementation details, please refer to [3].

H1c The avg. performance of *A*III* variants (using the more informed heuristic) is better than that of *A*II* variants.

H1d *Heuristic-based Element Selection* improves the avg. performance of *A*III* variants.

In this experiment, the solution space is not pruned by limiting the priority queue size, which ensures that a global optimum is found. However, a timeout of 120 s is set for each computation. We tested all combinations of the various improvements, resulting in a total number of 12 A* variants. *A*II* is used as baseline and can be extended with *Search Space Reduction (R)* and *Adaptive Mapping Orientation (M)*. The new A* variant *A*III* that uses the more informed heuristic can be combined with improvements *R*, *M*, and also with *Heuristic-based Element Selection (S)*.

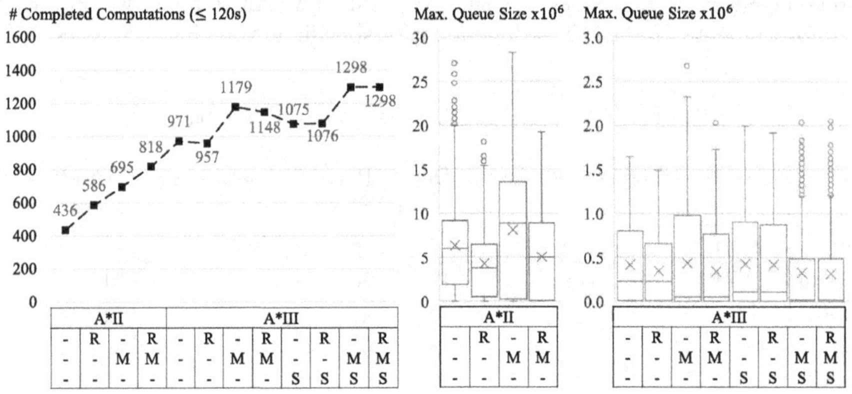

Fig. 3. Performance of A* variants

Figure 3 shows the number of computations (line chart) completed before the specified timeout of 120 s was reached. It also shows the maximum size of the priority queue (box plots) recorded in that time span for each of the 1600 computations. With no A* variant all computations could be finished. Comparing the baseline *A*II* with the fully supplemented variant *A*III-RMS*, three times more computations completed and the maximum size of the priority queue is about ten times smaller. The numbers indicate that *A*III* variants expand considerably less solutions resulting in much smaller priority queues and hence in a lower memory consumption than that of the *A*II* variants. The 436 computations completed with *A*II* took 13.07 s and required a maximum queue size of 1,175,633 in average while the 1298 computations completed with *A*III-RMS* took 8.78 s and a maximum queue size of 96,714 in average. Consequently, the baseline measure is clearly outperformed.

The results also indicate that each improvement positively affects the performance of A* variants. *Search Space Reduction (R)* considerably increased the number of completed computations for *A*II* variants but does not affect or slightly reduces that of *A*III* variants. However, it reduces the maximum queue size for every A* variant. *Adaptive Mapping Orientation (M)* has a higher positive impact on both *A*II* and *A*III* variants regarding the completed computations at the cost of an increased queue size. However, in combination with *Heuristic-based Element Selection (S)* it reduces the queue size. *Heuristic-based Element Selection (S)* itself results in an increased number of completed computations and reduced maximum queue size for the *A*III* variants. All in all, we see hypotheses H1a to H1d confirmed.

4.2 Similarity Computation Without Ensured Optimality

The second experiment addresses the similarity computation with a pruned solution space. Pruning becomes particularly necessary for large graphs due to the high memory consumption of the A* search. As pruning may cause a similarity error, we investigate the impact of different queue size limits on the accuracy in this experiment. We expect that the error decreases for higher limits of the priority queue. We compare the best A* variant from the previous experiment, i.e., *A*III-RMS*, with the baseline *A*II* regarding the computation time and similarity error for different queue size limits. We formulate the following hypotheses for the experiment:

H2a The accuracy of *A*III-RMS* is higher than that of *A*II* for a similar avg. computation time.

H2b The memory consumption of *A*III-RMS* is lower than that of *A*II* for a similar avg. computation time.

For each query graph, we store the highest similarity value obtained from all computations as the global optimum for assessing the similarity error. We do not set a timeout since computation time is restricted by the queue size limit.

Figure 4 depicts the results for selected queue size limits. The box plots show the similarity errors (top left) and the computation times (top right) for different queue size limits. For *A*III-RMS* with queue size limit of 10.000 four extreme outliers (with a maximum value of 642) are cut off. The graphs below plot the similarity error over the computation time (bottom left) and the computation time over the queue size limit (bottom right).

It can clearly be seen, that *A*III-RMS* outperforms *A*II* regarding the similarity error in terms of accuracy for similar average computation times. Consequently, H2a is confirmed. It is apparent that the similarity errors of *A*II* deviate more strongly than that of *A*III-RMS*, independent of the tested queue size limits. For a queue size limit of one, *A*III-RMS* has an average similarity error of 0.01 and a maximum error of 0.9 which seems acceptable for some use cases particularly in consideration of the computation times and errors with larger queue size limits. We observed that the queue size limit of *A*III-RMS* must be chosen about five to ten times smaller than that of *A*II* for achieving a similar computation time in average. Consequently, *A*III* has a considerably

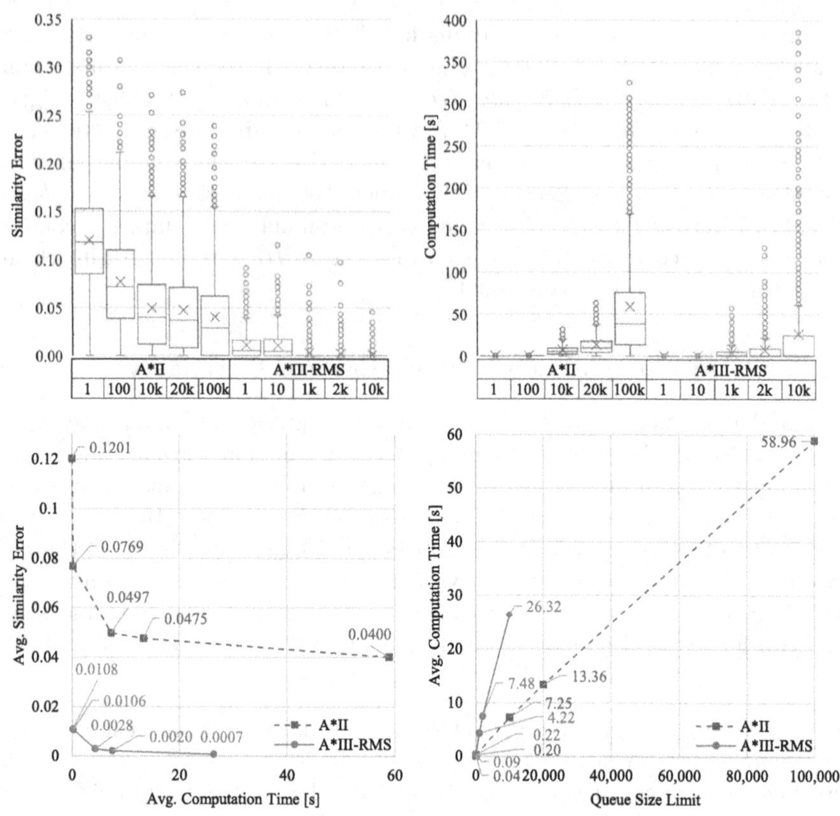

Fig. 4. Similarity error and computation time for different queue size limits

lower memory consumption than *A*II*, which confirms H2b. The computation time increases proportionally to the queue size limit. For *A*III-RMS*, the computation time increases more strongly for larger queue sizes in contrast to *A*II*.

5 Conclusion and Future Work

In this paper, we presented an improved similarity measure for assessing the similarity of semantic graphs whose labels are composed in an object-oriented manner. For such graphs, the efficient similarity computation is particularly challenging since their similarity is affected by structure and semantics. The measure discussed in this paper is based on A* search and is particularly suited for case-based reasoning as it can be combined with knowledge-intensive local similarity measures and outputs similarities and corresponding mappings usable for explanation and adaptation. We presented four complementary improvements that are suitable for enhancing the computation time and memory consumption of the similarity computation. We also demonstrated that the improvements considerably increase the accuracy of computations with pruned solution space.

In a next step, we plan to add an additional parameter to the measure for completing the A* search within a certain period or with limited memory consumption. Based on the given limits, the A* search is performed with minimal pruning that can be intensified dynamically if required. In future work, we also plan to integrate this measure with different retrieval approaches. For instance, Bergmann and Gil [2] presented a parallelized A*-based retrieval approach that enables to compute the top k graphs from the case base without fully computing the similarity for all graphs. To this end, the search process is parallelized for all graphs and the search terminates, when at least k searches have terminated and when the similarity of the k-best graphs is higher than all f-values of the remaining computations. The integration of the improved measure with MAC/FAC retrieval approaches seems also promising for performing knowledge-intensive similarity computations in an efficient manner.

Acknowledgements. This work is funded by the German Research Foundation (DFG) under grant No. BE 1373/3-3 and grant No. 375342983.

References

1. Bergmann, R. (ed.): Experience Management. LNCS, vol. 2432. Springer, Heidelberg (2002). https://doi.org/10.1007/3-540-45759-3
2. Bergmann, R., Gil, Y.: Similarity assessment and efficient retrieval of semantic workflows. Inf. Syst. **40**, 115–127 (2014)
3. Bergmann, R., Grumbach, L., Malburg, L., Zeyen, C.: ProCAKE: aprocess-oriented case-based reasoning framework. In: Case-Based Reasoning Research and Development: 27th ICCBR 2019, Workshop Proceedings (2019)
4. Bergmann, R., Lenz, M., Ollinger, S., Pfister, M.: Similarity measures for case-based retrieval of natural language argument graphs in argumentation machines. In: Barták, R., Brawner, K.W. (eds.) Proceedings of the Thirty-Second FLAIRS Conference, 2019, pp. 329–334. AAAI Press (2019)
5. Bergmann, R., Müller, G.: Similarity-based retrieval and automatic adaptation of semantic workflows. In: Nalepa, G.J., Baumeister, J. (eds.) Synergies Between Knowledge Engineering and Software Engineering. AISC, vol. 626, pp. 31–54. Springer, Cham (2018). https://doi.org/10.1007/978-3-319-64161-4_2
6. Burkhard, H.D., Richter, M.M.: On the notion of similarity in case-based reasoning and fuzzy theory. In: Pal, S.K., Dillon, T.S., Yeung, D.S. (eds.) Soft Computing in Case-Based Reasoning, pp. 29–45. Springer, London (2001). https://doi.org/10.1007/978-1-4471-0687-6_2
7. Champin, P.-A., Solnon, C.: Measuring the similarity of labeled graphs. In: Ashley, K.D., Bridge, D.G. (eds.) ICCBR 2003. LNCS (LNAI), vol. 2689, pp. 80–95. Springer, Heidelberg (2003). https://doi.org/10.1007/3-540-45006-8_9
8. Hoffmann, M., Malburg, L., Klein, P., Bergmann, R.: Using siamese graph neural networks for similarity-based retrieval in process-oriented case-based reasoning. In: Case-Based Reasoning Research and Development: 28th ICCBR 2020. LNCS, Springer (2020). Accepted for publication
9. Kendall-Morwick, J., Leake, D.: A study of two-phase retrieval for process-oriented case-based reasoning. Stud. Comput. Intell. **494**, 7–27 (2014)

10. Klein, P., Malburg, L., Bergmann, R.: Learning workflow embeddings to improve the performance of similarity-based retrieval for process-oriented case-based reasoning. In: Bach, K., Marling, C. (eds.) ICCBR 2019. LNCS (LNAI), vol. 11680, pp. 188–203. Springer, Cham (2019). https://doi.org/10.1007/978-3-030-29249-2_13
11. Li, Y., Gu, C., Dullien, T., Vinyals, O., Kohli, P.: Graph matching networks for learning the similarity of graph structured objects. In: Chaudhuri, K., Salakhutdinov, R. (eds.) Proceedings of the 36th International Conference on Machine Learning, ICML 2019. Proceedings of Machine Learning Research, vol. 97, pp. 3835–3845. PMLR (2019)
12. Ontañón, S.: An overview of distance and similarity functions forstructured data. CoRR **abs/2002.07420** (2020). http://arxiv.org/abs/2002.07420
13. Shemshadi, A., Sheng, Q.Z., Qin, Y.: Efficient pattern matching for graphs with multi-labeled nodes. Knowl. Based Syst. **109**, 256–265 (2016)
14. Sorlin, S., Solnon, C.: Reactive tabu search for measuring graph similarity. In: Brun, L., Vento, M. (eds.) GbRPR 2005. LNCS, vol. 3434, pp. 172–182. Springer, Heidelberg (2005). https://doi.org/10.1007/978-3-540-31988-7_16
15. Zhu, L., Ng, W.K., Cheng, J.: Structure and attribute index for approximate graph matching in large graphs. Inf. Syst. **36**(6), 958–972 (2011)

A Time-Series Similarity Measure for Case-Based Deviation Management to Support Flexible Workflow Execution

Erik Schake[1], Lisa Grumbach[1,2](✉), and Ralph Bergmann[1,3]

[1] Business Information Systems II, University of Trier, 54296 Trier, Germany
{s4ekscha,grumbach,bergmann}@uni-trier.de
[2] Trier University of Applied Sciences, 55761 Birkenfeld, Germany
[3] German Research Center for Artificial Intelligence (DFKI), Branch University of Trier, Behringstraße 21, 54296 Trier, Germany
ralph.bergmann@dfki.de

Abstract. Our objective is to develop an approach based on case-based reasoning that detects and handles unforeseen deviations that occur in flexible workflow execution. With a case-based approach we aim at supporting the continuation of a deviant workflow execution by utilizing successfully completed processes, where similar deviations emerged. As a first step, this work introduces a novel similarity measure based on time sequence similarity that is able to compare running and completed workflow instances. We implemented and evaluated our approach in the ProCAKE framework. The proposed similarity measure achieves promising results considering runtime and similarity assessment.

Keywords: Knowledge management · Process management · Case-based reasoning · Flexibility by deviation

1 Introduction

Digitalization is advancing in today's business. Small and medium-sized enterprises (SMEs) appear to be lagging behind compared to large companies. Process-aware information systems [1] are well established for standardized processes, but they lack support for flexibility, which is often required in SMEs and may lead to competitive advantages. Additionally, in SMEs there are often few experts who are responsible for certain processes. The knowledge about how things are done is implicit, not stored digitally and information is often only shared orally. These experts usually deviate and perform processes due to their expertise and experiences without losing control or missing the objective, but rather optimizing the process [19]. Tracing these processes automatically and using them for process control may simplify the transfer and preservation of "best practices". This in turn may lead to an increase of efficiency and enhanced assistance possibilities especially for inexperienced users. Furthermore, bypassing the system and thus a loss of knowledge and transparency is prevented.

I. Watson and R. Weber (Eds.): ICCBR 2020, LNAI 12311, pp. 33–48, 2020.
https://doi.org/10.1007/978-3-030-58342-2_3

A main characteristic of an adequate approach for SMEs is to allow unexpected deviations and support unforeseen changing circumstances. Thereby, the key challenge is to determine how to continue with the workflow, while still achieving a successful completion. Existing approaches either require a manual handling of upcoming deviations or an extensive modeling of expert knowledge, resulting in a large effort for knowledge acquisition and leading to high costs for maintenance [2,5,7,8,15,19,21]. To avoid these disadvantages we propose to utilize past experiences, more specifically, successfully completed processes that contain similar deviations. Applying case-based reasoning (CBR) seems to be promising, as previous made experiences are exploited for adapting to unknown situations. Our objective is to develop an approach based on CBR that handles deviations that occur in flexible workflow execution, but still guides the user by recommending adequate work items. As a first, but important step into this direction, this paper presents a novel similarity measure based on time sequence similarity that is able to compare running and completed workflow instances.

In the next section, we introduce the notions of workflow flexibility and deviation management as well as our pursued approach. Related similarity measures are sketched in Sect. 3. Our proposed similarity measure is presented in Sect. 4, while an evaluation of our concept is outlined in Sect. 5.

2 Deviation Management for Flexible Workflows

In this section our previous work on workflow flexibility and its limitations will be presented, before we introduce the idea of a case-based deviation management.

2.1 Workflow Flexibility

Flexible workflows have been focused in research for more than a decade [18]. Four different flexibility principles are distinguished [18]. *Flexibility by Design, Change* and *Underspecification* either require an entire awareness about all possible upcoming situations at design-time in order to manually model all possible alternatives, or a remodeling of the workflow is necessary at run-time. *Flexibility by Deviation* in contrast "is the ability for a process instance to deviate at runtime from the execution path prescribed by the original process without altering its process definition" [18]. Hence, the user is able to execute tasks that are not suggested as next activity, as the work list is only seen as a guideline. Thus, single instances may not fit to the process model. We therefore explicitly distinguish between modeled workflow, denoted as *de jure* and executed workflow, called *de facto* [1]. This, however, raises the problem of deciding how to continue with the deviating workflow to achieve a successful completion. To solve this problem we developed a workflow engine that facilitates flexibility by deviation.

2.2 Constraint-Based Workflow Engine

During the SEMAFLEX [11] and the SEMANAS [12] project we developed a flexible workflow engine based on constraints. We presented an approach [9], that allows flexible deviations from prescribed workflows, but still maintains control and recommends valid work items to some extent.

The proposed method is applied to imperatively modeled block-oriented workflows, which additionally comprise semantic information. Block-oriented workflows are constructed through a single root block element, which in turn consists of a single task node, a sequence of two block elements or a control-flow block. Start and end of control-flow blocks are clearly defined through control-flow nodes, of which three different types exist ($type \in \{+, \times, \circ\}$). These workflows are represented as semantic graphs (denoted as *NESTGraph*), where nodes and edges additionally link to semantic descriptions [3]. Figure 1 shows an excerpt of the workflow, which we further on used for evaluating our approach.

This workflow consists of six task nodes (blue rectangles), three data nodes (ovals), two control-flow nodes (red rhombuses), which represent an exclusive block ("×"), and one workflow node (blue rhombus). Additionally, the edges denote either control-flow (solid black lines), data-flow (solid grey lines, input/output relation) or part-of edges (dashed lines). Furthermore each node is associated with a semantic description (grey rectangles), which contains additional information, e.g. data node d_3 is assigned a *name* "volume" with a *value* of "1000000".

In our approach [9] we transform these imperative workflow models into declarative constraints, which indicate temporal dependencies between task activations, to be able to determine task activations and thus possible executions in a specific state of the workflow. A constraint satisfaction problem (CSP) is constructed on the basis of these generated constraints and logged task enactments. A solution of the CSP is searched for, which represents a valid enactment sequence of all tasks. Thus, with a CSP solution we are able to recommend which task to execute next. As we only trace task executions, deviations from this prescribed work list are permitted. Ideally, the user decides to do something else if s/he is sure that this is more appropriate in this specific situation than what the de jure workflow proposes. In such a case, constraints are violated but they can be retracted easily and fast at run-time in order to restore consistency. By regarding the remaining constraints, valid solutions can be computed and thus, the workflow engine is re-enabled to recommend further work items to complete the workflow.

However, a categorization of deviations and their cause is not considered until now. Several strategies for resolving inconsistencies and their limitations have been presented in [10]. Consider the example in Fig. 2, where the left upper row shows the initial situation and the second row represents the following step with an additionally executed task. Rectangles indicate tasks and edges represent the execution order. Blue-filled nodes were already executed, green ones are currently recommended and colorless nodes are not activated yet. In the left lower row there is an executed task, which is not in a valid order, thus a deviation occurred (marked in orange). The cause of the violation is not explicit without semantic knowledge and there may be different reasons and consequences. Tasks should be skipped either due to becoming obsolete or due to being executed but

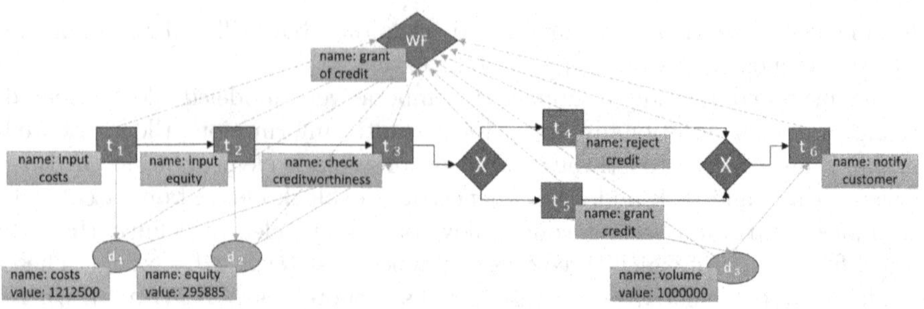

Fig. 1. Exemplary block-oriented semantic workflow graph (Color figure online)

without notice of the system (cf. a) in Fig. 2). Alternatively, task order should be adopted due to unknown reasons according to b) in Fig. 2.

This scenario is a simple type of deviation, but nevertheless requires a decision about which resolving strategy to apply. Besides, deviations might lead to additional deviations or might be more complex, which makes it impossible to determine similar strategies to handle all possible scenarios. Several approaches to deviation management exist, that utilize rules or knowledge which is specified beforehand [2,5,7,8,15,19]. CBRFlow [21] is a system that exploits conversational CBR to react to unexpected deviations. Business rules are used to model workflow run-time changes and may then be recommended in similar situations. To handle deviations, these approaches either require user interaction or domain knowledge resulting in a significant acquisition effort and limited usability.

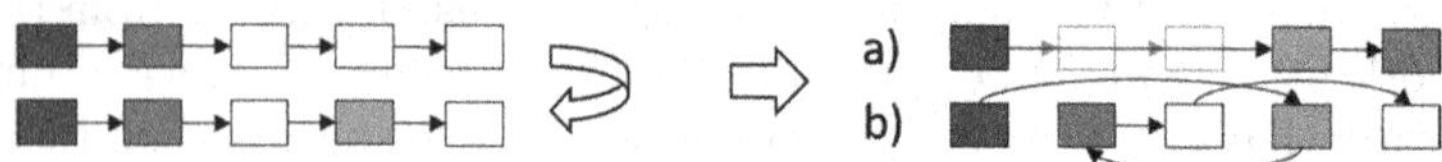

Fig. 2. Example sequential workflow with deviation and different interpretation

2.3 Case-Based Deviation Management

Our aim is to construct methods that can be applied in an automated manner and support the user without the need of manual intervention or prior knowledge acquisition. Therefore we focus on CBR as a technique to overcome the previously mentioned disadvantages. With a case-based approach we expect to support workflow continuation after a deviation by recommending adequate work items on the basis of similar cases. The overall approach is sketched in Fig. 3.

Case. As cases we regard all de facto workflows and their corresponding de jure workflow. The de jure workflow is block-oriented and the de facto workflow is a simple sequence of tasks, which were traced at run-time. This includes workflows with deviations as well as without deviations, as both cases might be useful for task recommendation.

Query. A running workflow instance, i.e a de facto workflow which is not completed yet, will be used as the query. This instance is a subsequence of a completed de facto workflow and contains at least one deviation (see orange-coloured node in Fig. 3) concerning its de jure workflow that occurred at the time of the request. The associated de jure workflow is also available.

Deviation Management. All phases of the CBR cycle are important for a holistic view of deviation management and lead to a self-learning system.

Retrieve. With an adequate similarity measure we aim at searching for similar de facto workflows whose subsequences match the current instance, containing a similar deviation compared to the query.

Reuse. This most similar case or even several similar cases might then be used to recommend tasks that were successive to the subsequence ending with the deviation (see green-coloured nodes in Fig. 3). In some circumstances, a simple transfer of the solution will not be reasonable, but rather an adaptation of the recommended remaining workflow part might be necessary.

Revise. As tasks are only recommended , the user is still able to execute a task, which was not part of the solution resulting from the reuse step. Thus, by continuing the query workflow, the solution might be revised.

Retain. When the query workflow has successfully terminated, its de facto workflow, containing the actual execution, can be integrated in the case base.

In this paper we focus on the retrieval phase and present a similarity measure that is necessary for this case-based approach. The de facto workflows that are compared are perceived as time series that consist of tasks with additional semantic information. Therefore an adequate similarity measure based on time sequence similarity is searched for.

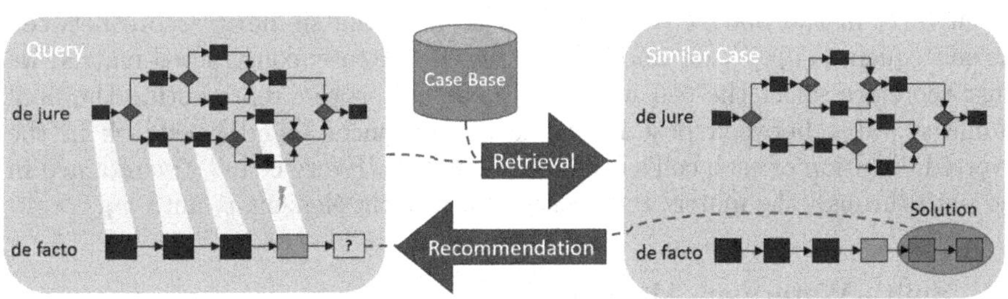

Fig. 3. Case-based approach for handling deviations (Color figure online)

3 Similarity Measures for Time Series

Two basic approaches of similarity measures for time series can be identified in literature. Either the series are transformed into a representation format, such as an n-dimensional vector, which then is compared, or the algorithm finds an alignment between both series which is then assigned a similarity score by aggregating local element similarities. Three promising approaches will be introduced in more detail in this section.

3.1 Dynamic Time Warping

Dynamic time warping (DTW) was originally developed to properly align distorted time series data collected from voice recordings [4,17]. Contrary to simple euclidean distance, which only evaluates distances between elements with the same timestamps, DTW allows elements to be warped onto elements with different timestamps. It therefore is resistant to compression and stretching.

Natively, DTW was defined using distance functions, however, since distances can be losslessly converted into similarity scores, we will present the algorithm using a similarity function. Given two sequences v and w with elements v_i ($i = 1, \ldots, m$) and w_j ($j = 1, \ldots, n$) to be compared, their leading elements are first set to a null value: $v_0 = w_0 = -$. The scoring matrix H is then constructed in the following way. Its first row and column are initialized to zero: $H_{0,j} = H_{i,0} = 0$ for $j = 0, \ldots, n$ and $i = 0, \ldots, m$. Every other cell's value can be calculated by the recursive function $H_{i,j}$:

$$H_{i,j} = \max \begin{cases} H_{i,j-1} + sim(v_i, w_j), & \text{step horizontally} \\ H_{i-1,j-1} + 2 * sim(v_i, w_j), & \text{step diagonally} \\ H_{i-1,j} + sim(v_i, w_j), & \text{step vertically} \\ 0 \end{cases}$$

A cell (k, l) in the matrix is interpreted to hold the similarity score between the subsequences $v_1 v_2 \ldots v_k$ and $w_1 w_2 \ldots w_l$. In the fully constructed matrix, we must therefore select the cell with the maximum score - representing the final similarity value between best matching subsequences - and backtrack in the inverted direction of each cell's original calculation. Every cell (i, j) contained in the path through the matrix represents a warp from element v_i onto w_j.

3.2 Smith-Waterman-Algorithm

Another adoption of finding subsequence alignments is the Smith-Waterman-Algorithm (SWA) [20]. Inspired by the Levenshtein distance, the alignment is found by successively either matching, inserting or deleting elements from one series with regard to the other.

Initialization of the scoring matrix is conducted equivalently to DTW, however, the scoring function itself differentiates the two approaches. Horizontal and vertical steps in the matrix represent either deletion or insertion (indels) of an element, while diagonal steps are interpreted as aligning two elements. Therefore, a penalty scheme must be introduced that assigns a negative score to any indel operation (cf. *penaltyInsertion* and *penaltyDeletion*). The scoring matrix is constructed in the following way:

$$H_{i,j} = \max \begin{cases} H_{i,j-1} + penaltyInsertion(b_j), & \text{insertion} \\ H_{i-1,j-1} + sim(a_i, b_j), & \text{match/mismatch} \\ H_{i-1,j} + penaltyDeletion(a_i), & \text{deletion} \\ 0 \end{cases}$$

Again, the highest score in the matrix represents the obtained similarity value. However, the path found by backtracking in the matrix must be interpreted differently. In contrast to DTW, only cells that originated from diagonal steps represent an alignment of those elements. Horizontally and vertically created cells represent insertions and deletions with regard to sequence v. This utilization of indel operations makes the measure very noise-resistant.

In addition to the similarity score, both DTW and SWA find series alignments which can be further exploited in the reuse phase of CBR. Their main difference is the interpretation of the found alignment path. SWA considers sequences to be equal if one is a subsequence of the other, whereas DTW considers sequences as equal if they are simply stretched or compressed versions of each other. The construction of quadratic matrices results in $O(n^2)$ comparisons. This however can be significantly lowered [14].

Zarka et al. [23] adopt SWA for an approach called trace-base reasoning. They utilize this method in order to find suggestions for workflow continuation in a mobile video editing suite by also incorporating a CBR approach. However, the context of deviations is not considered by the authors.

3.3 Weighted Vector Similarity

Contrary to the other two approaches which find series alignments by directly comparing the sequences, a similarity measure introduced by Gundersen [13] transforms the sequences into a vector representation. It is based on the assumption that recent tasks are most important when comparing processes.

Originally, this measure was defined on event sequences. Therefore we define the end of each task to be an event. Given n events, the sequence A is then transformed into a vector $V_A = (w_1, w_2, ..., w_n)$ with weights w_i depicting each event's importance in A based on its temporal position pos_i, calculated as follows:

$$w_i = \frac{1}{2^{\frac{end - pos_i}{h}}} \quad (1)$$

The halving distance h specifies the distance to the end where the events' importance is one half. Those weighted vector representations can now be compared by utilizing measures such as cosine similarity and relative component fraction.

The main strength of this measure is its efficiency having a computational complexity of only $O(n)$. Major drawbacks however include that it is not able to consider semantic similarity and can only compare entire sequences.

4 Similarity Measure for Deviating Workflows

In this section we first sketch specific properties of flexibility by deviation that are important for determining similarity. A pre-processing of the cases is described subsequently. Finally, the developed algorithm for similarity assessment[1] which is based on the previously presented approaches is introduced in detail.

4.1 Characteristics of Similarity for Deviating Workflows

The similarity measure has to deal with a subset relation between query and case, as the de facto workflow of the query has not terminated yet, whereas the de facto workflows of the cases are complete.

Another important aspect of the pursued similarity is that under certain conditions some mismatches of subsequences of case and query should have low or rather no influence on the similarity score. This refers to two aspects. On the one hand, we assume that differences with a greater temporal distance to the occurrence of the deviation should have a lower impact on the similarity. Therefore a weighting function will be included in the final similarity measure.

On the other hand, we incorporate a property of case and query which we call model-consistency. Any de facto workflow or any subsequence of a de facto workflow without a deviation, but conforming to the de jure workflow is denoted as model-consistent. In some cases, if case and query contain the same deviation but additionally differ in some other prior subsequences, which are both model-consistent, this difference might be ignored if it is not related to the deviation.

4.2 Pre-processing of the Case Base

The pre-processing algorithm is used to determine irrelevant workflow blocks in case and query which are excluded from similarity assessment by deleting these subsequences prior to comparison. This results in reduced cases and thus, a potentially less complex and faster similarity assessment. Furthermore, pre-processing can be done beforehand such that retrieval time is not affected but rather enhanced. As prerequisite, case and query need to be based on the same de jure workflow such that those subsequences might be deleted that belong to corresponding parts. This is necessary for a reasonable and meaningful comparison of reduced case and reduced query. As our overall approach is limited to block-oriented workflows we exploit the block structuring for this purpose. The pre-processing algorithm prepares the case base with further information which is used when a query arises. An example is presented in Fig. 4.

[1] An implementation is included in the ProCAKE framework V1.2 and publicly available under http://procake.uni-trier.de.

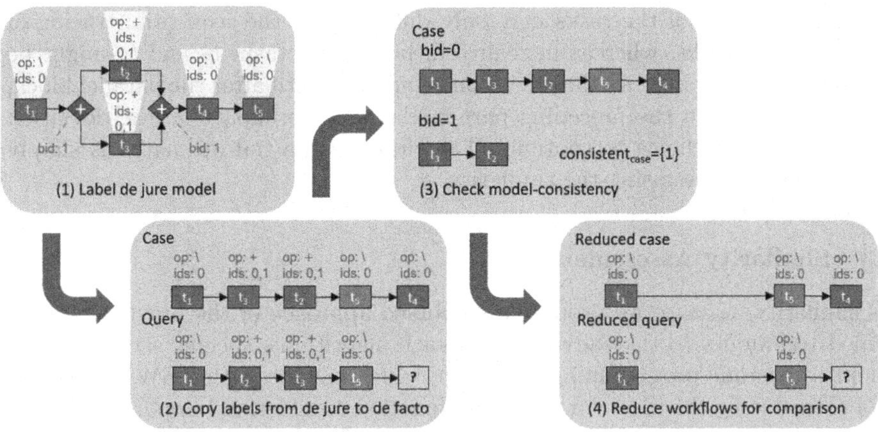

Fig. 4. Exemplary pre-processing (Color figure online)

Step 1. First, the nodes of the de jure workflow of each case are labeled. Every control-flow node pair, i.e. split and join node, is assigned a unique id, $bid \in blockids \subset \mathbb{N}$, and each task node t is labeled with certain information. This includes the operator of the nearest preceding control-flow node $op^t \in \{+, \times, \circ, \backslash\}$ that can be any type of control-flow node or "\", which denotes the highest level where tasks are not nested in a control-flow block. Furthermore, a set of ids, $ids^t \in \mathcal{P}(blockids)$, of all preceding control-flow split nodes that have not been joined until the currently regarded task node is added to denote the position concerning levels of nested workflow blocks.

Step 2. These labels are subsequently transferred to all corresponding de facto workflows of the cases. This can be done easily, since each task node in the de facto instance contains a reference id of the specific task of the de jure workflow.

Step 3. Model-consistency can be checked for each de facto workflow. For each $bid \in blockids$ the set of task ids $T_B = \{t | bid \in ids^t\}$ is extracted from the de facto workflow, preserving their sequential order, and validated by the constraint-based workflow engine. Every bid of consistent control-flow blocks is stored in a set $consistent \subseteq blockids$. In the example in Fig. 4 this is shown for the case workflow. The sequence for $bid = 0$ is not model-consistent, as a deviation is included (cf. position of t_5), whereas the subsequence for $bid = 1$ is model-consistent and this bid is thus added to $consistent$. The same procedure will be applied to the de facto workflow of the query.

Step 4. Prior to similarity assessment, query and cases can be reduced. If any bid coincides in the set $consistent$ of both query and case, every task t where $bid \in ids^t$ can be deleted from the de facto workflows. Hence, these tasks do not affect the similarity score. In the example in Fig. 4, $bid = 1 \in consistent_{case} = consistent_{query}$ and thus, t_2 and t_3 are deleted from both de facto workflows. In this case the omission of tasks of the parallel workflow block is reasonable, since the order of the tasks may only differ due to the sequential tracing of terminated tasks, whereas in reality in both cases tasks t_2 and t_3 might be executed in parallel. As the deviation occurs not until after the parallel block, the difference in the preceding part might have no impact on the deviation and the right choice to continue. Therefore this partial mismatch is simply ignored when assessing the similarity.

4.3 Similarity Assessment

As similarity measure we propose a combined approach of the previously mentioned techniques to take advantage of each algorithm's specific strengths. We adopt a dynamic programming approach, which includes either SWA or DTW, and extend it by the idea of a weighting function considering temporal ordering. Furthermore local task similarities include data-flow and semantic information. The similarity assessment can either be applied to reduced cases or non-reduced ones. We compare a de facto workflow of the query with m tasks to a de facto workflow of a case with n tasks.

Local Task Similarity. We define local task similarity sim_t of a query task q_i^t and a case task c_j^t as follows:

$$sim_t(q_i^t, c_j^t) = \frac{l_t * sim_N(q_i^t, c_j^t) + l_i * sim_{df}(in_{q_i^t}, in_{c_j^t}) + l_o * sim_{df}(out_{q_i^t}, out_{c_j^t})}{l_t + l_i + l_o} \quad (2)$$

This value is composed of task, input and output similarity, each assigned a respective weight l_t, l_i, l_o. sim_N represents an aggregated similarity score of the semantic description of the task nodes. sim_{df} describes the similarity of input and output data nodes respectively. The set of input data nodes of the query $in_{q_i^t}$ is compared to the set of input data nodes of the case $in_{c_j^t}$ by finding the best possible mapping. The same is applied to the sets of output data nodes $(out_{q_i^t}, out_{c_j^t})$. These three local similarities are finally summed up and normalized by the sum of all weights.

Scoring Matrix. The scoring matrix that combines either SWA or DTW with a temporal distance factor and the presented local similarity is defined as follows:

$$H_{i,j} = max \begin{cases} H_{i-1,j-1} & + wTemp_i * ALG_{i,j}(diagonal), \\ H_{i-1,j} & + wTemp_i * ALG_{i,j}(vertical), \\ H_{i,j-1} & + wTemp_i * ALG_{i,j}(horizontal), \\ 0 \end{cases} \quad (3)$$

As starting point the first row and column are initialized to 0, $\forall j : 0, \ldots, n : H_{0,j} = 0$ and $\forall i : 0, \ldots, m : H_{i,0} = 0$. The stepping function $ALG_{i,j}$ differs depending on which algorithm is used. Equations 4 and 5 show both variants.

$$SWA_{i,j}(x) := \begin{cases} sim_t(q_i^t, c_j^t) & \text{if } x = \text{'diagonal'}, \\ penaltyDeletion(q_i^t) & \text{if } x = \text{'horizontal'}, \\ penaltyInsertion(c_j^t) & \text{if } x = \text{'vertical'}, \\ 0 & \text{otherwise} \end{cases} \tag{4}$$

$$DTW_{i,j}(x) := \begin{cases} 2 * sim_t(q_i^t, c_j^t) & \text{if } x = \text{'diagonal'}, \\ sim_t(q_i^t, c_j^t) & \text{if } x = \text{'horizontal'}, \\ sim_t(q_i^t, c_j^t) & \text{if } x = \text{'vertical'}, \\ 0 & \text{otherwise} \end{cases} \tag{5}$$

This score is further multiplied by the weight depending on temporal distance. Therefore, Eq. 1 will be adapted as follows. Here, m is the length of the query, as this serves as baseline for the similarity calculation. The halving time as a parameter is assigned a value $h \in [0, m]$.

$$wTemp_i = \frac{1}{2^{\frac{m-i}{h}}} \tag{6}$$

Similarity Score. The non-normalized overall similarity score sim_{raw} can be obtained by searching for the largest value in the last row of the matrix. By limiting this search to $H_{m,j}$ for $0 < j \leq n$, it is ensured that the found alignment always ends with the last task of the query, thus, $sim_{raw} = H_{m,k}$ with $H_{m,k} > H_{m,j}$ for all $j \in \{0, \ldots, n\} \backslash \{k\}$.

To normalize the obtained score, it must be divided by the maximum possible score with regard to the query. In SWA, local positive similarity values are only aggregated when stepping diagonally in the matrix, hence, the maximum possible score can be calculated by finding the amount of diagonal steps in the alignment. In contrast, DTW adds a positive value to the score when stepping in either direction. Let $align = \{(0,0), \ldots, (m,k)\}$ denote all cells from the alignment path. Let $diag = \{(i_0, j_0), \ldots, (i_p, j_p)\} \subseteq align$ denote all cells that originated from a diagonal step and let $other = align \backslash diag$ denote all other assignments. Normalized similarity is then calculated as follows:

$$sim_{defacto}^{SWA}(q, c) = \frac{sim_{raw}}{\sum\limits_{(i,j) \in diag} wTemp_i} \tag{7}$$

$$sim_{defacto}^{DTW}(q, c) = \frac{sim_{raw}}{\sum\limits_{(i,j) \in diag} 2 * wTemp_i + \sum\limits_{(i,j) \in other} wTemp_i} \tag{8}$$

5 Evaluation

We evaluated our method by comparing it to a baseline approach. Bergmann and Gil, who developed the NESTGraph formalism, presented a graph-based similarity measure for modeled workflows [3]. They utilize heuristic A* search in order to find a mapping m that assigns nodes and edges from graph A to nodes and edges of graph B. Given such a legal mapping m, local similarities between the mapped elements are calculated and aggregated into a global similarity score.

While many related approaches have been researched [6,16,22] that all utilize workflow mappings, the method presented by Bergmann and Gil constitutes an exception to these mostly infeasible proposals for searching the mappings. Therefore, their A* approach will serve as the baseline similarity algorithm.[2] We want to show that our approach outperforms A* both regarding the obtained ranking when a retrieval is performed, and regarding overall retrieval times. To validate this, three hypotheses are considered:

H1 For every query instance, our approach will retrieve the *best case* from the case base at a higher or equal rank compared to the A* approach.
H2 Using pre-processing, rankings will be as high or higher than without.
H3 Our overall retrieval times are significantly lower than those of A*.

As prerequisite, we must clarify how we identify the best case from the case base for each query. Through communication with field experts, we modeled a realistic de jure workflow, based on a credit grant process, consisting of 31 task nodes, 18 data nodes and 4 control-flow blocks. As queries, non-terminated workflow instances were created which contain at least one deviation at the end with regard to the process model. Based on a pool of realistic deviations, randomly chosen ones were further included in the queries.

Then, a matching *best case* was constructed for every query through insertions of tasks leading to the termination of the query workflow. Additionally, not more than three deviations from the pool which are not included in the query have been added to this case. However, model-consistent passages may have been replaced with different but still model-consistent passages in order to evaluate pre-processing. Those generated instances were then inserted into the case base. Thereby, each query is associated with exactly one *best case*. The case base was filled up with additional 27 cases, each of which contains at least as much deviations with regard to every query as their respective *best cases*.

We performed a simple linear retrieval using the A* approach and our approaches with and without pre-processing for every query, respectively. Each retrieval produces a ranking of the cases based on their respective similarities to the query. The rank of each query's *best case* is shown in Fig. 5. In 50% of the retrievals, A* performs as well as at least two configurations of our approaches.

[2] Note that, in contrast to our approach, A* additionally searches for mappings between the two graphs' edges which accounts for approximately half of the runtimes. Furthermore, due to resource restrictions, the search queue is limited to 10000 entries which may hinder the algorithm from finding the overall best mapping.

However, in the other half, it produces significantly poorer results. In no case does it outperform all of our approaches regarding the ranking. Thus, hypothesis H1 is approved. Most of the time it does not matter whether pre-processing was applied or not. Only in queries 6 and 14, the utilization of pre-processing improves the rankings significantly. There are also queries (5,11,13) where it may even impair the results. However, with the exception of query 11, this is due to already poor results of DTW when no pre-processing is being applied. Thus, hypothesis H2, only holds partially.

The retrieval times of the approaches differ by several orders of magnitude even after correction for edge mapping. In our sample, mean retrieval time using SWA or DTW was 45 ms in contrast to A* taking 13437 ms on average[3]. Preprocessing can reduce runtimes even further. This shows a significant advantage of our approach and verifies hypothesis H3.

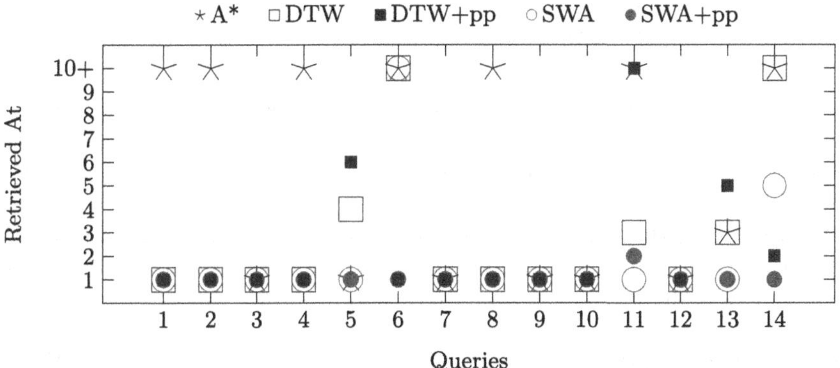

Fig. 5. Similarity ranking for best matching cases (Color figure online)

6 Conclusion and Future Work

We presented an approach for a case-based deviation management in the context of flexible workflow execution. In this paper we focused on the retrieval phase and therefore proposed a similarity measure that is able to compare completed and running workflow instances where a deviation occurred. Therefore we utilized time sequence similarity enhanced by a weighting factor that determines the temporal distance to the deviation. Furthermore, we presented a pre-processing method for the case base in order to ignore differences that result from the simple sequential tracing of tasks in the de facto workflows. We implemented the developed algorithms in ProCAKE and evaluated our similarity measure in

[3] Retrieval time of the A* approach was corrected for edge mapping which accounts for approximately halve of the runtime. The experiments were conducted on a personal computer with an 8-core Intel Core i7-6700 CPU @3.4 GHz and 32 GB of RAM.

comparison to a graph-based mapping algorithm based on A* search. The runtime and similarity assessment comparison shows promising results. As we aim at supporting workflow continuation with a retrieved similar case, an evaluation of usefulness is still pending. Therefore recommended tasks after the deviation, resulting from the most similar case, need to be rated.

Furthermore, as future work the remaining phases of the CBR cycle that were not considered in detail until now, but rather briefly sketched, will be investigated. Adaptation methods will be developed in order to increase the suitability of the solution for the query. Therefore the existing constraints that are processed by the workflow engine, will be taken into account, as they represent the de jure workflow, actual information about the de facto workflow as well as additional semantic information, e.g. state of the constraints (valid vs. violated).

Additionally, the application of the presented pre-processing algorithm needs to be refined. The results of the evaluation already indicate that the reduction cannot be applied reasonably in every condition, but rather needs to be weighed. The decision, whether model-consistency should be more important than regarding additional differences between case and query, should rather be made based upon the de jure workflow. Data-flow dependencies could be taken into account or a manual decision about which workflow block simply needs to be model-consistent during case comparison, for example depending on the type of control-flow block (parallel vs. exclusive), could be considered. In case of an exclusive block, the reduction would result in equal treatment of excluding task executions, even if they possibly have a totally different impact on the deviation or rather on the continuation after the deviation. A concept for deciding in which circumstances reduction of case and query is appropriate will be elaborated.

Acknowledgements. This work is part of the research project SEMANAS and is funded by the Federal Ministry of Education and Research (BMBF), grant no. 13FH013IX6.

References

1. van der Aalst, W.M.P.: Business process management - a comprehensive survey. ISRN Softw. Eng. **2013**, 1–37 (2013)
2. Adams, M., ter Hofstede, A.H.M., van der Aalst, W.M.P., Edmond, D.: Dynamic, extensible and context-aware exception handling for workflows. In: On the Move to Meaningful Internet Systems 2007: CoopIS, DOA, ODBASE, GADA, and IS, OTM Confederated International Conferences, Vilamoura, Portugal, 25–30 November 2007, Proceedings, Part I, pp. 95–112 (2007)
3. Bergmann, R., Gil, Y.: Similarity assessment and efficient retrieval of semantic workflows. Inf. Syst. **40**, 115–127 (2014)
4. Berndt, D.J., Clifford, J.: Using dynamic time warping to find patterns in time series. In: KDD Workshop, vol. 10, pp. 359–370 (1994)
5. Casati, F., Ceri, S., Paraboschi, S., Pozzi, G.: Specification and implementation of exceptions in workflow management systems. ACM Trans. Database Syst. **24**(3), 405–451 (1999)

6. Dijkman, R., Dumas, M., Van Dongen, B., Krik, R., Mendling, J.: Similarity of business process models: metrics and evaluation. Inf. Syst. **36**(2), 498–516 (2011)
7. Döhring, M., Zimmermann, B., Godehardt, E.: Extended workflow flexibility using rule-based adaptation patterns with eventing semantics. In: Informatik 2010: Service Science - Neue Perspektiven für die Informatik, Beiträge der 40. Jahrestagung der GI, Band 1, Leipzig, Deutschland, pp. 195–200 (2010)
8. Grambow, G., Oberhauser, R., Reichert, M.: Event-driven exception handling for software engineering processes. In: Daniel, F., Barkaoui, K., Dustdar, S. (eds.) BPM 2011. LNBIP, vol. 99, pp. 414–426. Springer, Heidelberg (2012). https://doi.org/10.1007/978-3-642-28108-2_40
9. Grumbach, L., Bergmann, R.: Semaflex: a novel approach for implementing workflow flexibility by deviation based on constraint satisfaction problem solving. Expert Syst. (2019)
10. Grumbach, L., Bergmann, R.: Towards case-based deviation management for flexible workflows. In: Proceedings of the Conference LWDA, Berlin, Germany, 30 September–2 October 2019, pp. 241–252 (2019)
11. Grumbach, L., Rietzke, E., Schwinn, M., Bergmann, R., Kuhn, N.: SEMAFLEX - semantic integration of flexible workflow and document management. In: Proceedings of the Conference LWDA, Potsdam, Germany, 12–14 September 2016, pp. 43–50 (2016)
12. Grumbach, L., Rietzke, E., Schwinn, M., Bergmann, R., Kuhn, N.: SEMANAS - semantic support for grant application processes. In: Proceedings of the Conference LWDA, Mannheim, Germany, 22–24 August 2018, pp. 126–131 (2018)
13. Gundersen, O.E.: Toward measuring the similarity of complex event sequences in real-time. In: Agudo, B.D., Watson, I. (eds.) ICCBR 2012. LNCS (LNAI), vol. 7466, pp. 107–121. Springer, Heidelberg (2012). https://doi.org/10.1007/978-3-642-32986-9_10
14. Mueen, A., Keogh, E.: Extracting optimal performance from dynamic time warping. In: Proceedings of the 22nd ACM SIGKDD International Conference on Knowledge Discovery and Data Mining, pp. 2129–2130 (2016)
15. Müller, R., Greiner, U., Rahm, E.: $\mathrm{A_{gent}W_{ork}}$: a workflow system supporting rule-based workflow adaptation. Data Knowl. Eng. **51**(2), 223–256 (2004)
16. Obweger, H., Suntinger, M., Schiefer, J., Raidl, G.: Similarity searching in sequences of complex events. In: 2010 4th International Conference on Research Challenges in Information Science - Proceedings, RCIS 2010, pp. 631–640 (2010)
17. Sakoe, H., Chiba, S.: Dynamic programming algorithm optimization for spoken word recognition. IEEE Trans. Acoust. Speech Sig. Process. **26**(1), 43–49 (1978)
18. Schonenberg, H., Mans, R., Russell, N., Mulyar, N., van der Aalst, W.M.P.: Towards a taxonomy of process flexibility. In: Proceedings of the Forum at the CAiSE 2008 Conference, Montpellier, France, 18–20 June 2008, pp. 81–84 (2008)
19. da Silva, M.A.A., Bendraou, R., Robin, J., Blanc, X.: Flexible deviation handling during software process enactment. In: Workshops Proceedings of the 15th IEEE International Enterprise Distributed Object Computing Conference, EDOCW 2011, Helsinki, Finland, 29 August–2 September 2011, pp. 34–41 (2011)
20. Smith, T.F., Waterman, M.S.: Identification of common molecular subsequences. J. Mol. Biol. **147**(1), 195–197 (1981)
21. Weber, B., Wild, W., Breu, R.: CBRFlow: enabling adaptive workflow management through conversational case-based reasoning. In: Funk, P., González Calero, P.A. (eds.) ECCBR 2004. LNCS (LNAI), vol. 3155, pp. 434–448. Springer, Heidelberg (2004). https://doi.org/10.1007/978-3-540-28631-8_32

22. Wombacher, A., Rozie, M.: Evaluation of workflow similarity measures in service discovery. In: Service-Oriented Electronic Commerce, Proceedings zur Konferenz im Rahmen der MKWI 2006. Gesellschaft für Informatik eV (2006)
23. Zarka, R., Cordier, A., Egyed-Zsigmond, E., Lamontagne, L., Mille, A.: Similarity measures to compare episodes in modeled traces. In: Delany, S.J., Ontañón, S. (eds.) ICCBR 2013. LNCS (LNAI), vol. 7969, pp. 358–372. Springer, Heidelberg (2013). https://doi.org/10.1007/978-3-642-39056-2_26

Process Trace Classification for Stroke Management Quality Assessment

Giorgio Leonardi, Stefania Montani(✉), and Manuel Striani

DISIT, Computer Science Institute, Università del Piemonte Orientale, Alessandria, Italy
stefania.montani@uniupo.it

Abstract. Stroke is a medical condition where poor blood flow to the brain may result in cell damage, possibly leading to patient's death or disability. Acute stroke care is best performed in dedicated and well-organized centers. Medical process trace classification can support stroke management quality assessment, since it allows to verify whether better-equipped Stroke Centers actually implement more complete processes, suitable to manage complex patients as well. In our previous work, we developed a semantic similarity metric able to compare process traces. In this paper, we adopt such a metric to perform k-Nearest Neighbour (k-NN) classification in the field of stroke management; moreover, we present an alternative classification approach based on deep learning techniques. Experimental results have shown the feasibility of deep learning classification for stroke management quality assessment, which performed better than the application of the semantic similarity metric. Improvements and future research in this direction will therefore be considered. Difficulties in classifying patients treated in less-equipped hospitals also suggest to identify and manage possible organizational problems.

Keywords: K-NN classification · Deep learning · Process traces

1 Introduction

A stroke is a medical condition where poor blood flow to the brain can result in cell death. Approximately 1.1 million inhabitants of Europe suffer a stroke each year and, because of the aging population, the absolute number of stroke is expected to dramatically increase in the near future: by 2025, 1.5 million European people will suffer a stroke each year [5].

Acute stroke care in hospitals is best performed in organized Stroke Units, where patient outcomes are better than those of patients managed in general medical or neurological wards [13].

The European Stroke Organisation (ESO) Stroke Unit Certification Committee has worked on the definition of evidence-based needs for acute stroke care, in order to stimulate the certification of more advanced stroke care facilities. The Committee has thus established 2 certification levels: (1) ESO Stroke Units (SUs) and (2) ESO Stroke Centers (SCs) [28]. ESO Stroke Centers must meet

I. Watson and R. Weber (Eds.): ICCBR 2020, LNAI 12311, pp. 49–63, 2020.
https://doi.org/10.1007/978-3-030-58342-2_4

all the requirements of an ESO Stroke Unit, and additionally should provide more advanced diagnostic and therapeutic equipment, have a larger staff and have expertise on rare or complex stroke subtypes.

In Italy, the Ministry of Health has codified the two levels of stroke care in 2015, along the lines explained above. However, significant organizational problems are still observed not only in SUs, but sometimes also in SCs[1]. Therefore, a thorough analysis of medical processes is needed, in order to verify if the actual performance of an hospital is coherent with its declared level.

In this paper, we propose to tackle the above needs by considering stroke management process traces (i.e., the sequences of activities actually executed on the single patients at the hospital at hand, and logged in the hospital information system). Traces can be interpreted as *cases* [1]; the identification of the k Nearest-Neighbour (k-NN) cases and k-NN classification (distinguishing between the SU class and the SC class) can then be implemented, to verify if the logged activities are coherent with the level assigned to a given hospital, in a quality assessment perspective.

In particular, we have realized classification according to two different approaches:

- in the first approach, we have adopted a trace similarity metric, able to take into account temporal information as well as domain knowledge, that we published in recent years [22,23]. By exploiting this metric, we have implemented k-NN trace classification;
- in the second approach, we have adopted a deep learning strategy [17]. Specifically, we have resorted to an architecture based on Long Short Term Memory (LSTM) networks [11] to extract *deep* features from process traces, and to the Euclidean distance for k-NN classification in this feature space.

The first experimental results obtained by means of the metric in [22,23] were not very satisfactory. We obtained a good improvement by separating the SC class into two subclasses, in order to better distinguish between more complex and simpler patients. The analogous separation, however, did not provide an analogous amelioration in the SU class. Overall, we obtained much better results (in both experiments) by resorting to the deep learning strategy; indeed, deep learning techniques are being increasingly adopted and proving successful in process classification and prediction, as described in Sect. 2. Our first experiments suggest to further investigate in this direction in the future. Difficulties in classifying traces within the SU class (experienced with deep learning as well) also suggest to identify and manage possible organizational problems.

The paper is organized as follows: in Sect. 2 we summarize related work. In Sect. 3 we detail our approaches to stroke trace classification for quality assessment. In Sect. 4 we present experimental results, while Sect. 5 is devoted to discussion and conclusions.

[1] https://www.sanita24.ilsole24ore.com/art/medicina-e-ricerca/2017-04-14/stroke-unit-merce-rara-strutture-e-personale-dati-lontani-dm-702015-162809.php?uuid=AEEhud5.

2 Related Work

The management of processes and process traces is nowadays an established area of research within the Case Based Reasoning (CBR) community, as testified by the workshops on Process Oriented CBR (PO-CBR) which have been co-located with the International Conference on CBR, where the most recent one was held in 2019[2].

In particular, process trace comparison has been tackled in, e.g., [12], which introduces a distance definition able to combine a contribution related to activity similarity and a contribution related to delays between activities, and in [22,23], where activity similarity is dealt with in a semantic way (see also Sect. 3.1).

Trace comparison can be adopted to support process prediction/classification [6], a task which exploits the activities logged in process traces to make predictions about the future of a running trace (such as, e.g., the remaining time to complete the work, the next activity to be executed, the needed resources), or to classify the trace on the basis of some categorical or numerical performance properties (as in our work). Process prediction and classification can be useful both for a better planning of the needed resources, and for quality assessment, by means of the identification of non-compliances with respect of the expected performance.

In the literature, most works in this field are focused on the prediction of the next activity in a running process trace. While classical business process management approaches use an explicit model representation such as a state-transition model [16] or an Hidden Markov Model [14], a more recent research direction exploits deep learning.

In particular, several authors rely on Recurrent Neural Networks (RNNs) [27], and more specifically on Long-Short-Term Memory (LSTM) networks [11]. The idea in RNNs is to preserve the results of previous calculations with memories, i.e., with feedback connections that provide a parameter sharing across different parts of the model. In LSTM a cell state, more complex than the memory cell in basic RNNs, is introduced, where information can be added or removed by gated structures [11]; this solution reduces the training time. LSTM can potentially learn the complex dynamics within the temporal ordering of input sequences; therefore, they are well suited to manage the sequential data of process activity logs. Specifically, they can also manage long-distance dependencies between activities. Indeed, in LSTM networks a long-term memory can be implemented, where the information flows from cell to cell with minimal variations, keeping certain aspects constant during the processing of all inputs.

In [32], the authors use LSTM networks to predict the type of the next activity of an ongoing process trace and the time until the next activity (its timestamp). The network architecture consists of a shared LSTM layer that feeds two independent LSTM layers specialized in predicting the next activity and in predicting times, respectively. The experiments show that the LSTM approach outperforms model-based approaches. The work in [8] proposes a different

[2] https://iccbr2019.com/workshops/process-oriented-case-based-reasoning/.

network architecture which comprises two LSTM hidden layers. An empirical evaluation shows that this approach sometimes outperforms the approach of [32] at the task of predicting the next activity. In [7] the authors combine the approach in [8] with the idea of interleaving shared and specialized layers from [32] to design prediction architectures that can handle large numbers of activity types. The paper in [10], on the other hand, is more generally devoted to classification. In this work, RRNs are used in a system designed to solve any classification problem (including next activity prediction) based on activity sequences.

In [21] the authors propose to predict the next activity using a multi-stage deep learning approach. In this approach, each activity is first mapped to a feature vector. Next, transformations are applied to reduce the input dimensionality, by extracting n-grams and applying a hash function; then, the input is passed through two Autoencoder layers. The main idea behind Autoencoders is to reduce the input into a latent space with fewer dimensions and then try to reconstruct the input from this representation. By reducing the number of variables which represent the data, the model is forced to learn how to keep only meaningful information, from which the input is reconstructable. In [21], the transformed input is finally processed by a feed-forward Neural Network responsible for the next activity prediction.

A different approach [20] relies on Convolutional Neural Networks (CNNs) [3]. CNNs operate by exploiting multiple convolution operators: a convolution is an operation which takes a filter and multiplies it over the entire area of the input. Convolution layers are then followed by pooling layers, meant to further reduce dimensionality. In particular, in [20] the authors resort to the inception architecture. The inception architecture [31] uses kernels of varied size in a convolution layer to capture features at different levels of abstraction: it processes information at different scales and then aggregates them to efficiently extract relevant features. The authors have obtained better results in predicting the next activity with respect to LSTM architectures in their experiments.

Overall, our approach is thus inserted in a very active research panorama, which is recently focusing on promising deep learning solutions.

Interestingly, deep learning is being progressively considered in CBR research as well (see, e.g., [4,29]), even if - to the best of our knowledge - not yet for trace classification/prediction. Our work can therefore be seen as an innovative contribution in this field.

3 Medical Process Trace Classification

This section presents the technical details of our work.

In particular, Subsect. 3.1 summarizes the main characteristics of the metric, defined in [22,23], which we have used in this paper for stroke trace classification.

Subsect. 3.2 provides a description of the deep learning architecture we have tested as an alternative to this classical approach.

3.1 Classification Through Semantic Trace Comparison

As a first strategy to process trace classification, we have implemented a k-NN classification approach, resorting to the metric we described in [22,23], which is a semantic extension of the edit distance [19].

Indeed, every process trace is a sequence of activities, each one stored with its execution starting and ending times, and an activity is basically a symbol (plus the temporal information).

In the metric in [22,23], thus, we first take into account activity types, by calculating a modified edit distance which we have called **Trace Edit Distance** [22,23]. As the classical edit distance [19], Trace Edit Distance tests all possible combinations of editing operations that could transform one trace into the other one. However, if domain knowledge allows to organize activities in an ontology or a taxonomy, as we have done in the field of stroke (see Fig. 1), the cost of a *substitution* is not always set to 1: indeed, we can adopt a more **semantic** approach, and apply Palmer's distance [26], to impose that the closer two activities are in the semantic structure, the less penalty we introduce for substitution.

Trace Edit Distance $trace_{NGLD}(P, Q)$ is then calculated as the Normalized Generalized Levenshtein Distance (NGLD) [33] between two traces P and Q (interpreted as two strings of symbols). Formally, we provide the following definitions:

Definition 1: Trace Generalized Levenshtein Distance.
Let P and Q be two traces of activities, and let α and β be two activities. The Trace Generalized Levenshtein Distance $trace_{GLD}(P, Q)$ between P and Q is defined as:

$$trace_{GLD}(P, Q) = min\{\sum_{i=1}^{k} c(e_i)\}$$

where $(e_1, \ldots, e_k)$ transforms P into Q, and:

- $c(e_i) = 1$, if e_i is an activity insertion or deletion;
- $c(e_i) = dt(\alpha, \beta)$, if e_i is the substitution of α (appearing in P) with β (appearing in Q), with $dt(\alpha, \beta)$ being Palmer's distance [26] between the two substituted activities.

Definition 2: Trace Edit Distance (Trace Normalized Generalized Levenshtein Distance).
Let P and Q be two traces of activities, and let $trace_{GLD}(P, Q)$ be defined as in Definition 1 above. We define Trace Edit Distance $trace_{NGLD}(P, Q)$ between P and Q as:

$$trace_{NGLD}(P, Q) = \frac{2 * trace_{GLD}(P, Q)}{|P| + |Q| + trace_{GLD}(P, Q)}$$

where $|P|$ and $|Q|$ are the lengths (i.e., the number of activities) of P and Q respectively.

CLASS BROWSER

Class Hierarchy 

- Emergency phase actions
  - EM Diagnostic procedures
    - EM blood test
    - EM brain parenchyma examination
      - EM brain CT
      - EM brain CT with CA
      - EM brain MR without DWI
      - EM DWI brain MR
      - EM DWI/PWI brain MR
      - EM perfusion CT
    - EM cardiac examination
    - EM neurological evaluation
    - EM neurovascular assessment
  - EM pre-hospital events
  - EM therapy
- Hospitalization phase actions
  - H consultations
  - H diagnostic procedures
    - H brain parenchyma Evaluation
      - H brain CT
      - H brain CT with CA
      - H brain MR
      - H brain MR with CA
      - H DWI brain MR
    - H cardiac diagnostic procedures
      - H transesophageal echocardiogram
      - H transthoracic echocardiogram
    - H cardiac evaluation
    - H neurovascular diagnostic procedures
    - H screening procedures
    - H thorax X-Ray
  - H monitoring procedures
  - H patient management procedures
  - H therapy

Fig. 1. An excerpt from the domain taxonomy.

The minimization of the sum of the editing costs allows one to find the optimal alignment between the two traces being compared. Given the optimal alignment, we can then take into account temporal information. Indeed, starting and ending times allow to get information about activity duration, as well as qualitative (e.g., Allen's *before*, *overlaps*, *equals* etc. [2]) and quantitative temporal constraints (e.g., delay length, overlap length [15]) between pairs of consecutive activities.

In particular, we compare the durations of aligned activities by means of a metric we called **Interval Distance** [22,23]. Interval distance calculates the normalized difference between the length of two intervals (representing activity durations in this case).

Moreover, we take into account the temporal constraints between two pairs of subsequent aligned activities on the traces being compared (e.g., activity A and B in trace P; the aligned activities A' and B' in trace Q). We quantify the distance between their qualitative constraints (e.g., A and B overlap in trace P; A' meets B' in trace Q), by resorting to a metric known as **Neighbors-graph Distance** [22,23]. If Neighbors-graph Distance is 0, because the two pairs of activities share the same qualitative constraint (e.g., A and B overlap in trace P; A' and B' also overlap in trace Q), we compare quantitative constraints by properly applying Interval Distance again (e.g., by calculating Interval Distance between the two overlap lengths).

In the metric in [22,23], these three contributions (i.e., Trace Edit Distance, Interval Distance between durations, Neighbors-graph Distance or Interval Distance between pairs of activities) are finally put in a linear combination with non-negative weights.

3.2 Deep Learning Classification

Inspired by existing literature contributions, we have tested a deep learning approach for stroke trace classification.

In particular, motivated by the successful examples described in Sect. 2 (see, e.g. [8,32]), we have defined and tested an LSTM-based architecture, which is described in Fig. 2.

In this approach, process traces are first pre-processed by converting each activity into a integer by means of an hashing layer; the overall trace is therefore converted into a feature vector. The architecture then exhibits two LSTM block, composed of 32 and 16 units (respectively) with *tanh* activation function and followed by a dropout layer, which randomly forces a fraction of the input units to be ignored at each update during training time, to help prevent overfitting [30].

The *deep* features produced by the following fully connected layer with *Relu* activation function can then be provided as an input to a k-NN classifier. Specifically, we resorted to the open source tool Weka [9] and to the Euclidean distance to perform k-NN classification in this feature space.

All parameters were set experimentally.

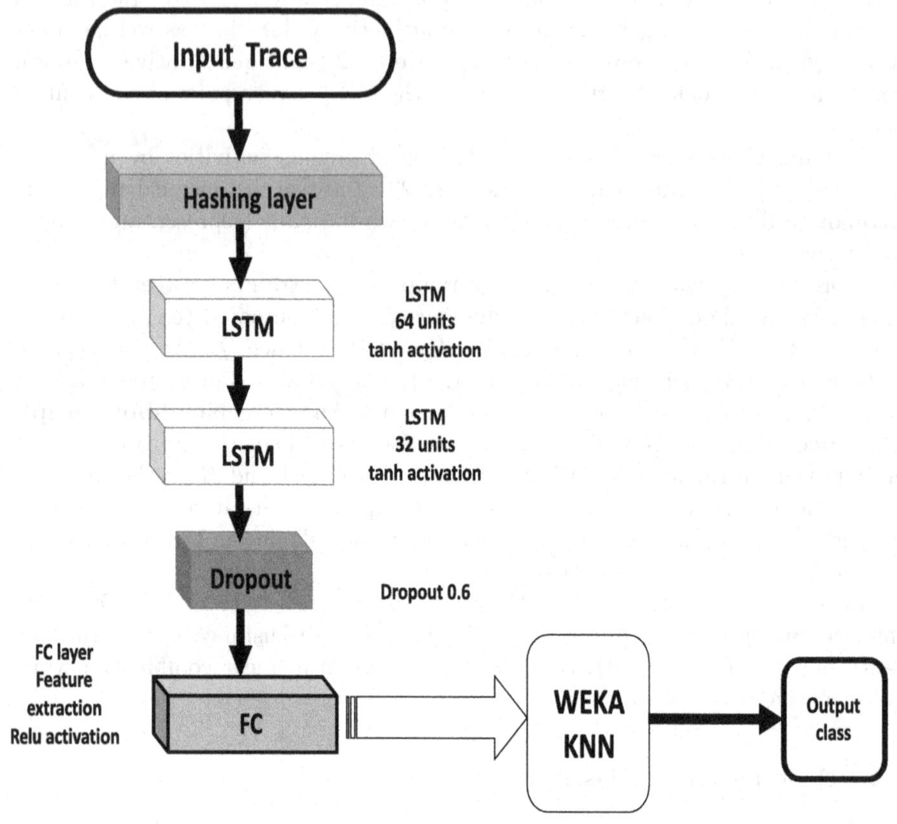

Fig. 2. LSTM-based architecture

4 Experimental Results

Our dataset was comprised of 5013 process traces, composed by a number of activities ranging from 10 to 25 (16 on average). In particular, 2629 traces were generated in a SC, while 2384 were generated in a SU.

The deep learning approach was realized and tested by means of the tool TensorFlow[3].

Details of the results are presented in the following subsections.

[3] https://www.tensorflow.org/.

4.1 Semantic Trace Comparison: Classification Results

In our experiments on classification relying on semantic trace comparison, we conducted a 9-NN classification (k = 9 was the optimal parameter setting automatically calculated by Weka [9]. Anyway, we also conducted a sensitivity analysis, which demonstrated that results did not change significantly when changing the value of k). Results are shown in Tables 1 and 2.

Table 1. Results (I) obtained by K-NN classification with semantic trace comparison, by class

Class	Precision	Recall	F-Measure	Specificity
SU	0.73	0.59	0.65	0.69
SC	0.54	0.69	0.60	0.59
Weighted average	0.63	0.64	0.63	0.64

Table 2. Results (II) obtained by K-NN classification with semantic trace comparison

MCC	K-stat	Accuracy
0.27	0.27	0.63

Table 3 also reports the confusion matrix for the LSTM-based classifier, for the sake of completeness.

Table 3. Confusion matrix obtained by K-NN classification with semantic trace comparison

	SU	SC
SU	1745	639
SC	1213	1416

As it can be observed from the tables, results are quite poor, reinforcing the need to test different classification strategies.

Following the suggestion of medical experts, we made a second experiment. In this case, we separated the SC class into two subclasses, in order to distinguish between traces generated on particularly complex patients, and traces generated on simpler patients. Such a distinction was made by experts referring to: (i) clinical data and patient's characteristics, available in the hospital information system (such as, e.g., the presence of co-morbidities), and (ii) the presence of specific activities in the trace (such as procedures for managing uncommon and problematic stroke types) or of repeated diagnostic/monitoring steps (such as frequent Computer Assisted Tomographies, to monitor the evolution over time of a particularly critical situation). Classification accuracy improved significantly within the SC traces, as shown in Tables 4 and 5.

Table 4. Results (I) obtained by K-NN classification with semantic trace comparison within the SC patients, by class

Class	Precision	Recall	F-Measure	Specificity
SC complex (905 traces)	0.59	0.72	0.65	0.80
SC simple (1724 traces)	0.88	0.80	0.84	0.72
Weighted average	0.78	0.78	0.77	0.75

Table 5. Results (II) obtained by K-NN classification with semantic trace comparison within the SC patients

MCC	K-stat	Accuracy
0.50	0.49	0.78

On the other hand, when implementing the same distinction within the SU class, we did not obtain significantly better results with respect to the initial experiment. Some discussion can be found in Sect. 5.

4.2 Deep Learning: Classification Results

Tables 6 and 7 report the results obtained by the tool Weka in 5-NN classification (in this case, k = 5 was the optimal parameter setting automatically calculated by Weka [9]), when *deep* features were provided by the LSTM architecture depicted in Fig. 2. As it can be seen, with respect to the adoption of semantic trace comparison, this approach provided a better classification performance.

Table 6. Results (I) obtained by LSTM + K-NN classification, by class

Class	Precision	Recall	F-Measure	Specificity
SU	0.73	0.72	0.73	0.76
SC	0.75	0.76	0.75	0.72
Weighted average	0.74	0.74	0.74	0.74

Table 8 also reports the confusion matrix for the LSTM-based classifier, for the sake of completeness.

Table 7. Results (II) obtained by LSTM + K-NN classification

MCC	K-stat	Accuracy
0.48	0.48	0.74

Table 8. Confusion matrix obtained by the LSTM + K-NN classification

	SU	SC
SU	1713	671
SC	620	2009

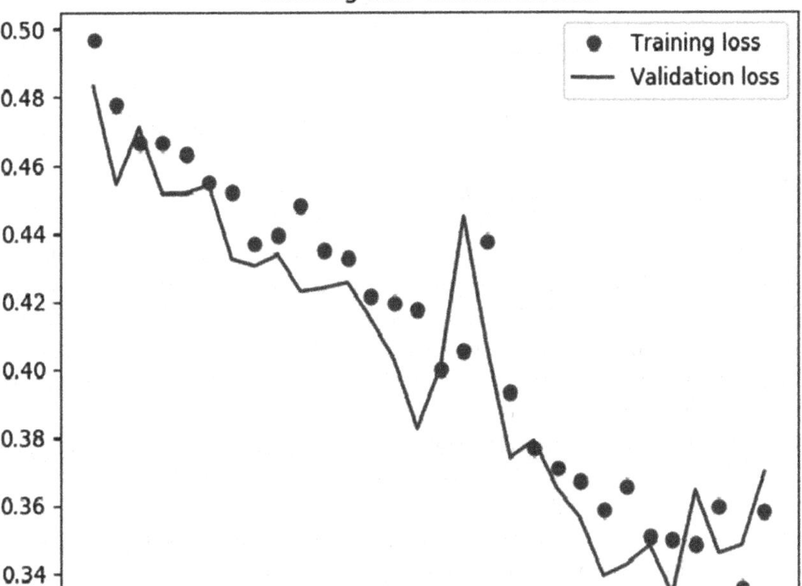

Fig. 3. LSTM loss per epoch

Figure 3 shows the evolution of the loss, depending on the number of epochs. As it can be observed from the figure, experimentally, working at 30 epochs represented a good compromise, able to reduce the loss value without increasing too much the computational effort (15 min were required for computation at 100 epochs, on Intel Xeon E3 - 2.70 GHz 4 processors with 4 GB RAM).

Also in this case, we repeated the experiment by distinguishing between more complex patients and simpler patients. The deep learning strategy provided a

Table 9. Results (I) obtained by LSTM + K-NN classification within the SC patients, by class

Class	Precision	Recall	F-Measure	Specificity
SC complex (905 traces)	0.90	0.90	0.90	0.95
SC simple (1724 traces)	0.95	0.95	0.95	0.90
Weighted average	0.93	0.93	0.93	0.92

Table 10. Results (II) obtained by LSTM + K-NN classification within the SC patients

MCC	K-stat	Accuracy
0.85	0.85	0.93

much higher accuracy when working within the SC class patients (see Tables 9 and 10), while results did not improve much within the SU class patients.

5 Discussion and Conclusions

In this paper, we have proposed two very different approaches to stroke trace classification. The first approach relies on a semantic similarity metric, followed by k-NN classification. The second approach adopts deep learning techniques.

Our first experimental results have shown that the more traditional approach, based on the semantic similarity metric, is not very successful, while the deep learning strategy has performed better.

The rather poor results obtained by the semantic metric have improved significantly when focusing on the SC class, and distinguishing between more complex patients and simpler patients, suggesting that two types of processes are actually carried out, depending on the patient condition - which makes sense from the medical viewpoint; however, an analogous improvement was not observed when working within the SU traces. Interestingly, an analogous output was observed also when applying deep learning. We thus make the hypothesis that SUs are much more heterogeneous than SCs, and more affected by organizational problems, which may limit their capacity to apply the right protocol to the right patient. Further experiments will be needed to support this claim.

As a more general consideration on our experimental results, we can conclude that deep learning, which is nowadays frequently chosen by the business process management community as a tool for trace prediction and classification, is indeed a promising approach, to be further investigated in the future. To this end, we will make other experiments, and consider different architectures as well, such as, e.g., convolutional inception modules [20,31].

Since deep learning methods operate as black boxes, and it can difficult to provide a meaning for the abstracted *deep* features, or to justify misclassification, we will also consider the issue of explainability. To this end, we will investigate whether it is possible to adapt the knowledge-based strategy we adopted in [18].

Last but not least, we also believe that further improvements of classification results, by both the approaches evaluated in this paper, might be obtained by resorting to a trace abstraction technique, such as the one described in [24,25]. Such an approach can hide irrelevant details, that could lead to misclassification, while keeping the most important information in the trace. This research direction will be considered in our future research as well.

References

1. Aamodt, A., Plaza, E.: Case-based reasoning: foundational issues, methodological variations and systems approaches. AI Commun. **7**, 39–59 (1994)
2. Allen, J.F.: Towards a general theory of action and time. Artif. Intell. **23**, 123–154 (1984)
3. Alom, M.Z., et al.: A state-of-the-art survey on deep learning theory and architectures. Electronics **8**(3), 292 (2019)
4. Amin, K., Kapetanakis, S., Althoff, K.-D., Dengel, A., Petridis, M.: Answering with cases: a CBR approach to deep learning. In: Cox, M.T., Funk, P., Begum, S. (eds.) ICCBR 2018. LNCS (LNAI), vol. 11156, pp. 15–27. Springer, Cham (2018). https://doi.org/10.1007/978-3-030-01081-2_2
5. Bejot, Y., Bailly, H., Durier, J., Giroud, M.: Epidemiology of stroke in Europe and trends for the 21st century. La Presse Medicale **45**(12, Part 2), e391–e398 (2016). QMR Stroke
6. Breuker, D., Matzner, M., Delfmann, P., Becker, J.: Comprehensible predictive models for business processes. MIS Quart. **40**, 1009–1034 (2016)
7. Camargo, M., Dumas, M., González-Rojas, O.: Learning accurate LSTM models of business processes. In: Hildebrandt, T., van Dongen, B.F., Röglinger, M., Mendling, J. (eds.) BPM 2019. LNCS, vol. 11675, pp. 286–302. Springer, Cham (2019). https://doi.org/10.1007/978-3-030-26619-6_19
8. Evermann, J., Rehse, J.R., Fettke, P.: Predicting process behaviour using deep learning. Decis. Support Syst. **100**, 129–140 (2017)
9. Hall, M., Frank, E., Holmes, G., Pfahringer, B., Reutemann, P., Witten, I.H.: The WEKA data mining software: an update. SIGKDD Explor. **11**(1), 10–18 (2009)
10. Hinkka, M., Lehto, T., Heljanko, K., Jung, A.: Classifying process instances using recurrent neural networks. In: Daniel, F., Sheng, Q.Z., Motahari, H. (eds.) BPM 2018. LNBIP, vol. 342, pp. 313–324. Springer, Cham (2019). https://doi.org/10.1007/978-3-030-11641-5_25
11. Hochreiter, S., Schmidhuber, J.: Long short-term memory. Neural Comput. **9**(8), 1735–1780 (1997)
12. Kapetanakis, S., Petridis, M., Knight, B., Ma, J., Bacon, L.: A case based reasoning approach for the monitoring of business workflows. In: Bichindaritz, I., Montani, S. (eds.) ICCBR 2010. LNCS (LNAI), vol. 6176, pp. 390–405. Springer, Heidelberg (2010). https://doi.org/10.1007/978-3-642-14274-1_29
13. Kjellstrom, T., Norrving, B., Shatchkute, A.: Helsingborg declaration 2006 on European stroke strategies. Cerebrovasc. Dis. **23**, 229–241 (2007)
14. Lakshmanan, G.T., Shamsi, D., Doganata, Y.N., Unuvar, M., Khalaf, R.: Markov prediction model for data-driven semi-structured business processes. Knowl. Inf. Syst. **42**(1), 97–126 (2015)
15. Lanz, A., Weber, B., Reichert, M.: Workflow time patterns for process-aware information systems. In: Proceedings of BMMDS/EMMSAD, pp. 94–107 (2010)

16. Le, M., Gabrys, B., Nauck, D.: A hybrid model for business process event prediction. In: Bramer, M., Petridis, M. (eds.) SGAI 2012, pp. 179–192. Springer, London (2012). https://doi.org/10.1007/978-1-4471-4739-8_13
17. LeCun, Y., Bengio, Y., Hinton, G.E.: Deep learning. Nature **521**(7553), 436–444 (2015)
18. Leonardi, G., Montani, S., Striani, M.: Deep feature extraction for representing and classifying time series cases: towards an interpretable approach in haemodialysis. In: Proceedings of the 33rd International Florida Artificial Intelligence Research Society Conference, FLAIRS 2020, Miami, Florida, AAAI Press (2020)
19. Levenshtein, A.: Binary codes capable of correcting deletions, insertions and reversals. Sov. Phys. Dokl. **10**, 707–710 (1966)
20. Di Mauro, N., Appice, A., Basile, T.M.A.: Activity prediction of business process instances with inception CNN models. In: Alviano, M., Greco, G., Scarcello, F. (eds.) AI*IA 2019. LNCS (LNAI), vol. 11946, pp. 348–361. Springer, Cham (2019). https://doi.org/10.1007/978-3-030-35166-3_25
21. Mehdiyev, N., Evermann, J., Fettke, P.: A multi-stage deep learning approach for business process event prediction. In: Loucopoulos, P., Manolopoulos, Y., Pastor, O., Theodoulidis, B., Zdravkovic, J., (eds.) 19th IEEE Conference on Business Informatics, CBI 2017, Thessaloniki, Greece, 24–27 July ,2017, Volume 1: Conference Papers, pp. 119–128. IEEE Computer Society (2017)
22. Montani, S., Leonardi, G.: Retrieval and clustering for business process monitoring: results and improvements. In: Agudo, B.D., Watson, I. (eds.) ICCBR 2012. LNCS (LNAI), vol. 7466, pp. 269–283. Springer, Heidelberg (2012). https://doi.org/10.1007/978-3-642-32986-9_21
23. Montani, S., Leonardi, G.: Retrieval and clustering for supporting business process adjustment and analysis. Inf. Syst. **40**, 128–141 (2014)
24. Montani, S., Leonardi, G., Striani, M., Quaglini, S., Cavallini, A.: Multi-level abstraction for trace comparison and process discovery. Expert Syst. Appl. **81**, 398–409 (2017)
25. Montani, S., Striani, M., Quaglini, S., Cavallini, A., Leonardi, G.: Semantic trace comparison at multiple levels of abstraction. In: Aha, D.W., Lieber, J. (eds.) ICCBR 2017. LNCS (LNAI), vol. 10339, pp. 212–226. Springer, Cham (2017). https://doi.org/10.1007/978-3-319-61030-6_15
26. Palmer, M., Wu, Z.: Verb semantics for english-Chinese translation. Mach. Transl. **10**, 59–92 (1995)
27. Pascanu, R., Gülçehre, Ç., Cho, K., Bengio, Y.: How to construct deep recurrent neural networks. In: Bengio, Y., LeCun, Y., (eds.) 2nd International Conference on Learning Representations, ICLR 2014, Banff, AB, Canada, 14–16 April 2014, Conference Track Proceedings (2014)
28. Ringelstein, E.B., et al.: European stroke organisation recommendations to establish a stroke unit and stroke center. Stroke **44**(3), 828–840 (2013)
29. Sani, S., Wiratunga, N., Massie, S., Cooper, K.: kNN sampling for personalised human activity recognition. In: Aha, D.W., Lieber, J. (eds.) ICCBR 2017. LNCS (LNAI), vol. 10339, pp. 330–344. Springer, Cham (2017). https://doi.org/10.1007/978-3-319-61030-6_23
30. Srivastava, N., Hinton, G.E., Krizhevsky, A., Sutskever, I., Salakhutdinov, R.: Dropout: a simple way to prevent neural networks from overfitting. J. Mach. Learn. Res. **15**(1), 1929–1958 (2014)
31. Szegedy, C., et al.: Going deeper with convolutions. In: IEEE Conference on Computer Vision and Pattern Recognition, CVPR 2015, Boston, MA, USA, 7–12 June 2015, pp. 1–9. IEEE Computer Society (2015)

32. Tax, N., Teinemaa, I., van Zelst, S.J.: An interdisciplinary comparison of sequence modeling methods for next-element prediction. *CoRR*, abs/1811.00062 (2018)
33. Yujian, L., Bo, L.: A normalized levenshtein distance metric. IEEE Trans. Pattern Anal. Mach. Intell. **29**, 1091–1095 (2007)

Technical Session: Applications in Health

Using Case-Based Reasoning to Predict Marathon Performance and Recommend Tailored Training Plans

Ciara Feely[1(✉)], Brian Caulfield[2], Aonghus Lawlor[2], and Barry Smyth[2]

[1] ML Labs, University College Dublin, Dublin, Ireland
Ciara.Feely@ucdconnect.ie

[2] Insight Centre for Data Analytics, University College Dublin, Dublin, Ireland
{brian.caulfield,aonghus.lawlor,barry.smyth}@ucd.ie

Abstract. Training for the marathon, especially a first marathon, is always a challenge. Many runners struggle to find the right balance between their workouts and their recovery, often leading to sub-optimal performance on race-day or even injury during training. We describe and evaluate a novel case-based reasoning system to help marathon runners as they train in two ways. First, it uses a case-base of training/workouts and race histories to predict future marathon times for a target runner, throughout their training program, helping runners to calibrate their progress and, ultimately, plan their race-day pacing. Second, the system recommends tailored training plans to runners, adapted for their current goal-time target, and based on the training plans of similar runners who have achieved this time. We evaluate the system using a dataset of more than 21,000 unique runners and 1.5 million training/workout sessions.

Keywords: CBR for health and exercise · Marathon running · Race-time prediction · Plan recommendation

1 Introduction

With the advent of wearable and mobile devices it has become increasingly routine for runners to track their training using apps such as Strava, RunKeeper, and MapMyRun. Researchers are harnessing this data to learn about how people exercise [1,2], to provide personalised training advice [3–6] and motivational support [7–11], to predict their performance potential [12,13], and even to provide them with real-time advice and guidance as they compete [14].

This work focuses on *recreational* (non-elite) marathon runners, although the ideas described should be equally applicable to other running distances (ultras, half-marathons, 10 km's etc.) and endurance sports (cycling, triathlon, skiing, speed skating etc.). Its main technical contribution is to support marathon runners as they train, in two ways. Firstly, we predict a runner's target race-time, based on their current training progress. This is important because it helps to

I. Watson and R. Weber (Eds.): ICCBR 2020, LNAI 12311, pp. 67–81, 2020.
https://doi.org/10.1007/978-3-030-58342-2_5

set appropriate race-day expectations for runners, helping them to better plan their race, but it also allows them to calibrate and fine-tune their training. Secondly, if runners wish to adjust their training – perhaps by targeting a faster or slower marathon time – then we describe a technique to generate a tailored training plan based on their current training habits and their new goals. In what follows, we describe and evaluate how both of these tasks can be fulfilled using case-based reasoning (CBR) by leveraging a case-base of more than 1.5 million training sessions logged by more than 21,000 marathoners. CBR is an appropriate method for these tasks as, for race-time prediction, the training completed by runners can be seen as the problem part, and race-time as the solution. Conversely, for training plan recommendation, the desired marathon finish-time is the problem, while the training plan is the solution.

2 Related Work

Fitness and exercise applications are popular targets for machine learning research, in part because of the volume of data that is now available, as people track their activities online, but also because of the wealth of interesting problems that exist when it comes to helping people to exercise safely and train effectively. The world of sports and fitness has been exploring the data captured by wearable sensors to solve a variety of tasks related to exercise, personalised training, motivation, and athlete performance [1–11]. Recently, case-based reasoning and other machine learning techniques have been utilised to support marathoners on race-day by providing them with real-time pacing advice [14].

A key task in this work is to predict future marathon times using training/workout data. This task is not new, but previous approaches have focused on either using a full complement of training/workout data or past race-times to generate predictions; see [12,13,15,16]. Instead, we predict future race-times at various points during a training programme using incomplete training/workout data. Recently, the work of [17–20] used case-based reasoning ideas to accurately predict marathon performance but required runners to have completed at least one recent marathon. This means that these approaches are not suitable for first-time marathoners or novices. A key objective of the present work is to address this shortcoming, by using training/workout data, which even first-timers will generate at scale, instead of past marathon times.

Our second task involves recommending new training plans to runners. Such a virtual coaching assistant has long been discussed in the literature [6,21,22] but progress has been limited to some notable early efforts [23]. It is a challenging problem because generating a training plan depends on a complex mix of physiological and sport-specific factors as well as personal preferences. But this is precisely why a CBR approach is appealing: by reusing existing training plans (or parts of existing plans) from similar runners, we can provide a runner with tailored training recommendations without the need for an explicit domain model.

3 A CBR Approach to Marathon Training

Training for a marathon requires 12–16 weeks of dedicated effort, with most runners following carefully scripted training programmes based on their goals and ability. A typical week involves 3–6 training sessions, usually different types of runs: some short (5–10 km), some longer (15–30 km), some slow, some fast. Some runs introduce hills to build strength while others focus on stamina or recovery. As training progresses, new types of sessions encourage the physiological adaptations necessary for race-day. In other words, training for a marathon involves a complex mixture of workouts carefully balanced with rest and recovery.

By harnessing workout data, we provide runners with feedback as their training progresses. Predicting their likely marathon time will help runners to evaluate their progress, while the ability to make training recommendations will help them to adapt their otherwise *one-size-fits-all* training plan. In what follows, we will describe how we do this, but first we need to transform the time-series data from training sessions into a suitable representation for case-based reasoning.

3.1 From Training/Workout Sessions to Cases

The dataset used in this work includes approximately 1.5 million training activities by over 21 thousand marathon runners (73% male, 27% female) who completed either Dublin, London, or New York Marathons during the period 2014 – 2017; see Table 1. The anonymised dataset was produced by users of the popular mobile and web-based running app, Strava,[1] which has been made available as part of a data sharing agreement with the authors. The activities in the dataset all occur during a 16-week period directly before a marathon. This period was chosen as marathon plans are typically 12–16 weeks however, it is possible that some runners trained for less or more than 16 weeks. Each activity includes timing, distance, and elevation data sampled at 100 m intervals.

More formally, for a runner, r, we denote their training data as $T(r)$, a time-ordered sequence of training activities; see Eq. (1).

$$T(r) = \{A_1(r), A_2(r), \ldots, A_n(r)\} \tag{1}$$

Each activity, $A_i(r) = (d, P)$, includes the number of days before the race (d) and a list of paces at 100 m intervals for the activity (P). A runner's activities can be aggregated by week to extract key weekly features, including:

1. The *number of sessions* in the current week;
2. The *total weekly distance* in kms;
3. The *mean pace* for the week in mins/km;
4. The *longest run distance*;
5. The *fastest/slowest 10 km/5 km/1 km paces*.

[1] www.strava.com.

These features were chosen as they have been found to capture important aspects of marathon training in the past [16]. For example, the number and duration of *long-runs* is often cited as an important success criteria while, long-distance pacing typically correlates with marathon times.

In addition to these features that represent the current week of training, we also calculate the corresponding features for the training period up to and including the current week (e.g. *longest run distance* to date). Thus, for each runner r, we can generate a feature-based description for training week w, $F(r, w)$. Figure 1 demonstrates how the training of a runner in week 12 is transformed into a suitable feature representation.

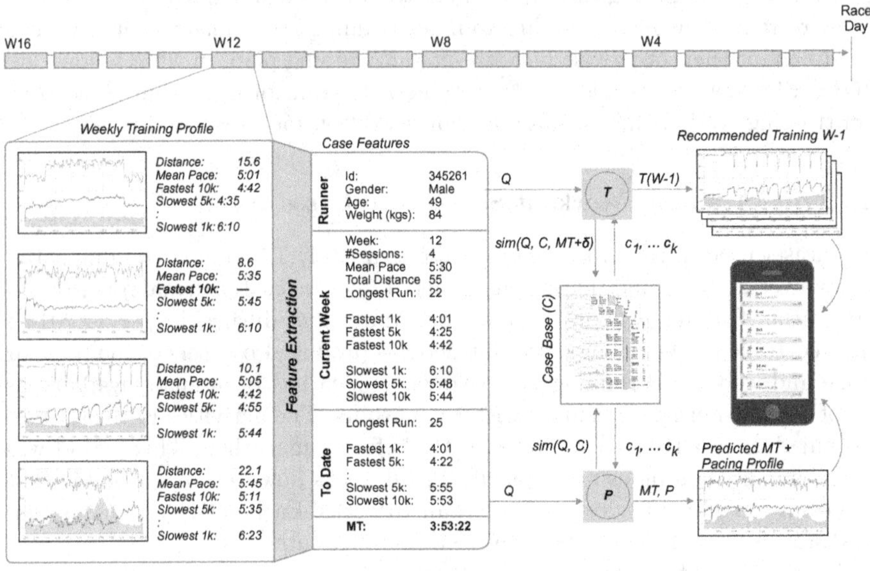

Fig. 1. An overview of a case-based reasoning system for supporting marathoners during their training by predicting (P) their estimated marathon time and by recommending (R) tailored training plan for an adjusted marathon time.

We generate a case $(C(r, w))$, representing r's training during week w, by associating $F(r, w)$ with their marathon time, $MT(r)$, and also a pointer to their next week of training, $C(r, w-1)$; see Eq. (2). These cases can be used in two ways: (a) to predict a runner's marathon time at week w, using the MT components of similar cases; and (b) to recommend next week's training, using the $C(r, w-1)$ component of similar cases for a revised goal-time $(MT + \delta)$.

$$C(r, w) = \{F(r, w), MT(r), C(r, w-1)\} \tag{2}$$

When building a case-base of training activities we separate male and female runners because the physiological differences between men and women have a significant bearing on training and performance. We also generate separate case-bases for each week of training, based on the feature-based description for a training week, $F(r,w)$, previously described. The marathon time $MT(r)$ for a case $C(r,w)$ encodes r's marathon time in w weeks time and relates this to a specific week (week w) of training. It would not be appropriate to reuse such a case at a very different point in their training cycle, even for a similar runner.

3.2 Task 1: Predicting Goal Race-Times

The use-case for the first task is common: runner r in week w of training wishes to estimate their likely marathon time for race-day; the estimated time is not their *current* marathon time but rather their expected *future* marathon time, w weeks from now, based on their training to date. This is useful to know for a number of reasons. It helps r set appropriate race-day expectations and provides some level of confidence that their training is on-track, depending on whether the predicted time matches their goal. In addition, many marathon training programmes are parameterised with respect to a runner's goal marathon time – e.g., a long run session might include 5–10 km at *marathon pace* – so it is important to have an accurate estimate to work with.

To predict the marathon time of a runner r in week w, we use r's current week of training as a query, and compute a standard Euclidean distance metric to identify the k most similar cases to r in the appropriate case-base (based on gender and training week). The predicted marathon time is the weighted average of the times for these similar runners; see P in Fig. 1. It is worth noting, but not discussed further here, that we can also recommend a suitable pacing plan to help the runner achieve this time on race-day, by reusing pacing profiles of the marathons completed by the k most similarly trained runners as in [17,20].

3.3 Task 2: Recommending Tailored Training Programmes

To understand the use-case for the second task, imagine runner r has completed week 10 of their training plan and their predicted marathon time is 245 min. Given how well their training has gone so far, they decide that they want to break the iconic 4-h finish-time. Should they change their training plan to improve their chances of finishing faster? If so, how? What would a 4-h plan look like for them? Alternatively, if r's training is proving to be too much of a challenge, they may wish to reduce their expectations and look for a training plan that suits a 4.5 h finish. What might this plan look like with 10 weeks of training still to go?

Instead of using r's current training as a query to predict a marathon finish-time, we instead use their current training *and* their *revised* target time as a query to identify a new case, $C(r',w)$ from a runner r' who achieved the new target time (± 1 min), such that $C(r',w)$ is maximally similar to $C(r,w)$. Then, we can recommend $C(r',w{-}1)$ from the $C(r',w)$ case as r's next week of training.

Note, for this task we focus on a single most similar case for r, rather than retrieving and reusing k similar cases. The main reason for this is that since runners can be following different types of training plans, it may not make sense to try and combine these training plans from a recommendation perspective. That being said, it may make sense to offer r a choice of similar runners and therefore a choice of possible training for the following week.

3.4 From Single Weeks to Multiple Weeks

So far the focus has been on matching runner cases based on a single current week of training. Since many marathon programmes are designed around 4-week training blocks – during which training intensity ramps-up and then down to allow for recovery before the next block – it is also worth considering a longer, 4-week training period during prediction and recommendation. One way to do this is to extend our representations so that each case encodes the features of the previous 4 weeks of training.

Another option – and the one proposed here – is to use an ensemble approach to combine the predictions produced by similar cases for the 4 weeks including and preceeding the current week. For example, for week $w = 10$, we generate 4 predictions using the case-bases for weeks 10, 11, 12, and 13, and the final prediction is produced from the median of these individual predictions.

One problem with the above approach is that runners who are on similar training plans can sometimes be out of sync with respect to their individual training weeks so that some weeks are "out of sequence". To deal with this, we also implement a variation of this 4-week ensemble such that the case-bases used are produced by first *ordering* the 4 training weeks in ascending order of training-load (longest run distance for now). For example, for week $w = 10$, we use cases from weeks 10, 11, 12, 13, but we order them based on their longest run distance. So the $w - 3$ case-base contains the shortest training week for runners, the $w - 2$ case-base contains the next shortest training week etc. The advantage of this approach is that it facilitates a better alignment between the training weeks of runners over a 4-week period.

Obviously, the advantage of these ensemble approaches is that predictions are based on an extended view of training, rather than a single-week snapshot, which may lead to more accurate predictions. In what follows we will refer to the first ensemble approach as the *unordered* ensemble – to indicate that the weeks have not been ordered by training-load – and the second technique as the *ordered* ensemble.

Training plan recommendations can also take advantage of these extended approaches in a straightforward way, by using the ensemble methods to generate a (more accurate) race-time prediction and then using this single predicted time as the basis for the subsequent training plan recommendation as described previously.

4 Evaluation

We test the performance of our approach to race-time prediction and training plan recommendation using the Strava dataset referenced previously. In what follows we describe this dataset in detail, and the evaluation methodology, before presenting key results for the prediction and recommendation tasks.

4.1 Setup

The details of the dataset used in this study are summarised in Table 1. It includes approximately 5,000 female runners who completed their marathon in 3–5 h and over 15,000 male runners who completed their marathons in up to 5 h; while the original dataset included some sub 3-h females and some slower (>5 h) males and females, these were relatively rare and excluded from this evaluation. Using this dataset we generate case-bases of weekly marathon training sessions for male and female runners, as previously described.

Each of the evaluations that follow adopt a similar, tenfold cross validation methodology, separating test and training data for the male and female case-bases for each week of training. During each iteration we extract 10% of the cases to use as test queries with case-bases constructed from the remaining cases.

For the prediction task we calculate the RMSE between the predicted marathon time and known marathon time for each test case. For the training-plan recommendation task we compare the recommended training plan to the corresponding plan for the test runner, to determine how its training load varies under different target time adjustments; we will discuss the details of this in due course.

In preparation for this evaluation we tested overall prediction accuracy for different values of k (the number of cases retrieved and reused) finding that accuracy improved (RMSE decreased) as k increased, before stabilising for $k \geq 15$. These results are not shown here for reasons of space but we use the $k = 15$ setting for the evaluations that follow.

4.2 Prediction Error by Training Week

One of the unique features of this work is the ability to generate marathon time predictions at any point in a runner's training plan, not just at the completion of training. As such, it is important to understand how prediction accuracy changes as training progresses.

Figure 2 shows the results of this analysis for men and women and for each of the 3 CBR variants (single-week vs unordered 4-week vs ordered 4-week). As we might expect, prediction error falls steadily as training progresses, for men and women, and for each variant. A notable exception is one week before race-day for the single-week version, where RMSE increases slightly. This can be explained by the so-called *marathon taper* during which some runners significantly reduce their training load, so that they are rested for their race. Runners vary in when, how and even if they taper, so it is likely that the increase in error for the single-week representation exists because of a lack of taper consistency among the single-week cases, which is less problematic in the 4-week ensembles.

The 4-week variants produce more accurate predictions than the single-week approach, with the ordered variant consistently producing the most accurate predictions overall, for each week and for men and women.[2] In each case, for men and women, the weekly differences in error between the ordered 4-week variant and both the single-week and un-ordered 4-week variants are all statistically significant (based on a one-sided t-test with $p < 0.01$). As a base-line, to further support the validity of the CBR approach, a linear regression model was fitted to each week of data. The results are omitted due to space constraints however,

Table 1. A summary of the dataset used in this study for runners of Dublin, London, and New York marathons in the period 2014–2017. The table includes gender and age information as well as mean (and standard deviation) data for age, race-time (minutes), number of weekly activities, and weekly distance).

City	Year	Sex	Runners	Age	Race-Time	Activites/Wk	Distance/Wk
Dublin	2014	F	52	37±7	251.69±23.66	2.97±1.19	31.35±10.6
		M	305	38±7	225.86±32.11	3.53±1.75	39.61±17.67
	2015	F	81	38±7	252.6±25.02	3.43±1.34	35.61±12.76
		M	496	38±8	222.32±32.5	3.62±1.83	39.64±18.33
	2016	F	180	39±8	248.7±26.7	3.49±1.53	35.91±14.83
		M	918	39±7	222.56±30.08	3.59±1.73	40.0±17.42
London	2015	F	535	38±8	239.45±30.19	3.52±1.57	38.79±14.55
		M	2091	39±8	210.2±34.76	4.0±2.21	45.21±22.03
	2016	F	881	38±8	239.2±31.4	3.6±1.56	38.76±15.19
		M	3088	40±8	211.31±35.89	4.13±2.37	45.99±23.07
	2017	F	1427	38±8	243.76±30.19	3.57±1.78	37.68±14.41
		M	4056	40±9	213.91±36.62	4.24±2.39	46.33±23.13
NYC	2015	F	324	37±8	244.21±27.5	3.61±1.42	38.84±13.99
		M	1374	40±8	225.21±35.37	3.63±1.66	42.07±19.95
	2016	F	693	37±8	245.31±28.68	3.64±1.59	38.11±14.96
		M	2180	40±8	225.34±34.14	3.64±1.72	41.55±18.86
	2017	F	1193	36±8	245.67±29.35	3.62±1.52	39.21±16.61
		M	3274	40±8	225.01±33.94	3.68±1.66	42.27±19.18

[2] Prediction estimates are more accurate for women than for men, echoing similar findings by [17] when using previous marathon times to predict future PBs.

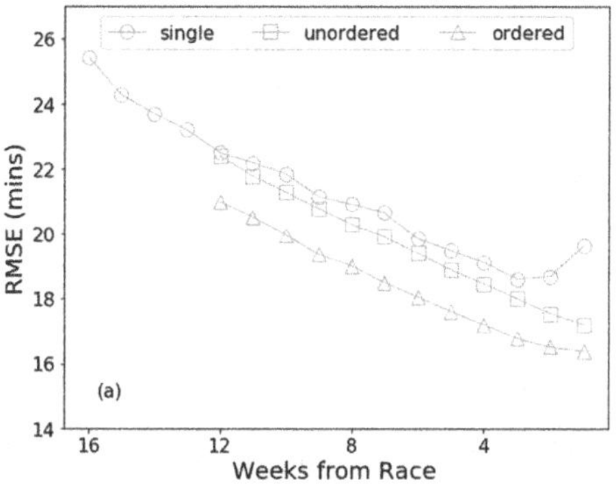

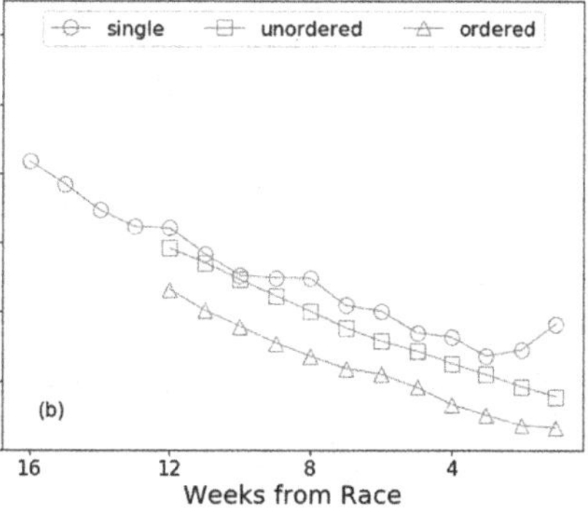

Fig. 2. The prediction error (RMSE in minutes) by training week for (a) men and (b) women using the weekly and 4-week variants.

the linear regression model was statistical significantly ($p < 0.01$) less accurate than the single-week variant (and therefore both 4-week variants).

Indeed, predictions made 10 weeks before race-day, by the ordered variant, are as accurate as the predictions made by the single-week variant 5–6 weeks later. This is an important difference because, as mentioned earlier, having an accurate estimate of marathon time helps to inform subsequent training; workouts are often expressed relative to marathon pace. Thus, the availability of more accurate marathon predictions, earlier in training, has the potential to significantly optimise training.

4.3 Prediction Stability

While accuracy is important, it is not the only consideration when it comes to selecting a variant to use in practice. For example, if predictions tend to vary from week to week, then runners may be less likely to trust in them and therefore less likely to heed the advice and recommendations being made. To evaluate this, in Fig. 3 we calculate the absolute difference in the predicted marathon times between consecutive weeks for each runner and present the average difference for male and females and for each week of training and CBR variant.

Figure 3 shows that, in addition to enjoying better prediction accuracy, the 4-week variants also produce significantly more stable predictions, week on week. For example, 8 weeks from race-day, the single week variant generates an average prediction that differs from the previous week by approximately 9–10 min. By comparison, the 4-week variants produce predictions that differ from the previous week by only about 4 min; a useful side-effect of the ensemble prediction approach. In this case, the unordered variant produces more stable predictions for men and women than the ordered variant. The differences between the 4-week variants and the single-week variant are statistically significant based on a one-sided t-test with $p < 0.01$.

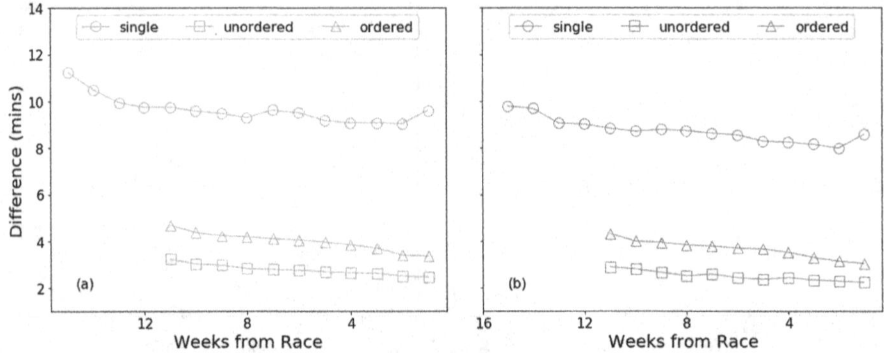

Fig. 3. The absolute difference in consecutive weekly predictions by training week for (a) men and (b) women using the weekly and 4-week variants.

4.4 Prediction Error by Ability

Fig. 4 plots the prediction error by runner ability – using their actual marathon times as a proxy for ability – for men and women at 10, 6, and 2 weeks before race-day. For reasons of space, we only show the results for the 4-week ordered variant, which proved to be the most accurate overall.

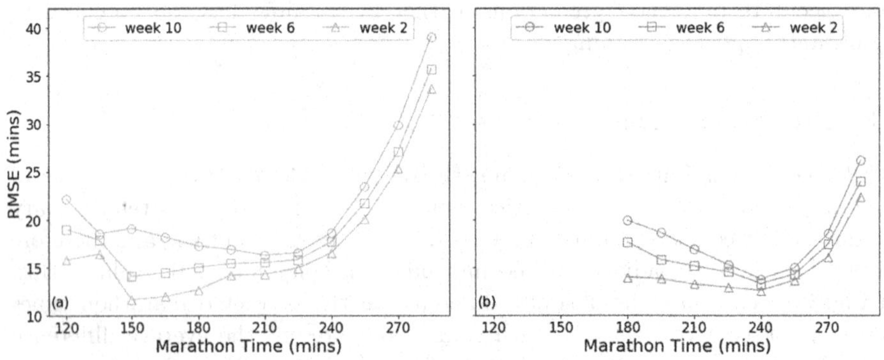

Fig. 4. The prediction error (RMSE in minutes) by marathon time (mins) for (a) men and (b) women using the weekly and 4-week variants.

Error rates increase significantly for slower runners (males >225 min and females >240 min) with the most accurate predictions associated with finish times of 210 min for male runners and 240 min for female runners. This is at least partly due to the distribution of marathon times in the training data: most of the training data is for runners in the 3–4 h finish-time range with relatively fewer faster and slower runners, leading to a paucity of training cases at the extremes, and less reliable predictions as a result.

There is a similar increase in error for faster (<210 min) females as there are relatively few of these in the dataset; the effect is less pronounced for faster males although still present. Generally speaking, we can also see how earlier predictions (week 10) tend to be less accurate regardless of gender or finish-time.

Another explanation for the significant increase in prediction error for the slower runners is that their training plans will tend to be less specific than those for faster runners and, as a result, may provide fewer or less reliable signals that can be used for prediction. For example, beginner training plans will tend to focus on helping a runner to *finish* the marathon distance, rather than achieve a particular time, and as such there will be less of a focus on pace, leading to less reliable 'fastest pace' features.

4.5 Evaluating Training Plan Recommendations

Evaluating training plan recommendations is less straight forward as there is no direct ground-truth to compare the recommendations to; after all, the aim is to suggest a training plan that is *different* (harder or easier) from the current plan for a given runner. Ideally, these recommended plans should be evaluated as part of a live-user trial – perhaps by obtaining user feedback on their desirability or suitability or by evaluating whether they lead to better outcomes, if and when users adopt them.

Such a study is beyond the scope of the present work. Instead, we propose a *plausibility* test by measuring how the *training load* of the recommended plans compares to the runner's default plan: we compare their recommended next-week of training to their current next-week training plan. If a runner requests a plan for a marathon time that is faster ($\delta < 0$) than their current predicted marathon time, then the recommended plan should have a higher training load than their current plan, and vice versa if they request a plan for a slower ($\delta > 0$) marathon time. We use two measures of training load: (1) the average pace for the week; and (2) total weekly distance. Higher training loads should be associated with faster weeks or longer weeks or both. We calculate the percentage difference, with respect to the runner's current plan, for distance and pace.

The results are shown in Figs. 5 and 6 for weeks 4, 6 and 8 of training using the ordered variant. We compare the recommendations produced when runners request plans that are associated with marathon times that are 5, 10, 15, and 20 min faster or slower than their current *predicted* marathon time. The results are generally consistent with expectations: when runners request training plans that are faster than their current predicted finish-time ($\delta < 0$) then mean weekly pace tends to speed-up (a negative % difference as in Fig. 5) while total weekly distance tends to increase (a positive % difference as in Fig. 6). The reverse is true when they request a plan for a slower marathon time.

The changes in pace exhibit a very strong correlation with δ ($R^2 > 0.92$ for men and women). The changes in weekly distance are also strongly correlated with δ for men ($R^2 > 0.90$), but less so for women ($R^2 > 0.66$ on average). The relative changes in distance tend to be greater (for a given δ) than the corresponding changes in pace. For example, for males to improve their predicted time by 15 min, means they will have to increase their weekly distance by up to 5% and speed-up by 2–3%.

While not definitive, these results are encouraging. Recommending new training plans is a very challenging recommendation task; conventional recommendation techniques have largely focused on recommending simple, atomic items (books, music, movies) rather than complex items, such as training plans, which are made up of a complex mix of components and factors. The fact that we can generate training plan recommendations that are consistent with a runner's modified goals is an encouraging start. And since these plans are based on the real training plans of similar runners, this increases the chances that they will be well received by runners.

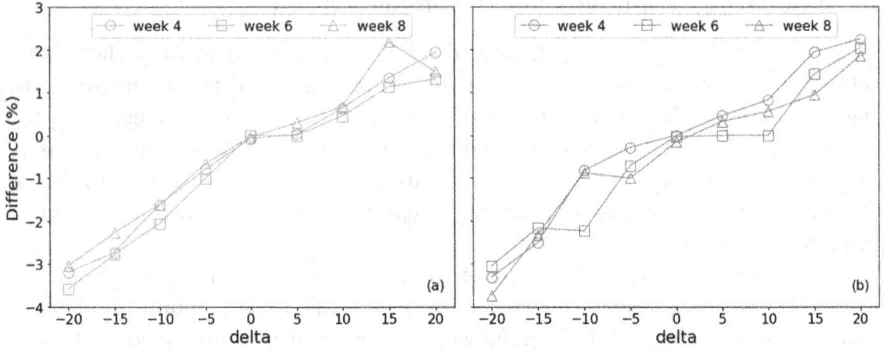

Fig. 5. The difference in mean weekly pace (mins/km) for training plans based on adjusted goal-times for (a) men and (b) women during training weeks 4, 6, and 8. Note: $\delta < 0$ implies the goal-time is δ minutes *faster* than the runner's current predicted time.

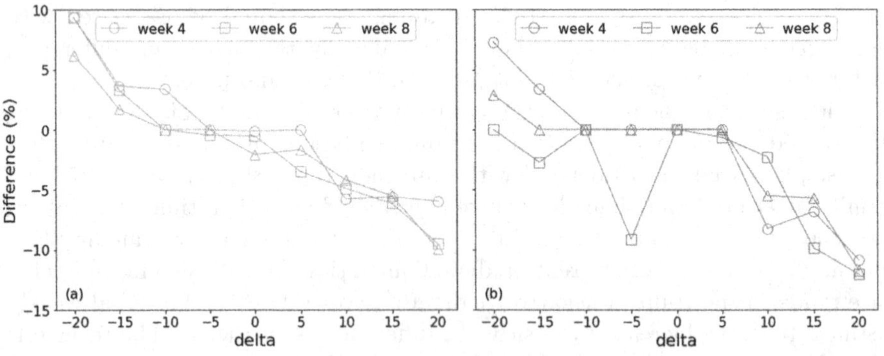

Fig. 6. The difference in mean weekly distance (km) for training plans based on adjusted goal-times for (a) men and (b) women during training weeks 4, 6, and 8. Note: $\delta < 0$ implies the goal-time is δ minutes *faster* than the runner's current predicted time.

5 Conclusions

In this paper, we described an initial study about how raw training/workout data that is routinely collected by fitness apps can be used to support runners as they train for the marathon. We focused on two important tasks in particular: (a) race-time predictions, as training progresses; and (b) recommending tailored training plans to runners if their goals change during training. A number of CBR variations were described – reusing the training and racing experiences of similar runners – and evaluated. The results are promising. It was possible to predict marathon finish-times with a reasonable degree of accuracy and to recommend training plans that are consistent with a runner's changing goals. Unlike the work of [17–20], which required runners to have run multiple marathons, this approach is suitable for novice and veteran runners alike, because it is based on current training data, with no requirement for previous marathon experience.

There are many opportunities to extend this research and improve the results obtained. We are currently developing a Strava companion app for providing predictions and recommendations to users based on their logged training sessions, making it possible to evaluate how users respond to this advice, and whether their performances improve as a result. Further representation improvements are also feasible, for example, by including heartrate data as a signal for effort and intensity during training, or by using time-series analysis techniques [24–26] to detect different types of training sessions. Another option is to employ feature analysis and selection techniques to determine which features are best predictors for race-time, as well as investigating different multi-week representations. Additionally, it is planned to transform the predictions and recommendations into a format that the runners could more easily interpret by providing upper and lower bounds, alongside average values for the race-time and weekly training completed by the similar runners retrieved from the case-base.

Finally, although the focus of this work has been exclusively on marathon runners, it is straightforward to adapt these techniques for other running distances, from shorter 5k, 10k and half-marathon races to longer ultra marathons, and it should also be possible to apply the work to other endurance sports such as cycling, triathlons, adventure racing, skiing and even skating.

Acknowledgments. Supported by Science Foundation Ireland through the Insight Centre for Data Analytics (12/RC/2289_P2) and the SFI Centre for Research Training in Machine Learning (18/CRT/6183).

References

1. Gasparetti, F., Aiello, L.M., Quercia, D.: Evaluating the efficacy of traditional fitness tracker recommendations. In: Proceedings of the 24th International Conference on Intelligent User Interfaces: Companion, IUI 2019, pp. 15–16, ACM, New York (2019)

2. Schneider, O.S, MacLean, K.E., Altun, K., Karuei, I., Wu, M.M.: Real-time gait classification for persuasive smartphone apps: Structuring the literature and pushing the limits. In: Proceedings of the 2013 International Conference on Intelligent User Interfaces, IUI 2013, pp. 161–172. ACM, New York (2013)
3. Cau, F.M., Mancosu, M.S, Mulas, F., Pilloni, P., Spano, L.D.: An intelligent interface for supporting coaches in providing running feedback. In: Proceedings of the 13th Biannual Conference of the Italian SIGCHI Chapter: Designing the next interaction, CHItaly 2019, Adova, Italy, September 23–25, pp. 6:1–6:5 (2019)
4. Mulas, F., Pilloni, P., Manca, M., Boratto, L., Carta, S.: Using new communication technologies and social media interaction to improve the motivation of users to exercise. In: Second International Conference on Future Generation Communication Technologies (FGCT 2013), London, United Kingdom, November 12–14, pp. 87–92 (2013)
5. Boratto, L., Carta, S., Iguider, W., Mulas, F., Pilloni, P.: Predicting workout quality to help coaches support sportspeople. In: Proceedings of the 3rd International Workshop on Health Recommender Systems, HealthRecSys 2018, co-located with the 12th ACM Conference on Recommender Systems (ACM RecSys 2018), Vancouver, BC, Canada, October 6, pp. 8–12 (2018)
6. Monteiro-Guerra, F.M. , Rivera-Romero, O., Luque, L.F., Caulfield, B.: Personalization in real-time physical activity coaching using mobile applications: A scoping review. IEEE J. Biomed. Health Inform. (2019)
7. Boratto, L., Carta, S., Fenu, G., Manca, M., Mulas, F., Pilloni, P.: The role of social interaction on users motivation to exercise: A persuasive web framework to enhance the self-management of a healthy lifestyle. Pervasive Mob. Comput. **36**, 98–114 (2017)
8. Pilloni, P., Piras, L., Carta, S., Fenu, G., Mulas, F., Boratto, L.: Recommender system lets coaches identify and help athletes who begin losing motivation. IEEE Comput. **51**(3), 36–42 (2018)
9. Buttussi, F., Chittaro, L., Nadalutti, D.: Bringing mobile guides and fitness activities together: A solution based on an embodied virtual trainer. In: Proceedings of the 8th Conference on Human-Computer Interaction with Mobile Devices and Services, MobileHCI 2006, pp. 29–36, ACM, New York (2006)
10. Hosseinpour, M., Terlutter, R.: Your personal motivator is with you: A systematic review of mobile phone applications aiming at increasing physical activity. Sports Med. **49**, 1425–1447 (2019)
11. Mulas, F., Carta, S., Pilloni, P., Manca, M.: Everywhere run: A virtual personal trainer for supporting people in their running activity. In: Proceedings of the 8th International Conference on Advances in Computer Entertainment Technology, ACE 2011, Lisbon, Portugal, November 8–11, p. 70 (2011)
12. Bartolucci, F., Murphy, T.B.: A finite mixture latent trajectory model for modeling ultrarunners' behavior in a 24-hour race. J. Quant. Anal. Sports **11**(4), 193–203 (2015)
13. Keogh, A., Smyth, B., Caulfield, B., Lawlor, A., Berndsen, J., Doherty, C.: Prediction equations for marathon performance: A systematic review. Int. J. Sports Physiol. Perform. **14**(9), 1159–1169 (2019)
14. Berndsen, J., Smyth, B., Lawlor, A.: Pace my race: Recommendations for marathon running. In: Proceedings of the 13th ACM Conference on Recommender Systems, pp. 246–250. ACM (2019)

15. Claudino, J.G., Capanema, D.d.O., de Souza, T.V., Serrão, J.C. , Machado Pereira, A.C., Nassis, G.P.: Current approaches to the use of artificial intelligence for injury risk assessment and performance prediction in team sports: A systematic review. Sports Med. Open **5**, 28 (2019)
16. Doherty, C., Keogh, A., Davenport, J., Lawlor, A., Smyth, B., Caulfield, B.: An evaluation of the training determinants of marathon performance: A meta-analysis with meta-regression. J. Sci. Med. Sport (2019)
17. Smyth, B., Cunningham, P.: Running with cases: A CBR approach to running your best marathon. In: Aha, D.W., Lieber, J. (eds.) ICCBR 2017. LNCS (LNAI), vol. 10339, pp. 360–374. Springer, Cham (2017). https://doi.org/10.1007/978-3-319-61030-6_25
18. Smyth, B., Cunningham, P.: A novel recommender system for helping marathoners to achieve a new personal-best. In: Proceedings of the Eleventh ACM Conference on Recommender Systems, RecSys 2017, Como, Italy, August 27–31, pp. 116–120 (2017)
19. Smyth, B., Cunningham, P.: Marathon race planning: A case-based reasoning approach. In: Proceedings of the Twenty-Seventh International Joint Conference on Artificial Intelligence, IJCAI 2018, July 13–19, Stockholm, Sweden, pp. 5364–5368 (2018)
20. Smyth, B., Cunningham, P.: An analysis of case representations for marathon race prediction and planning. In: Cox, M.T., Funk, P., Begum, S. (eds.) ICCBR 2018. LNCS (LNAI), vol. 11156, pp. 369–384. Springer, Cham (2018). https://doi.org/10.1007/978-3-030-01081-2_25
21. Zahran, L., El-Beltagy, M., Saleh, M.: A conceptual framework for the generation of adaptive training plans in sports coaching. In: Hassanien, A.E., Shaalan, K., Tolba, M.F. (eds.) AISI 2019. AISC, vol. 1058, pp. 673–684. Springer, Cham (2020). https://doi.org/10.1007/978-3-030-31129-2_62
22. Schneider, H.: Adapting at run-time: Exploring the design space of personalized fitness coaches. In: Proceedings of the 22Nd International Conference on Intelligent User Interfaces Companion, IUI 2017 Companion, pp. 173–176, ACM, New York (2017)
23. Fister Jr., I., Fister, I.: Generating the training plans based on existing sports activities using swarm intelligence. In: Patnaik, S., Yang, X.-S., Nakamatsu, K. (eds.) Nature-Inspired Computing and Optimization. MOST, vol. 10, pp. 79–94. Springer, Cham (2017). https://doi.org/10.1007/978-3-319-50920-4_4
24. Senin, P., Lin, J., Wang, X., Oates, T., Gandhi, S., Boedihardjo, A.P., Chen, C., Frankenstein, S.: GrammarViz 3.0: Interactive discovery of variable-length time series patterns. ACM Trans. Knowl. Discov. Data **12**(1), 10:1–10:28 (2018)
25. Berlin, E., Laerhoven, K.V.: Detecting leisure activities with dense motif discovery. In: The 2012 ACM Conference on Ubiquitous Computing, Ubicomp 2012, Pittsburgh, PA, USA, September 5–8, pp. 250–259 (2012)
26. Cheng, H.-T.: Learning and recognizing the hierarchical and sequential structure of human activities. PhD thesis, Carnegie Mellon University, Pittsburgh, PA, USA (2013)

Classifying Breast Cancer Tissue Through DNA Methylation and Clinical Covariate Based Retrieval

Christopher L. Bartlett(✉), Guanghui Liu, and Isabelle Bichindaritz

Intelligent Bio Systems Laboratory, Biomedical and Health Informatics,
State University of New York at Oswego, 7060 NY-104, Oswego, NY 13126, USA
cbartle3@oswego.edu

Abstract. In the current era of medicine where clinicians and researchers alike are seeking to personalize treatment plans to individuals, the integration of clinical data with microarray data is surprisingly absent. With this in mind, clinical covariate data was used to pre-select previously classified breast cancer tissue, and employ these classifications to new test cases. The pool of retrieved cases was then reduced further by investigating similar DNA methylation patterns. We first compared breast cancer tissue to normal tissue samples. This work was then extended to differentiating triple-negative breast cancer samples from ER-positive samples followed by investigating these subtypes at a genomic region level. In order to use the clinical covariate data, categorical distance measures were used to locate similar cases before being narrowed down with numeric DNA methylation data. Classification was then carried out using a novel, confidence-based procedure that automatically retrieves solved cases for each test sample until a threshold is met. We find that integrating clinical covariates increases the accuracy within our constructed two-stage system as opposed to using microarray data alone. Further, we outperformed random forest, naive bayes and kNN after refining the cases to a genomic region level.

Keywords: Machine learning · Case-based reasoning · Bioinformatics · Breast cancer · k-nearest neighbor

1 Introduction

In this current era of personalized medicine, clinicians have sought after methods which specifically target the patient through carefully tailored treatment plans. Throughout this movement, clinical and molecular profiles are constructed and managed in unison for advanced treatment. While this is becoming more prevalent on the frontlines of healthcare, the integration is surprisingly absent in 'omics research. The term 'omics collectively refers to genomics, proteomics, epigenomics and similar fields. Here, analysts are typically focused on a specific subtype of 'omics data while paying little attention to the clinical information

I. Watson and R. Weber (Eds.): ICCBR 2020, LNAI 12311, pp. 82–96, 2020.
https://doi.org/10.1007/978-3-030-58342-2_6

that define the research sample. Even in studies that span across 'omics, these primary variables are neglected. As these clinical variables are more descriptive, they increase focus and lend to a more explainable outcome. Therefore, it is the intent of this research study to couple a stable epigenetic biomarker, DNA methylation, with clinical data through a case-based reasoning structure built for classifying breast cancer samples. The clinical variables that were selected are the well-distinguished covariates age group, method of therapy, and race. Several studies have found age [4,9], therapy [7,14], and race [12] to have a significant effect on DNA methylation levels, making these common confounding variables. With this in mind, we hypothesize that drawing similarities to cases in the case base using these clinical covariates will aid in finding similar samples. Further, we assert that adding clinical covariates will improve diagnostic accuracy.

Specifically, this paper uses CBRMiC (Case-Based Reasoning for Microarray Classification), an R package designed by the authors to use clinical and microarray data for classification tasks. CBRMiC makes use of two iterative feature selection algorithms, computes distance matrices for categorical and numeric data, and classifies using a novel procedure that finds the optimal number of cases for each sample based on a confidence metric.

This paper outlines the methods used to be able to apply case-based reasoning (CBR) and instance-based learning to methylation data, most often analyzed through statistical methods. With four primary processes, retrieve, reuse, revise and retain, CBR is a powerful tool with a transparent problem-solving process. When a new case is presented to a CBR system, the similarity between the new case and previously solved cases (called the case base) is used to retrieve the most similar historic cases (the retrieve step). Then, the problem resolution of the prior cases can either be used to solve the new case (reuse step), or modified to fit any differences (revise step). Finally, the new case is stored in memory to be used in the future (retain step). The measure of similarity is often the most crucial, especially when there are different types of data as is the case within this paper. The most widely used similarity measures are often distance-based functions that compute the distance between cases using some or all of the attributes that define the case. A popular distance measure for numerical data is Euclidean distance (used within this study) though the addition of clinical data requires a categorical distance metric (discussed in Sect. 3.3). Processed DNA methylation is typically in the form of β values. β values are an estimation of the methylation levels between 0 and 1 with 0 being completely non-methylated and 1 being completely methylated. As such, these values are numerical.

Case-based reasoning (CBR) within the domain of microarray analysis is mostly unexplored, especially for epigenetic data. The primary foundation for CBR is its ability to consistently update with new cases, and adapt prior solutions to fit a new problem. Within microarray analysis, however, problems exist that make updating and adaptation particularly difficult. The first problem is the high dimensionality with few samples. There are thousands of features for a small subset of samples (specifically 485,000 for the standard chipset used in DNA methylation), and these samples are often imbalanced between cases and controls. A second problem is that technical variations, called "batch effects", often exist. Batch effects are alterations of the data that occur when different laboratories, technicians, or different equipment collects the data. Even when the same technicians operate on the same equipment within the same laboratory, subtle varying factors such as the amount of humidity can alter expression levels. These effects can be controlled to some degree through pre-processing, but need to be performed again when new cases are investigated. Lastly, clinical variables are all but ignored in any prior ventures in case-based reasoning for microarray analysis. Typically, researchers investigate similarities in genetic expression levels while disregarding whether samples are similar on a phenotypical level. [16] performed a multiple'omics study across 14 different cancer types and found that integrating clinical variables led to improved prognostic performance, while [13] found that clinical integration increased prediction performance. It is plausible that investigating samples that are similar on a clinical level as well as on a microbiological level will lend to more precise case selection, and therefore greater precision in identifying samples.

Methylation data require a preprocessing pipeline leading to improved analysis, as this article shows. First, potential confounding factors such as batch effects (discussed in Sect. 2.1) are eliminated. Following, methods which cluster the probes into possible functional regions for gene transcription are applied. Feature selection methods are also tested to further refine and select appropriate probes. Eventually, these probes are grouped into genomic regions.

This paper shows that the integration of clinical covariates improves the accuracy over microarray data alone. Further, we compare our results with four other classification algorithms. We have outperformed one of these algorithms during the first two tasks, before outperforming three after refining to a genomic region level.

Specifically, we offer the following significant contributions:

1. **Clinical and microarray integration:** A methodology that integrates clinical and microarray data, in the form of DNA methylation values. To the best of the author's knowledge, this is one of the first papers to take clinical covariate factors into account.
2. **Tailored case retrieval for each sample:** A method which locates a custom-tailored number of similar cases for each sample based on an automatically defined level of confidence in each of the stored cases. Varying the number of cases upon retrieval for each test case, and the method through which it is performed are both novel contributions.
3. **Multi-level case elaboration and refinement which examine biological and statistical differences:** Significantly different methylation levels in the DNA found at a high-order cluster of probes that serve similar functions were utilized and compared. Lastly, these probes are mapped to genetic regions to capture their precise influence upon the gene.
4. **One of the first applications of CBR using methylation data:** While studies using gene expression data in a CBR context have been performed previously, very few applications using methylation data have been produced.

2 Background

The term epigenetics was first introduced into modern biology by Conrad Waddington as a means of defining interactions between genes and their products that result in phenotypic variations. Waddington's landscape presents a cell becoming more differentiated as time goes on. One of the events that can cause this differentiation is methylation. Methylation is a covalent attachment of a methyl group to cytosine. Cytosine (C) is one of the four bases that construct DNA and one of only two bases that can be methylated. While adenine can be methylated as well, cytosine is typically the only base that's methylated in mammals. Once this methyl group is added, it forms 5-methylcytosine where the 5 references the position on the 6-atom ring where the methyl group is added. Under the majority of circumstances, a methyl group is added to a cytosine followed by a guanine (G) which is known as CpG. While the methyl group is added onto the DNA, it doesn't alter the underlying sequence but it still has profound effects on the expression of genes and the functionality of cellular and bodily functions. Methylation at these CpG sites has been known to be a fairly stable epigenetic biomarker that usually results in silencing the gene. Further, the amount of methylation can be increased (known as hypermethylation) or decreased (known as hypomethylation) and improper maintenance of epigenetic information can lead to a variety of human diseases.

DNA methylation, tested with a chip known as a microarray, has recently become more prevalent in genetic research studies in oncology. This paper proposes to apply these findings in a study of the diagnostic accuracy of DNA methylation signatures for classifying breast cancer samples when samples are first compared on a clinical level. The first study will be breast cancer samples versus normal tissue samples, while the second study is classifying two specific subtypes of breast cancer. These subtypes are ER-positive samples and Triple Negative samples. Breast cancer cells can be hormone receptor-positive, hormone receptor-negative or triple-negative. Hormone receptor-positive samples have either estrogen (ER) receptors, progesterone (PR) receptors or both. ER-positive breast cancer, specifically, is the most common type of breast cancer that's currently diagnosed. Triple-negative breast cancer cells do not have estrogen or progesterone receptors and do not make much of the protein called HER2. These cancers tend to grow and spread faster and do not respond to hormone therapies or drugs that target HER2. Due to the common nature of ER-positive breast cancer, and the aggressive nature of Triple Negative breast cancer, we sought a method that could help distinguish the two.

2.1 Research Background

An additive nonparametric margin maximum for case-based reasoning method (ANMM4CBR) was proposed in [15]. ANMM4CBR focuses on the retrieving and reusing stages of CBR and feature selects using additive nonparametric margin maxima. The nonparametric margin maximum is defined based on the nearest between-class distance maximization and the furthest within-cluster distance minimization. They first perform pre-selection and then cluster using hierarchical clustering. Finally, they apply an additive approach where, at each iteration, a feature is selected. When a feature is selected, for each sample the nearest between-class neighbor and furthest within-cluster neighbor may change. They state that maintaining the distance between any two samples in each iteration is computationally expensive and therefore maximize instead of directly optimizing. This allows them to test each feature on a training set and select the top-ranked. In order to reduce redundancy among features, they assign weights to training samples and update the weights where a sample that has a larger margin will receive a lower weight. Surprisingly, their case base is samples in one class. Testing with 10, 20, 30, 40 and 50 iterations on 4 different datasets, ANMM4CBR performed better than LogitBoost, SVM and kNN at every iteration on colon cancer. For leukemia, small round, blue cell tumors (SRBT), and global cancer map (GCM) data, ANMM4CBR had comparable results but did not outperform the others.

[2] built a framework with the kNN classifier as its backing. Also using gene expression data, they tested on child leukemia, colon cancer and prostate cancer. First, they preprocess the training data. Beginning with feature selection, they apply a Balanced Iterative Random Forest (BIRF) algorithm to select the relevant features (discussed further in Sect. 3.5). They follow this stage with dimensionality reduction through principal component analysis and weight features either through eigenvalues or a genetic algorithm. If classes are imbalanced, they oversample using the SMOTE algorithm. During testing, samples are reduced to the selected features and kNN is used to retrieve similar cases. Revision and retention is not employed through their framework. On leukemia, the best results were with a k of 5 which resulted in an average accuracy of 73%. A balanced accuracy of 93% was achieved on the colon data, and 98% on the prostate data.

More recently, [10] proposed a CBR method that visualizes results. The CBR system was rather straight-forward, retrieving cases through a distance measure, though their specialization was in the explainability. Qualitative attributes between cases were shown using rainbow boxes, where labeled and colored rectangles extend through columns that represent the cases, clearly showing what was similar or dissimilar between cases. Quantitative attributes are provided in scatter plots that center on the query case and accurately display the similar cases.

In the domain of instance-based retrieval methods is the work of [3]. Constructed for gene expression data, [3] proposed a modified k-nearest neighbor algorithm. Their methodology consists of projecting the data through the gene expression values, computing the center of each class, and computing the distance between each class item and the center of the class. With this data, they compute each item's weight. They then compute the distance between the center of the class and a test point and pick the smallest and largest of these distances (D_s and D_l). Neighbors are selected within the circles created with radius D_s and D_l, with the distances between the test item and these neighbors calculated to determine the strength of the neighbors. The test point is then assigned to the class with the highest summation of item strength.

3 Methods

Methylation data for breast cancer (BRCA,[1]) was downloaded from The Cancer Genome Atlas (TCGA,[2]) using the R package TCGAbiolinksGUI [6]. Molecular data was filtered for only the Illumina Human Methylation 450 microarray platform and prepared as an RStudio object. This data pertained to 892 samples and the 485,577 probes that exist on the Illumina Human Methylation 450 beadchip. The methylation β values were then extracted. β values are an estimation of the methylation levels between 0 and 1 with 0 being completely non-methylated and 1 being completely methylated. Tissue samples were either from the primary cancer tumor, normal breast tissue (typically from the opposite, non-cancerous breast), or the metastasized site. For the validation set, cancer tumor tissue was subsetted to only those samples having an ER positive or a Triple Negative status. Similarly, the BRCA clinical data was downloaded. Variables of interest in the clinical data were the age at initial diagnosis, race, and therapy method.

3.1 Data Preprocessing

Metastatic tissue samples (those pertaining to the metastasized site, not the primary cancer site) were discarded from the methylation data, as well as samples from males. Age group was determined based on which decade the sample's diagnosed age fell into. A sample extracted from an individual who was diagnosed with breast cancer at age 45 would be in group 4, while a sample from someone who was diagnosed at age 53 would be in group 5 for example. Batch effects were then located and removed using the R package ComBat. TCGA barcodes have a plate identifier, and this identifier was used to determine the batch. After pre-processing and batch correction, 782 cancer samples, 96 normal samples and 364,464 features (DNA methylation probes) were used. These probes were then used to locate differentially methylated regions (DMR) using the TCGAbiolinks R package. Differentially methylated regions are clusters of probes that are a possible functional region for gene transcriptional regulation. Here, this process served as a feature reduction mechanism using a biological methodology. The number of features were reduced to 8,722. Once this data was constructed, it was passed into the CBRMiC system where it was tested.

3.2 System Overview

Retrieval and classification was carried out using an author-constructed R package called CBRMiC. CBRMiC is a modular system that allows a user to split

[1] https://portal.gdc.cancer.gov/projects/TCGA-BRCA.
[2] https://www.cancer.gov/tcga.

data into K-folds, perform class balancing, undergo feature selection, calculate distance matrices for categorical and numeric features and finally classify.

When a dataset is loaded in, it is split into training and testing folds. Information is gleaned from the training folds so that it may serve as a case base for the testing folds. The training data can then be class-balanced and/or feature selected prior to distance calculation.

3.3 Distance Measures

Distance for the microarray features is calculated for a novel test case using Euclidean distance, while clinical (categorical) variables are calculated using either the Goodall3 or Lin measures [5]. The Goodall measure tries to normalize the similarity between two objects by the probability that the similarity value observed could be observed in a random sample of two points. A higher similarity is assigned to a match if the value is infrequent. In its third iteration, the measurement assigns a higher similarity if the matching values are infrequent regardless of the frequencies of the other values. To contrast, the Lin measure assigns a higher weight to mismatches on infrequent values and if there are few other infrequent values. A lower weight is assigned to mismatches if either of the mismatching values are frequent or if there are several values that have frequency in between the mismatching values. Operating these measures results in a distance matrix where test samples have a notated distance to each of the stored cases in the case base.

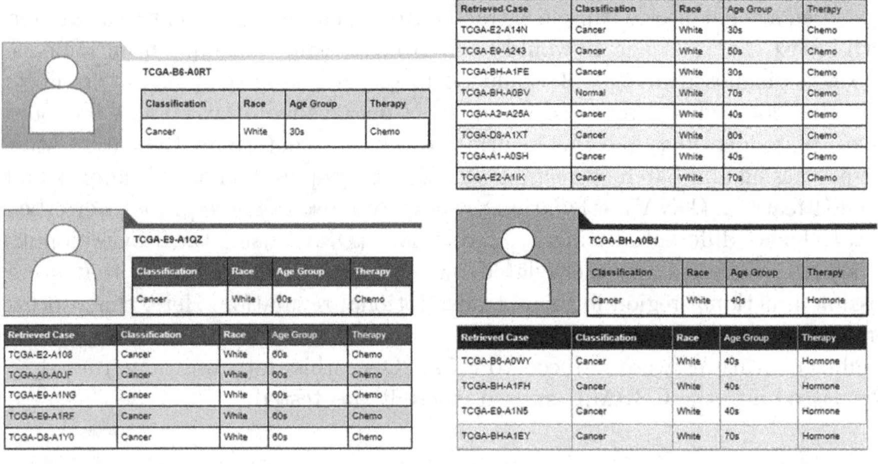

Fig. 1. Three query cases and their retrieved cases using the two-stage process. Retrieved cases are based upon similar clinical covariate data as well as a similar microarray signature.

3.4 Retrieval Framework

During classification, similar cases are retrieved for each test sample using a confidence metric. This confidence metric is the computed average of all distances to samples of a different classification minus the average of all distances to samples from the same classification for each case in the case base (shown in Algorithm 1). To frame it in terms of finding a cancerous sample among normal samples, the best cancer sample during training would have the highest average distance to all normal samples and the lowest average distance to all cancer samples. These values are normalized, giving this prototypical case a perfect score of 1.0 to imply 100% confidence.

Algorithm 1: Constructing a confidence table

```
Input: Distance matrix of cases and distances, Table of cases and their
classification label
Output:Table of cases and their confidence levels
Result: Construct a table of cases and confidence levels
for each case c_c do
    get all samples of the same class as c_c;
    get all samples of the different class as c_c;
    get distances for same class samples;
    get distances for different class samples;
    D_s c = mean distance for samples in the same class;
    D_d c = mean distance for samples in the different class;
    confidence level for c_c = D_d c - D_s c;
    add c_c and its confidence level to confidence table;
end
normalize confidence table;
return confidence table
```

During the two-stage process, cases in the case base are retrieved for each test case by first finding cases with a similar age group, therapy method and race (shown in Algorithm 2). This method uses the clinical covariate distance matrix calculated with the categorical distance measures outlined above to determine the distance between the test case and the case base. Then, once a pool of these cases has been retrieved, it is further refined using a Euclidean distance matrix from the DNA methylation features. Cases are continuously retrieved based on each case's confidence value until a threshold is reached. While this paper uses a threshold of 1.0 in its methods, a threshold greater than 1.0 can be established if the user wishes to retrieve more cases. In this manner, a distinct number of cases in the case base are retrieved for each test case. The classification label assigned to a testing case is then the majority label of the retrieved training cases. An example of this methodology in action is depicted in Fig. 1. In this figure, three randomly selected query cases are paired with their retrieved cases. Each query case has a different number of retrieved cases, though they share highly similar clinical traits which aids to the power and explainability of our system.

To summarize, our method is distinguished from the traditional k-Nearest neighbor through its usage of two distance matrices (one computed with a categorical distance measure and one computed with a numeric distance measure), and a confidence threshold that tells the algorithm when to cease retrieving cases.

Algorithm 2: The two stage retrieval process in CBRMiC

```
Input: Clinical covariate distance matrix C, Microarray distance matrix M
Output: Retrieved cases for a query case q
Result: Two Stage Retrieval Process
for a query case q do
    for every case c in C do
        Retrieve nearest case c from C;
        if current confidence > confidence threshold then
            stop;
        else
            current confidence = confidence of c + current confidence;
            Retrieve next nearest case c;
        end
    end
    for every retrieved case from C do
        Retrieve next nearest case m from M;
        if current confidence > confidence threshold then
            stop;
        else
            current confidence = confidence of m + current confidence;
            Retrieve next nearest case m;
        end
    end
end
return Retrieved cases for case q
```

3.5 Feature Selection

Feature selection algorithms used were Balanced Iterative Random Forest (BIRF), and random KNN (rKNN). BIRF was introduced in [1] and begins with the entire set of features and reduces features with zero importance value at each iteration. It continues to do so while the classification error rate of the training set is less than the classification error of the validation set. At this point, it considers the training set as being overfitted and concludes. rKNN is discussed in [11] and is an ensemble of k-Nearest Neighbor models that are constructed from a random subset of the input variables. A support criterion is used to rank features until the most relevant features can be used for classification. Additionally, it was tested with only the microarray data being used to retrieve cases until the confidence threshold was achieved and again with the two-stage clinical and microarray process.

4 Results

4.1 Test for Confounding Clinical Variables

To test whether the clinical variables had a significant effect on DNA methylation when comparing cancer and normal tissue samples, we first computed the average methylation for the samples using the differentially methylated regions. Then, each sample's average was separated into its respective age group, therapy group or racial group with samples having an NA status being excluded. A series of single-factor ANOVAs was used to determine if this status had a significant effect on the sample's average methylation level. For the samples used to differentiate breast cancer tissue from normal tissue, age group was found to have a significant effect on the average methylation level ($F(7{,}855) = 2.29$, $p = 0.025$). Therapy group was not found to have a significant effect on the average methylation level ($F(3, 573) = 1.79$, $p = 0.147$). Racial group also did not have a significant effect on the average methylation level ($F(4, 874) = 1.93$, $p = 0.102$).

A similar test was performed for the validation set of Triple Negative and ER Positive samples.The average methylation per sample was calculated using the differentially methylated regions. Each sample's average was separated into its respective age group, therapy group or racial group depending on the test. Again, null values were removed. A series of single-factor ANOVAs was used to determine if these groups had a significant effect on the sample's average methylation levels. For the samples used to differentiate ER positive from Triple Negative tissue, age group was again found to have a significant effect on the average methylation level ($F(6{,}125) = 2.40$, $p = 0.03$). Therapy group ($F(2{,}82) = 2.30$, $p = 0.10$) and racial group ($F(3{,}128) = 1.53$, $p = 0.20$) were again found to have non-significant effects.

Despite the non-significant effects in therapy and racial group for our datasets, we decided to continue with their usage since there were important differences between the groups, and also due to the support from the medical literature.

4.2 Classification Tasks

Two different stages were conducted, with the first being a subjectively easier classification task while the second was a more arduous task to validate the constructed system by trying to identify specific subtypes. The first task was accurately identifying whether a new sample (query case) was cancerous breast tissue or normal breast tissue. For this test, 782 cancer samples and 96 normal tissue samples were used. After identifying the differentially methylated regions, 8,722 features remained corresponding to probes on the DNA methylation chip. Once this data was constructed, it was passed into the CBRMiC system where it was tested with and without the two feature selection algorithms and with each of the categorical distance measures. These tests were performed using tenfold cross validation.

The second task was to try and differentiate two specific subtypes of breast cancer: ER Positive breast cancer and Triple Negative breast cancer. 48 ER positive samples and 84 Triple Negative samples were found and used in the TCGA BRCA dataset that met our selection criteria. After preprocessing and differentially methylated region analysis, 1,123 features remained. It is important to note that these samples were also used in the previous series of analyses. The tests within the CBRMiC followed the same methodology as the first task.

4.3 First Task: Cancer Classification

For these tests, a confidence threshold of 1.0 was set. Balanced accuracy (computed using the average of per-class accuracy), the F statistic and the Kappa statistic were used for performance metrics. Table 1 has the results for CBRMiC.

As a means of comparison, four other classification algorithms were tested. A kNN algorithm that uses a distance weight of $1/d$ where d corresponds to the distance and k is found through cross-validation was tested. During this test, the optimal k was found to be 10. Random Forest with 500 iterations, a Support Vector Machine (SVM) and Naive Bayes were also tested. These tests were conducted using the Waikato Environment for Knowledge Analysis (WEKA) [8]. Additionally, we tested CBRMiC using microarray data alone. Table 2 displays the results of these tests with our algorithm for comparison (the microarray stage uses the rKNN and Goodall algorithms).

Table 1. Testing results for classifying cancer tissue versus normal tissue using a two-stage process. (8,722 features)

Feature selection	Categorical distance measure	Balanced accuracy	F statistic	Kappa statistic
No	Lin	94.25%	0.98	0.84
No	Goodall	95.04%	0.98	0.84
BIRF	Lin	95.96%	0.98	0.88
BIRF	Goodall	96.68%	0.98	0.88
rKNN	Lin	95.05%	0.98	0.85
rKNN	Goodall	96.79%	0.98	0.85

Table 2. We compared our method, CBRMiC with four traditional algorithms, as well as using microarray data alone.

Algorithm	Balanced accuracy	F statistic	Kappa statistic
SVM	97.9%	0.98	0.93
kNN	97.85%	0.98	0.93
Naïve Bayes	97.4%	0.98	0.93
CBRMiC(rKNN, Goodall)	96.79%	0.98	0.85
CBRMiC(Microarray alone)	96.75%	0.99	0.91
Random Forest	95%	0.98	0.92

4.4 Second Task: Cancer Subtype

As aforementioned, the second series of tests was to try and differentiate two specific subtypes of breast cancer: ER Positive breast cancer and Triple Negative breast cancer. This stage follows the same pipeline as in the first task. Table 3 displays the results with our two-stage algorithm.

Similarly, four comparison methods were tested following the same paradigm as with the cancer versus normal tissue dataset. The results of these tests are available in Table 4 (the microarray stage uses the rKNN and Goodall algorithms).

Table 3. Testing results for classifying ER Positive versus Triple Negative breast cancer tissue using only the DNA methylation data (1,123 features).

Feature Selection	Categorical distance measure	Balanced accuracy	F statistic	Kappa statistic
No	Lin	76.61%	0.69	0.54
No	Goodall	75.56%	0.68	0.52
BIRF	Lin	75.15%	0.67	0.52
BIRF	Goodall	73.88%	0.64	0.47
rKNN	Lin	77.69%	0.71	0.58
rKNN	Goodall	77.55%	0.70	0.57

Table 4. We again compared CBRMiC with four traditional algorithms, as well as using microarray data alone.

Algorithm	Balanced accuracy	F statistic	Kappa statistic
Random forest	80.35%	0.83	0.63
Naïve Bayes	79.9%	0.81	0.60
kNN	78.15%	0.81	0.58
CBRMiC(rKNN, Goodall)	77.55%	0.70	0.57
CBRMiC(Microarray)	77.06%	0.69	0.55
SVM	69.65%	0.74	0.44

4.5 Initial Findings

As shown, our proposed algorithm outperformed random forest during the first task and SVM during the second task. Further, it can outperform using microarray data alone. While our two-stage algorithm performed better than one traditional algorithm at each of these tasks, we believed that it would produce stronger results when refining the cases to a genomic region level. As the high dimensionality was reduced through integrating probes to a gene level, we believed the additional dimension of the clinical covariate data would aid in differentiating samples.

4.6 Effect of Clinical Covariate Integration

First, we looked to see if integrating the clinical covariates had a significant effect. A series of paired-samples two-tailed t-tests with an alpha of 0.05 were conducted to determine if integrating the clinical covariate variables had a significant effect on the balanced accuracy, F statistic, and Kappa statistic. We utilized the scores obtained when using only the microarray data, and when using the clinical variables in our two-stage process. While we did not observe a significant increase when differentiating cancer from normal samples, we did find a significant increase for ER Positive and Triple Negative samples. Specifically, we found a significant effect on the balanced accuracy ($t(5) = -3.238$, $p = 0.022$), a significant effect on the F statistic ($t(5) = -3.415$, $p = 0.018$) and a significant effect on the Kappa statistic ($t(5) = -3.627$, $p = 0.015$). The effect on balanced accuracy is shown in Table 5. A possible explanation of why we did not observe the significant effect for our first dataset is that the cancer versus normal dataset holds a greater number of samples and a greater number of features. Without the larger sample and feature size, the algorithm may require more data through which to differentiate the samples and draw upon the clinical covariate differences to a greater degree. More tests will need to be conducted to determine whether this theory is correct.

Table 5. Effect of integrating clinical covariates on the balanced accuracy

Balanced accuracy			
Microarray	**Two-stage**	Paired samples t-test	
72.55	**76.61**	Mean	
71.92	**75.56**	72.95	76.073
69.24	**75.15**	Variance	
69.24	**73.88**	13.621	2.201
77.69	**77.69**	P(Two-tailed)	
77.06	**77.55**	0.022	

4.7 Case Refinement for Subtype Classification

After these initial tests, we wished to see if refining the cases further would increase our ability to differentiate cancer subtypes. Towards this end, we mapped each DNA methylation probe after DMR analysis to its associated gene and genomic region. Probes within each genomic region had their mean β value calculated. After mapping and calculating the means for each genomic region, 133 regions for the ER positive and Triple Negative data existed. Tests were performed with the two-stage process, as well as with the traditional algorithms as a means of comparison. A k of 15 was chosen when testing the kNN algorithm. As displayed in Table 6, our proposed two-stage algorithm outperformed

Naive Bayes, kNN, and SVM. Additionally, we re-display results prior to case refinement to show that associating probes to genomic regions increased classification accuracy for our proposed method. This indicates that initial hypotheses were correct that integrating methylated probes to a genomic level would not only reduce dimensionality, but lead to better performance from our constructed system.

Table 6. Results of a case refinement stage where probes were mapped to associated genomic regions. Comparisons were made with traditional algorithms at this stage, and results prior to case refinement are reshown to display the effect of the refinement.

Algorithm	Balanced accuracy	F statistic	Kappa statistic
Random forest	78.15%	0.81	0.58
CBRMiC(rKNN, Goodall)	78.08%	0.71	0.59
Naïve Bayes	77.22%	0.79	0.55
kNN	76.65%	0.80	0.56
SVM	53%	0.54	0.07
Before Case Refinement			
CBRMiC(rKNN, Goodall)	77.55%	0.70	0.57

5 Discussion

Results indicate that integrating clinical covariates performs better than microarray data alone within our proposed system during all tasks, and holds strong results after refining the cases to a genomic region level. During the first task, our two-stage system CBRMiC outperformed random forest, outperformed SVM during the second task, and outperformed Naive Bayes, kNN and SVM after case refinement. We believe that this current iteration of CBRMiC performs stronger on datasets with reduced dimensionality and will seek to strengthen the system to more appropriately handle the high dimensionality of DNA methylation data. We believe that a further increase in performance may occur with the addition of other clinical variables, so that there are more dimensions through which to differentiate the samples. Future directions will be to evaluate the confidence metric and search for other mathematical formulae to instill a single value upon samples as a means of determining how well that sample lends itself towards classification. We would also like to test our methodology on other independent datasets as well as incorporating other clinical information. Still, we have found results that display the utility of integrating clinical covariates with microarray information as well as the strength of using case-based reasoning for cancer classification.

References

1. Anaissi, A.: Case-base retrieval of childhood leukaemia patients using gene expression data, January 2013
2. Anaissi, A., Goyal, M., Catchpoole, D.R., Braytee, A., Kennedy, P.J.: Case-based retrieval framework for gene expression data. Cancer Inform. **14**, 21–31 (2015). https://doi.org/10.4137/CIN.S22371
3. Ayyad, S.M., Saleh, A.I., Labib, L.M.: Gene expression cancer classification using modified k-nearest neighbors technique. Biosystems **176**, 41–51 (2019). https://doi.org/10.1016/j.biosystems.2018.12.009
4. Bell, J.T., et al.: Epigenome-wide scans identify differentially methylated regions for age and age-related phenotypes in a healthy ageing population. PLoS Genet. **8**(4) (2012). https://doi.org/10.1371/journal.pgen.1002629
5. Boriah, S., Chandola, V., Kumar, V.: Similarity measures for categorical data: A comparative evaluation. In: Proceedings of the 2008 SIAM International Conference on Data Mining (2008). https://doi.org/10.1137/1.9781611972788.22
6. Colaprico, A., et al.: Tcgabiolinks: An R/bioconductor package for integrative analysis of TCGA data. Nucleic Acids Res. (2015). https://doi.org/10.1093/nar/gkv1507
7. Flanagan, J.M., et al.: Platinum-based chemotherapy induces methylation changes in blood dna associated with overall survival in patients with ovarian cancer. Clin. Cancer Res. **23**(9), 2213–2222 (2016). https://doi.org/10.1158/1078-0432.ccr-16-1754
8. Hall, M., Frank, E., Holmes, G., Pfahringer, B., Reutemann, P., Witten, I.H.: The WEKA data mining software: An update. SIGKDD Explor. **11**(1), 10–18 (2009)
9. Horvath, S., et al.: Aging effects on DNA methylation modules in human brain and blood tissue. Gen. Biol. **13**(10) (2012). https://doi.org/10.1186/gb-2012-13-10-r97
10. Lamy, J.B., Sekar, B., Guezennec, G., Bouaud, J., Séroussi, B.: Explainable artificial intelligence for breast cancer: A visual case-based reasoning approach. Artif. Intell. Med. **94**, 42–53 (2019). https://doi.org/10.1016/j.artmed.2019.01.001
11. Li, S., Harner, E.J., Adjeroh, D.A.: Random KNN feature selection - A fast and stable alternative to random forests. BMC Bioinforma. **12**(1), 450 (2011). https://doi.org/10.1186/1471-2105-12-450, http://www.biomedcentral.com/1471-2105/12/450
12. Song, M.A., et al.: Racial differences in genome-wide methylation profiling and gene expression in breast tissues from healthy women. Epigenetics **10**(12), 1177–1187 (2015). https://doi.org/10.1080/15592294.2015.1121362
13. van Vliet, M.H., Horlings, H.M., van de Vijver, M.J., Reinders, M.J., Wessels, L.F.: Integration of clinical and gene expression data has a synergetic effect on predicting breast cancer outcome. PLoS ONE **7**(7) (2012). https://doi.org/10.1371/journal.pone.0040358
14. Yang, G.S., et al.: Differential DNA methylation following chemotherapy for breast cancer is associated with lack of memory improvement at one year. Epigenetics, 1–12 (2019). https://doi.org/10.1080/15592294.2019.1699695
15. Yao, B., Li, S.: ANMM4CBR: A case-based reasoning method for gene expression data classification. Algorithm. Mol. Biol. **5**(1), 1–11 (2010). https://doi.org/10.1186/1748-7188-5-14
16. Zhu, B., et al.: Integrating clinical and multiple omics data for prognostic assessment across human cancers. Sci. Rep. **7**(1), 1–13 (2017). https://doi.org/10.1038/s41598-017-17031-8

A New Adaptation Phase for Thresholds in a CBR System Associated to a Region Growing Algorithm to Segment Tumoral Kidneys

Florent Marie(✉), Julien Henriet, and Jean-Christophe Lapayre

FEMTO-ST Institute, University Bourgogne-Franche-Comté, CNRS, DISC, 16 route de Gray, 25030 Besançon, France
{florent.marie,julien.henriet,jean-christophe.lapayre}@univ-fcomte.fr

Abstract. Image segmentation is an abundant topic for computer vision and image processing. Most of the time, segmentation is not fully automated, and a user is required to guide the process in order to obtain correct results. Yet, even with programs, it is a time-consuming process. In a medical context, segmentation can provide a lot of information to surgeons, but since this task is manual, it is rarely executed because of time. Artificial Intelligence (AI) is a powerful approach to create viable solutions for automated treatments. In this paper, we reused a case-based reasoning (CBR) system previously developed to segment renal parenchyma with a region growing algorithm and we completed its adaptation phase allowing a better adjustment of parameters before segmentation. Compared to the previous system, we added an adaptation for the thresholds values in addition to the adaptation of the seeds coordinates. We compared several versions of our new adaptation in order to determine the best and we confronted it with a deep learning approach realized in similar conditions.

Keywords: Case-Based Reasoning · Convolution Neural Network · Segmentation · Cancer tumour · Healthcare imaging · Artificial Intelligence

1 Introduction

Nephroblastoma, also called Wilms tumour, is one of the most frequent abdominal tumours observed in young children, representing 5 to 14% of malignant paediatric tumours, and affects kidney. Because of tumour's presence, the kidney can be very deformed and hard to segment. Radiologists and surgeons need 3-Dimensional (3D) representations of the tumour and the border organs in order to establish the diagnosis and to plan the surgery

Segmentation is one of the key steps in the construction of such a 3D representation. During this process, each pixel of all scans has to be affected to one and only one region. Each region represents a given structure (right or left kidney, medullas, tumours, muscles, veins, cavities, etc.). The problem resides

I. Watson and R. Weber (Eds.): ICCBR 2020, LNAI 12311, pp. 97–111, 2020.
https://doi.org/10.1007/978-3-030-58342-2_7

in the unforeseeable nature of the situation of the kidneys and radiologists and surgeons must lead and verify the segmentations of more than 200 scans manually for each patient in order to improve the therapy, which, in practice, is out of the question since the segmentation leading by a surgeon or a radiologist using actual tools requires 6 to 8 h.

Artificial Intelligence (AI) is a powerful tool capable of automatically performing image segmentation, but its performance is highly dependent on the quantity and quality of the available data. A knowledge approach helps to limit this dependence. In [16], we privileged the use of a CBR system coupled with a region growing algorithm, in order to perform kidney segmentation reached by a nephroblastoma. The main contribution of [16] was the adaptation of the seeds coordinates which ensured that they were well placed in the parenchyma of the pathologic kidney before starting segmentation. Despite the improvement in the results, the experiments highlighted the need to extend the adaptation step to the second type of parameters, namely thresholds, to avoid leakage phenomena that could severely deteriorate the accuracy of the yielded segmentations. In [15], we completed our work with a training method for CNN, but dedicated to the segmentation of nephroblastoma, called $OV^2ASSION$.

In this paper, we will first briefly present our platform dedicated to the segmentation of scanner images in children, COLISEUM-3D, before focusing on the CBR system for the segmentation of the pathological kidney. In particular, we will present a second adaptation dedicated to the threshold values used during segmentation by region growth so that the system itself is able to modify these values to find an optimal combination better adapted to the new problem.

2 Related Work

Many methods exist for image segmentation and some are commonly used for medical applications. Huang *et al.* realized a recent and complete survey describing popular algorithms for breast tumour segmentation [10]. Thresholding is the simplest way to compute a segmentation but, as a histogram-based method, it is not very efficient for noisy images such as US images or CT-scans. Clustering is another classical method where pixels are divided into several groups and given feature vectors for each of them. Yet, results widely depend on initialization. Region-based methods such as watershed and region-growing algorithms have a similar problem. On the one hand, the watershed technique tends to produce over-segmentation because each basin in the image corresponds to a different region. In contrast, region-growing needs to be initialized with seeds. Most often, parameters are manually determined. Seeds and threshold values are respectively placed in the images and defined allowing to calculate a criterion to drive the regions growing. Mohammed *et al.* developed a process for automatic seed point selection in order to segment Nasopharyngeal Carcinoma (NC) from microscopy images, using probability maps [18]. Another way would be to enhance the region-growing process with Artificial Intelligence (AI). Despite its sensitivity to noise and a phenomenon of recurrent leakage, the region-growing algorithm is fast and efficient.

Many research studies relative to segmentation enhanced by AI using CBR [5, 19, 20], genetic algorithms [6], knowledge stored in ontologies [2, 3, 11, 23], Markov random fields [12] and Deep learning [14].

Though, in recent studies, Deep Learning appears to give the most accurate results. This technique requires a lot of data in order to be trained. In contrast, CBR gives an advantage to knowledge and enriches itself following its experiments [13]. A large number of CBR systems designed for Health Science (CBR-HS) can be found in [1, 7–9, 17, 21, 22]. For instance, Saraiva *et al.* [22] designed a CBR and RBR (Rule Based Reasoning) system as a decision support system for diagnosis of gastrointestinal cancer. Petrovic *et al.* [21] worked on a CBR-HS to retrieve and adapt the best radiotherapy for patients. Gu *et al.* [7] realized a CBR system for diagnosis of breast cancer. In the image segmentation field, Perner [19] designed a system for segmentation of brain images with a cut histogram method. Frucci and Perner [5] adapted and improved this system with a watershed method. Burgos *et al.* [2] created another CBR system to retrieve the best segmentation process following the input images but for an agricultural application. This approach is inspired by Perner's one. Another interesting application was made by Ficet-Cauchard *et al.* [4]. The architecture of an interactive system allows the user to use a set of freely selectable and configurable modules to perform a particular image processing task as image segmentation.

3 Materials and Methods

This part presents the material and method aspect of our work. A first section describes our COLISEUM-3D platform. Then, an overview of our CBR system for kidney segmentation is showed as a part of the platform. The main section concerns the update of the adaptation process for seeds position and especially for thresholds values.

3.1 COLISEUM-3D

COLISEUM-3D (**COL***laborative plateform with artificial* **I***ntelligence for* **SE***gmentation of t***U***moral kidney in* **M***edical images in* **3D**) is a platform dedicated to the segmentation of scanner images for the detection of different abdominal structures in children. The structures of interest are the parenchyma of the pathological kidney, the corresponding renal cavities, the nephroblastoma and the blood vessels (arteries and veins). The platform inputs are the different images of the patient to be segmented. These images can be taken in vascular time (when the contrast product is in the patient vessels) or in late time (when this contrast product is evacuated through the kidney cavities) depending on the structures of interest. Its output is a final and single segmentation of these structures. An overview of the platform is showed in Fig. 1.

COLISEUM-3D is organized in layers, themselves made up of modules, as shown in Fig. 1 and explained below:

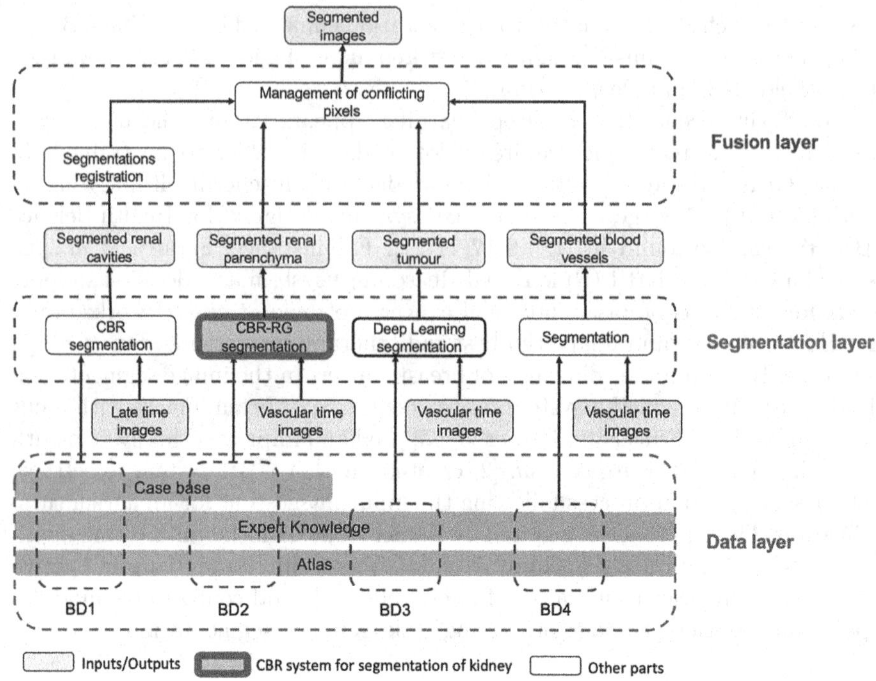

Fig. 1. Overview of COLISEUM-3D platform

- The data layer includes all the available data on which to base the solution of segmentation problems. It is itself divided into 3 sub-layers: the atlas, expert knowledge and the case base;
- The segmentation layer produces the different segmentations from the different inputs. It is composed of 4 distinct modules, each dedicated to the segmentation of a particular structure. Currently, a CBR system is used to segment the renal parenchyma and a Deep learning approach (presented in [15]) focuses on the segmentation of nephroblastoma;
- The fusion layer then merges the different segmentations in order to produce a single result. This involves label conflict resolutions.

3.2 CBR System for Segmentation of Pathological Kidney

Our system is an update of the one developed in our previous paper [16], dedicated to segmentation of renal parenchyma deformed by the presence of a nephroblastoma, and is presented in Fig. 2. The input of the CBR system is a new CT-scan to segment. It searches in the case base the closer image already segmented (source case) for reuse its solution. For this search, It calculates a similarity value for each stored case and extracts the source case with the highest similarity during a retrieval phase. Then, extracted parameters of segmentation are adapted to the current case through an adaptation phase. These adapted parameters are used to perform a new segmentation thanks to an region growing algorithm. Finally, the result is evaluated by an expert and stored in the case base as new source case if the segmentation is relevant.

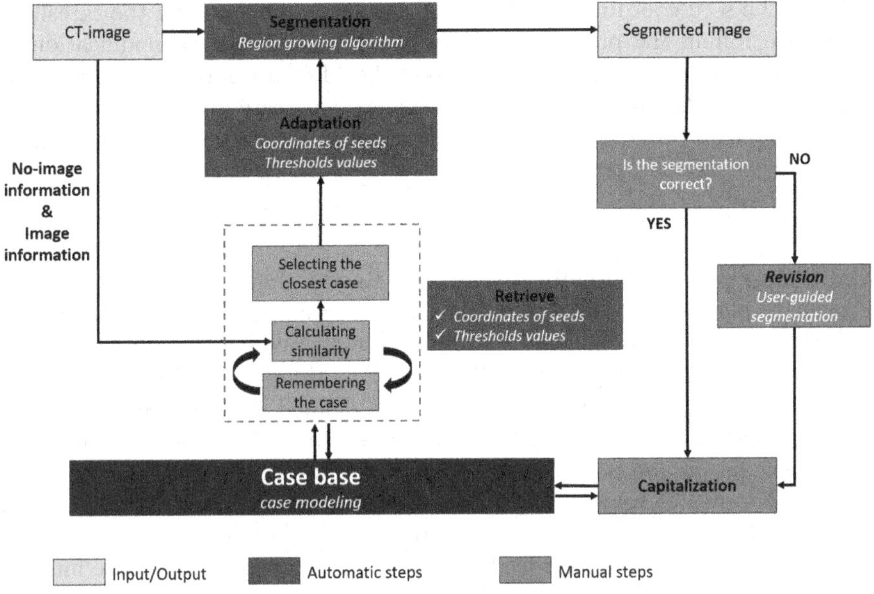

Fig. 2. Overview of our CBR system

Figure 3 describes the case structure. This case structure is an enhancement of the one used in the previous version of this tool and presented in [16]. The solution part is updated to take into consideration new criteria used during the new adaptation phase. In addition, we added the following items: intensity of seeds' pixels, area, center of mass and orientation of segmentation.

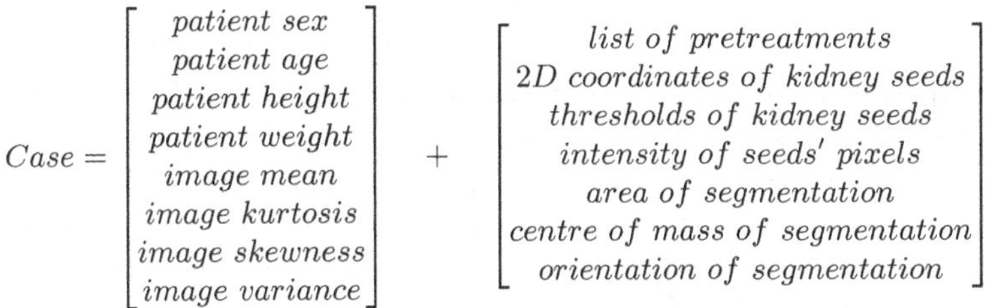

$$Case = \begin{bmatrix} patient\ sex \\ patient\ age \\ patient\ height \\ patient\ weight \\ image\ mean \\ image\ kurtosis \\ image\ skewness \\ image\ variance \end{bmatrix} + \begin{bmatrix} list\ of\ pretreatments \\ 2D\ coordinates\ of\ kidney\ seeds \\ thresholds\ of\ kidney\ seeds \\ intensity\ of\ seeds'\ pixels \\ area\ of\ segmentation \\ centre\ of\ mass\ of\ segmentation \\ orientation\ of\ segmentation \end{bmatrix}$$

Description of problem part **Description of solution part**

Fig. 3. The case model of the CBR: problem part and solution part

3.3 Adaptation Phase

The adaptation phase aims to automatically modify the parameters of region growing algorithm in order to maximize the relevance of the result. According to the algorithm presented in [16], there are two main types of parameters to be modified: the seed coordinates (used to initialize the process) and the threshold values (controlling the propagation/growth of the regions). A modification of these parameters, even minimal, may infer big difference for the resulting segmentation. It is therefore paramount to achieve to create an adaptation phase robust enough in order to ensure the efficiency of the system. The number of seeds is never modified and the system only use the ones that come from the retrieval phase.

Adaptation of the Coordinates of the Seeds. Part of the adaptation is to correctly place the seeds in the image. In [16], we suggested an algorithm to adapt the coordinates of the seeds. We automatically inferred the correct position of seeds, considering the grey-level intensity I of the pixel and extending step by step the neighborhood until finding it. We defined a coherence interval CI for each object to segment, corresponding to an interval of grey-level intensity a seed must be in, and a procedure to verify if a seed belongs to its dedicated region. This previous version outperformed a Level-Set technique (Dice equal to 75%) and FCN-8s (59%). In this work, we made some updates about the way we search the best position for seeds. First, we use a specific coherence interval CI for each retrieved seed in regards of a benchmark intensity i_{seed}. This value corresponds to the intensity of the pixel used to host the seed in the stored case. Secondly, the coherence interval CI is now dynamic around i_{seed} following an iteration value z. During a first step, the algorithm looks for a pixel with an exact intensity value i_{seed} in a window 50×50. If no position is found, the procedure starts from scratch by incrementing the value z. We limit the search of a better pixel intensity in a window in order to avoid seed placement in distant structures with an average intensity close from renal parenchyma. As a result, the test to verify the relevance of a seed position has changed as below:

$$\begin{aligned} \forall seed,\ isCorrectlyPlaced(seed) = true \ \ if \ \ I(seed) \in CI_{seed} \\ with\ CI_{seed} = [i_{seed} - z, i_{seed} + z] \end{aligned} \tag{1}$$

Adaptation of the Thresholds of the Seeds. As the region growth algorithm is very sensitive to initialization (different initial conditions have a lot of impact on the result), it is essential to adapt the position of the seeds. But this adaptation is not enough to guarantee the quality of the calculated segmentation and it is common that even with good coordinates, growth of seeds leads to an aberrant result. The problem is that the position adaptation does not prevent the leakage phenomenon in complex and sometimes low contrast images. If the location of the seeds plays a role in this, the sensitivity of the algorithm to this phenomenon depends strongly on the threshold values used.

The adaptation of the values of the thresholds aims at optimizing the values of 2 thresholds (local and global) per seed and determining an optimal combination. This implies designing a function that quantifies the quality of a segmentation (or the error) in order to maximize it (or respectively minimize it).

The Evaluation Criteria. This function is based on 3 different criteria to characterize the calculated segmentation compared to the segmentation of the reference case. These 3 criteria correspond to the calculation of the first 3 geometrical moments. The geometrical moment of order ij, for an image in which each pixel has for coordinates (x, y) and for value $I(x, y)$, has for expression :

$$m_{ij} = \sum_x \sum_y x^i y^j I(x, y) \tag{2}$$

The first criterion m_{00} is the order time 0. In a segmentation in which the pixel values are binary (0 for the *background* and 1 for the segmented object), this is equivalent to calculating the area, in number of pixels, of the segmentation. Using Eq. 2, we end up with :

$$m_{00} = \sum_x \sum_y I(x, y) \tag{3}$$

The second criterion is the center of mass, or center of inertia, C_m with coordinates $(\bar{x}, \bar{y})$:

$$\bar{x} = \frac{m_{10}}{m_{00}} \qquad \bar{y} = \frac{m_{01}}{m_{00}} \tag{4}$$

Finally, the third criterion θ allows to characterize the orientation of the segmentation in space :

$$\theta = \frac{1}{2} arctan\left(\frac{2m_{11}}{m_{20} - m_{02}}\right) \tag{5}$$

The Score Function. In addition to these criteria, we have built a function *score* in order to evaluate the quality of a proposed segmentation. This function is itself composed of sub-functions calculating a score for each criterion :

$$scoreGlobal = (a * scoreSup + b * scoreCdM + c * scoreOrient)/(a + b + c) \tag{6}$$

Where *scoreSup*, *scoreCdM* and *scoreOrient* are the scores on the area criterion, the center of mass criterion and the shape orientation criterion respectively. a, b and c are weight values which make it possible, if necessary, to give more weight to one criterion in relation to another in the calculation. Let x_{seg} be the x parameter calculated for the segmentation of the case to be solved and x_{ref} the parameter x obtained for the segmentation of the retrieved case. The scores are calculated by performing the difference $|x_{seg} - x_{ref}|$ and by standardizing them in order to delete the difference in scale of values between the 3 criteria.

Threshold Adaptation Algorithm. In order to determine an optimal combination of parameters, we have defined the search intervals IR_{local} and IR_{global} around the reference thresholds $thresholdLocal_{ref}$ and $thresholdGlobal_{ref}$ such that:

$$\begin{aligned} IR_{local} &= [thresholdLocal_{ref} - \alpha, thresholdLocal_{ref} + \alpha] \\ IR_{global} &= [thresholdGlobal_{ref} - \alpha, thresholdGlobal_{ref} + \alpha] \end{aligned} \tag{7}$$

where α is a value to control the extent of the search. In order to limit the complexity of the problem, we have used a maximum of 3 seeds to initiate the segmentation. We have favored a heuristic approach that allows us to efficiently explore a small part of the possibilities in order to obtain an acceptable solution, i.e. one that can be medically exploited. We have used the DICE and IU indices in order to validate the segmentations obtained in relation to the manual segmentation done by physicians.

Algorithm 1 proceeds by several stages for adapting the thresholds. First of all, the *seg* segmentation is calculated a first time with the list of seeds *lseeds* directly from the retrieval process. This provides the initial score as a basis for finding a better combination of thresholds. The score calculation uses the weights a, b and c as defined in Eq. (6). They must be defined empirically to maximize the quality of the segmentations. Indeed, modifying these weights impacts the different criteria (area, center of mass and orientation) in the definition of a optimal segmentation and therefore modifies the results of the CBR system. For each seed of the *lseeds*, all possible pairs $(threshold_{local}, threshold_{global})$ are explored, in accordance with the following search intervals α, by setting the other values and then the segmentation produced by each of them is evaluated. If the score of the new segmentation is higher than that of the previous one, the new threshold values are retained, otherwise, the old values are reassigned. The algorithm returns the list of seeds, with adapted thresholds to the current problem.

4 Results

This section presents our experiments and the results obtained. The first part presents the way the experiments have been performed. The second part shows our results for the determination of the best combination of weights for thresholds adaptation and highlights the interest of our adaptation phase in the CBR system. Finally, the segmentations obtained with this CBR system are compared to the ones obtained with a CNN in the lart part of this section.

4.1 Database, Initial Hypothesis and Conditions, and Evaluation Process

In order to evaluate the second stage of adaptation (modification of thresholds), the experiments are based on a database of 33 CT-scans segmented using a region growth manually guided by an expert, giving as many different cases. The cases are extracted from the examinations of 3 different patients, which we will name

Algorithm 1. Adaptation of seeds threshold values

```
Require: image, lseeds, infoSeg_ref, α, a, b, c
Ensure: lseeds
  seg ← segmentation(image, lseeds)
  scoreArea ← calculScoreArea(seg, infoSeg_ref.area)
  scoreCoM ← calculScoreCoM(seg, infoSeg_ref.centerOfMasse)
  scoreOrient ← calculScoreOrient(seg, infoSeg_ref.orientation)
  scoreGlobal ← a * scoreArea + b * scoreCoM + c * scoreOrient
  for each seed s of lseeds do
     localThreshold_ref ← s.localThreshold
     globalThreshold_ref ← s.globalThreshold
     for i from −α to α do
        for j from −α to α do
           localThreshold_temp ← s.localThreshold
           globalThreshold_temp ← s.globalThreshold
           s.localThreshold ← localThreshold_ref + i
           s.globalThreshold ← globalThreshold_ref + j
           seg ← segmentation(image, lseeds)
           scoreArea ← calculScoreSup(seg, infoSeg_ref.area)
           scoreCoM ← calculScoreCdM(seg, infoSeg_ref.centerOfMasse)
           scoreOrient ← calculScoreOrient(seg, infoSeg_ref.orientation)
           scoreGlobal_new ← a * scoreArea + b * scoreCoM + c * scoreOrient
           if scoreGlobal_new > scoreGlobal then
              scoreGlobal ← scoreGlobal_new
           else
              s.localThreshold ← localThreshold_temp
              s.globalThreshold ← globalThreshold_temp
           end if
        end for
     end for
  end for
  return lseeds
```

here respectively P1, P2 and P3. Table 1 summarizes the information on the constitution of this base. Note that we limit ourselves here for each patient to the sections in which the pathological kidney is present. Therefore, it does not refer to the entire examination. Finally, we have 33 images used to build the case base and 150 images to evaluate the system.

In order to improve the quality of the calculated segmentations, post-processing was applied to the images output from the CBR system. The renal parenchyma is organized in 2 distinct tissues, the cortex and the medulla. Actually, surgeons did not distinguish these 2 tissues during their segmentations considered as ground truth. But the region growing algorithm distinguished them sometimes. The post-processing consists of therefore applying a filling algorithm in order to merge these 2 structures in one.

Table 1. Case base for evaluation of our CBR system

	Nb of images	Nb of images in the base	Nb of tested images
P1	40	12	28
P2	55	13	42
P3	88	8	80
Total	183	33	150

4.2 Determination of Optimal Weights

The threshold adaptation step uses an overall score so that the system is able to assess the relevance of a segmentation associated with a combination of threshold values. The expression for the global score was given by Eq. (6). It uses a set of 3 weights a, b and c determining the influence of each criterion in the calculation. The determination of these weights is empirical. In this part, we experiment the adaptation of the threshold values for the seeds, according to Algorithm 1, with different triplets (a, b, c).

Four versions of the adaptation algorithm called respectively AdaptV0, AdaptV1, AdaptV2 and AdaptV3 are evaluated and faced to the lack of adaptation :

AdaptV0 Algorithm with adaptation of seeds positions only.
AdaptV1 Algorithm with a triplet weight (1,0,0).
AdaptV2 Algorithm with a triplet weight (a,b,c) without nomalization.
AdaptV3 Algorithm with a triplet weight (a,b,c) with nomalization.

Table 2 presents the results obtained for patients P1, P2 and P3 indicating, Dice scores for each of them. The score is determined for a patient at one time by considering the whole examination as one and the same 3D image. This method gives more relevant results than average because it is free from a calculation bias that can artificially decrease or increase the score. A large number of weight combinations was tested during the experiments but only the results of a sample of these combinations are presented. Without adaptation, we obtained a Dice score from 0.245 to 0.543. An adaptation of seed position only succeeded to significantly improve the performances for all patients. This improvement increases with a fully adaptation step. AdaptV1 achieves Dice index between 0.817 and 0.867 . The introduction of 2 additional criteria by AdaptV2 allows to have a clear improvement. AdaptV3 corresponding to a willingness to correct a methodological bias in the calculation of the criteria by standardizing them between 0 and 1. The best results are achieved for the triplet $(20, 10, 1)$ enabling a better mean segmentation accuracy for patients P1 and P3. These results also show that it is difficult to find an optimal (a, b, c) weight triplet for all patients. Some triplets may give the best result on one and the worst on another. The $(20, 10, 1)$ triplet appears to be the most relevant here because it provides good segmentations on all patients tested, but it is likely to lose relevance on others.

Table 2. Global Dice measures obtained by the region growth segmentations guided by our CBR system with adaptation of the seeds positions and thresholds.

	NoAdapt	AdaptV0	AdaptV1	AdaptV2 (1,150,4500)	AdaptV3 (1,1,1)	AdaptV3 (8,2,1)	AdaptV3 (20,10,1)
P1	0.455	0.620	0.826	0.826	0.651	0.806	0.830
P2	0.245	0.319	0.817	0.824	0.816	0.827	0.824
P3	0.543	0.712	0.867	0.888	0.899	0.882	0.897

Figure 4 highlights the importance of this new adaptation phase in our CBR system, as well as its effectiveness, with a series of examples. For the 4 images presented, the system failed to correctly segment the renal parenchyma when the threshold adaptation is missing (which corresponds to the previous version of this CBR [16]). For these 4 cases, the activation of the adaptation phase significantly increased the quality of the result, even if it did not manage to produce a perfect segmentation.

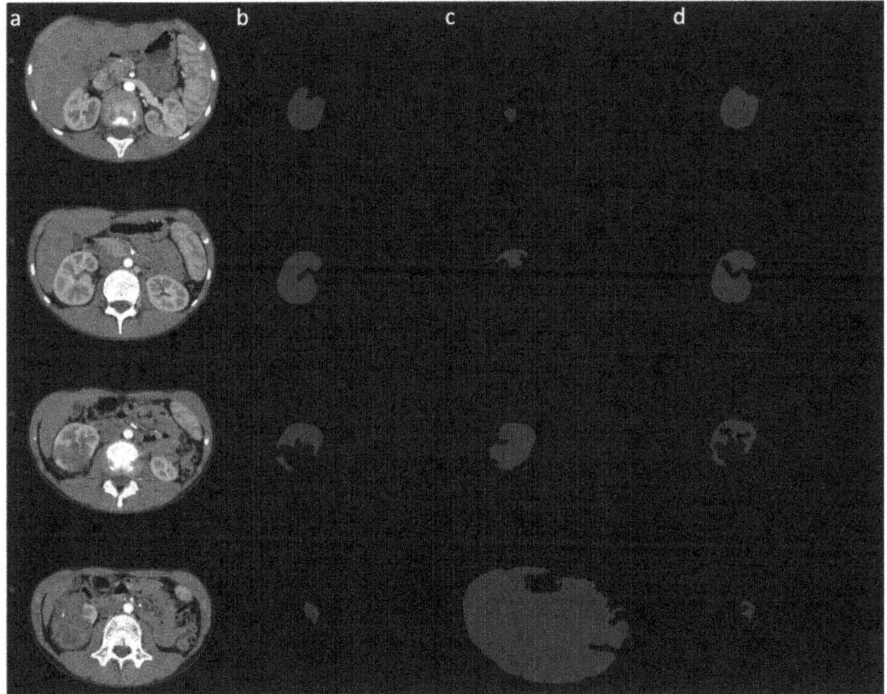

Fig. 4. Results of the region growth segmentation of different CT-scans (a) : (b) ground truths (c) without threshold adaptation (d) with threshold adaptation using triplet (20,10,1)

4.3 Comparaison with $OV^2ASSION$ Approach for Segmentation of Tumoral Kidneys

We have finally compared the segmentations obtained by CBR system (with its complete adaptation phase) to the ones obtained using a CNN (FCN-8s), trained according to our $OV^2ASSION$ method from [15], for the segmentation of the pathological renal parenchyma. The interest is that this method places the CNN in a favorable situation (segmentations to be calculated close to those included in the learning set LS) and optimizing the segmentation accuracies. The case base of the CBR system is identical to that of the previous experiments. The same patients P1, P2 and P3 have been used for these tests. We have used CBR with its complete adaptation phase (seeds' coordinates and threshold values), with the weight combination $(20, 10, 1)$. To perform the comparison under similar conditions, we set up the method $OV^2ASSION$ with a gap $g = 4$ and a vector $(V_4)_1$. The constitution of both of the databases is presented in Table 3. Only the number of data for P3 is significantly different (twice as many important for FCN-8s).

Table 3. Contents of the databases for CBR and FCN-8s

	Total Nb of images	**Nb of images case base of CBR**	**Nb of images learning set of FCN-8s** ($g = 4$)
P1	40	12	8
P2	55	13	11
P3	88	8	18

Table 4 presents the scores of Dice and IoU of both approaches, calculated only on missing images on the bases. For all patients, the CBR system is reached, thanks to its adaptation phase, to calculate segmentations more accurate than those proposed by FCN-8s. Both of the systems deliver performance very close for P3 with an advantage in favour of the CBR system. The pathological kidney of P3 has a healthy appearance on a large number of slices, this may explain why the CNN also manages to give good results. However, CBR keeps a superior performance while relying on a weaker database than FCN-8s (8 images versus 18).

5 Discussion and Future Work

Our results showed that our CBR system could significantly improve the accuracy of kidney parenchyma segmentation with a region growing algorithm, despite strong deformations induced by the presence of nephroblastoma. These good results are strongly linked to the existence of an adaptation of the seeds positions and thresholds. This one allows first of all to improve the likelihood that the seeds are properly placed and ensure better threshold values to lead

Table 4. Comparison of Dice and IoU scores for the segmentation of renal parenchyma (pathological) between our CBR system (with full adaptation) and FCN-8S trained according to the $OV^2ASSION$ method

	RàPC-CR with full adaptation		**FCN-8s** $OV^2ASSION$ $g = 4$	
	Dice	**IoU**	**Dice**	**IoU**
P1	0.830	0.710	0.763	0.617
P2	0.824	0.700	0.729	0.574
P3	0.897	0.814	0.881	0.788

the segmentation despite the small size of data base which is a medical constraint we have to deal with. A performance comparison when this adaptation is activated or disabled has clearly highlighted this contribution. On the other hand, the CNN showed poorer performance under the same conditions despite an advantageous situation allowed by the $OV^2ASSION$ method. The main limitation of the current system, however, remains the small size of the case base, which cannot be fully compensated for by adaptation. Of course, this limitation becomes all the more problematic when the kidney of the considering patient is of an original (unexpected) aspect (considering the system case-base). Beyond the question of a novel shape/position of the tumour (and therefore of the kidney by extension), there is also the problem of the laterality of the nephroblastoma. There are situations in which the characteristics of the kidney to be segmented may be very close to a stored case, which should logically lead to a relevant segmentation, but for which the pathological kidney is on the other side in this new target problem in relation to this stored case. This then leads to an inability of the system to compute a correct segmentation when all the conditions are met. The consequence is an under-exploitation of the knowledge available by the system, implying the need to complete the case base to maintain its efficiency and to predict the mirror cases. If we add the fact that including new cases is very time-consuming, the optimal exploitation of this knowledge is an essential point to work on. The relevance of the scoring criteria used for the adaptation of the thresholds, namely area, center of mass and orientation of the segmented form, should also be questioned. These criteria appear to be very interesting to describe the image but they are insufficient in use to guarantee the convergence of the algorithm towards the best possible segmentation. Thus, determining the weights to be given for each of these criteria remains an area of improvement.

Other futur works will be considered in order to improve this CBR system results. First, the determined weights are the best for the tested data but there is no guarantee there are for all patients. Further experiments are required in order to optimize these weight values. For example, the combination of weights (a, b, c) could be also integrated in the case solution. Second, our adaptation step does not allow all the differences between the stored cases and the new cases to be solved. It would be interesting to be able to design a modular adaptation capable of building an original solution from several different solutions stored in the database according to the relevance of their different parts.

6 Conclusion

The core of this work has enabled us to propose a segmentation solution by AI to extract the renal parenchyma from CT-scans, with the important lock of the limited amount of available data. This solution uses a Case Based Reasoning (CBR) system to guide a region growth algorithm. In particular, we have imagined an adaptation phase for the main initialization parameters of such an algorithm, namely the seed coordinates and the threshold values. We were able to demonstrate the efficiency of this adaptation and the clear improvement of induced performance. The presence of this adaptation has strongly limited leakage phenomena, which are common when a segmentation by growth of regions is performed. This adaptation has also increased the probability of segmenting the desired structure by correctly placing the seeds in the image.

Acknowledgments. The authors wish to thank Pr Frédéric Auber, Dr Marion Lenoir-Auber and Dr Yann Chaussy of the *Centre Hospitalier Régional Universitaire de Besançon* for their expertise with nephroblastoma and for achieving the manual segmentations with help of Loredane Vieille. The authors thanks *European Community* (*European FEDER*) for financing this work by the *INTERREG V*, the *Communauté d'Agglomération du Grand Besançon* and the *Cancéropôle Grand-Est*.

References

1. Attig, A., Perner, P.: Incremental learning of the model for watershed-based image segmentation. In: Barneva, R.P., Brimkov, V.E., Aggarwal, J.K. (eds.) IWCIA 2012. LNCS, vol. 7655, pp. 209–222. Springer, Heidelberg (2012). https://doi.org/10.1007/978-3-642-34732-0_16
2. Burgos-Artizzu, X.P., Ribeiro, A., Tellaeche, A., Pajares, G., Fernández-Quintanilla, C.: Improving weed pressure assessment using digital images from an experience-based reasoning approach. Comput. Electron. Agric. **65**(2), 176–185 (2009)
3. Colliot, O., Camara, O., Bloch, I.: Integration of fuzzy spatial relations in deformable models–application to brain MRI segmentation. Pattern Recogn. **39**(8), 1401–1414 (2006)
4. Ficet-Cauchard, V., Porquet, C., Revenu, M.: CBR for the reuse of image processing knowledge: a recursive retrieval/adaptation strategy. In: Althoff, K.-D., Bergmann, R., Branting, L.K. (eds.) ICCBR 1999. LNCS, vol. 1650, pp. 438–452. Springer, Heidelberg (1999). https://doi.org/10.1007/3-540-48508-2_32
5. Frucci, M., Perner, P., di Baja, G.S.: Case-based reasoning for image segmentation by watershed transformation. In: Perner P. (eds) Case-Based Reasoning on Images and Signals. SCI, vol. 73. Springer, Heidelberg. https://doi.org/10.1007/978-3-540-73180-1_11
6. Golobardes, E., Llora, X., Salamó, M., Martı, J.: Computer aided diagnosis with case-based reasoning and genetic algorithms. Knowl.-Based Syst. **15**(1), 45–52 (2002)
7. Gu, D., Liang, C., Zhao, H.: A case-based reasoning system based on weighted heterogeneous value distance metric for breast cancer diagnosis. Artif. Intell. Med. **77**, 31–47 (2017)

8. Henriet, J., Lang, C.: Introduction of a multiagent paradigm to optimize a case-based reasoning system designed to personalize three-dimensional numerical representations of human organs. Biomed. Eng. Appl. Basis Commun. **26**(05), 1450060 (2014)
9. Henriet, J., Leni, P.E., Laurent, R., Salomon, M.: Case-based reasoning adaptation of numerical representations of human organs by interpolation. Expert Syst. Appl. **41**(2), 260–266 (2014)
10. Huang, Q., Luo, Y., Zhang, Q.: Breast ultrasound image segmentation: A survey. Int. J. Comput. Assist. Radiol. Surg. **12**(3), 493–507 (2017). https://doi.org/10.1007/s11548-016-1513-1
11. Hudelot, C., Atif, J., Bloch, I.: Fuzzy spatial relation ontology for image interpretation. Fuzzy Sets Syst. **159**(15), 1929–1951 (2008)
12. Kato, Z., Zerubia, J., et al.: Markov random fields in image segmentation. Found. Trends® Sig. Process. **5**(1–2), 1–155 (2012)
13. Kolodner, J.: Case-Based Reasoning. Morgan Kaufmann (2014)
14. Litjens, G., et al.: A survey on deep learning in medical image analysis. Med. Image Anal. **42**, 66–88 (2017)
15. Marie, F., Corbat, L., Chaussy, Y., Delavelle, T., Henriet, J., Lapayre, J.C.: Segmentation of deformed kidneys and nephroblastoma using case-based reasoning and convolutional neural network. Exp. Syst. Appl. **127**, 282–294 (2019)
16. Marie, F., Corbat, L., Delavelle, T., Chaussy, Y., Henriet, J., Lapayre, J.-C.: Segmentation of kidneys deformed by nephroblastoma using case-based reasoning. In: Cox, M.T., Funk, P., Begum, S. (eds.) ICCBR 2018. LNCS (LNAI), vol. 11156, pp. 233–248. Springer, Cham (2018). https://doi.org/10.1007/978-3-030-01081-2_16
17. Marling, C., Montani, S., Bichindaritz, I., Funk, P.: Synergistic case-based reasoning in medical domains. Expert Syst. Appl. **41**(2), 249–259 (2014)
18. Mohammed, M.A., Ghani, M.K.A., Hamed, R.I., Abdullah, M.K., Ibrahim, D.A.: Automatic segmentation and automatic seed point selection of nasopharyngeal carcinoma from microscopy images using region growing based approach. J. Computat. Sci. **20**, 61–69 (2017)
19. Perner, P.: An architecture for a CBR image segmentation system. Eng. Appl. Artif. Intell. **12**(6), 749–759 (1999)
20. Perner, P.: Why case-based reasoning is attractive for image interpretation. In: Aha, D.W., Watson, I. (eds.) ICCBR 2001. LNCS (LNAI), vol. 2080, pp. 27–43. Springer, Heidelberg (2001). https://doi.org/10.1007/3-540-44593-5_3
21. Petrovic, S., Khussainova, G., Jagannathan, R.: Knowledge-light adaptation approaches in case-based reasoning for radiotherapy treatment planning. Artif. Intell. Med. **68**, 17–28 (2016)
22. Saraiva, R., Perkusich, M., Silva, L., Almeida, H., Siebra, C., Perkusich, A.: Early diagnosis of gastrointestinal cancer by using case-based and rule-based reasoning. Expert Syst. Appl. **61**, 192–202 (2016)
23. Trzupek, M., Ogiela, M.R., Tadeusiewicz, R.: Intelligent image content semantic description for cardiac 3D visualisations. Eng. Appl. Artif. Intell. **24**(8), 1410–1418 (2011)

Predicting the Personal-Best Times of Speed Skaters Using Case-Based Reasoning

Barry Smyth[1(✉)] and Martijn C. Willemsen[2]

[1] Insight Centre for Data Analytics, University College Dublin, Dublin, Ireland
Barry.Smyth@ucd.ie

[2] Jheronimus Academy of Data Science, Eindhoven University of Technology, Eindhoven, The Netherlands
M.C.Willemsen@tue.nl

Abstract. Speed skating is a form of ice skating in which the skaters race each other over a variety of standardised distances. Races take place on specialised ice-rinks and the type of track and ice conditions can have a significant impact on race-times. As race distances increase, pacing also plays an important role. In this paper we seek to extend recent work on the application of case-based reasoning to marathon-time prediction by predicting race-times for speed skaters. In particular, we propose and evaluate a number of case-based reasoning variants based on different case and feature representations to generate track-specific race predictions. We show it is possible to improve upon state-of-the-art prediction accuracy by harnessing richer case representations using shorter races and track-adjusted finish and lap-times.

Keywords: CBR for health and exercise · Speed skating · Race-time prediction · Case representation

1 Introduction

Speed skating has a long history as a popular winter sport. The International Speed Skating Union was founded in 1892 and long-track speed skating has been an Olympic sport since 1924 [1]. Olympic events include sprints (500/1000 m), middle distance (1500 m) and long distance (3,000/5,000/10,000 m) races, which impose different physiological, fitness, and pacing demands on skaters. Fast skating requires a high degree of technical skill, physical strength and dexterity: the crouched body position with low knee and body angles, which is optimal over shorter distances, is exceedingly difficult to maintain over longer distances [1,2]. Speed skating is also a time-trial event, with two skaters competing in separate

Supported by Science Foundation Ireland through the Insight Centre for Data Analytics under Grant Number 12/RC/2289P2.

I. Watson and R. Weber (Eds.): ICCBR 2020, LNAI 12311, pp. 112–126, 2020.
https://doi.org/10.1007/978-3-030-58342-2_8

lanes, so their performance mostly depends on their own abilities. Choosing a pacing strategy that is optimal, given the distance, track, competition, and the skater's own ability is a challenge and it is interesting to consider whether we can help skaters to achieve new personal-best (PB) times by recommending more appropriate pacing strategies.

There is a growing interest in the use of machine learning techniques in sports for performance prediction [3]. For example, recent research by [4–6] has considered performance prediction among marathon runners, where pacing also plays a role, showing how case-based reasoning can be used for PB prediction and pacing recommendation. Briefly, by reusing a case-base of past *race progressions*, each documenting the progress of a runner from a non-PB to a PB race, it was possible to predict challenging but achievable PBs for runners with upcoming races, based on the PBs of similar runners, and also to recommend a pacing plan to help a runner achieve their predicted PB time.

In this paper we explore whether this approach can be adapted to predict the race-times of skaters, bearing in mind that there are important and obvious differences between speed skating and marathon running. For example, speed skaters compete over a range of distances and thus there is an opportunity to create cases using multiple past races over different distances, unlike the marathon-to-marathon format of the cases used by [4–6]. This also facilitates prediction for distances that the target skater has not yet raced. While weather conditions are no doubt important in marathons, such factors were not considered by [4–6]; although a simple weather adjustment was use for ultra-running prediction by [7]. In skating the condition of the ice and the environment of the track are significant enough that they need to be included, especially since a skater's prior races will tend to take place on a variety of different tracks; we will describe how to normalise performances with respect to different tracks.

The remainder of this paper is organised as follows. In the next section we introduce speed skating as our domain of interest, discussing the important aspects of the sport, summarising the dataset that we will use, and highlighting the main research questions that we wish to answer. Following this, we will present our main technical contribution, by describing a case-based approach to predicting track-specific race-times. In fact, we will describe a number of variants of this approach, which differ in terms of the race histories that are used in cases, and the way that they are used. Finally, before concluding, we will describe a detailed evaluation to compare the prediction accuracy of these different variants, showing how significant improvements in prediction accuracy can be achieved relative to the state-of-the-art baseline approach proposed by [4, 8].

2 An Introduction to Speed Skating

Speed skating is a unique sport that combines endurance and power with pacing strategy and racing aerodynamics. In this section we briefly review the major features of the sport before describing the details of the dataset used by this work. We then go on to outline the key research questions that will be considered by this research.

2.1 The Anatomy of Speed Skating: Skaters and Races

Long-track speed skating is typically performed on an 400 m artificial ice-rink (see Fig. 1) over the following distances:

1. *Sprint:* 500 m (comprising one straight end and one lap) and 1,000 m (2.5 laps);
2. *Middle Distance:* 1500 m (an opening of 300 m, with 3 additional laps) is an important distance because it combines elements of sprint and endurance skating;
3. *Endurance:* 3,000 m (7.5 laps), 5,000 m (12.5 laps) and 10 km (25 laps), all of which demand a considerable degree or pacing strategy from skaters.

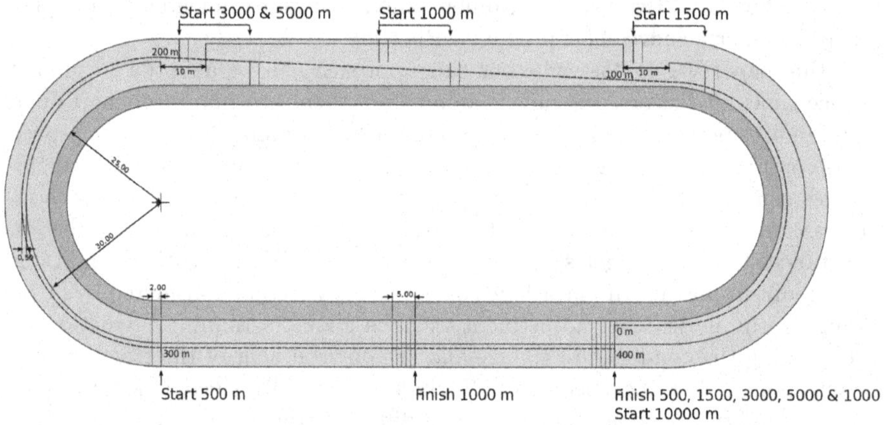

Fig. 1. The dimensions of a standard speed skating track and race configurations; image provided courtesy of wikipedia.org

In competition, skaters achieve similar high speeds to cyclists: elite sprinters reach 60 km/h while endurance skaters sustain average speeds in the 45–50 km/h range. During a race, skaters have access to very limited information on their performance – unlike runners and cyclists, GPS devices are useless as most tracks are semi-covered or completely indoor – and typically they only have access to their 400 m lap-times. Speed skating also places very different physical demands on athletes, compared with running or cycling: the crouched body position and low knee and trunk angles that are required for aerodynamic skating are physiologically challenging because they restrict blood-flow to the active muscles [1]. This makes it especially difficult for skaters to maintain good form and pacing over longer distances.

2.2 The Importance of Pacing

Previous research has focused on the pacing strategies used by elite skaters for shorter [2,9] and longer distances [10]. For sprint distances (500/1000 m), pacing does not play a significant role and the best approach is typically an *all-out* strategy with skaters going as fast as possible from the start and maintaining this speed, as best they can, until the finish [9]. However, for distances $\geq$1500 m, which combine elements of anaerobic and aerobic exertion, pacing plays an increasingly important role [11,12]. If a skater starts too fast, then they run the risk of slowing during the final stages of a race, and research has shown how maintaining a high speed in the 3rd lap (from 700–1,100 m) of 1,500 m races is critical for faster finishing times; see also the work of [13] for an analysis of a similar phenomenon among marathon runners.

Pacing is even more important in long-distance races, but in a way that differs from marathon running. For example, in elite long-distance skating negative splits – where the skater achieves a faster second-half time than first-half time – are more rare than in elite long-distance running, likely due to the physiological constraints and reduced blood-flow that is associated with good skating form.

For non-elite skaters lap-times typically slow as a race unfolds but the degree of slowing depends on the race distance: shorter races present with more significant slowdowns between laps than longer races, which are associated with more consistent pacing. As with marathons, how skaters pace their races is important when it comes to identifying similar skaters, thus motivating the importance of lap-times as part of case representations.

While previous research has focused on small samples of elite speed skaters, in this paper we focus on much larger samples of amateur and sub-elite speed skaters. Usually amateur skaters are still learning *how* to race, and thus any improvements to their pacing may enhance their PB prospects. Indeed, the pacing issue is exacerbated for non-elite skaters with respect to longer distances, in part because there are fewer opportunities to compete over longer distances, compared with elites; in other words non-elite skaters have fewer racing experiences when they need them.

2.3 The Dutch Speed Skating Data Set

The dataset used in this study was collected from http://www.osta.nl and comprises 329,080 race records from 15,590 unique Dutch skaters; thus each individual skater is associated with an average of 21 races. The races took place between September 2015 and January 2020 and race distances included all of the common distances, 500 m, 700 m, 1,000 m, 1,500 m, 3 km, 5 km, and 10 km. Each race record includes information about the skater (their name/id, gender, age), the race date, distance and track, and the skater's performance (finish-time and segment/lap-times, whether or not the result was a personal-best, and various age/gender rankings).

Skater Demographics: Speed skating is a somewhat unusual sport. In the data set skaters ranged in age from 4 to 84 years-old, but as shown in Fig. 2 most skaters are young, between the ages of 10 and 18 years-old, and once they graduate from high-school and go on to college most leave the sport, unless they

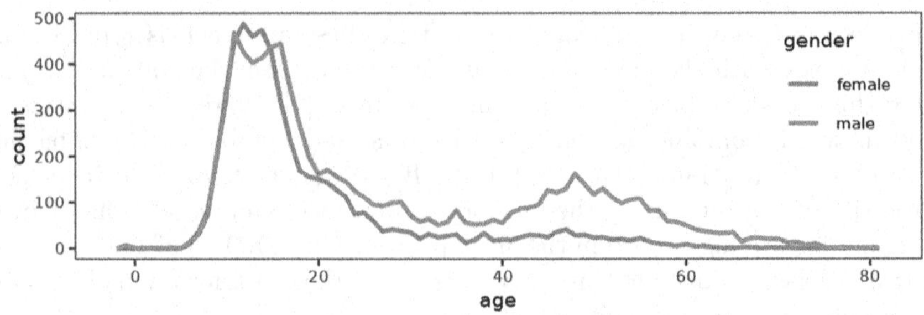

Fig. 2. Age distribution of skaters in the Dutch data set

are especially competitive. However, it is not unusual for skaters to return to the sport in their 40's, especially men, perhaps as their own children start to compete. In the Netherlands there exists a large population of older skaters who remain active at so-called *masters* level. There is even an official national masters championship.

Race Histories: There are 4 major categories of skaters in the dataset (Fig. 3: *pupils* are younger than 12 years old and only compete over shorter distances (100 m and 300 m, which are not in the data set, and 500 m, 700 m and 1000 m which are present); the majority of races are completed by *junior* skaters between 13 and 18 years old, mostly in races up to 3000 m; *senior* and *masters* skaters more frequently compete in 5 km and 10 km races, although they still remain rare compared to shorter distances, in part at least because the economics of ice-rinks make longer races more costly. The 500 m races are the most common by far because skaters often combine them with another distance on the same day or at the same event.

Track Types and Track Conditions: Track type and the ice conditions are important factors that influence performance. The quality of the ice can have an impact on race-times and is determined by a variety of factors including humidity and temperature. Outdoor or semi-covered tracks require frequent reconditioning of the ice (often every 20–30 min), while air-conditioned, closed-roof tracks provide more stable conditions, which are conducive to faster racing; high-altitude tracks are also considered to be faster [10], due to reduced air-resistance, but they are not present in the Dutch data set.

The data set contains records for a variety of track types, including: fully enclosed, air-conditioned tracks like the one in Heerenveen (HV), which hosts many international races; enclosed tracks without air-conditioning, typically with direct ventilation; semi-closed tracks with some cover, but that are otherwise exposed to the elements; and fully outdoor tracks without any cover at all. Figure 4 shows the mean 500 m race-times for a variety of different tracks and track types, and serves to highlight just how important track types are when

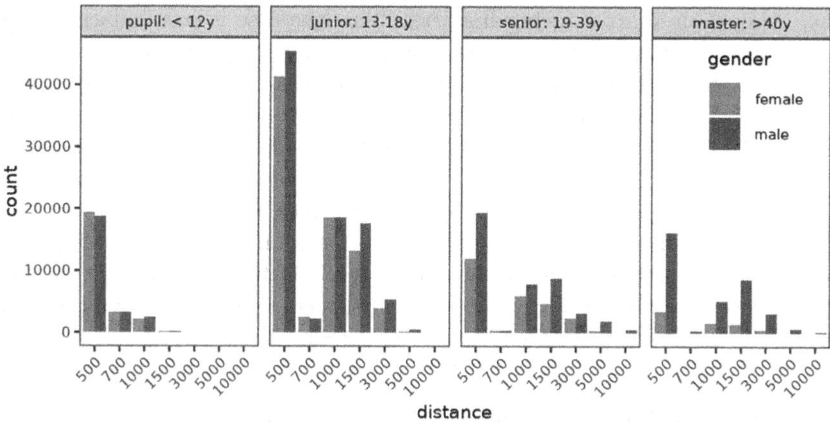

Fig. 3. Speed skaters by age category and distance.

it comes to finish-times. The fastest air-conditioned tracks are associated with finish-times that can be >10% faster that outdoor tracks (e.g. ≈45 s vs ≈53 s, for HV vs AM).

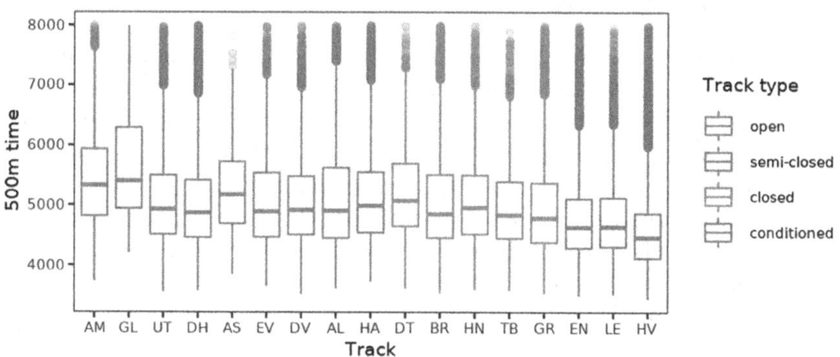

Fig. 4. Boxplots of 500 m times by track; note times are in hundreds of a second.

2.4 Research Questions

The main research question to be explored in this work is whether it is possible to accurately predict track-specific, personal-best times for skaters based on their previous racing histories. Unlike the work of [4,5,8], which relied on marathon race records from the same course, in this work each skater can be represented by a more diverse mix of race distances across a variety of tracks. As such, the main question becomes whether it is possible to predict the performances of skaters over distances that are longer than they are used to, and for different types of tracks, using their shorter racing histories. This use-case is particularly important to younger skaters because, when younger skaters graduate from shorter sprints to longer endurance races they can benefit from advice about realistic goal-times and pacing strategies.

For a given distance, differences in finish-times depend on track conditions, but they also depend on the skaters. Therefore it is not enough to simply apply a *one-size-fits-all* weighting to account for track differences when trying to predict track-specific finish-times. For example, some tracks might attract very young or much older skaters, who tend to be slower, while faster tracks like Heerenveen (HV) tend to attract more competitive skaters, who want to improve their PB, or those who wish to qualify for national championships.

3 Predicting Track-Specific Race-Times

Our approach to predicting finish-times is fundamentally case-based in nature: to predict a finish-time for some skater s and distance d we reuse the finish-times of skaters with similar race histories. To do this we describe a number of different ways to represent race histories with or without track-specific adjustments, and outline how the resulting case-bases can be used to generate predictions.

3.1 From Races to Cases

The work of [4,8] proposed pairing a runner's non-PB marathon time (and 5 km split-times) with their PB time (and split-times). The equivalent representation in the present work would, for a given target distance, d, pair a skater's non-PB race for d, $nPB(s,d)$, with their PB time for d, $PB(s,d)$ as per Eq. 1; each race, is represented by a finish-time, lap-times and a track id. In other words, to predict the finish-time for s for an upcoming 3,000 m race, requires a case-base that is made up of PB/non-PB times for 3,000 m races by other skaters. In what follows we refer to this as the *nPB* case representation (c_{nPB}) and it will serve as the *baseline* against which to judge the variations that follow.

$$c_{nPB}(s,d) = \Big\langle nPB(s,d) \mid PB(s,d) \Big\rangle \tag{1}$$

While this baseline remains valid in the present work, we are also interested in predicting a target distance PB by using previous races from shorter (more common) distances. Thus, one variation pairs a skater's PB and lap-times for shorter distances with their PB for a longer target distance, d, as in Eq. 2; in this study the target distances used are 500 m, 1,000 m, 1,500 m, 3,000 m, and 5,000 m. We refer to this as the *PB* representation (c_{PB}).

$$c_{PB}(s,d) = \Big\langle PB(s,d')\ \forall_{d'<d} \mid PB(s,d) \Big\rangle \tag{2}$$

In this way each case encodes additional performance information for s – their finish-times (and lap-times) for multiple shorter races – but these times are also personal-best times, reflecting recent *best-efforts* over these distances. This contrasts with the *nPB* representations, where it is less clear if the transition from nPB to PB is representative of a typical progression for a skater, or an artefact of the pairing of an outlier nPB with a very good PB. Moreover, the pacing patterns reflected in the lap-times of these shorter distance PBs encode important information about the type of pacing employed by a skater, which is important when it comes to finding cases that are similar in terms of their finish-times and pacing strategy: a sprinter will likely use a different pacing strategy on a 3000 m than an endurance skater, for example.

Of course, we can also combine the *nPB* and *PB* representations, so that cases for some race distance d are made up of a nPB race for that distance and PB races for shorter distances, as shown in Eq. 3, which we refer to as the *combined* representation (c_{com}).

$$c_{com}(s,d) = \left\langle PB(s,d') \ \forall_{d'<d} \ , nPB(s,d) \mid PB(s,d) \right\rangle \tag{3}$$

3.2 Adapting for Track Variations

Given that track conditions can have a material impact on finish-times we also produce modified versions of the above case representations, which use adjusted finish-times to reflect these conditions. In our initial analyses we found that simple adjustments for mean times per track (as reflected in Fig. 4) did not improve our predictions, because there are many confounding factors at play, such as different track-specific populations and type of races.

Since many skaters in our dataset have race times for a specific distance, on different tracks, we can estimate within-person adaptations that overcome most of these confounds. For each skater and each distance we calculate a PB for each track they have raced on, and then fit a multilevel regression model to this data to estimate within-person, track-specific differences relative to a single reference track. The fixed effects of this multilevel regression model provide the adjustments that can be used to standardise the finish-times of all races relative to the reference track.

$$c'_{nPB}(s,d) = \left\langle nPB'(s,d) \mid PB'(s,d) \right\rangle \tag{4}$$

$$c'_{PB}(s,d) = \left\langle PB'(s,d') \ \forall_{d'<d} \mid PB'(s,d) \right\rangle \tag{5}$$

$$c'_{com}(s,d) = \left\langle PB'(s,d') \ \forall_{d'<d} \ , nPB'(s,d) \mid PB'(s,d) \right\rangle \tag{6}$$

These adjusted finish-times can then be used to produce new versions of our *nPB, PB* and *combined* case representations, as shown in Eqs. 4–6, by replacing *raw* timing data with *normalised*, track-adjusted timing data, as indicated by nPB' and PB'.

3.3 Generating Predictions

For a given skater s and race distance d we predict their finish-time (using one of the representations outlined above) by using the past races of s to identify the k nearest cases, using a standard Euclidean distance similarity metric. As in the work of [4,5,8], male and female skaters are separated so that the predictions for male skaters are generated from the cases of male skaters, and vice versa for females; this is because of the performance differences that exist between the sexes due mainly to physiological differences. We also separate younger skaters ($\leq$20 years-old) from older skaters ($\geq$40 years-old) to facilitate a later age-based comparison.

Then a prediction is generated based on the distance-weighted mean of the target distance PB times from these cases ($PB(s', d)$ or $PB'(s', d)$ as appropriate, where s' denotes a similar, nearest-neighbour skater). If adjusted timings are used then ($PB'(s', d)$) then obviously the resulting prediction needs to be transformed back into an actual finish-time for the target track. As an aside, it is worth noting that to predict a pacing plan for the target race we can adopt a similar approach to that described in [4,8], by computing the average relative lap-times from the k nearest cases. However, we do not focus on this particular task further in this paper.

4 Evaluation

In this section we provide a detailed analysis of prediction accuracy, comparing the baseline *nPB* approach originally described in [4,8] to the alternatives proposed in this work.

4.1 Data and Methodology

We use the Dutch dataset introduced earlier to produce different case-bases for three common target distances (1,500 m, 3,000 m, and 5,000 m), using the different case representations (nPB, PB, and combined), and timing data (raw times versus adjusted times). This leads to 18 (3 $\times$ 3 $\times$ 2) individual case-bases for prediction. Note that the different target distances have quite different race characteristics: there are $\approx$48k 1,500 m races, each with 4 lap times, compared with $\approx$16k 3,000 m races (each with 8 lap times) and $\approx$2.7k 5,000 m races (with 13 lap times per race). The longer distances also facilitate richer *PB* representations because there are more shorter component PB distances. Thus a 5,000 m *PB* or *combined* case will have significantly more features than a 5,000 m *nPB* case, because of its extra component PB cases, and their lap-times.

We adopt a standard 10-fold cross-validation approach to evaluate prediction accuracy across these variations and for different values of k (1, 3, 5, 10. 20, 50). During each fold/iteration we select a random 10% of cases to use as test problems with the remaining 90% of cases used as the training case-base. Each test problem is solved (generating a race-time prediction) and compared to the known race-time for that test problem. For each prediction we calculate a percentage error and compute an average error across the folds for each variation.

4.2 Prediction Error vs k

To begin, it is informative to explore how prediction error varies with k, the number cases retrieved to make a prediction, and how this depends on the target distance, representation, and whether or not track-adjusted timings are used. Figure 5 shows the results, separately for each combination of (a) target distance, (b) representation, and (c) timings.

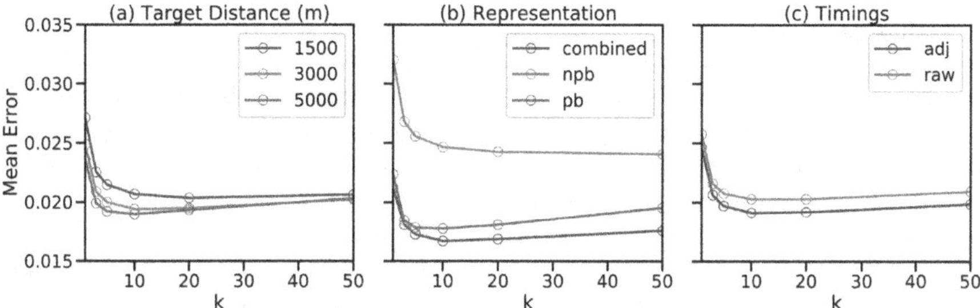

Fig. 5. The mean error rates by k (the number of similar cases reused) for different (a) target distances, (b) representations, and (c) timings (raw versus track-adjusted).

In general, as we might expect, the accuracy of predictions improves with k, up to a point, and on average the best overall errors are available for values of k in the range 10–20. It is also clear that the accuracy of the predictions, for a given value of k, depends on the target distance, representation and timing and it is worth discussing these accuracy differences further before proceeding.

The different error rates between the target distances can be explained by the number and quality of the features used during prediction. Since the error rates in Fig. 5(a) are averaged over all representations and timings, then cases for longer target distances tend to use more features, since the *combined* and *PB* representations will be made up of additional PB races and because longer races will be made up of more lap-time features. This explains the lower *combined* and *PB* error rates in Fig. 5(a). Moreover, since these longer distances are predominantly skated by the more skilled skaters, they are more predictable even at lower k. However, for larger k, the error goes up, most likely because there are fewer records for the longer distances and a larger k results in less representative similar cases being reused. This does not apply to the 1500 m distance, which still benefits from larger k due to the much larger number of available race records, and good similar cases can still be found even up to $k = 50$.

A related argument can be applied to explain the error differences by representation, in Fig. 5(b): the *combined* cases contain more features than the *PB* cases which, in turn, contain more features than the *nPB* cases. In addition, it is reasonable to expect that the PB races used in the *PB* and *combined* cases will be of *higher quality*, from a prediction viewpoint, than the lone nPB races in the *nPB* cases. That being said, the improved error rates for the *combined* cases over the *PB* cases indicates that these nPB races do add still value.

Figure 5(c) presents a like-for-like comparison in terms of the number and types of features in cases, the only difference being whether raw timings or track-adjusted times are used. The difference in error is more modest across values of k but indicates a benefit accruing to the track-adjusted timings.

In summary then, the novel case representations (*PB* and *combined*) and track-adjusted timings proposed in this work lead to more accurate predictions than the baseline *nPB* representation from [4,8].

4.3 Best Performers

Given the sensitivity of prediction to k, the target distance, the case representation, and the timings used, it is appropriate to examine the single best performing k for each combination of distance, representation, and timings, so that we can compare individual systems (single case-based predictors) more directly.

Figure 6 presents a table of these *best performers* for each of the 18 unique combinations of distance, representation, and timings. Each row of the table represents a single case-based predictor, with its corresponding value of k, and shows the mean and standard error of the prediction errors produced by the 10-fold cross-validation. The table is arranged in blocks by target distance (1,500 m, 3,000 m, and 5,000 m) and within each block the *baseline* and *best* performing variants are indicated.

We can see that best predictors, for a given combination of distance, representation, and timing, produce their most accurate predictions for different values of k, from 3 to 50, although in most cases the best value of k is either 10 or 20. The *combined* representation using track-adjusted times provides the most accurate predictions, regardless of target distance, with significant improvements with respect to the baseline, as shown. For example, when predicting 1,500 m times, the *combined, track-adjusted* variant generates predictions with a mean error of 0.0154 and a standard error of 0.0015, as compared with 0.0298 and .0016 for the baseline; a relative error improvement of more than 48% due to the *combined, track-adjusted* approach. As the target distances increase the improvements for the *combined, track-adjusted* variant, relative to the baseline, decrease, but remain significant; we observe a relative error improvement of 29% and 21% for 3,000 m and 5,000 m races, respectively.

It is interesting to note that these results appear somewhat at odds with the average prediction errors by target distance from Fig. 5(a), where shorter distances were associated with larger errors. While this is true in general – Fig. 5(a) averages over all representations and times for a given distance – the much higher error for the *nPB* cases for the 1500 m tends to increases the overall error rate. When we compare the *single, best performing* system for each distance, then the shorter distances have lower best-errors. This may be due to the fact that there are many more 1,500 m cases to choose from than there are for the 3,000 m or 5,000 m distances, as previously discussed.

d	rep	t	k	mean	SEM	
1500	combined	adj	20	0.0154	0.0015	*Best*
1500	combined	raw	20	0.0156	0.0016	
1500	pb	adj	20	0.0161	0.0032	
1500	pb	raw	10	0.0168	0.0034	
1500	npb	adj	50	0.0279	0.0016	
1500	npb	raw	50	0.0298	0.0016	*Baseline*
3000	combined	adj	10	0.0171	0.0017	*Best*
3000	combined	raw	10	0.0177	0.0018	
3000	pb	adj	10	0.0172	0.0024	
3000	pb	raw	10	0.0178	0.0027	
3000	npb	adj	20	0.0219	0.0017	
3000	npb	raw	50	0.0240	0.0018	*Baseline*
5000	combined	adj	10	0.0166	0.0003	*Best*
5000	combined	raw	10	0.0173	0.0003	
5000	pb	adj	5	0.0179	0.0003	
5000	pb	raw	3	0.0197	0.0003	
5000	npb	adj	10	0.0196	0.0003	
5000	npb	raw	50	0.0211	0.0003	*Baseline*

Fig. 6. Mean and standard error of prediction errors for the best performing value of k for each of the 18 case-base variants.

Figure 6 also indicates that the *PB* representation is also associated with significantly lower errors than *nPB*; the latter has fewer, lower quality features than the former. Moreover, for any given combination of distance and representation, the best track-adjusted timing cases offer improved errors compared to the use of raw timings; although the difference for a given distance and representation tends to be modest and is not commonly statistically significant.

4.4 On Gender and Age

The work of [4,8] highlighted different marathon-time prediction errors for men versus women: women enjoyed superior prediction accuracy, a result that is consistent with the notion that female runners tend to pace their marathons more evenly than men, and therefore are more predictable in their finish-times; see [14]. We consider a similar question here, by examining male and female prediction accuracy, and also the accuracy associated with younger ($\leq$20) and older ($\geq$40) skaters. We do this for two approaches – the *best* overall approach (*combined* representation with *track-based timing adjustments*) and the *baseline* (nPB with raw timings) – for the three target distances (1,500 m, 3,000 m, and 5,000 m).

We define a *relative advantage* score for gender and for age as shown in Eq. 7, so that the relative advantage for males versus females, for the baseline, is one minus the baseline error rate for males divided by the baseline error rate for females; thus, if $RelAdv_{baseline}(males, females) < 0$, then it means that the baseline error rate for males is *higher* (worse) than the baseline error rate for females, and vice versa.

$$RelAdv_{alg}(x, y) = 1 - \frac{error(x)}{error(y)} \tag{7}$$

Figure 7 presents the scores for the *best* and *baseline* approaches, for the target distances, comparing error rates for gender and age. $RelAdv_{best}(males, females) > 0$ in Fig. 7(a) means that the *best* approach produces more accurate predictions for men than for women. But $RelAdv_{baseline}(males, females) < 0$, indicating that the baseline produces more accurate predictions for women than for men, as with [4,8] for marathons. A similar pattern is observed in Fig. 7(b), comparing younger and older skaters: For the *best* approach the race-times of younger skaters are predicted more accurately $RelAdv_{best}(younger, older) > 0$ than older skaters, but for the *baseline* approach the finish-times of older skaters are predicted more accurately, $RelAdv_{baseline}(younger, older) < 0$ (except in the case of the 5,000 m target distance).

It is not clear why these approaches perform in this way, but it indicates that the *best* approach offers a more balanced prediction accuracy than the *baseline* approach, as well as its better overall accuracy. For example, the mean absolute relative advantage of the *best* approach is ≈0.05, for gender and age, indicating that the mean errors between genders and ages differ by only about 5%. This is compared with corresponding scores of 0.08 and 0.19 for *baseline*, indicating a much greater imbalance between genders and between age categories.

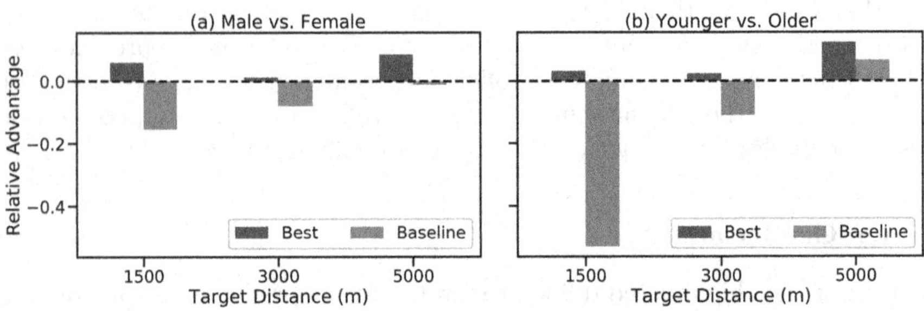

Fig. 7. A comparison of the relative error rates for the *best* and *baseline* approaches with respect to gender and age. A *relative advantage* score <0 for gender means females enjoy more accurate predictions than men, using a given approach, and a similar score for age means older skaters enjoy better predictions than younger skaters.

5 Conclusions

This paper extends the original work of [4,8], on predicting finish-times for marathon runners, in a number of important ways. First, we apply the techniques described by [4,8] to the very different sport of speed skating. Second, we propose an alternative case representation which is better suited to speed skating by representing case uses multiple races that are shorter than the target race; this in turn addresses one of the key shortcomings of the [4,8] approach, which required runners to have run at least one marathon in the past. Finally, given the importance of track conditions in speed skating we also proposed a technique for normalising race-times across a wide range of tracks. The results of a large-scale evaluation demonstrate the benefits of the new approaches that have been proposed. Using these approaches it has been possible to significantly reduce the prediction error compared with the baseline approach of [4,8].

The ideas presented in this work are general enough that they may also be applicable to marathons and other sports. For example, in marathon running, course conditions may have a significant impact on performance, which speaks to the value of a similar timing adjustment for marathon races to the one presented here for speed skating. Moreover, since many marathoners will run shorter races too (5k's, 10k's, half-marathons), then the idea of including PBs over shorter distances is also likely to be worthwhile. We also plan to extend our current work to include pacing recommendations as was the case for marathon races [5,6] to help skaters to achieve their predicted PB times and even help skaters to tackle a first race over a new, longer distance.

References

1. Konings, M.J., Elferink-Gemser, M.T., Stoter, I.K., van der Meer, D., Otten, E., Hettinga, F.J.: Performance characteristics of long-track speed skaters: a literature review. Sports Med. **45**, 505–516 (2015). https://doi.org/10.1007/s40279-014-0298-z
2. Hettinga, F.J., De Koning, J.J., Schmidt, L.J.I., Wind, N.A.C., MacIntosh, B.R., Foster, C.: Optimal pacing strategy: from theoretical modelling to reality in 1500-m speed skating. Br. J. Sports Med. **45**, 30–35 (2011)
3. Bartolucci, F., Murphy, T.B.: A finite mixture latent trajectory model for modeling ultrarunners' behavior in a 24-hour race. J. Quant. Anal. Sports **11**(4), 193–203 (2015)
4. Smyth, B., Cunningham, P.: Running with cases: a CBR approach to running your best marathon. In: Aha, D.W., Lieber, J. (eds.) ICCBR 2017. LNCS (LNAI), vol. 10339, pp. 360–374. Springer, Cham (2017). https://doi.org/10.1007/978-3-319-61030-6_25
5. Smyth, B., Cunningham, P.: An analysis of case representations for marathon race prediction and planning. In: Cox, M.T., Funk, P., Begum, S. (eds.) ICCBR 2018. LNCS (LNAI), vol. 11156, pp. 369–384. Springer, Cham (2018). https://doi.org/10.1007/978-3-030-01081-2_25

6. Smyth, B., Cunningham, P.: A novel recommender system for helping marathoners to achieve a new personal-best. In: Proceedings of the Eleventh ACM Conference on Recommender Systems, RecSys 2017, Como, Italy, 27–31 August 2017, pp. 116–120 (2017)
7. McConnell, C., Smyth, B.: Going further with cases: using case-based reasoning to recommend pacing strategies for ultra-marathon runners. In: Bach, K., Marling, C. (eds.) ICCBR 2019. LNCS (LNAI), vol. 11680, pp. 358–372. Springer, Cham (2019). https://doi.org/10.1007/978-3-030-29249-2_24
8. Smyth, B., Cunningham, P.: Marathon race planning: a case-based reasoning approach. In: Proceedings of the Twenty-Seventh International Joint Conference on Artificial Intelligence, IJCAI 2018, Stockholm, Sweden, 13–19 July 2018, pp. 5364–5368 (2018)
9. Muehlbauer, T., Schindler, C., Panzer, S.: Pacing and sprint performance in speed skating during a competitive season. Int. J. Sports Physiol. Perform. **5**, 165–176 (2010)
10. Muehlbauer, T., Panzer, S., Schindler, C.: Pacing pattern and speed skating performance in competitive long-distance events. J. Strength Cond. Res. **24**, 114–119 (2010)
11. Muehlbauer, T., Schindler, C., Panzer, S.: Pacing and performance in competitive middle-distance speed skating. Res. Q. Exerc. Sport **81**, 1–6 (2010)
12. Stoter, I.K., MacIntosh, B.R., Fletcher, J.R., Pootz, S., Zijdewind, I., Hettinga, F.J.: Pacing strategy, muscle fatigue, and technique in 1500-m speed-skating and cycling time trials. Int. J. Sports Physiol. Perform. **11**, 337–343 (2016)
13. Smyth, B.: Fast starters and slow finishers: a large-scale data analysis of pacing at the beginning and end of the marathon for recreational runners. J. Sports Anal. **4**(3), 229–242 (2018)
14. Trubee, N.W.: The effects of age, sex, heat stress, and finish time on pacing in the marathon. Ph.D. thesis, University of Dayton (2011)

Technical Session: New Paradigms

Clood CBR: Towards Microservices Oriented Case-Based Reasoning

Ikechukwu Nkisi-Orji[1(✉)], Nirmalie Wiratunga[1], Chamath Palihawadana[1], Juan A. Recio-García[2], and David Corsar[1]

[1] School of Computing Science and Digital Media, Robert Gordon University, Aberdeen AB10 7GJ, Scotland, UK
{i.o.nkisi-orji,n.wiratunga,c.palihawadana,d.corsar1}@rgu.ac.uk

[2] Department of Software Engineering and Artificial Intelligence, Universidad Complutense de Madrid, Madrid, Spain
jareciog@fdi.ucm.es

Abstract. CBR applications have been deployed in a wide range of sectors, from pharmaceuticals; to defence and aerospace to IoT and transportation, to poetry and music generation; for example. However, a majority of these have been built using monolithic architectures which impose size and complexity constraints. As such these applications have a barrier to adopting new technologies and remain prohibitively expensive in both time and cost because changes in frameworks or languages affect the application directly. To address this challenge, we introduce a distributed and highly scalable generic CBR system, Clood, which is based on a microservices architecture. This splits the application into a set of smaller, interconnected services that scale to meet varying demands. Experimental results show that our Clood implementation retrieves cases at a fairly consistent rate as the casebase grows by several orders of magnitude and was over 3,700 times faster than a comparable monolithic CBR system when retrieving from half a million cases. Microservices are cloud-native architectures and with the rapid increase in cloud-computing adoption, it is timely for the CBR community to have access to such a framework.

Keywords: Cloud CBR · Mircoservices · Elasticsearch · CBR framework

1 Introduction

Several case-based reasoning (CBR) development frameworks and toolkits have been introduced to the CBR community [13–15]. These have been extended for recommender systems [8] and textual CBR [12] and more recently for self-management systems [1]. However many of these CBR systems are mostly implemented with monolithic architectures such as desktop standalone applications,

J. A. Recio-García—Supported by the Spanish Committee of Economy and Competitiveness (TIN2017-87330-R).

I. Watson and R. Weber (Eds.): ICCBR 2020, LNAI 12311, pp. 129–143, 2020.
https://doi.org/10.1007/978-3-030-58342-2_9

with heavy demands due to siloed in-memory batch processing. This is not compatible with recent software development trends, which are increasingly using REST APIs[1] for communication with cloud computing platforms.

Cloud computing is a term used to describe the use of remote hardware and software to deliver on-demand computing services through a network (usually the Internet). In the past, applications or programs were run from software downloaded on to a physical computer or server. In contrast cloud computing lets users access these applications through the internet. Implementing software applications in the cloud offer several benefits which include efficient/cost reduction, scalability, mobility, and disaster recovery. Distribution of CBR applications and cases enables, MapReduce type algorithms to exploit the parallelism opportunity that is to be had with pair-wise similarity computations [19]. Interestingly, CBR has also been applied to support cloud provisioning, whereby similar Amazon Web Services (AWS)[2] configurations are recommended given a characterisation of a user's compute task [9]. This helps the user to make decisions about the types of cloud services for the given task. But having to monitor resource utilisation and change service requirements accordingly is a challenge which in turn has paved the way for microservice based architectures.

A CBR framework using a microservice based architecture provides (amongst other things) flexibility in both the technology being used (e.g., programming language) as well as dynamic scalability that can adapt to user application demands (e.g., spikes in casebase querying, seasonal effects). This is because, individual microservices are independently scaled and developed such that the overall system architecture is a scalable distributed application [6]. Importantly, the computation of services are stateless since they are automatically provisioned only when needed and then stopped when no longer required. This is particularly advantageous to CBR in situations where there is in-memory demand due to its inherent nature of being a lazy learner.

In this paper we discuss how the CBR cycle can be organised into multiple microservices and how service discovery is facilitated between these independent components using rest communications. A microservice is considered efficient when the system is loosely coupled and highly cohesive [10]. Identifying which functionalities within the CBR cycle should be decoupled and organising them into microservices is a key design challenge that we address in this paper. We do this by introducing, Clood[3], a generic open-source CBR cloud-based microservice framework, and make the following key contributions:

- create a novel design using the microservice paradigm for CBR;
- introduce, Clood, an extensible open source microservice CBR framework[4];
- evaluate the scalability of the retrieval phase on a recommender task; and

[1] An architectural style and approach for communication based on representational state transfer (REST) that is often used in web services development.

[2] https://aws.amazon.com.

[3] Clood is "Cloud" in Scottish dialect.

[4] Clood CBR repository: https://github.com/RGU-Computing/clood.

- identify areas of future development that are essential for the sustainability of CLOOD CBR.

Rest of the paper is organised as follows; in Sect. 2 we discuss existing frameworks, jCOLIBRI and *myCBR*. The design paradigm appears in Sect. 3 and the CLOOD implementation is discussed in Sect. 4. Results from a scalability experiment with half a million cases is presented in Sect. 5 followed by conclusions and future directions in Sect. 6.

2 Related Work in CBR Development Architectures

There are two well-established open-source frameworks for building CBR applications: *myCBR* and COLIBRI, though they follow different approaches and support different phases of the CBR application development.

myCBR[5] has been a tool for researchers and practitioners over the last ten years [16]. This framework is focused on the developing of a knowledge model for representing cases and computing similarity through the myCBR-workbench tool [2]. This knowledge model can be instantiated through the building blocks and functionality provided by the myCBR-SDK, that is a Java library following a classical monolithic software architecture. However, their authors have recently presented the *myCBR* Rest API which exposes the functionality of both myCBR-SDK and myCBR-workbench through a RESTful API [1]. Instead of forcing users to integrate their *myCBR* systems into a Java environment, this novel API enables users to model a CBR system using myCBR's workbench and then deploying the application as a web service. The goal is to make it easier to build, test, compare and deploy CBR applications.

COLIBRI, on the other hand, is focused on the development of a wide range of CBR applications [11]. As a platform, COLIBRI offers a well defined architecture for designing CBR systems, a reference implementation of that architecture: the jCOLIBRI framework [13], and several development tools that aid users in the implementation and sharing of new CBR systems and components. These tools have been integrated in the COLIBRI *Studio* development environment [14]. Both tools make up the COLIBRI platform following a two layer architecture. jCOLIBRI is the white-box layer of the architecture: a framework for developing CBR applications in Java. This framework represents the bottom layer of the platform. It includes most of the code required to implement a wide collection of CBR systems: Standard, Textual, Knowledge-Intensive, Data-Intensive, Recommender Systems, and Distributed CBR applications. It also includes evaluation, maintenance and casebase visualisation tools. All this functionality has established jCOLIBRI as a reference CBR framework with more than 35K downloads[6]. However, jCOLIBRI still follows the same monolithic Java architecture like *myCBR* and is not suitable for modern web environments.

[5] http://mycbr-project.org.

[6] http://gaia.fdi.ucm.es/research/colibri/jcolibri.

The need for both these platforms to evolve into web services architecture is clear. However, there are different approaches to implement this evolution. *myCBR* proposes wrapping its existing java components as web services. It is a straightforward option but has several drawbacks. Mostly, the wrapping of the existing java components does not allow to take advantage of the capabilities of cloud architectures regarding availability or scalability. The alternative option is to create a cloud-based CBR framework from scratch in order to exploit the features of modern cloud architectures. This is the option adopted by CLOOD, that can be considered as a re-implementation of the functionalities provided by the jCOLIBRI and *myCBR* frameworks, but instead of wrapping its existing java components, it redesigns entirely the CBR architecture for the cloud. In this manner, CLOOD adopts the CBR architecture defined in COLIBRI based on a pre/post-CBR-cycle to load/release required resources. CLOOD also reproduces the case structure representation based on a composite pattern, and the similarity computation through global/local similarity functions that both jCOLIBRI and *myCBR* implement.

In summary, our goal is to create a cloud architecture that is able to provide the same functionalities using familiar methods currently being used in jCOLIBRI and, thereafter, further integrate existing web services found in *myCBR*. As we will present in the following section, CLOOD re-implements jCOLIBRI's methods using modern web services technologies such as Elasticsearch or JSON-based communications that extend the existing capabilities of the framework regarding flexibility and data-intensive processing.

3 Microservices Design Paradigm for CBR

A microservice is an independent process which can carry out specific tasks in isolation [6]. These should be deployed, tested and scaled independently for a single functional responsibility; such as similarity, ranking, casebase editing, etc. Key to this architecture are the concept of serverless functions also referred to as *Function-as-a-Service* (FaaS) [3] - logic that is split into small code snippets and executed in a managed compute service. Well known examples include AWS Lambda and Google Cloud Functions[7].

3.1 Clood Architecture

Fig. 1 shows a high-level overview of the system's design consisting of 3 main components: REST API; serverless functions (compute service); and data service. The core CBR tasks – retrieve, reuse, revise, retain – are implemented as serverless computing functions. Functions can interact with external applications (e.g., a dashboard) and internally with other functions through REST APIs. Decomposition of the CBR cycle into smaller functions provides flexibility to introduce similarity functions and deploy them independently. Such functions will also include relevant knowledge container provisions. The post-cycle

[7] http://aws.amazon.com/lambda and http://cloud.google.com/functions.

or maintenance tasks, like forgetting cases or recomputing footprint cases can be confined to the Retain service. The data service is used as the casebase which allows the serverless functions to query and retrieve. Data sources and connectors forming the pre-cycle communicate with the casebase once they are synced with the data service. Data sources can either be external or within the cloud platform which gives flexibility for the community to use existing data sources. An important distinction here with the pre-cycle is that it remains lean (as compared to jCOLIBRI, or *myCBR*); in that it does not involve loading cases into memory once cases are made persistent.

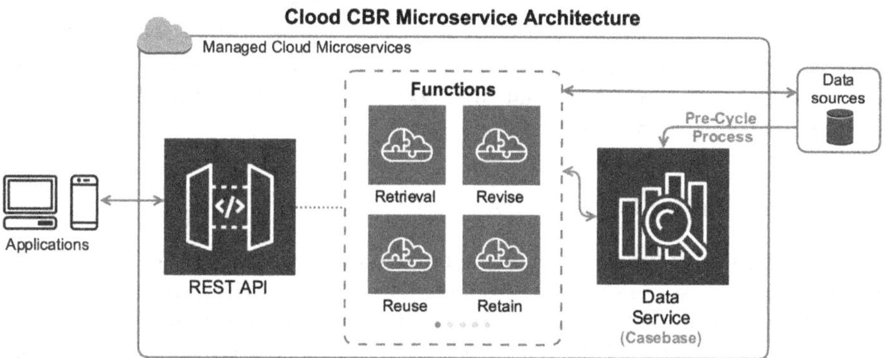

Fig. 1. Proposed CLOOD CBR architecture diagram

3.2 The Casebase

Popular CBR systems like jCOLIBRI keep the casebase in memory during operation. An in-memory casebase guarantees speed when interacting with the casebase but will incur massive costs to scale up for big data. Also, using the CBR system in a distributed manner can be problematic with in-memory casebase as memory is an expensive resource even on the cloud. In the serverless architecture, we maintain the casebase in the data service. The data service is a NoSQL full-text distributed search engine for all types of data. Elasticsearch and Solr are popular examples of such distributed, scalable open-source search tools for textual, numerical, geospatial, structured, and unstructured data. These tools provide a significant improvement regarding the representation of cases in previous CBR frameworks, because the case structure does not need to be fixed. Therefore, the cases in the casebase can have different attributes, and similarity metrics are applied according to each particular data types. Moreover, as these search tools are built on Apache Lucene, they are extendable, allowing users to write custom similarity metric scripts against a data index. Accordingly, the type of operations that would normally occur in-memory can be done in the data store index which is usually file-based[8].

3.3 Local Similarity

A subset of the serverless functions for the retrieve phase are used to generate similarity scripts to measure local similarity. These metric functions perform retrieval from the casebase at the attribute level. Each generated similarity function script depends on the data type of the attribute. Supported data types include string, numeric, boolean, date and object. Some similarity metrics, such as metrics to retrieve exact matches, are in-built in several distributed search engines that can be used for the data service. A suitable data service should enable the implementation of custom similarity metrics functions to support other local similarity functions that are used for CBR retrieval in the jCOLIBRI and *myCBR* frameworks.

3.4 Global Similarity

The global similarity function which aggregates local similarities determines the order in which cases are retrieved from the casebase and their ranking. Both a weighted and non-weighted form can be used to identify the nearest neighbours and is managed directly by the data service. Each local similarity function script is executed in the data service, in response to a single query, to obtain the global similarity as a sum. Custom scripts can be created as needed to vary the weights associated with different attributes. These weights can be dynamically modified for each retrieval task or alternatively remain static for all queries. The latter corresponds to learning an attribute weighting scheme that is used unchanged with every casebase query; whilst the former provides the opportunity to change attribute weights to suit the query context. The default global aggregation can be replaced with a custom aggregation script; whilst this does offer greater flexibility it will also incur greater computing memory when working with medium to large casebases since all the cases that are returned by the local functions will be held in memory (as with the monolithic organisation of jCOLIBRI and *myCBR*).

3.5 Implication for CBR Cycle

The major improvement over the architectures used by jCOLIBRI and *myCBR* is the lack of a two-layer persistence strategy. In previous frameworks there is a need to load cases into memory from a persistence media such as a database, text file, etc. However, the use of the CLOOD data service allows to manage cases directly from its internal data index.

Absence of the two-layer persistence strategy, has an immediate impact on the application structure because unlike previously where a *pre-cycle* step was

[8] Elasticsearch index store http://www.elastic.co/guide/en/elasticsearch/reference/7.6/index-modules-store.html (accessed May 14, 2020).

needed prior to the CBR cycle itself for loading cases into memory, this is no longer required. However Clood maintain the possibility of executing a pre-cycle (or its complementary post-cycle) in order to perform additional pre/post-processing of the data, if the CBR system requires it.

Another significant benefit of cloud-based technologies is concurrency, which directly creates the opportunity to execute CBR processes in parallel. This feature is quite limited in current frameworks and is also very relevant in order to parallelise time-consuming algorithms such as kNN or noise removal methods such as BBNR (Blame-based noise reduction), CRR (Conservative Redundancy Removal), RENN (Repeated Edited Nearest Neighbour), RC (Relative Cover), or ICF (Iterative Case Filtering) [5].

4 Clood CBR System

Clood is implemented using python functions following the design paradigm presented in Sect. 3. These functions run on Amazon Web Services (AWS) Lambda, which is the serverless event-driven computing service of AWS. The casebase uses the AWS ES service and the client application is implemented with JavaScript and HTML using the AngularJS framework[9]. Using a test application provided by jCOLIBRI[10] we describe the Clood implementation (see Fig. 2) and discuss how CBR functionality is achieved with cloud capabilities. Services that are not core to CBR operations include Cognito which is used for authenticated access to the system and Cloud Watch which is used to collect and monitor event logs.

4.1 Casebase Using Elasticsearch

Elasticsearch (ES) is an open-source highly distributed and horizontally scalable full-text search engine with various capabilities built on Apache Lucene [7]. ES uses RESTful interfaces to manipulate its schema-free JSON document store and performs searches at very high speeds maintaining an index that is about 20% the size of the indexed documents [18]. Compared to traditional database management systems, the ES "index" is somewhat like the database table as queries are executed against the index. While there are several schema-free databases with search capability to choose from, we choose ES as the data service in our implementation because of its popularity and close integration with existing cloud service providers.

Although it is "schema-free", ES internally generates a schema based on the field (attributes/columns) values of documents to be indexed. Relying on an ES-generated schema can be problematic in some cases. For example, a field for storing alphanumeric values can be designated as numeric by ES if the first documents to be indexed have numeric values only for that field. In order to

[9] http://angularjs.org.

[10] http://gaia.fdi.ucm.es/research/colibri/jcolibri/doc/apidocs/es/ucm/fdi/gaia/jcolibri/test/test1/package-summary.html (accessed May 14, 2020).

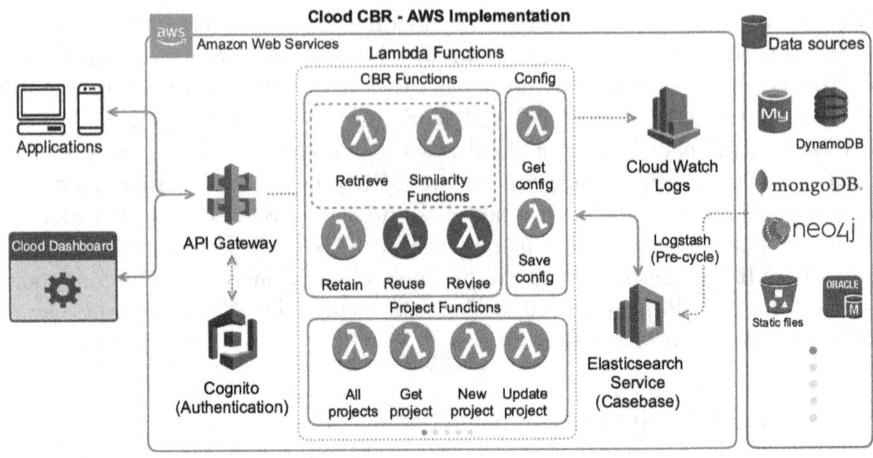

Fig. 2. CLOOD CBR implementation on AWS

avoid undesirable field properties, we create an explicit mapping which indicates the data type to be stored for each field in the casebase. The ES index "mapping" is comparable to the database schema as it describes the fields (columns) in the JSON documents along with their data types.

An explicit index mapping supports the specification of how a field's values should be indexed and the local similarity metric to be used for retrieving the values of that field. Where possible, we delay specifying the local similarity function for a field until retrieval time for greater flexibility. This is because the index specification for a field cannot be modified once data is added to the index. With query script similarity functions supplied at retrieval time, the method of retrieval can be varied without having to modify the underlying index mapping. Introducing a new attribute to an existing casebase can be done by extending the index mappings with the new field. The structure of cases that do not have values for newly created fields will remain unchanged. CLOOD's serverless functions interact with ES by HTTP requests and responses using a python Elasticsearch client, elasticsearch-py[11]. The casebase is a separate service which can be hosted anywhere with exposed API end-points further highlighting the distributed nature of CLOOD.

4.2 Clood Similarity Functions

Table 1 shows the local similarity metric functions that are currently implemented on CLOOD, reproducing some relevant functions available in jCOLIBRI and *myCBR*. Although several similarity metrics are currently missing in CLOOD, the goal here is to demonstrate the potential of the framework and to encourage code contributions in the future. Each similarity metric is

[11] http://elasticsearch-py.readthedocs.io/en/master (accessed May 14, 2020).

implemented as a python function which generates and returns a *Painless* script[12] that can be executed on ES during retrieval operations. Painless is the scripting language that is specifically designed for writing inline and stored scripts on ES. Generated scripts for the local similarity of each case attribute are combined into a single multi-match query script at retrieval.

Table 1. Clood's local similarity metrics

Data type	Similarity metric	Description
All	Equal	Similarity based on exact match
String	EqualIgnoreCase	Case-insensitive string matching
	BM25	TF-IDF similarity with TF normalisation based on Okapi BM25 ranking function
	Semantic USE	Similarity based on the similarity of vector representations
Numeric	Interval	Similarity of two numbers inside an interval
	INRECA	Similarity following the INRECA More is Better and Less is Better
	McSherry	Similarity following the McSherry More is Better and Less is Better
Enum	EnumDistance	Similarity of values based on their relative positions within an enumeration
Date	ClosestDate	Similarity depending on the extent two dates are to each other

McSherry, INRECA, Interval and EnumDistance are re-implementations of local similarity metrics found in jCOLIBRI. For textual CBR, we specifically implemented the Semantic local similarity metric (Semantic USE) for text content, using the Universal Sentence Encoder (USE) which embeds texts in a dense vector space of 512 dimensions [4]. This vector representation is generated using a lite version of USE based on the Transformer architecture[13] [17] and is stored as a dense vector field on ES. Textual retrieval follows the same process of generating the vector representation of a query string. Afterwards, the Semantic USE local similarity function measures the cosine similarity between query vectors and documents' vectors to identify the most semantically similar content.

4.3 REST API

REST APIs are stateless in that the API server does not remember the state of its clients and every call to an end-point is independent of other calls. REST

[12] http://www.elastic.co/guide/en/elasticsearch/painless/master/painless-guide.html (accessed May 14, 2020).

[13] http://github.com/tensorflow/tfjs-models/tree/master/universal-sentence-encoder (accessed May 14, 2020).

API uses existing protocols such as HTTP for Web APIs. As a result, client applications do not need additional software to use the service. REST improves portability to different types of platforms since all interactions are completed through universally understood interfaces. With CLOOD, each REST API end-point is a serverless function. The replication of an end-point and the resources allocated to it vary to meet changing demands without affecting the other end-points. REST APIs are created and published using the API Gateway (see Fig. 2) and Table 2 summarises the major REST API end-points of CLOOD.

CLOOD is able to concurrently manage multiple CBR applications (use-cases) referred to as "project" in Table 2. The system's capabilities can be easily extended by introducing new serverless functions (e.g., similarity functions, reuse functions, revise functions). Functions that will become part of the REST API are specified in a YAML file along with their access protocols.

Table 2. CLOOD's REST API end-points

End-point	Request method	Description
/project	HTTP GET	Retrieves all the CBR projects
/project/{id}	HTTP GET	Retrieves a specific CBR project with specified id
/project	HTTP POST	Creates a new CBR project. The details of the project are included as a JSON object in the request body
/project/{id}	HTTP PUT	Updates the details of a CBR project. Modifications are included as a JSON object in the request body
/project/{id}	HTTP DELETE	Removes a CBR project with specified id
/case/{id}/list	HTTP POST	Bulk addition of cases to the casebase of the project with specified id. Cases are included in the request body as an array of objects
/retrieve	HTTP POST	Performs the retrieve task
/retain	HTTP POST	Performs the retain task
/config	HTTP GET	Retrieves the system configuration
/config	HTTP POST	Adds or updates the system configuration

4.4 Clood CBR Dashboard

Client applications can perform CBR operations through the RESTful API end-points of CLOOD. The CLOOD CBR client application is a light-weight HTML and JavaScript implementation that is able to manage multiple CBR projects through API calls. Figure 3 shows the interface for specifying the attributes of a project's casebase. CLOOD system's configuration provides guidance on allowed operations when specifying attributes. For example, it indicates that the Interval local similarity metric only applies to numeric attributes. Once the attribute specifications are completed, CLOOD generates an index mapping for the case representation on ES.

Name	Data Type	Similarity Metric	
caseId	String	None	Remove
HolidayType	Enum	Enum Distance	Remove
Price	Integer	INRECA Less	Remove
NumberOfPersons	Integer	Interval	Remove
Region	String	Semantic USE	Remove
Transportation	String	Equal	Remove

Fig. 3. Specifying attributes for a casebase.

Attribute (Type)	Attribute value	Weight	Solution	Retrieve strategy
caseId (String)	caseId	1		Best Match
HolidayType (String)	Skiing	2		Best Match
Price (Integer)	Price		☑	Minimum
NumberOfPersons (Integer)	2	3		Best Match
Region (String)	Egypt	1		Best Match
Transportation (String)	Plane	1		Best Match
Duration (Integer)	3		☑	Minimum

Fig. 4. Retrieve stage query specification.

Logstash is an open-source data processing pipeline from the ES stack for ingesting data into ES[14]. Using Logstash, cases can be added to a CLOOD's

[14] http://www.elastic.co/guide/en/logstash/current/input-plugins.html (accessed May 14, 2020).

casebase from multiple data sources including files (e.g., CSV file), databases with JDBC interfaces (e.g., MySQL), and NoSQL databases (e.g., MongoDB). However, we also include a file upload utility for adding cases from CSV files through a RESTful end-point and which should be sufficient for file sizes that will not overwhelm the Web browser.

The retrieve operation begins with specifying some attribute values along with weights for aggregating the local similarity measures. Attributes with known values become part of the problem space while attributes with unknown values form the solution space. Furthermore, a retrieve strategy can be specified per attribute as shown on the user interface in Fig. 4. For example, the Best match can be retrieved for one attribute while the Mean of the k best matches retrieved for another attribute. The k nearest neighbours to retrieve and the global similarity method can also be specified at the retrieve phase.

A reuse interface displays the retrieval results for reuse. The recommended case (candidate solution) mixes the user-supplied attribute values with the retrieved values for unknown attribute values. The k most similar cases to the query case are also presented for possible reuse. The reuse button against a retrieved case is used to make it the recommended case. The recommended case can be revised by adjusting it as required. Afterwards, the case can be retained by adding to the casebase.

5 Evaluation

A scalability test is conducted to evaluate Clood based CBR application, to examine how resource demands both on the casebase and the serverless CBR functions are met. We expect a fairly consistent compute performance for different CBR tasks across different project sizes (compared to a jCOLIBRIapplication). We focus on case retrieval for evaluation since it is the most commonly performed and time-consuming stage of the CBR cycle.

5.1 Experimental Setup and Dataset

Six CBR projects of increasing casebase sizes (10, 10^2, 10^3, 10^4, 10^5, and 540, 394) were created from a used cars dataset[15] (1.35 GB CSV file), and case retrieval efficiency compared with Clood and jCOLIBRI. A case has 25 attributes[16] describing the physical attributes of a car (e.g., colour), identification attributes (e.g., vehicle identification number), and location attributes (e.g., region, state, coordinates), and the listing price.

In the comparative study, 10 nearest neighbours (NN) are retrieved with Equal similarities (Table 1) using the following query.

---

[15] http://www.kaggle.com/austinreese/craigslist-carstrucks-data/data (accessed February 25, 2020).

[16] Dataset attributes are `id`, `url`, `region`, `region_url`, `price`, `year`, `manufacturer`, `model`, `condition`, `cylinders`, `fuel`, `odometer`, `title_status`, `transmission`, `vin`, `drive`, `size`, `type`, `paint_color`, `image_url`, `description`, `county`, `state`, `lat`, `long`.

```
{ 'year':'2017', 'manufacturer':'ford', 'model':'focus',
'condition':'good', 'fuel':'gas', 'title_status':'clean',
'transmission':'automatic', 'drive':'4wd',
'size':'compact', 'paint_color':'grey' }
```


Time taken by the Retrieval function (Retrieve time) is recorded which for CLOOD, consists of: the time spent to dynamically generate a query using the appropriate similarity functions for the query case, retrieve the 10 NN of the query case from the casebase, generate a recommended case for reuse using specified reuse strategy, and generate a response through the API. We do not include the time lapse between the client application and the API endpoints as that is very dependent on the network connection speed and client's platform resources. For jCOLIBRI, Retrieve time is measured in the cycle phase consisting of: the time spent to retrieve the similarity configuration, perform NN scoring over the cases (in-memory), and select the 10 best cases. jCOLIBRI was run on a Windows 10 PC having 6th generation Intel core i7 processor and 16 GB RAM with 2GiB Java heap size. CLOOD uses AWS Lambda functions for its operations while the casebase was hosted on a single cluster of the AWS ES Service with 2GiB and 1 vCPU (t2.small.elasticsearch instance).

5.2 Results and Discussion

Figure 5 shows the average case retrieve times for CLOOD and jCOLIBRI on log scales with standard deviations as error bars. jCOLIBRI was marginally faster on the smallest casebase (10) but the superior performance of CLOOD is apparent with increasing casebase sizes. Similar case retrieval times were obtained by both systems at about casebase size of 100 cases; however at casebase size of 1,000, CLOOD was 5.5 times faster than jCOLIBRI and at casebase size of 540,394, CLOOD was 3,737 times faster than jCOLIBRI. Close examination of CLOOD's Retrieve time spent on the ES casebase when measured separately (Query time) shows to have increased due to time spent querying the casebase (see Fig. 6). We used the smallest AWS ES instance, and we expect Query time to improve when using an ES instance with improved resources. Also, several optimisation techniques can be employed to improve Query time. In the current implementation, we apply each local similarity function to the target attribute of every case in the casebase. An improvement can optimise the querying process such that it uses filters to reduce the number of similarity computations. For example, in the query above where the 'year' must match '2017', we can apply the year limit as a filter when matching 'manufacturer' so that it only searches for 'ford' in 2017 models.

The use of cloud services typically involves usage costs. The microservice architecture with pricing per run-time keeps the costs minimal. For example, running the CloodCBR system with core services (Lambda and ES and data transfer) costs 14 USD a month. In comparison, a similar monolith system hosted

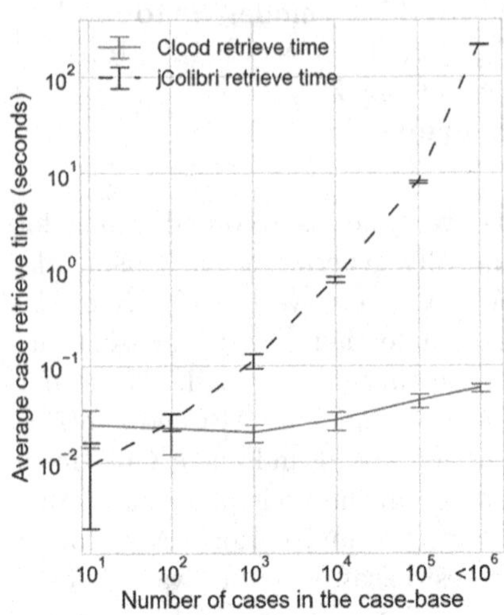

Fig. 5. Case retrieve times as casebase size increases. Both axes are log scales.

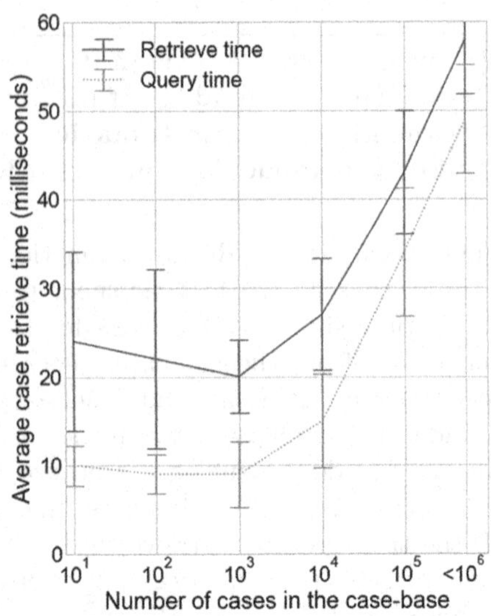

Fig. 6. CLOOD retrieve times compared to the query times. X-axis is a log scale.

on a medium-sized AWS machine (t3a.medium and 50 GB storage) costs 22 USD a month (cost estimates as of April 2020).

6 Conclusion

We introduced CLOOD CBR, a novel microservices-oriented CBR framework which leverages the serverless architecture for CBR operations and a distributed data storage service (Elasticsearch) for CBR knowledge persistence. Implementation of the extensible CLOOD CBR framework is an ongoing open-source project. We demonstrated the robustness of CLOOD on a CBR project of half a million cases and showed how CLOOD is scalable for different project sizes. Ongoing work for the future sustainability of CLOOD include extending support for additional similarity and data types (e.g., *myCBR*'s table similarity); and include functions for reuse and revise, casebase maintenance and visualisation. Also, overcoming the performance bottleneck of handling the intermediate results of local similarity functions in-memory, when implementing custom global similarity functions, is beneficial for extending the capabilities of CLOOD. We intend to make CLOOD a Python library to reuse the CLOOD Elasticsearch similarity functions for the community and add seamless integration for deploying on more cloud providers.

References

1. Bach, K., Mathisen, B.M., Jaiswal, A.: Demonstrating the myCBR rest API. In: Demo Session of the 27th International Conference on CBR (2019)

2. Bach, K., Sauer, C.S., Althoff, K., Roth-Berghofer, T.: Knowledge modelling with the open source tool myCBR. In: CEUR Workshop Proceedings, KESE@ECAI, vol. 1289. CEUR-WS.org (2014)
3. Castro, P., Ishakian, V., Muthusamy, V., Slominski, A.: Serverless programming (function as a service). In: 2017 IEEE 37th International Conference on Distributed Computing Systems (ICDCS), pp. 2658–2659. IEEE (2017)
4. Cer, D., et al.: Universal sentence encoder. arXiv preprint arXiv:1803.11175 (2018)
5. Cummins, L., Bridge, D.: On dataset complexity for case base maintenance. In: Ram, A., Wiratunga, N. (eds.) ICCBR 2011. LNCS (LNAI), vol. 6880, pp. 47–61. Springer, Heidelberg (2011). https://doi.org/10.1007/978-3-642-23291-6_6
6. Dragoni, N., et al.: Microservices: yesterday, today, and tomorrow. Present and Ulterior Software Engineering, pp. 195–216. Springer, Cham (2017). https://doi.org/10.1007/978-3-319-67425-4_12
7. Gormley, C., Tong, Z.: Elasticsearch: The Definitive Guide: A Distributed Real-time Search and Analytics Engine. O'Reilly Media Inc., Sebastopol (2015)
8. Jorro-Aragoneses, J.L., Recio-Garcia, J.A., Diaz-Agudo, B., Jiménez-Diaz, G.: Recolibry-core: a component-based framework for building recommender systems. Knowl.-Based Syst. **182**, 104854 (2019)
9. Minor, M., Schulte-Zurhausen, E.: Towards process-oriented cloud management with case-based reasoning. In: Lamontagne, L., Plaza, E. (eds.) ICCBR 2014. LNCS (LNAI), vol. 8765, pp. 305–314. Springer, Cham (2014). https://doi.org/10.1007/978-3-319-11209-1_22
10. Pahl, C., Jamshidi, P.: Microservices: a systematic mapping study. In: CLOSER (1), pp. 137–146 (2016)
11. Recio-García, J.A., Díaz-Agudo, B., González-Calero, P.A.: The COLIBRI platform: tools, features and working examples. In: Montani, S., Jain, L. (eds.) Successful CBR Applications-2, pp. 55–85. Springer, Heidelberg (2014). https://doi.org/10.1007/978-3-642-38736-4_5
12. Recio, J.A., Díaz-Agudo, B., Gómez-Martín, M.A., Wiratunga, N.: Extending jCOLIBRI for textual CBR. In: Muñoz-Ávila, H., Ricci, F. (eds.) ICCBR 2005. LNCS (LNAI), vol. 3620, pp. 421–435. Springer, Heidelberg (2005). https://doi.org/10.1007/11536406_33
13. Recio-García, J.A., González-Calero, P.A., Díaz-Agudo, B.: jCOLIBRI2: a framework for building CBR systems. Sci. Comput. Program. **79**, 126–145 (2014)
14. Recio-Garcia, J.A., González-Calero, P.A., Diaz-Agudo, B.: Template-based design in COLIBRI studio. Inf. Syst. **40**, 168–178 (2014)
15. Roth-Berghofer, T., Recio-Garcia, J.A., Severing-Sauer, C., Althoff, K.D., Diaz-Agudo, B.: Building CBR applications with myCBR and COLIBRI. In: Proceedings of 17th UK Workshop on CBR, pp. 71–82. University of Brighton (2012)
16. Stahl, A., Roth-Berghofer, T.R.: Rapid prototyping of CBR applications with the open source tool myCBR. In: Althoff, K.-D., Bergmann, R., Minor, M., Hanft, A. (eds.) ECCBR 2008. LNCS (LNAI), vol. 5239, pp. 615–629. Springer, Heidelberg (2008). https://doi.org/10.1007/978-3-540-85502-6_42
17. Vaswani, A., et al.: Attention is all you need. In: Advances in Neural Information Processing Systems, pp. 5998–6008 (2017)
18. Voit, A., Stankus, A., Magomedov, S., Ivanova, I.: Big data processing for full-text search and visualization with elasticsearch. Int. J. Adv. Comput. Sci. Appl. **8**(12), 18 (2017)
19. Zhong, Z., Xu, T., Wang, F., Tang, T.: Text CBR framework for fault diagnosis and prediction by cloud computing. Math. Probl. Eng. **2018**, 1–10 (2018)

Holographic Case-Based Reasoning

Devi Ganesan(✉) and Sutanu Chakraborti

Indian Institute of Technology Madras, Chennai 600036, TN, India
{gdevi,sutanuc}@cse.iitm.ac.in

Abstract. In this paper, we present a novel extension of CBR that allows cases to be more proactive at problem solving, by enriching case representations and facilitating richer interconnectedness between cases. We empirically study the improvements resulting from a holographic realization on experimental datasets. In addition to making CBR more cognitively appealing, the idea has the potential to lend itself as an elegant general CBR formalism of which diverse realizations of CBR can be viewed as instances.

Keywords: Case-based reasoning · Case base maintenance · Holonic cases · Holographic reasoner · Cognitive CBR · CBR formalism

1 Introduction

Case-Based Reasoning (CBR) is founded on the central premise of reusing past experiences to solve problems, and this is particularly effective in ill-defined domains, where sufficiently rich logical or mathematical models of the domain are unavailable. In a help desk domain where the goal is to answer user queries on malfunctioning of a software, no domain model of the software is available for model-based diagnosis, but logs of past episodes of problems solving can be exploited to build a CBR diagnosis system. Thus, one appeal of CBR is in its ability to reduce human (expert) effort needed to engineer rich top down domain knowledge. In this respect, CBR seems, on the surface, to share some commonalities with Machine Learning (ML) which uses bottom up methods, largely driven by induction, to acquire knowledge. Unsurprisingly, there is a growing trend in the CBR community to embrace state-of-the-art ML techniques, for instance those from the field of Deep Learning, to CBR. In reality, however, CBR is a problem solving paradigm, broad enough in its scope, to elegantly embrace both top down and bottom up approaches effectively to solve a problem in a given domain. We hold the view that to bring back CBR to the centre stage of AI, it is imperative to appreciate CBR as a paradigm closely driven by the problem specific to the domain under consideration, rather than as a toolkit (like a set of ML algorithms) that can be easily adapted to suit diverse problem needs but is distanced from the nuances of the actual problems being solved.

Dijkstra had once remarked: "Computer science should be called computing science for the same reason why surgery is not called knife science". In saying

I. Watson and R. Weber (Eds.): ICCBR 2020, LNAI 12311, pp. 144–159, 2020.
https://doi.org/10.1007/978-3-030-58342-2_10

so, he intended to point out the futility in trying to understand the solution technique (the knife) without a keen appreciation of the problem at hand (the patient anatomy). Machine Learning methods are analogues of knives that can dissect a wide range of problems, starting from very simple ones (apples) to very complex ones (a human patient). Their effectiveness depends on the extent to which its user is aware of the problem complexities. CBR, on the other hand is a paradigm for problem solving, for performing a surgery, which may use the knife of Machine Learning when appropriate, but may need several other tools as well. In particular, CBR critically relies on a top down model of the domain, that decides the representation of cases, and in particular, the knowledge containers required by the reasoner, viz. cases, vocabulary, similarity and adaptation knowledge [23].

Bottom up methods, such as Machine Learners that induce similarity knowledge from data accumulated over time, can feed into these knowledge containers and can be used effectively in many situations to alleviate knowledge engineering bottleneck. The way top down knowledge is traded off for bottom up knowledge, or vice versa, is a key design choice that differentiates CBR systems deployed till date in diverse domains. Knowledge rich domains (i.e. domains where the domain knowledge is readily available) may rely more on top down knowledge, while knowledge light domains rely more on bottom up learners to compensate for absence of rich domain knowledge [9]. Irrespective of the nature of domains, however, the design choice is critically guided by the need to minimize what we call the "representation gap": the information loss incurred by an expert in the process of recording his problem solving experiences in the CBR knowledge containers. The effectiveness of a CBR system in a given domain is critically dependent on how well this representation gap is bridged.

In this paper, we propose the concept of holographic CBR, that aims at bridging this representation gap by breaking free of certain presuppositions implicit in conventional CBR systems. One such presupposition is that cases are passive knowledge containers, and hence case addition or deletion does not affect the rest of the case base. Clearly, human memories are more interesting; the experience of encountering a new problem and solving it, not only adds this experience passively to our storehouse of experience, but can lead to a re-organization of the remaining set of experiences, as well. Holographic CBR is founded on the philosophy that cases can be made more proactive in problem solving by embedding in them a richer model of how they relate to the CBR system as a whole. In practical terms, it involves enriching the representation of cases; in particular, each case can have its own local similarity, adaptation and vocabulary knowledge, which it can use, in addition to shared knowledge containers, to refer to other cases and collaborate in order to arrive at a solution to the problem. We show that holographic CBR not only leads to more cognitive realizations of CBR, but also offers us a fresh perspective that allows us to picture conventional CBR, and a large class of CBR realizations reported in literature in specific domains, as special instances of holographic CBR systems.

In Sect. 2, we discuss the inspiration behind the holographic conception from disciplines as diverse as physics, biology and organization structures. In Sect. 3, we discuss basic ideas of holographic CBR. Section 4 illustrates the essential idea by way of two realizations of holographic CBR. In Sect. 5, we discuss how our work relates to other work in literature, and how it can be further extended. Section 6 summarizes our main conclusions.

2 Holographic Systems

The conventional view in neuroscience in the earlier part of the last century was that specific memories were confined to specific locations in the brain. This viewpoint was advocated, for example by Wilder Penfield, a Canadian neurosurgeon [17], who experimented by electrically stimulating various brain regions of epileptic patients. In the mid-nineties, there was a surprise in store for the neuroscience community, when Karl Lashley's three decades of research culminated in evidences contrary to Penfield's findings. Lashley had trained rats to run a maze, and then surgically removed portions of their brains, with the aim of completely removing the regions in their brains responsible for their maze running abilities [13]. Interestingly, he discovered that irrespective of the brain region that was removed, their memories refused to perish. Lashley was joined by Karl Pribram, who hypothesized that the only explanation of Lashley's findings would be that memories, instead of being localized at specific brain regions, were distributed throughout the brain [20]. Whatever was true with rats was also true with humans, in that patients with portions of the brain selectively removed did not have specific memories wiped out; rather they could hazily reconstruct most of what was known before the surgery. To quote Talbott [28], who provides an engaging account of Pribram's findings, "Individuals who had received head injuries in car collisions and other accidents never forgot half of their family, or half of a novel they had read". This phenomenon can be attributed to non-localized or holographic memories, where each component contains an imprint of the whole. The name "holographic" pervades study of complexity in diverse areas such as biology, physics and organizational systems. For example, holism [26] is a method of study which believes that the whole is greater than the sum of the parts; the term 'holon' [12] refers to a system that is both a whole and a part; a hierarchy of such self-regulating holons is called a holarchy [12].

We were tempted to explore if ideas of holographic systems can inspire the engineering of systems more adept at simulating aspects of cognition. The traditional view of CBR is analogous to that of Penfield's in neuroscience, in that the cases are treated as isolated pieces of knowledge that do not interact with each other. One fallout of such an assumption is in case base maintenance, where cases can be deleted from the case base, or fresh cases can be added, without affecting the rest of the case base. This is clearly inconsistent with cognitive findings on human memory, where a new experience is known to affect related memories in interesting ways that facilitate the creation of abstractions. Similarly, forgetting may not be localized to just one specific experience, but may result in the blurring out of a class of memories associated with the experience being lost. These observations gave rise to the design hypothesis that in a holographic model of CBR, the cases need not only be isolated passive pieces of knowledge but can be proactively interconnected with other cases in ways more interesting that explored by conventional CBR systems. It is through the interconnectedness of cases, that a model where the whole is greater than the sum of parts, can be realized.

3 Holographic CBR

Let us use an analogy to convey the essential idea behind holographic CBR. Consider three different settings.

Setting 1: Let us consider the case of a person X who attempts to float an organization to address requirements from client Y. X hires a set of employees with diverse skillsets to address the client needs. X also hires a project manager who acts as a mediator between the team members and Y. Y issues a query to the mediator, who facilitates interaction between the project members, and responds back to Y with a solution. The mediator has some coarse knowledge about the skills of the team members, which helps in directing client queries to one or more of them. The fine-grained knowledge of how best to get the problem solved, by collaborating with each other, rests with each team member. So a team member may receive a query from the mediator and choose to solve it; alternately, she may direct it to another member whom she reckons to be more appropriate for the job. In certain cases, the team member may like to get more clarity from the mediator regarding the client query, and in case the mediator is not sure herself, she may approach the client to get a clarification. In the course of interaction with team members, the mediator may update her knowledge of skills of the team members, and the team members keep enriching their knowledge of the organization as a whole. Such an evolution of the mediator, along with the team members, renders the system more competent in addressing subsequent queries.

Setting 2: This is a hypothetical variant of Setting 1, where X hires a mediator who has a complete knowledge of the skillsets of each team member. Given a client query, the mediator solves it by assembling inputs from her members. In comparison to Setting 1, the team members are passive, in that their role is limited to answering queries from the mediator. They do not collaborate with others, and have no knowledge either of the client query, or of the skillsets of others in their project team.

Setting 3: This is yet another variant of Setting 2, in which the mediator attempts to answer the client query, all by herself, on behalf of X. In case she is not able to do so, she requests X to hire another employee having certain skills. Employees thus progressively are added on demand, provided X agrees, given his budget constraints and his level of confidence in the mediator. Each employee, while being distinct to each other in terms of skills and competencies, is fully aware of his or her role in the broader context of the problem being solved.

In the context of a CBR system, the client Y is analogous to the user who presents a query to a CBR system, X is the designer of the CBR system, the

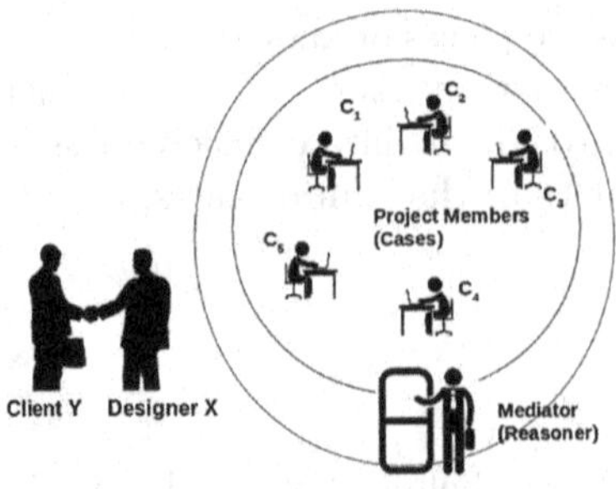

Fig. 1. Mediator analogy

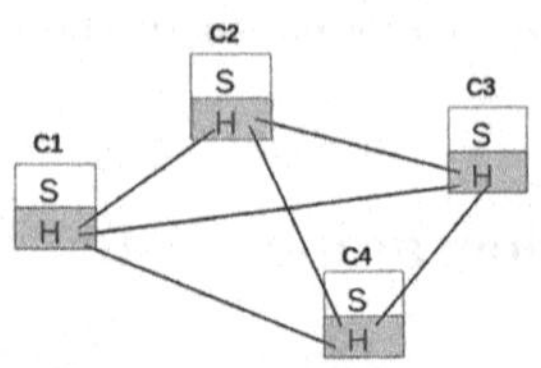

Fig. 2. Cases with Solo (S) and Holo (H) components

mediator is the case-based reasoner put in place by X to address the needs of Y, and the project members are the cases $C_1, C_2, .., C_5$. This analogy is shown in the schematic shown in Fig. 1. Setting 2 is the case of traditional CBR, where the mediator (the reasoner) has full access to knowledge of cases. The reasoner uses the knowledge of similarity to identify cases that may be useful, gets solutions from them, and combines these solutions using adaptation knowledge to answer the query posed by Y. Both similarity and adaptation knowledge are centralized and available exclusively to the reasoner. In contrast, Setting 3 is holographic, and Setting 1 is semi-holographic. We refer to the CBR systems in Settings 1, 2 and 3 as SH (for semi-holographic), TR (for traditional) and HG (for holographic) respectively.

In HG, the case base is grown on demand. Each case, in addition to storing a representation of the specific problem it solves, has knowledge of the reasoning goals as well as knowledge of how it relates to the other cases. SH can be conceived of striking a middle ground between the extremes of TR and HG, where the cases are richer than those in traditional case bases. Since cases only have local models of related cases, but are not equipped with the model of the case base as a whole, they are critically reliant on the reasoner (mediator) to dictate the retrieval process.

In Sect. 1, we had discussed that effectiveness of a CBR system can be improved by minimizing the information loss incurred by an expert in the process of recording his experiences of problem solving in the knowledge containers provided by CBR. It is clear that the loss is maximal in TR, and minimal in HG, with SH striking a middle ground. In HG, the cases have the highest autonomy in that each case has a reasonably good model of the goals of the CBR system, and also of the knowledge contained in every other case. We can visualize a spectrum of CBR applications ranging from TR to HG, through SH. As we move from TR to HG, the cases start having a richer representation of knowledge contained in other cases, as well as of the overall goals of problems solving. Henceforth, we shall use the term holographic to refer to systems that are either SH or HG. In a holographic setting, each case has two components which we call the solo component (referred to as the S component henceforth) and the holo component (referred to as the H component henceforth). The S component is the traditional problem-solution part and represents the individual experience that the case stands for. The H component, on the other hand embodies the essence of the proposed holographic setting, in that it defines the role of the case in relation to the case base and the underlying domain knowledge as a whole. We can picture the cases interacting with each other via their H components (see Fig. 2). Interestingly, such a holographic realization entails a change in our perspective of knowledge containers in CBR. The H component in cases facilitates localization of adaptation and similarity knowledge within each case; in other words, unlike in traditional CBR where knowledge containers other than cases are centralized, in a holographic setting, adaptation and similarity knowledge get distributed across the case base in holographic CBR. It may be noted that the scheme still allows for capturing aspects of domain knowledge that are shared by all cases, outside those in H components via the global knowledge resources possessed by the reasoner. Secondly, the H component of each case can capture diverse forms of relationships of a case with other cases in the case base. We envisage that the H component of each case can be used to capture how a case has been used, and its direct associations with other cases as well, so that any case maintenance operation would, no longer, be agnostic to this more general notion of ensuring case base competence. A schematic representation of a holographic reasoner for the problem of predicting animal names is given in Fig. 3. It is interesting to observe that both the reasoner and the cases have the same structure in a holographic reasoner. The reasoner holds the global knowledge containers and uses them to solve the larger problem of predicting the animal name given its representation. Each of the cases also hold the same kind of knowledge containers locally and, hence, can be called 'holonic'. These holonic cases use their local knowledge containers to solve the problem that they individually stand for. The problem part is pictorially depicted in the schematic diagram and it can correspond to any type of representation chosen by the case based designer for the problem part of experiences.

4 Realization of a Holographic Reasoner

In this section, we discuss the realization of a holographic reasoner in two settings: knowledge-rich and knowledge-light domains. A knowledge-rich domain is one where the domain knowledge is readily available. In practice, there are many domains where domain knowledge is not available readily or is costly to acquire in terms of time. We refer to such domains as knowledge-light domains.

Knowledge-Rich Domain. A key difference between a conventional and a holographic reasoner is with respect to the case addition process. In conventional settings, the reasoner is fully responsible for adding new cases to the case base. Whereas, in a holographic reasoner, this responsibility is shared among the cases. In the following pseudocode, the function `ADD_CASE` of `HOLOGRAPHIC_REASONER` describes how the case addition process varies between a knowledge-rich and knowledge-light settings. In a knowledge-rich setting, the holographic reasoner

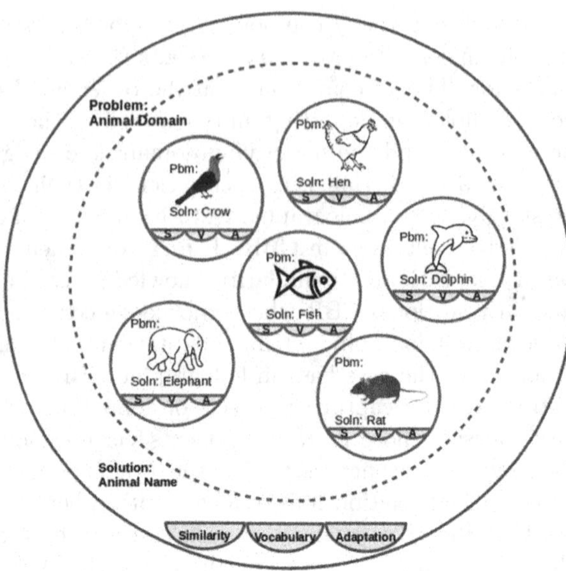

Fig. 3. Holographic Reasoner - A Schematic Diagram; S, V, A (in each case) stand for the local Similarity, Vocabulary and Adaptation knowledge containers respectively.

(mediator) uses the global similarity knowledge to direct an incoming case with its problem and solution components to its most similar case (a team member) in the case base. The global similarity knowledge, which can be shallow (coarse) compared to the local similarity knowledge in cases, enables the reasoner to quickly reach the relevant area of the problem space. Next, the most similar case spawns a case addition process that tries to predict a solution for the incoming problem, that is, it forms an expectation. This is explained by the functions `ADD_CASE`, `PREDICT` in the pseudocode for class `HOLONIC_CASE_KRICH`. If it faces an expectation failure, then it engages in a conversation with the domain expert. The expert feedback, together with a pointer to the new case, is stored as part of the local vocabulary as explained in the function `GET_EXPERT_FEEDBACK`. It is important to note that addition of a new case is performed by an existing case itself when there is an expectation failure. Thus, the responsibility for case addition lies not only with the reasoner but is also shared among the cases. On the other hand, if a case does not face an expectation failure, then it may choose not to do anything further or continue to add the new case to case base. This depends on constraints such as case base size, response time, etc. as known to the case base designer. In the `PREDICT` function, it is possible that the query gets redirected multiple number of times and it terminates only when a case finds itself to be the most similar one to the query.

Knowledge-Light Domain. In knowledge-light domains, a holographic reasoner does not have a domain expert to interact with. The knowledge-light setting is more like a conventional reasoner where the new cases are added to the case base as they arrive. Hence, the case acquisition process does not include any interaction with the domain expert. Instead, a holonic case could spawn a process to learn bottom up abstractions from their neighbourhood as shown by the function INTROSPECT in the class HOLONIC_CASE_KLIGHT. The H component of cases will now contain the parameters corresponding to the local model of abstraction, which could be any machine learning model such as Logistic Regression or Bayesian Classifier. This is like a human problem solver trying to learn something by observing their fellow problem solvers rather than asking the domain expert directly.

```
Class HOLOGRAPHIC_REASONER
 Vocabulary, Similarity, Adaptation, Case
      Base // Global Knowledge Containers
 Function ADD_CASE (newProblem, newSolution)
   If the domain is knowledge-rich:
     MostSimilarCase = RETRIEVE (newProblem)
     If MostSimilarCase is not null:
          MostSimilarCase.ADD_CASE (
               newProblem, newSolution)
     Else: //Adds the first case
          newCase = new HOLONIC_CASE_KRICH()
          newCase.Problem = newProblem
          newCase.Solution = newSolution
          GET_EXPERT_FEEDBACK (newCase)
          Store newCase in the CaseBase

   Else If the domain is knowledge-light:
        newCase = new HOLONIC_CASE_KLIGHT()
        newCase.Problem = newProblem
        newCase.Solution = newSolution
        Store newCase in the CaseBase

 Function RETRIEVE (incomingProblem)
   If CaseBase contains zero cases: Return
        null
   Else: Return the case in the CaseBase that
         is most similar to the
        incomingProblem according to the
        global Similarity knowledge

 Function PREDICT (incomingProblem)
   //The prediction process of the
        holographic reasoner  invokes the
        prediction process of the most
        similar case
   MostSimilarCase = RETRIEVE (
        incomingProblem)
   Return MostSimilarCase.PREDICT (
        incomingProblem)

------------------------------------------

Class HOLONIC_CASE_KRICH
 Problem, Solution //Solo Components
 Local Vocabulary, Local Similarity, Local
      Adaptation //Holo Components
 CaseBase // pointer to reasoner's case base
 Function ADD_CASE(newProblem, newSolution)
   If PREDICT(newProblem) matches Solution:
       //No Expectation Failure; No Case
            Addition
       Return null
   Else:
       newCase = new HOLONIC_CASE_KRICH()
       newCase.Problem = newProblem
       newCase.Solution = newSolution
       GET_EXPERT_FEEDBACK (newCase)
       Store newCase in the CaseBase

 Function PREDICT (incomingProblem)
   //MostSimilarCase is that case in the
        local neighbourhood (including self)
        which is most similar to the
        incomingProblem and is determined
        using the Local Vocabulary and Local
        Similarity knowledge.
   If MostSimilarCase is this holonic case
        itself: Return Solution
   Else: //Invokes the prediction process of
        the most similar case
       Return MostSimilarCase. PREDICT (
            incomingProblem)

 Function GET_EXPERT_FEEDBACK (newCase)
   Get feedback from a domain expert as to
        why the new case is being added, what
         feature-value pairs differentiate
        the new case from itself, etc. Update
         the Local Vocabulary to include the
        feedback and pointers to locally
        added cases.

------------------------------------------

Class HOLONIC_CASE_KLIGHT
 Problem, Solution //Solo Components
 Local Vocabulary, Local Similarity, Local
      Adaptation //Holo Components
 CaseBase //pointer to reasoner's case base
 Model // to store model parameters
 Function ADD_CASE(newProblem, newSolution)
   newCase = new HOLONIC_CASE_KLIGHT()
   newCase.Problem = newProblem
   newCase.Solution = newSolution
   Store newCase in the CaseBase

 Function PREDICT (incomingProblem)
   Predict a solution for the incomingProblem
         using Model
   Return the above prediction

 Function INTROSPECT ()
   //Invoked by reasoner (say after the case
        base reaches a certain size)
   Model = learn a model over the local
        neighbourhood , for example, a
        logistic regression model over the
        ten nearest neighbours
```

Observations from Experimental Datasets. Next, we present our observations on the characteristics of a holographic reasoner in the light of its realization on experimental datasets.

Knowledge-Rich Domain. The zoo case base from UCI repository [7] is an instance of a knowledge-rich domain and the nature of its domain (viz. animals) facilitates the authors themselves to play the role of a domain expert. It is a simple database containing 17 Boolean-valued attributes, 7 classes of animals and 101 data instances. On this case base, we realized both a holographic reasoner and a conventional case-based reasoner. In both the reasoners, global similarity knowledge was represented using the following two weight vectors: $S0$, a uniform weight vector and $S1$ emphasizing the attributes *feathers, aquatic, backbone, legs* three times over the rest. We did not employ any global or local adaptation knowledge. In the holographic setting, the expert gives her feedback using a list of entries where each entry is of the form `{feature_id:feature_value}`. For example, suppose the reasoner is adding a case *dolphin* to its case base and the most similar case is *dogfish*. Then, *dogfish* would face an expectation failure when it tries to predict the class of *dolphin* (as dolphin is a mammal). Expert feedback in this example could be `{milk_feeding:True}`. The holonic cases store the expert feedback together with a pointer to the newly created cases. The local vocabulary of a holonic case corresponds to those attributes used by an expert for giving feedback. Jaccard coefficient was used for estimating local similarity. In the conventional reasoner, we also found the footprint set [27], which is a minimal set of cases that has the same competence (problem-solving ability) as the entire case base. Competence based maintenance algorithms, such as the footprint algorithm, compress the case base in a post-facto way i.e. compression happens only after the experiences are stored. In terms of the representation gap, the damage is already done. In contrast, a holographic reasoner is capable of doing pre-facto compression i.e. it can compress the case base while adding the experience itself. While the post-facto compression relies purely on the cases to reduce the case base size, the pre-facto approach is able to acquire the knowledge enabling compression from the domain expert herself. This can facilitate the

Table 1. Observations on a knowledge-rich domain: zoo case base; $S0$: uniform weight vector and $S1$: weight vector that emphasizes *feathers, aquatic, backbone, legs* thrice over others. Results are based on 3-fold cross validation.

Reasoner type	Global similarity	No. of cases added	Case base size	Test accuracy %
Conventional (full CB)	$S1$	67.3	67.3	96.2
Conventional (footprint)	$S1$		13.6	94.3
Holographic	$S1$		**13.3**	**97.0**
Holographic	$S0$	67.3	11.3	94.3

reducing of knowledge gap between a reasoner and the domain expert. Table 1 shows the total number of cases added by the reasoner to its case base, the resulting case base size and the prediction accuracy. It can be observed from the table that the holographic reasoner performs best both in terms of case base compression and performance when the global similarity knowledge is $S1$. This can be attributed to the impact of domain knowledge acquired in the form of expert feedback. It can also be observed that when the global similarity knowledge is coarse ($S0$), the holographic reasoner is still able to achieve better compression and performance comparable to the footprint set. Hence, it makes it suitable for domains where one could not easily get a rich global similarity measure and may prefer to begin with a simple global similarity measure, progressively learning local similarities based on expert feedback.

Knowledge-Light Domains. The datasets used are CPU from OpenML [29] and Wine from UCI repository [7]. The CPU dataset contains 209 instances with 7 attributes and the task is to predict the relative cpu performance (regression). The Wine dataset contains a total of 178 cases with 13 attributes and 3 classes. The task is to predict the quality of wine given its attribute values (classification). For regression, the case-based reasoner (traditional as well as holographic) uses the distance-weighted average of the 3-nearest neighbours' predictions. Each holonic case learns a Locally Weighted Linear Regression (LWLR) [5] model over its neighbourhood. For classification, the holonic cases learn a naive Bayes classifier to model their local neighbourhood. The independence assumption in naive Bayes has an advantage for small-sized case bases because the algorithm is known to predict well even with small-sized training data. As elaborated in the previous sections, the H components of cases store the LWLR parameters and conditional probabilities in the regression and classification settings respectively. In our experiments, the size of the local neighbourhood is fixed empirically to be 10. It is important to note that knowledge-light holographic realizations in practice can be far more sophisticated in terms of richness of holonic case representations and processes they can spawn. The examples above use relatively simplistic ML tools to illustrate the essential idea. In particular, it is easy to see that the holographic perspective can accommodate richness in both top down and bottom up knowledge, hence most existing CBR systems can be viewed as instances of the general holographic CBR conception (see Sect. 5).

Here, we are interested in studying whether the global competence of cases increase in a holographic setting. In all our experiments in knowledge-light setting, the reasoner combines the solutions of the three nearest neighbours to solve the query problem. This process of combining the solutions of multiple cases in some appropriate way to solve the target problem is called compositional adaptation. Retention score [15] is a global competence measure suited for such scenarios and estimates the retention quality of a case based on its ability to cover highly retainable cases with the support of a few but highly retainable cases. This is achieved by a recursive formulation in the lines of PageRank [16]. We do not go into the details of this formulation but would like to emphasize the following fact: *retention scores can be used to order the cases in descending*

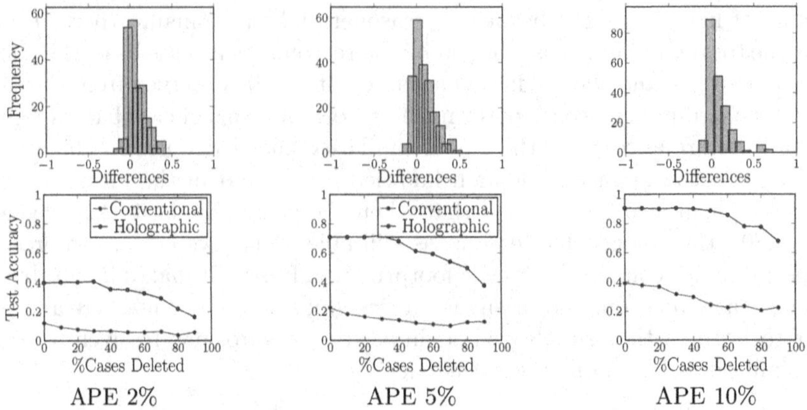

Fig. 4. Results on regression dataset (CPU); The top row shows the histograms of differences in retention scores (holographic – traditional) corresponding to the different settings of Acceptable Prediction Error (APE) shown in the bottom row.

Fig. 5. Results on classification dataset (Wine).

order of their global competence. In our experiments, we have used a variation of retention scores called *weighted retention scores* in which every set of cases that solves a target problem is weighed by its problem solving ability. After measuring the retention scores of cases in conventional and holographic settings, we plotted a *histogram of their differences* (holographic – traditional) to see if the differences are more skewed towards the positive side. This would indicate that a holographic design has resulted in an increase of competence for many cases. We also tested the effectiveness of the increased competence by progressively deleting the case base and observing its impact on the performance of reasoner on test data. We would expect a holographic reasoner to perform better than a conventional one even as the case base is progressively shrunk in size.

Figure 4 shows the results on the regression dataset. The top row shows the histograms for different settings of Acceptable Prediction Error (APE). APE is the percentage error allowed in the reasoner's predictions and is typically fixed by the user for the regression task. The more the right-skewedness, the better is the holographic design in terms of case competence. In the CPU dataset, as the histograms are skewed towards the right, it can be inferred that there is an increase in the case competence under the holographic design. Holographic design is consistently better than the conventional ones with increase in the progressive reduction of case base size. In Fig. 5, the histogram is skewed towards the right, hence, increased competence of cases in this holographic design becomes evident.

5 Discussion and Related Work

In this paper, we have restricted our scope to demonstrating the effect of holographic realizations on case addition, though in practice we need to have a mechanism for case deletion as well. We envisage two kinds of deletions: soft and hard. It is easy to see that holonic cases carry information about their local neighbourhood even after the neighbouring cases are deleted. We call this soft deletion. Though this increases the robustness of reasoner, in cases where we deliberately want to delete a (noisy) case, this may be undesirable, and a hard deletion is called for. In soft deletion, the H components of neighbours are retained, and is analogous to employees taking leave in a holarchic organization. In hard deletion, the H components of neighbours are updated before a case is deleted; this is analogous to handover-takeover processes in an organization, when an employee leaves the organization (is fired). Another interesting aspect not discussed in the paper is the impact of the order in which cases are acquired by a holographic reasoner. We can draw inspiration from how a child progressively acquires a storehouse of experience she encounters when systematically guided by an adult. Educational material for children aims at presenting experiences in an order that facilitates highest compression thereby improving the learning experience, where lessons are not merely recorded as facts, but are richly connected to each other. Reorganization of case interconnections over time to facilitate more effective retrieval is out of scope of this paper, though it opens up interesting area for future work.

In his work on Dynamic Memory [24], Roger Schank had emphasized the role of expectation failures in triggering the need for explanations and consequent generalization of memory structures. An event of visiting a restaurant like McDonald's where one has to pay before one eats, may lead to expectation failure for someone used to paying after eating in a restaurant. She would then attempt to find an explanation, generalize her memory structures and accommodate the new experience. This may involve creating a specific dimension (an attribute) that discriminates between the two categories of restaurants. Thus, while specific details of most restaurant trips are forgotten and abstracted out ("mushed up", to use Schank's terminology), some restaurant trips (like the McDonald's trip) are thus more influential than others in effecting changes to our memory structures. In the holographic setting, these changes that a case causes should be recorded in its H component during insertion, so that the influence of the case is preserved even when the case is deleted. Ideally, active processes must be spawned by the H component of cases as new cases are inserted, deleted or updated, to make changes to similarity and adaptation knowledge of related cases, facilitate case-to-case direct connections, or record and preserve influence of the case on the underlying representations. In the context of maintenance, H components can also potentially carry explanations pertaining to poorly aligned cases. The holographic setting can also accommodate bottom up knowledge induced from data in local similarity and adaptation knowledge containers in holonic cases to complement top down knowledge, thereby alleviating the knowledge acquisition bottleneck that plagued Schank's conceptualization limiting its practical use.

Several classical CBR systems can be thought of as instances of the more general holographic CBR framework. Aspects of it are ideologically close to the proposed holographic design for a knowledge rich domain. PROTOS [4] is a case-based reasoner built to serve as a learning apprentice system for heuristic based classification. It is interesting to see that many ideas in PROTOS such as difference links, efficient retrieval, expert feedback were aimed at overcoming limits of traditional CBR systems. In the early days of CBR, knowledge-rich reasoners such as CYRUS [25] and CELIA [21] were built to demonstrate the cognitive aspects of CBR. In CYRUS, which is an attempt to model the reconstructive model of memory, the cases are stored as hierarchically indexed facts. CELIA aims at modelling the passage from a novice to expert; the cases are composed of interconnected case snippets. Knowledge-intensive CBR systems like CREEK [1] reinforce the importance of integrating general domain knowledge with CBR systems and having rich knowledge representations. Some other interesting works to explore in this direction include the CREEK-based knowledge-intensive conversational CBR system [10] and Bayesian-Network powered CBR system [2]. The holographic perspective shows these as instantiations of the same umbrella framework, and is also suggestive of more proactivity on the part of cases that can be realized if the full potential of holographic CBR is exploited, by realizing richly interconnected cases that spawn active processes, and are empowered to influence H components of related cases, and generate explanations for failures.

Distributed CBR [19] is a terminology used in the CBR community to indicate research efforts towards organising knowledge in single versus multiple case bases and processing knowledge using single versus multiple agents. There are also many agent-based CBR approaches where knowledge is distributed such as [3,14,18,22] where the focus is on knowledge modelling, architecture and building of CBR based systems. Unlike domain specific engineering realizations such as distributed CBR, holographic systems are inspired differently: they are aimed at repositioning a broad spectrum of CBR applications (including distributed CBR systems) based on how they attempt to reduce the representation gap: all that is lost of the intent with which a case is being recorded, in the process of its representation. Such a repositioning has an essential cognitive appeal in that it helps us get to the heart of appreciating discrepancies in system effectiveness with respect to a human expert who solves problems using experiential reasoning. In future, it would be interesting to accommodate the study of analogical reasoning in a comprehensive way into the fold of holographic systems.

A related perspective is from the very recent work by Susan Craw et al. [6] where the authors present connections of CBR to cognitive models. In particular, the authors refer to the dichotomy between two modes of thought as identified by Kahneman [11]. While fast thinking relies on instinctive, unconscious, frequent and stereotypical decision making, slow thinking is more deliberative, conscious, logical and calculating. Slow thinking can correct errors made by fast thinking. In the CBR context, Craw et al. [6] suggest that simple retrieve/reuse may fall in the realm of fast thinking and this is appropriate when case base alignment is high, i.e. similar problems do indeed have similar solutions. On the other hand, in the face of poor alignment deliberate slow processes (say, complicated adaptation or multiple redirections) should intervene. It is compelling to picture the S and H components as facilitating fast and slow thinking respectively. Finally, we note that there are some recent claims that Deep Neural Networks (DNN) exhibit holographic behaviour [8]. However, there has been no understanding of the equivalents of holons and the organisational structure inside a DNN. DNNs do not facilitate the integration of top down knowledge about the domain, thus restricting their scope of applications in the context of CBR, where a problem-centric view, that allows for flexible integration of top down and bottom up is called for.

6 Conclusion

The historical roots of CBR can be traced to the seminal work by Roger Schank on dynamic memory [24] where he proposed mechanisms for creation and update of memory structures to account for abstraction, generalization, and goal based reminding (as in analogical reminding) which play a central role in modelling cognition. However, the cognitive emphasis in memory based reasoning waned over time. On occasions, machine learning techniques appeared to present easier alternatives to a principled mix of top down and bottom up knowledge that the CBR paradigm would ideally exploit reasoning based on representations, that are rich, and yet not too difficult to acquire to facilitate experiential problem solving. The concept of holographic reasoner is an attempt to bring back to perspective a wider set of possibilities than conventional CBR systems can offer, while showing its ability to position diverse CBR realizations in a unifying framework.

In living systems, every cell has in its nucleus (analogous to the H component) an imprint of the design of the organism as a whole. Not unlike the organism it is part of, every cell has a digestive, respiratory, nervous an immune system. This is remarkably different from a brick which is perhaps barely aware of the design of the building, of which it is a part. The design almost wholly resides in the mind of the designer. The difference between the ideal holonic case and the traditional case in CBR is one of that between the cell and the brick. As we foray into the ambitious realms of Artificial General Intelligence (AGI), we speculate holographic systems may well hold clues, if not answers, to design of computational models of cognition that can address certain limitations of traditional approaches.

References

1. Aamodt, A.: Knowledge-intensive case-based reasoning in CREEK. In: Funk, P., González Calero, P.A. (eds.) ECCBR 2004. LNCS (LNAI), vol. 3155, pp. 1–15. Springer, Heidelberg (2004). https://doi.org/10.1007/978-3-540-28631-8_1
2. Aamodt, A., Langseth, H.: Integrating Bayesian networks into knowledge-intensive CBR. In: AAAI Workshop on Case-Based Reasoning Integrations, pp. 1–6 (1998)
3. Bach, K., Reichle, M., Reichle-Schmehl, A., Althoff, K.D.: Implementing a coordination agent for modularised case bases. In: Proceedings of 13th UKCBR@ AI, pp. 1–12 (2008)
4. Bareiss, E.R., Porter, B.W., Wier, C.C.: Protos: an exemplar-based learning apprentice. In: Machine Learning, pp. 112–127. Elsevier (1990)
5. Cleveland, W.S., Devlin, S.J.: Locally weighted regression: an approach to regression analysis by local fitting. J. Am. Stat. Assoc. **83**(403), 596–610 (1988)
6. Craw, S., Aamodt, A.: Case based reasoning as a model for cognitive artificial intelligence. In: Cox, M.T., Funk, P., Begum, S. (eds.) ICCBR 2018. LNCS (LNAI), vol. 11156, pp. 62–77. Springer, Cham (2018). https://doi.org/10.1007/978-3-030-01081-2_5
7. Dheeru, D., Karra Taniskidou, E.: UCI machine learning repository (2017). http://archive.ics.uci.edu/ml
8. Gan, W.C., Shu, F.W.: Holography as deep learning. Int. J. Mod. Phys. D **26**(12), 1743020 (2017)
9. Ganesan, D., Chakraborti, S.: An empirical study of knowledge tradeoffs in case-based reasoning. In: Proceedings of IJCAI, pp. 1817–1823 (2018)
10. Gu, M., Aamodt, A.: A knowledge-intensive method for conversational CBR. In: Muñoz-Ávila, H., Ricci, F. (eds.) ICCBR 2005. LNCS (LNAI), vol. 3620, pp. 296–311. Springer, Heidelberg (2005). https://doi.org/10.1007/11536406_24
11. Kahneman, D.: Thinking, Fast and Slow. Macmillan, New York (2011)
12. Koestler, A.: The Ghost in the Machine. Macmillan, New York (1968)
13. Lashley, K.S.: In search of the engram. In: Physiological Mechanisms, p. 454 (1950)
14. Leake, D.B., Sooriamurthi, R.: When two case bases are better than one: exploiting multiple case bases. In: Aha, D.W., Watson, I. (eds.) ICCBR 2001. LNCS (LNAI), vol. 2080, pp. 321–335. Springer, Heidelberg (2001). https://doi.org/10.1007/3-540-44593-5_23
15. Mathew, D., Chakraborti, S.: A generalized case competence model for casebase maintenance. AI Commun. **30**(3–4), 295–309 (2017)
16. Page, L., Brin, S., Motwani, R., Winograd, T.: The PageRank citation ranking: bringing order to the web. Technical report, Stanford InfoLab (1999)
17. Penfield, W., Gage, L.: Cerebral localization of epileptic manifestations. Arch. Neurol. Psychiatry **30**(4), 709–727 (1933)
18. Pla, A., LóPez, B., Gay, P., Pous, C.: eXiT* CBR. v2: distributed case-based reasoning tool for medical prognosis. Decis. Supp. Syst. **54**(3), 1499–1510 (2013)
19. Plaza, E., McGinty, L.: Distributed case-based reasoning. Knowl. Eng. Rev. **20**(3), 261–265 (2005)
20. Pribram, K.H.: Brain and Perception: Holonomy and Structure in Figural Processing. Psychology Press, London (2013)
21. Redmond, M.: Distributed cases for case-based reasoning: facilitating use of multiple cases. In: Proceedings of AAAI, vol. 90, pp. 304–309 (1990)
22. Reichle, M., Bach, K., Althoff, K.D.: Knowledge engineering within the application-independent architecture seasalt. Int. J. Knowl. Eng. Data Mining **1**(3), 202–215 (2011)

23. Richter, M.M.: Knowledge Containers. Readings in Case-Based Reasoning. Morgan Kaufmann Publishers, Burlington (2003)
24. Schank, R.C.: Dynamic Memory: A Theory of Reminding and Learning in Computers and People, vol. 240. Cambridge University Press, Cambridge (1982)
25. Schank, R.C., Kolodner, J.L.: Retrieving information from an episodic memory or why computers' memories should be more like people's. In: Proceedings of IJCAI, vol. 2, pp. 766–768 (1979)
26. Smuts, J.C.: Holism and Evolution. Ripoll Classic, Moscow (1926)
27. Smyth, B., McKenna, E.: Competence models and the maintenance problem. Comput. Intell. **17**(2), 235–249 (2001)
28. Talbot, M.: The Holographic Universe. HarperCollins, New York (1991)
29. Vanschoren, J., Van Rijn, J.N., Bischl, B., Torgo, L.: OpenML: networked science in machine learning. ACM SIGKDD Explor. Newslett. **15**(2), 49–60 (2014)

Technical Session: Explanations

Good Counterfactuals and Where to Find Them: A Case-Based Technique for Generating Counterfactuals for Explainable AI (XAI)

Mark T. Keane[1,2,3] and Barry Smyth[1,2(✉)]

[1] School of Computer Science, University College Dublin, Dublin, Ireland
{mark.keane,barry.smyth}@ucd.ie
[2] Insight Centre for Data Analytics, University College Dublin, Dublin, Ireland
[3] VistaMilk SFI Research Centre, University College Dublin, Dublin, Ireland

Abstract. Recently, a groundswell of research has identified the use of counterfactual explanations as a potentially significant solution to the Explainable AI (XAI) problem. It is argued that (i) *technically*, these counterfactual cases can be generated by permuting problem-features until a class-change is found, (ii) *psychologically*, they are much more causally informative than factual explanations, (iii) *legally*, they are GDPR-compliant. However, there are issues around the finding of "good" counterfactuals using current techniques (e.g. *sparsity* and *plausibility*). We show that many commonly-used datasets appear to have few "good" counterfactuals for explanation purposes. So, we propose a new case-based approach for generating counterfactuals, using novel ideas about the *counterfactual potential* and *explanatory coverage* of a case-base. The new technique reuses patterns of good counterfactuals, present in a case-base, to generate analogous counterfactuals that can explain new problems and their solutions. Several experiments show how this technique can improve the counterfactual potential and explanatory coverage of case-bases that were previously found wanting.

Keywords: CBR · Explanation · XAI · Counterfactuals · Contrastive

1 Introduction

In recent years, there has been a tsunami of papers on Explainable AI (XAI) reflecting concerns that recent advances in machine learning may be limited by a lack of transparency (see e.g., [1, 2]) or by government regulation (e.g., GDPR in the EU, see [3, 4]; for reviews [5–7]). Historically, Case-Based Reasoning (CBR) has always given a central role to explanation, as predictions can readily be explained by cases, akin to human reasoning from precedent/example [8–12]). Indeed, Kenny & Keane's [13, 14] *twin systems approach*, explicitly maps black-box deep-learning systems into CBR systems to find *post-hoc* explanatory cases for their predictions. Typically, CBR uses "factual cases"; nearest *like* neighbors that explain why a prediction was made [14]. But, recently, another class of explanatory cases is attracting interest, *counterfactual cases*; nearest *unlike* neighbors that explain how a prediction might be changed. For example, a loan

I. Watson and R. Weber (Eds.): ICCBR 2020, LNAI 12311, pp. 163–178, 2020.
https://doi.org/10.1007/978-3-030-58342-2_11

application system might explain its decision to refuse a loan by presenting a factual case: "*you were refused because a previous customer had the same salary as you and they were refused a loan for this amount*". In contrast, the same loan system might, arguably, provide a better explanation by presenting a counterfactual case; effectively saying "*if you asked for a slightly lower amount you would have been granted the loan*". Researchers championing the use of counterfactual explanations, argue that they provide better solutions to the XAI problem [7, 15–18] (see Sect. 2).

In this paper, we consider counterfactual explanations from a CBR perspective. Though any CBR system can explain its predictions directly using counterfactual cases, here, we assume a twin-system context [13, 14]; where some opaque machine-learning model (e.g., deep learning model) generating predictions to be explained by finding case-based explanations from a twinned CBR[1]. We assess how many "good" counterfactuals are available in a given case-base (i.e., ones that are easily comprehended by people). So, we systematically map the topology of "good" counterfactuals in different case-bases, what we call their *counterfactual potential* (see Sect. 2). Initially, we perform an analysis of 20 frequently-used case-bases from the ML/CBR literature (see Sect. 3). To presage our results, to our surprise, we find that in most case-bases "good" counterfactuals are quite rare. This leads us to the novel notion of *explanatory coverage* by analogy to *predictive coverage* [19–21], from which we develop and evaluate a new case-based technique for counterfactual generation in XAI (Sects. 4 and 5).

2 Counterfactual Explanation: Promise, Problems and Prospects

Intuitively, counterfactual explanations seem to provide better explanations than factual ones; nearest-unlike-neighbor (NUN) explanations are better than nearest-like-neighbor (NLN) explanations[2]. Imagine you using the drink-&-drive app, DeepDrink, that can predict whether you are under/over the alcohol limit for driving. DeepDrink knows your physical profile and when you tell it (i) how many drinks you have taken, (ii) your recent food intake and (iii) when you started drinking, it predicts you are *over the limit* explaining it with a *factual case*; saying that a person with a similar profile to you was also over the limit when they were breathalysed (see Table 1). This explanation is reasonable but perhaps less informative than a *counterfactual case*; which would tell you that someone with your profile who drank a similar amount over a longer period, ended up being under the limit (see "good" counterfactual in Table 1). The counterfactual directly tells you more about the causal dependencies in the domain and, importantly, provides you with "actionable" information (i.e., if you stopped drinking for 30 min you could be under the limit). Technically, counterfactuals can tell you about the feature

[1] This context assumes an existing (albeit opaque) model to which cases can be presented to find predictions/labels; all counterfactual-generation techniques make this assumption, though there is some discussion around whether the training data would also always be accessible (obviously, we assume the training-data/case-base is available).

[2] Though NUNs have been studied in CBR (e.g., [22, 23]), few consider counterfactual cases (aka NUNs) for explanation; [24, 25] are exceptions but they viewed NUNs as being more important as confidence indicators with respect to decision boundaries.

differences that affect the decision boundary around a prediction. Accordingly, [20] define counterfactual explanations as statements taking the form:

Score y was returned because variables V had values (v1, v2, ..). If V had values (v1′, v2′ …), and all others remain constant, score y′ would have been returned.

where, in our example, score y would be the class "over the limit" and y' the class "under the limit". Recently, researchers championing counterfactual cases for XAI have argued that psychologically, technically and legally they provide better explanations than other techniques for XAI [7, 16, 17, 26–29].

Table 1. A query case paired with a "Good" and a "Bad" Counterfactual from the Blood Alcohol Content (BAC) case-base with the feature-differences between them (shown in bold italics)

Features	Query case	"Good" Counterfactual	"Bad" Counterfactual
Weight	**80 kg**	80 kg	80 kg
Duration	**1 h**	***1.5 h***	***3 h***
Gender	**Male**	Male	***Female***
Meal	**Empty**	Empty	***Full***
Units	**6**	6	***6.5***
Bac Level	**Over**	Under	Under

2.1 Counterfactual Promise

Many have argued that counterfactual thinking has a promising role to play in explanation from philosophical, psychological, computational and legal perspectives. Philosophers of science have argued that true causal explanation only emerges from contrastive propositions, using counterfactuals [30, 31]. Psychologists have also shown that counterfactuals play a key role in human cognition and emotion, eliciting spontaneous causal thinking about what might have been the case [15, 16, 32]. Byrne [16] has explicitly related this literature to the XAI problem, laying out the different ways in which counterfactuals could be used (see also [7, 33]). For example, as counterfactuals engender more active causal thinking in people, they are more likely to facilitate "human in the loop" decision making [16]. Recently, Dodge et al. [34] assessed explanations of biased classifiers using four different explanation styles and found counterfactual explanations to be the most effective. In AI, Pearl [27] has proposed an influential structural Bayesian approach to counterfactuals that can test the fairness of AI systems, but it has been less used in explanation generation (e.g., see [35, 36]). In the XAI literature, the use of counterfactuals has been used to counter popular post-hoc perturbation approaches (e.g., LIME; [37, 38]), with many researchers arguing that counterfactuals provide more robust and informative post-hoc explanations [18, 26, 38–40]; these "counterfactualists" have also argued that counterfactual explanations are GDPR compliant [4, 39].

2.2 Counterfactual Problems

However, the promise of counterfactuals for XAI comes with a number of problems; the three main ones being prolixity, sparcity and plausibility.

Prolixity. Currently, most XAI systems generate counterfactuals using random perturbation and search, making them somewhat *prolix* [4, 17]; that is, many counterfactuals may be produced for a given prediction from which a "good" one must be filtered (e.g., in the loan system, one could be shown counterfactuals for every $10 incremental change in one's salary). Stated simply, this prolixity is handled by filtering counterfactuals on the minimally-changed features to the query case that flip the prediction (i.e., the nearest unlike neighbor). So, [20] propose the following loss function, L:

$$L(x, x', y', \lambda) = \lambda(f(x') - y')^2 + d(x, x') \quad (1)$$

$$arg \min_{x'} \max_{\lambda} L(x, x', y', \lambda) \quad (2)$$

where x is the vector for the query case and x' is the counterfactual vector, with y' being the desired (flipped) prediction from f (..) the trained model, where acts as the balancing weight. In formula (2), λ balances the closeness of the counterfactual to the query case against making minimal changes to the query case while delivering a prediction change, using the L1 norm weighted by median absolute deviation (MAD). This technique claims to find minimally-mutated counterfactuals, solving the prolixity problem (see [17, 39, 40] and [39] for *diversity* between counterfactuals).

Sparcity. These methods also profess to solve the *sparcity* problem. All commentators argue that good explanatory counterfactuals need to be *sparse*; that is, they need to modify the *fewest* features of the query case. For example, Table 1 shows, for the blood alcohol domain, two different counterfactuals, one with a 1-feature change and another with a 4-feature change, with the sparcity of the former making it better than the latter. Wachter et al. [4] argue that the L1 norm delivers sparse counterfactuals, though many of these appear to still involve high numbers of feature-differences (e.g., >4, see [40]). Importantly, the argument for sparcity is a psychological one that has not been specifically tested in the XAI literature. Typically, AI researchers propose sparcity is important because of human working memory limits [41, 42], but we argue that people prefer sparse counterfactuals because of limits on human category learning. For example, [43] have shown that when people are learning categories for unfamiliar items they prefer single-feature changes between to-be-learned items over multiple-feature changes, because it makes the learning task easier (unless there is additional domain knowledge on dependencies between features). Based on this evidence, we operationalize the *sparcity* of "good" counterfactuals (as items with 1 or 2 feature differences) versus "bad" counterfactuals (those with >2 feature changes). This definition helps us develop the novel idea of the *counterfactual potential* of case-bases, based on quantifying the "good" counterfactuals they contain (see Sects. 4 and 5).

Plausibility. The final problem is that of *plausibility*; that is, the counterfactuals generated by these methods may not be valid data-points in the domain or they may suggest feature-changes that are difficult-to-impossible. Classic examples of such counterfactuals in loan decisions, are explanations that propose increasing one's salary by an implausible amount (i.e., *if you earned $1M, you would get the loan*) or radically altering oneself (i.e., *if you changed gender, you would get the loan*). Plausibility is the least-solved problem facing counterfactual generation; many researchers propose to "lock" features (e.g., not allow *gender* change) or to get users to provide inputs on feature weights [40] (e.g., using interface sliders on salary boundaries). However, automated solutions to the plausibility problem are thin on the ground[3]. Our proposal is to *directly* generate counterfactuals analogically from the dataset, rather than producing them by "blind", random perturbation followed by filtering. As counterfactuals generated in this way are based on "real experiences" in the problem domain, they should be inherently plausible. However, this raises another question: namely, how many good counterfactuals "naturally" occur in case-bases, what is their *counterfactual potential.*

2.3 CBR's Prospects for Counterfactuals

Most techniques for generating counterfactuals for XAI perform random perturbations of a query case followed by a search to find minimally-different items that are close to the decision boundary (i.e., a NUN). These perturbation techniques can encounter problems, notably in meeting *sparcity* and *plausibility,* which may benefit from a case-based approach. Just as CBR has successfully explained predictions using factual cases [10, 25], perhaps it can also deliver counterfactual cases that are *sparse* and *plausible.* However, if CBR is to be used, we need to establish whether case-bases/datasets actually contain good counterfactuals, whether they have high counterfactual potential. We define a *good counterfactual* to be a NUN that differs from the query case by no more than 2 features. So, *counterfactual potential* can be computed from the feature-differences for all pairwise comparisons of cases in the case-base. If these comparisons find many "good" counterfactuals then the potential is high, if not then it is low. So, in our first experiment, we computed the counterfactual potential of 20 classic ML/CBR datasets, from the UCI repository [45]. From this analysis we develop the idea of *explanatory coverage* before proposing a novel case-based technique for counterfactual generation (Sect. 4). Finally, in Sect. 5, we report a set of experiments on five representative datasets to show how our technique can enhance counterfactual potential.

3 Experiment 1: Plotting Counterfactual Potential

In this experiment, we computed the counterfactual potential of 20 classic datasets from the UCI repository [45], ones that have been commonly used in many CBR papers. This analysis was done by computing the number of feature differences between all pairwise comparisons of cases in the case-base, noting the proportion of "good" counterfactuals found (i.e., $\leq$2 feature difference counterfactuals). This analysis provides us with an

[3] Rare recent attempts include Laugel et al.'s [44] method to "justify" generated counterfactuals using nearest neighbors in the training data, and [29] finding "feasible paths" to counterfactuals in the dataset; both methods attempt to *ground* counterfactuals in prior experience.

upper/lower bound on the potential of a case-base to deliver good counterfactuals. Obviously, in any specific CBR system, one might be able to adjust weights, how features are matched or *k*-values to find such counterfactuals, but such fine-tuning will not improve matters hugely if good counterfactual-cases are just not there.

3.1 Method: Data Sets and Procedure

Twenty UCI datasets were used in the experiment, selected on the basis of their common usage in CBR. We compared all pairings of query cases (one side of a decision boundary) to training cases (on the other side of a decision boundary) calculating the number of feature differences found in each.

3.2 Results and Discussion

Table 2 shows the counterfactual potential of the UCI datasets, as the percentage of counterfactuals from 1 to >5 feature-differences. The results show that "good" counterfactuals are rare[4]; in nearly every dataset, the 1-diff and 2-diff counterfactual categories

Table 2. Percent counterfactuals for feature-differences in 20 UCI datasets (expt.1)

DataSets	N of cases	Feat. no.	Class no.	N of pairs	1-diff	2-diff	3-diff	4-diff	>5-diff
Abalone	4177	10	8	15.6M	**0%**	**0%**	0%	0%	99.9%
Auto MPG	398	8	5	52.3k	**0%**	**0%**	0%	0.4%	99.6%
BAC	9291	7	2	19M	**0%**	**1.5%**	23%	3%	72%
Bupa liver	345	6	2	29k	**0%**	**0%**	0.1%	3.1%	96.8%
Credit	653	15	2	105.7k	**0%**	**0%**	0%	0%	99.9%
Cleveland heart	303	13	5	32.9k	**0%**	**0%**	0%	0.1%	99.9%
Ecoli	336	7	7	41k	**0%**	**0%**	0%	0.2%	99.8%
Glass	214	9	7	21.9k	**0%**	**0%**	0%	0%	99.9%
German credit	914	20	2	177k	**0%**	**0%**	0%	0%	99.9%
Horse colic	300	22	2	20.8k	**0%**	**0%**	0%	0%	99.9%
Indian liver	583	10	2	69.5k	**0%**	**0%**	0%	0%	99.9%
Ionosphere	351	34	2	28.3k	**0%**	**0%**	0%	0%	100%
Iris	150	4	3	7.5k	**0%**	**0.3%**	8.8%	91%	n/a
Sonar	208	60	2	10.8k	**0%**	**0%**	0%	0%	100%
Soybean (large)	307	26	19	43k	**0%**	**0%**	0.2%	0.6%	99.2%
Thyroid	2800	27	3	355.8k	**0%**	**0%**	0%	0%	99.9%
Votes	435	17	2	44.8k	**0%**	**0.3%**	0.9%	1.9%	88.8%
Wine-Italian	178	13	3	10.4k	**0%**	**0%**	0%	0%	100%
Wisconsin breast	699	9	2	110k	**0%**	**0%**	0%	0.4%	99.5%
Yeast	1484	8	10	855.3k	**0%**	**0%**	0.3%	4.8%	94.9%

[4] We extensively tested this Blood Alcohol Content (BAC) case-base [24, 25], but cannot report it for reasons of space. Using a mechanical model for estimating BAC, we generated several master-case-bases from which we sampled 50+ specific case-bases; across all of these case-bases, to our astonishment, we repeatedly found the same absence of good counterfactuals.

account for $<1\%$ of total counterfactuals. Most of the counterfactuals found have poor sparcity (i.e., >5 feature-differences) and would likely be hard for people to understand.

It should be noted that in the above, we determine feature differences using an exact match. Such an approach is inherently conservative with real-valued features. In practice, a matching tolerance could be used by, for example, treating two feature-values as equivalent if they are within 1% of each other. While this tolerance-matching improves the results (albeit in a somewhat *ad hoc* fashion), the fraction of good counterfactuals ($\leq$2 feature differences) still typically remains very low (see Sect. 5 for tests).

On the face of it, these results suggest that a case-based approach to counterfactual generation is a bad idea; if most datasets do not deliver good counterfactuals then case-based techniques seem bound to fail? However, as we shall see in the following sections, there are additional steps that can be used to meet and resolve this challenge.

4 A Case-Based Technique for Good Counterfactuals

Ironically, the above analysis suggests that CBR seems to have little to offer in using counterfactuals for XAI. For most case-bases good counterfactuals are rare, few query cases have associated good counterfactual cases. This may explain why the dominant counterfactual XAI techniques use perturbation, where synthetic counterfactuals are generated "blindly" from problem-cases and labelled using a machine-learning model, without reference to other known cases in the training set [18, 26, 38–40]. In contrast to these approaches, we believe that counterfactuals need to be explicitly grounded in known cases (*aka* the training data) to ensure plausibility. Hence, we developed a novel case-based technique for counterfactual-XAI which reuses patterns of good counterfactuals that already exist in a case-base, to generate analogous counterfactuals (as new datapoints) that can explain new target problems and their solutions. In generating new counterfactuals, these existing good counterfactuals provide 'hints' about what features can and should be adapted and plausible feature-values to use in them. This new technique relies on the notion of *explanatory competence* (see Sect. 4.1). Note, the context for the use of this method is a twin-system approach to XAI, where an opaque ML model is "explained" by twinning it with a more transparent CBR-system to find explanatory cases [13, 14]; hence, along with all other counterfactual-generation techniques, we assume an ML model is available to assign labels for any newly-generated synthetic case.

4.1 Explanatory Competence

The notion of *predictive competence* or simply *competence* (i.e., an assessment of an ML/CBR system's potential to solve a range of future problems) has proved to be a very useful development for AI systems [19–21]. For example, in CBR, predictive competence can assess the overall problem-solving potential of a system, to help avoid the utility problem as a case-base grows, to maintain case-bases and so on [19, 20]. A parallel notion of *explanatory competence* can also be applied to any case-base.

Just as the fundamental unit of (predictive) competence is a relation of the form *solves(c, c′)* to indicate that case/example *c* can be used to solve some target/query *c′*, the basic unit of explanatory competence is *explains(c, c′)* indicating that some case *c* can be used to explain the solution of *c′*; where the explanatory cases (*c*) are the counterfactuals of *c′*. So, the explanatory competence of a case-base *C* can be represented by a *coverage set* (Eq. 3) and explanatory competence can be estimated as the size of the coverage set as a fraction of the case-base (Eq. 4):

$$XP\_Coverage\_Set(C) = \{c' \in C \mid \exists c \in C - \{c'\} \,\&\, explains(c, c')\} \quad (3)$$

$$XP\_Coverage(C) = |XP\_Coverage\_Set(C)|/|C| \quad (4)$$

4.2 Leveraging Counterfactual Cases for Explanation

Although good counterfactuals are rare, in practice most case-bases should offer some examples where a query/problem-case can be associated with a good counterfactual, with or without some matching tolerance (as mentioned above). For example, in the Abalone dataset, even though there are few good counterfactuals (<1%), with a similarity tolerance of 0.02, ~20% of cases are found to have good counterfactuals; for the Liver dataset a tolerance of 0.025 results in ~4% of cases having associated good counterfactuals. Can these query-counterfactual case-pairs guide the search for novel (good) counterfactuals for new target problems that otherwise lack a good counterfactual?

Below, we refer to the pairing of a case and its corresponding good counterfactual as an *explanation case* (*XC*). For any given case-base, we can generate a corresponding case-base of these explanation cases for use during counterfactual generation; see Eqs. 5 and 6. By definition explanation cases are symmetric; either of the cases can be viewed as the query or counterfactual, which, in practice, means that each pair of unlike neighbours, which differ by ≤2 features, contributes two XCs to the XC case-base.

$$xc\left(c, c'\right) \Leftrightarrow class(c) \neq class(c') \,\&\, diffs(c, c') \leq 2 \quad (5)$$

$$XC(C) = \{(c, c') : c, c' \in C \,\&\, xc(c, c')\} \quad (6)$$

Each XC is associated with a set of *match-features (m)*, the features that are the same between the query and counterfactual (using a specified tolerance), and a set of *difference-features (d)*, the ≤2 features that differ between the query and counterfactual.

Figure 1(a) shows a two-class case-base of cases (*C*) with its corresponding *XCs* – *xc(x, x′)*, *xc(y, y′)*, and *xc(z, z′)* – along with two query cases (*p* and *q*), which have been classified by the underlying ML-model, and which now need to be explained. For our purposes, we assume that there are no existing good counterfactuals for *p* or *q* in *C*, hence the need to generate new good counterfactuals for them.

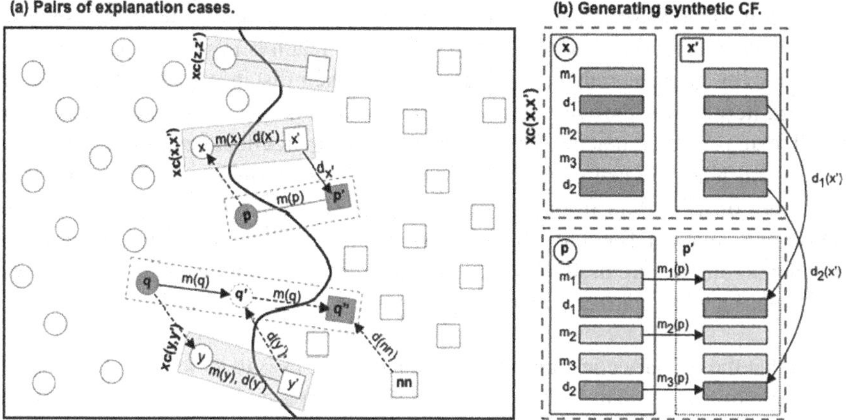

Fig. 1. An illustration of (a) a two-class case-base with 3 explanation cases; (b) how a synthetic counterfactual, *(p, p′)*, is generated from an existing explanation-case, *xc(x, x′)*.

4.3 A Case-Based Approach to Generating Good Counterfactuals

We propose a classical case-based reasoning approach to generating good counterfactuals by *retrieving*, *reusing*, and *revising* a nearby explanation case as follows:

1. First, we identify the XC case whose query is most similar to *p* while sharing p's class; this is *xc(x, x′)* in Fig. 1. Since *xc(x, x′)* has a good counterfactual, *x′*, and because the *p* is similar to *x*, then the intuition is that *x′* is a suitable basis for a new counterfactual *p′* to explain *p*. The *difference-features* between *x* and *x′*, which are solely responsible for the class change between *x* and *x′*, should play a critical role in constructing *p'*.
2. For each of the *match-features* in *xc(x, x′)*, we copy the *values* of these features in *p* to the new counterfactual *p′*. Similarly, for each of the *difference-features* in *xc(x, x′)* we copy their *values* from *x′* into *p′*. In this way, *p′* is a combination of feature values from *p* and *x′*. It differs from *p* in a manner that is similar to the way in which *x′* differs from *x* and, by construction, *p′* is a *candidate good counterfactual* because these differences amount to no more than two features. This transfer of values from *p* and *x′* into *p′* is illustrated in Fig. 1(b).
3. For *p′* to be *actually a* good counterfactual, it has to be a different class from *p*, which is not yet guaranteed. We determine the class of *p′* by using the underlying ML-model (from the twin-system) and, if it is different from *p*, then *p′* can be used directly as a good counterfactual to explain *p* (see Fig. 1(a)).
4. Sometimes, however, the class of the new counterfactual, after retrieval/reuse, is not different from the target query. For example, the new counterfactual *q′*, which is generated for *q* by reusing *xc(y, y′)* in Fig. 1(a), has the same class as *q*, because the combination of the match-feature values (from *q*) and difference-features (from *y′*) are not sufficient to change its class from that of *q*.
5. Since *q′* is not a valid counterfactual, we perform an *adaptation* step to *revise* the values of the difference-features in *q′* until there is a class change; note, we cannot

change the match-features in q' without increasing the number of feature differences with q. We can revise the values of the difference-features in q' in various ways, for example, by perturbing them to further increase their distance from q. However, we instead iterate over the *ordered nearest neighbours* of q with the same class as y', until there is a class change[5]. The values of the difference-features from each *nearest neighbour* leads to a new candidate, q'', and adaptation terminates successfully when the class of *q"* differs from that of *q;* if none of the *neighbours* produce a class change, then adaptation fails. In Fig. 1(a), when the difference-feature values from the neighbour, *nn,* are used to produce q'', the result is a class change, and so q'' can be used as a good counterfactual for q.

Note that the primary contribution of explanation cases is to identify and distinguish between common combinations of features (match-features and difference-features) that tend to participate in good counterfactuals. Depending on the domain this may reflect important relationships (causal or otherwise) that exist within the feature-space. In other words, the XCs tell us about which features *should* be changed (or held constant) when generating new counterfactuals in the feature-space near a query case.

Another advantage of this approach is that, because it reuses *actual feature-values* from *real cases,* it should lead to more plausible counterfactuals and, better explanations. This contrasts with perturbation approaches, which rely on arbitrary values for features (and may even produce invalid data-points) and is consistent with approaches that try to ground counterfactuals in the training data [28, 44]. However, [28, 44] still use prior experience in a less direct way; they justify/link the generated counterfactual to known data-points rather directly using those data-points to directly create the counterfactual, as we do here. Notably, this method reminds one of analogical extrapolation methods in CBR [46] and structural analogical transfer [47, 48].

Finally, though our approach may succeed in finding a suitable counterfactual without the need for the adaptation/revision step, it may be desirable to proceed with this step, nonetheless. This is because the adaptation step has the potential to locate a suitable counterfactual that is *closer to the query* than the candidate counterfactual produced by the retrieval step alone and finding counterfactuals that are maximally similar to the query is an important factor when it comes to explanation [17].

5 Experiment 2: Evaluating Explanation Competence

A *preliminary* evaluation of the above approach was carried out using five popular ML/CBR datasets to demonstrate how explanatory competence can be improved over the baseline level of good counterfactuals naturally occurring in a dataset. For the ML model used to validate the generated counterfactuals, we used a k-NN model, to determine whether the predicted counterfactual class differs from the test/query case, but other classifiers could also be used if available.

[5] More generally, for multi-class datasets, this adaptation can be modified to iterate over all ordered nearest neighbours with a *different class* to q, not just those with the same class as y'. This provides a larger pool of difference-feature values and increase the likelihood of locating a good counterfactual for q.

5.1 Method: Data and Procedure

Each of the datasets represent a classification task of varying complexity, in terms of the number of classes, features, and training examples. The task of interest, however, is not a classification one but an explanation one. As such we are attempting to generate good counterfactuals in order to *explain* target/query cases and their classes. The key evaluation metrics will be: (a) the fraction of target/query cases than can be associated with good counterfactuals (*explanatory competence*); and (b) the distance from the target/query case to the newly-generated good counterfactual (*counterfactual distance*).

As a baseline for explanatory competence we use the fraction of cases that can be associated with a good counterfactual in each case-base. In each dataset we use a matching tolerance of 1–2% with normalized features and the Minkowski similarity metric was used throughout; variations in these settings will increase the fraction of existing and generated good counterfactuals and future work will need to explore such matters more completely. As a corresponding baseline for counterfactual distance, we use the average distance between these cases and their good counterfactuals. A 10-fold cross-validation was used to evaluate the newly-generated counterfactuals, selecting 10% of the cases at random to use as queries, and building the XC case-base from the remaining cases. Then, we use the above technique to generate good counterfactuals for the queries, noting the fraction of the queries that can be associated with good counterfactuals, and the corresponding counterfactual distances, after the retrieval/reuse and adaptation steps. Results reported are the averages for the 10 folds for each dataset.

5.2 Results and Discussion: Explanatory Competence

The explanatory competence results are presented in Fig. 2, showing the explanatory competence (fraction of queries that can be explained) for the dataset (baseline), and for the synthetic counterfactuals generated after the retrieval and adaptation steps of our approach. The results show how explanatory competence can be significantly increased by our case-based-counterfactual technique. For example, on average only about 11% of the cases in these datasets can be associated with good counterfactuals (the average baseline competence when a tolerance is applied) but by retrieving and re-using explanation cases we can reach an average explanatory competence of just over 40%. Implementing the adaptation step further increases the explanatory competence just under 94%, on average. Notably, even datasets with very low baseline explanatory competence benefit from significant improvements in explanatory competence particularly when the adaptation step is used. For example, the 6,400 case Wine dataset (12 features and 7 classes) has a baseline explanatory competence of just 6%, but its 559 XC-cases can be used to achieve almost 90% in explanatory competence.

5.3 Results and Discussion: Counterfactual Distance

Of course, just because it is possible to generate a counterfactual for a query that has no more than 2 feature-differences, does not necessarily mean that the counterfactual will make for an ideal explanation, in practice. To test this would require a succession of live user-trials (currently planned), that are beyond the scope of the present work. As a proxy

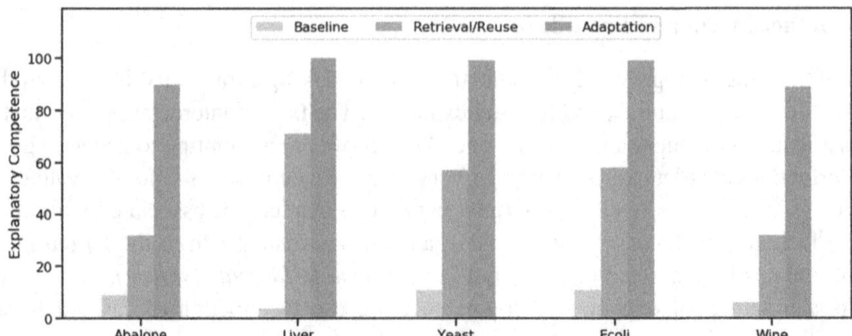

Fig. 2. The explanatory competence (XP_Coverage) of five case-bases/datasets, showing baseline competence and how competence increases by reusing and adapting explanation cases.

for the utility of the explanation, however, we can use the distance between the query and the generated counterfactual, on the grounds that counterfactuals which are closer to a query are more likely to serve as more useful explanations. Since counterfactual distance will vary from dataset to dataset, reflecting the nature of the feature space, we use a *relative counterfactual distance* (RCF) measure by dividing the counterfactual distances of the synthetic counterfactuals by the baseline counterfactual distance for the dataset. Thus, if RCF >1, then it indicates that the synthetic counterfactual is farther from the query that the average baseline counterfactual distance.

The results are presented in Fig. 3, which include the relative distance of the good counterfactuals produced by the retrieval/reuse and the adaptation steps for each dataset. We also show the relative distance results for an additional condition, *Closest*, which is defined as follows: when both the retrieval/reuse and adaptation steps lead to a good counterfactual, then choose the one with the lower counterfactual distance, otherwise if only one good counterfactual is produced then use its distance.

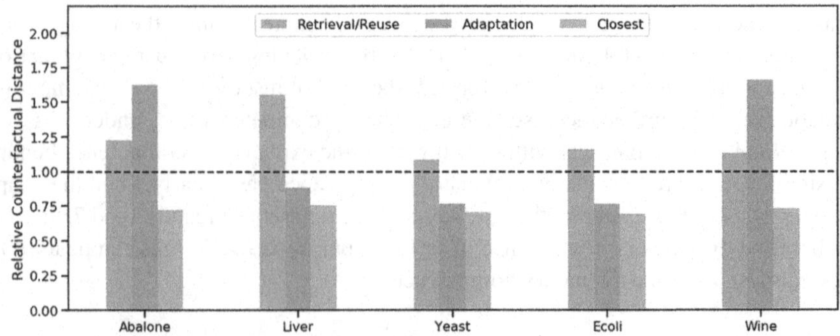

Fig. 3. The counterfactual distance of good counterfactuals produced for five case-bases/datasets, relative to the baseline counterfactual distance (between a query case and its counterfactual)

On average, good counterfactuals produced by the retrieval/reuse step are farther from the test query than the baseline counterfactual distance (RCF ≈ 1.2). In most cases the additional distance beyond the baseline is modest with the exception of the Liver dataset, where the retrieval/reuse step produces good counterfactuals that are 55% (RCF ≈ 1.55) more distant from the query than the baseline distance. The good counterfactuals produced by the adaptation step are closer to the test queries – the average RCF $\approx$ 1.1, and in 3 out of the 5 datasets the generated counterfactuals are closer than the baseline (RCF < 1). If we select the closest counterfactual, when both retrieval/reuse and adaptation produce one, then the RCF < 1 for all of the datasets. This further validates the need for, and quantifies the benefits of, the adaptation step: it provides an opportunity to choose a counterfactual that is significantly closer to the query.

6 Conclusions and Future Directions

In the last three years, there has been a significant upsurge in XAI research arguing for the computational, psychological and legal advantages of counterfactuals. Most of this work generates synthetic counterfactuals without reference to the training-data in the domain and, as such, can suffer from *sparsity* and *plausibility* deficits. In short, these methods do not guarantee the production of good counterfactuals and, may indeed, sometimes generate invalid data points. This state of affairs invites a case-based solution to counterfactual generation that leverages the prior experience of the case-base, adapting known counterfactual associations between query-problems and known cases. In this paper, we advance just such a technique and show how it can improve the counterfactual potential of many datasets. In developing this technique, we have (i) clarified the definition of good counterfactuals, (ii) proposed the new idea of explanation competence, (iii) reported significant new evidence for the utility of this novel technique.

This approach is *model agnostic*, in that it can operate with any underlying classifier (e.g., deep learner, decision tree, k-NN) once it has access to the features of training data, an agreed distance metric, and the dataset (see [49, 50] for a discussion of this issue). However, the approach makes some assumptions that might limit its utility beyond the datasets discussed. It assumes the availability of at least some explanation cases, which is typically feasible; even though good counterfactuals are rare they are seldom so rare as to exclude a minimally-viable explanation case-base, at least when a degree of matching tolerance is allowed for when computing feature similarities and differences; note, different degrees of matching tolerance, similarity metrics, and feature normalization strategies may have an impact on outcomes. The approach also assumes the availability of sufficiently accurate underlying ML-model (e.g., in a twin system) for the purpose of counterfactual validation, though this is an accepted assumption in all approaches. Finally, though previous psychological work supports our operational definition of good counterfactuals, more user testing is required; notions of *goodness* in general (see [2]) need to be squared with *sparcity goodness*. Notwithstanding this future research, from the current findings, it is clear that a CBR approach to counterfactuals has much to offer the explainable AI (XAI) problem.

Acknowledgements. This paper emanated from research funded by (i) Science Foundation Ireland (SFI) to the *Insight Centre for Data Analytics* under Grant Number 12/RC/2289_P2 and (ii) SFI and the Department of Agriculture, Food and Marine on behalf of the Government of Ireland to the *VistaMilk SFI Research Centre* under Grant Number 16/RC/3835.

References

1. Gunning, D.: Explainable artificial intelligence (XAI). Defense Advanced Research Projects Agency (DARPA), Web, vol. 2 (2017)
2. Gunning, D., Aha, D.W.: DARPA's explainable artificial intelligence program. AI Mag. **40**(2), 44–58 (2019)
3. Goodman, B., Flaxman, S.: European Union regulations on algorithmic decision-making and a "right to explanation". AI Mag. **38**(3), 50–57 (2017)
4. Wachter, S., Mittelstadt, B., Floridi, L.: Why a right to explanation of automated decision-making does not exist in the general data protection regulation. Int. Data Priv. Law **7**(2), 76–99 (2017)
5. Adadi, A., Berrada, M.: Peeking inside the black-box: a survey on Explainable Artificial Intelligence (XAI). IEEE Access **6**, 52138–52160 (2018)
6. Guidotti, R., Monreale, A., Ruggieri, S., Turini, F., Giannotti, F., Pedreschi, D.: A survey of methods for explaining black box models. ACM Comput. Surv. **51**(5), 93 (2018)
7. Miller, T.: Explanation in artificial intelligence. Artif. Intell. **267**, 1–38 (2019)
8. Leake, D.B.: CBR in context: the present and future. In: Case-Based Reasoning: Experiences, Lessons, and Future Directions, pp. 3–30 (1996)
9. Leake, D., McSherry, D.: Introduction to the special issue on explanation in case-based reasoning. Artif. Intell. Rev. **24**(2), 103–108 (2005)
10. Sørmo, F., Cassens, J., Aamodt, A.: Explanation in case-based reasoning–perspectives and goals. Artif. Intell. Rev. **24**(2), 109–143 (2005)
11. Schoenborn, J.M., Althoff, K.D.: Recent trends in XAI: In: Case-Based Reasoning for the Explanation of intelligent systems (XCBR) Workshop (2019)
12. Lipton, Z.C.: The Mythos of model interpretability. Queue **16**(3), 30 (2018)
13. Kenny, E.M., Keane, M.T.: Twin-systems to explain neural networks using case-based reasoning. In: Proceedings of the 28th International Joint Conference on Artificial Intelligence, IJCAI 2019, pp. 326–333 (2019)
14. Keane, M.T., Kenny, E.M.: How case-based reasoning explains neural networks: a theoretical analysis of XAI using *Post-Hoc* explanation-by-example from a survey of ANN-CBR twin-systems. In: Bach, K., Marling, C. (eds.) ICCBR 2019. LNCS (LNAI), vol. 11680, pp. 155–171. Springer, Cham (2019). https://doi.org/10.1007/978-3-030-29249-2_11
15. Byrne, R.M.J.: The Rational Imagination. MIT Press, Cambridge (2007)
16. Byrne, R.M.J.: Counterfactuals in explainable artificial intelligence (XAI): evidence from human reasoning. In: Proceedings of the Twenty-Eighth International Joint Conference on Artificial Intelligence, IJCAI 2019, pp. 6276–6282 (2019)
17. Wachter, S., Mittelstadt, B., Russell, C.: Counterfactual explanations without opening the black box: automated decisions and the GDPR. Harv. J. Law Tech. **31**, 841 (2018)
18. Guidotti, R., Monreale, A., Giannotti, F., Pedreschi, D., Ruggieri S., Turini. F.: Factual and counterfactual explanations for black box decision making. IEEE Intell. Syst. **34**(6), 14–23 (2019)
19. Smyth, B., Keane, M.T.: Remembering to forget. In: Proceedings of the 14th International Joint Conference on Artificial Intelligence, IJCAI 1995, pp. 377–382 (1995)
20. Smyth, B., McKenna, E.: Modelling the competence of case-bases. In: Smyth, B., Cunningham, P. (eds.) EWCBR 1998. LNCS, vol. 1488, pp. 208–220. Springer, Heidelberg (1998). https://doi.org/10.1007/BFb0056334
21. Juarez, J.M., Craw, S., Lopez-Delgado, J.R., Campos, M.: Maintenance of case-bases: current algorithms after fifty years. In: Proceedings of the Twenty-Seventh International Joint Conference on Artificial Intelligence, IJCAI 2018, pp. 5457–5463 (2018)

22. Delany, S.J., Cunningham, P., Doyle, D., Zamolotskikh, A.: Generating estimates of classification confidence for a case-based spam filter. In: Muñoz-Ávila, H., Ricci, F. (eds.) ICCBR 2005. LNCS (LNAI), vol. 3620, pp. 177–190. Springer, Heidelberg (2005). https://doi.org/10.1007/11536406_16
23. Kumar, R.R., Viswanath, P., Bindu, C.S.: Nearest neighbor classifiers: a review. Int. J. Comput. Intell. Res. **13**(2), 303–311 (2017)
24. Cunningham, P., Doyle, D., Loughrey, J.: An evaluation of the usefulness of case-based explanation. In: Ashley, K.D., Bridge, D.G. (eds.) ICCBR 2003. LNCS (LNAI), vol. 2689, pp. 122–130. Springer, Heidelberg (2003). https://doi.org/10.1007/3-540-45006-8_12
25. Nugent, C., Cunningham, P.: A case-based explanation system for black-box systems. Artif. Intell. Rev. **24**(2), 163–178 (2005)
26. Mittelstadt, B., Russell, C., Wachter, S.: Explaining explanations in AI. In: Proceedings of Conference on Fairness, Accountability, and Transparency, FAT 2019 (2019)
27. Pearl, J.: Causality, Cambridge University Press, Cambridge (2000)
28. Sokol, K., Flach, P.: Desiderata for interpretability: explaining decision tree predictions with counterfactuals. In: AAAI 20119, Doctoral Consortium, pp. 10035–10036 (2019)
29. Poyiadzi, R., Sokol, K., Santos-Rodriguez, R., De Bie, T., Flach, P.: FACE: feasible and actionable counterfactual explanations. In: Proceedings of the AAAI/ACM Conference on AI, Ethics, and Society, pp. 344–350 (2020). https://doi.org/10.1145/3375627.3375850
30. Woodward, J.: Making Things Happen. Oxford University Press, Oxford (2003)
31. Van Fraassen, B.C.: The Scientific Image. Oxford University Press, Oxford (1980)
32. Kahneman, D., Miller, D.T.: Norm theory: comparing reality to its alternatives. Psychol. Rev. **93**(2), 136–153 (1986)
33. Mueller, S.T., Hoffman, R.R., Clancey, W.J., Emery, A.K., Klein, G.: Explanation in human-AI systems. Florida Institute for Human and Machine Cognition (2019)
34. Dodge, J., Liao, Q.V., Zhang, Y., Bellamy, R.K., Dugan, C.: Explaining models: an empirical study of how explanations impact fairness judgment. In: Proceedings of the 24th International Conference on Intelligent User Interfaces, pp. 275–285 (2019)
35. Miller, T.: Contrastive explanation. arXiv preprint arXiv:1811.03163 (2018)
36. Russell, C., Kusner, M.J., Loftus, J., Silva, R.: When worlds collide: integrating different counterfactual assumptions in fairness. In: Advances in Neural Information Processing Systems, pp. 6414–6423 (2017)
37. Ribeiro, M.T., Singh, S., Guestrin, C.: Why should I trust you?. In: Proceedings of the 22nd ACM SIGKDD, pp. 1135–1144. ACM (2016)
38. Pedreschi, D., Giannotti, F., Guidotti, R., Monreale, A., Ruggieri, S., Turini, F.: Meaningful explanations of Black Box AI decision systems. In: Proceedings of AAAI 2019 (2019)
39. Mothilal, R.K., Sharma, A., Tan, C.: Explaining machine learning classifiers through diverse counterfactual explanations. In: Proceedings of the 2020 Conference on Fairness, Accountability, and Transparency, FAT 2020, pp. 607–617 (2020)
40. McGrath, R., et al.: Interpretable credit application predictions with counterfactual explanations. In: NIP Workshop on Challenges and Opportunities for AI in Financial Services, Montreal, Canada (2018)
41. Miller, G.A.: The magical number seven, plus or minus two: some limits on our capacity for processing information. Psychol. Rev. **63**(2), 81 (1956)
42. Alvarez, G., Cavanagh, P.: The capacity of visual STM is set both by visual information load and by number of objects. Psychol. Sci. **15**, 106–111 (2004)
43. Medin, D.L., Wattenmaker, W.D., Hampson, S.E.: Family resemblance, conceptual cohesiveness, and category construction. Cogn. Psychol. **19**(2), 242–279 (1987)
44. Laugel, T., Lesot, M.J., Marsala, C., Renard, X., Detyniecki, M.: The dangers of post-hoc interpretability: unjustified counterfactual explanations. In: Proceedings of the 28th International Joint Conference on Artificial Intelligence, IJCAI 2019, pp. 2801–2807 (2019)

45. Dua, D., Graff, C.: UCI Machine Learning Repository University of California, School of Information and Computer Science, Irvine, CA. http://archive.ics.uci.edu/ml (2019)
46. Lieber, J., Nauer, E., Prade, H.: Improving analogical extrapolation using case pair competence. In: Bach, K., Marling, C. (eds.) ICCBR 2019. LNCS (LNAI), vol. 11680, pp. 251–265. Springer, Cham (2019). https://doi.org/10.1007/978-3-030-29249-2_17
47. Veale, T., Keane, M.T.: The competence of sub-optimal theories of structure mapping on hard analogies. In: International Joint Conference on Artificial Intelligence, pp. 232–237 (1997)
48. Keane, M.T.: Analogical asides on case-based reasoning. In: Wess, S., Althoff, K.D., Richter, M.M. (eds.) EWCBR 1993. LNCS, vol. 837, pp. 21–32. Springer, Heidelberg (1994). https://doi.org/10.1007/3-540-58330-0_74
49. Karimi, A.H., Barthe, G., Balle, B., Valera, I.: Model-agnostic counterfactual explanations for consequential decisions. In: Proceedings of the 23rd International Conference on Artificial Intelligence and Statistics, AISTATS 2020, Palermo, Italy, vol. 108. PMLR (2020)
50. Sokol, K., Flach, P.: Explainability fact sheets: a framework for systematic assessment of explainable approaches. In: Proceedings of the 2020 Conference on Fairness, Accountability, and Transparency, FAT 2020, pp. 56–67 (2020)

CBR-LIME: A Case-Based Reasoning Approach to Provide Specific Local Interpretable Model-Agnostic Explanations

Juan A. Recio-García(✉), Belén Díaz-Agudo, and Victor Pino-Castilla

Department of Software Engineering and Artificial Intelligence,
Instituto de Tecnologías del Conocimiento,
Universidad Complutense de Madrid, Madrid, Spain
{jareciog,belend,vpino}@ucm.es
http://gaia.fdi.ucm.es

Abstract. Research on eXplainable AI has proposed several model agnostic algorithms, being LIME [14] (Local Interpretable Model-Agnostic Explanations) one of the most popular. LIME works by modifying the query input locally, so instead of trying to explain the entire model, the specific input instance is modified, and the impact on the predictions are monitored and used as explanations. Although LIME is general and flexible, there are some scenarios where simple perturbations are not enough, so there are other approaches like Anchor where perturbations variation depends on the dataset. In this paper, we propose a CBR solution to the problem of configuring the parameters of the LIME algorithm for the explanation of an image classifier. The case base reflects the human perception of the quality of the explanations generated with different parameter configurations of LIME. Then, this parameter configuration is reused for similar input images.

Keywords: Specific explanations · User experience · Model-agnostic explanations · Case-based explanations

1 Introduction

With the success of Machine Learning (ML) interpretability for ML systems have become an active focus of research. XAI research tries to solve several questions related to the increasing need for interpretable models, such as: How should interpretable models be designed? How do we evaluate the resulting explanations? What knowledge do we need for building explanations? How does interpretability change interactions between the AI systems and the users? What to explain? When to explain? How to deal with the fact that different users have different

Supported by the Spanish Committee of Economy and Competitiveness (TIN2017-87330-R) and UCM Research Group 921330.

I. Watson and R. Weber (Eds.): ICCBR 2020, LNAI 12311, pp. 179–194, 2020.
https://doi.org/10.1007/978-3-030-58342-2_12

expectations and explanation needs? From the CBR perspective, research in XAI has pointed out the importance of taking advantage of the human knowledge to generate and evaluate explanations [16,19].

At a high level, the literature distinguishes between two main approaches to interpretability: *model-specific* (also called transparent or white box) models and *model-agnostic* (post-hoc) surrogate models to explain black box models [12,13,24]. Transparent models are ones that are inherently interpretable by users. So, the easiest way to achieve interpretability is to use algorithms that create interpretable models, such as decision trees, nearest-neighbour or linear regression. However, the best performing models are often not interpretable, or they are interpretable only if features are few in number or where the model is sparse, and where the features have a readily understandable semantics [10]. Besides, for the sake of performance, it is typical to use ensembles of several models that cannot be interpreted, even if every single model could be interpreted, like in the random forest algorithm. Model-agnostic interpretation methods propose separating the explanations from the ML model. Although the main advantage is flexibility, as the interpretation methods can be applied to any model, some authors consider this type of post-hoc explanations as limited *justifications* because they are not linked to the real reasoning process occurring in the black box.

LIME [14] (Local Interpretable Model-Agnostic Explanations) is a well-known model agnostic model that attempts to understand the model by perturbing the input of data samples and understanding how the predictions change. The intuition to local interpretability is to determine which feature changes will have the most impact on the prediction. According to its authors, the algorithm fulfils the desirable aspects of a model-agnostic explanation system regarding flexibility. The LIME interpretation method can work with any ML model and is not limited to a particular form of explanation and representation. An essential requirement for LIME is to work with an interpretable representation of the input, like images or bag of words, that is understandable to humans. The output of LIME is a list of explanations, reflecting the contribution of each feature to the prediction of a data sample.

Although LIME is general and flexible, there are some scenarios where simple perturbations are not enough, so there are other approaches like Anchor [15] where perturbations variation depends on the dataset. Either in LIME or Anchor, the configuration variables are set up by default. However, the adequacy of the variables to the input query instance is critical to provide quality explanations. In fact, the type of modifications that need to be performed on the data to get proper explanations are typically *use case* specific. The authors gave the following example in their paper [14]: "a model that predicts sepia-toned images to be retro cannot be explained by presence or absence of superpixels".

In this paper, we propose a CBR solution to the problem of configuring the default parameters of the LIME algorithm for an image classifier. The case base reflects the human perception of the quality of the explanations generated with different parameter configurations of LIME. Then, this parameter configuration is reused to generate explanations for similar input images.

This paper is organized as follows: Sect. 2 presents related work, whereas Sect. 3 introduces the LIME algorithm and some of its limitations. Section 4 describes the CBR-LIME method and the case base elicitation process. In Sect. 5 we demonstrate the benefits of our approach using both off-line and on-line evaluations. Concluding remarks are discussed in Sect. 6.

2 Related Work

CBR can provide a methodology to reuse experiences and generate explanations for different AI techniques and domains of applications. Therefore, we can find several initiatives in the CBR literature to explain AI systems. Some relevant early works can be found in the review by [8]. For example, [19] presents a framework for explanation in case-based reasoning (CBR) focused on explanation goals, whereas [2] develops the idea of explanation utility, a metric that may be different to the similarity metric used for nearest neighbour retrieval.

Recently there is a relevant body of work on CBR applied to the explanation of black-box models, the so-called *CBR Twins*. In [6], authors propose a theoretical analysis of a post-hoc explanation-by-example approach that relies on the twinning of artificial neural networks with CBR systems. [9] combine the strength of deep learning and the interpretability of case-based reasoning to make an interpretable deep neural network. [4] investigates whether CBR competence can be used to predict confidence in the outputs of a black box system when the black box and CBR systems are provided with the same training data. [23] demonstrates how CBR can be used for an XAI approach to justify solutions produced by an opaque learning method, particularly in the context of unstructured textual data. As we can observe, most of these works are post-hoc explanation systems, where CBR follows the model-agnostic approach to explain black-box models. However, there are other works that, instead of explaining the outcomes of the model, they try to explain the similarity metrics [17].

Outside the CBR community, many algorithms follow the same model-agnostic approach than LIME. Partial dependence plots (PDP) show the marginal effect that one or two features have on the predicted outcome of a machine learning model [3]. The equivalent to a PDP for individual data instances is called individual conditional expectation (ICE) plot [5]. It displays one line per instance that shows how the instance's prediction changes when a feature changes. Other approaches, referred to as permutation feature importance, measure the increase in the prediction error of the model after permuting the feature's values [1].

The global surrogate model is an interpretable model that is trained to approximate the predictions of a black box model [13]. In contrast, local surrogates, such as LIME or Anchors [14,15], focus on explaining individual predictions. Another popular local surrogate model similar to LIME is SHAP [11]. It is based on the game theory concept of Shapley values and explains the prediction of an instance by computing the contribution of each feature to the prediction.

Once we have reviewed the most relevant contributions of CBR to XAI and presented an overview of model-agnostic explanation methods, the next section focuses on the LIME algorithm that is the basis of this paper.

3 Background

LIME focuses on training local surrogate models to explain individual predictions given by a global black-box prediction model. In a general way, it analyses the behaviour of the global prediction model through the perturbation of the input data.

In order to figure out what features of the input are contributing to the prediction, it perturbs the input data around its neighbourhood and evaluates how the model behaves. Then, it trains an interpretable local model that weights these perturbed data points by their proximity to the original input. This local model should be a good and explainable local approximation of the black-box model. Mathematically, it is formulated as follows [14]:

$$explanation(x) = \arg\min_{g \in G} L(f, g, \Pi_x) + \Omega(g) \tag{1}$$

This equation defines an explanation as a model $g \in G$, where G is a class of potentially interpretable models, such as linear models or decision trees. The goal is to minimize the loss function L that measures how close the explanation is to the prediction of the original model f given a proximity measure Π_x. This proximity measure defines the size of the neighbourhood around the predicted instance x that is used to obtain the explanation. Additionally, it is necessary to minimize the complexity (as opposed to interpretability) of the explanation $g \in G$, denoted as $\Omega(g)$.

Regarding the perturbation of the input data, it depends on its type. For tabular data, LIME creates new samples by perturbing each feature individually based on statistical indicators. For text and images, the solution is to remove words or parts of the image (called superpixels). Here, the user can also configure how these superpixels are computed and replaced. By default, LIME uses the Quickshift clustering algorithm [22] that finds areas with similar pixels using a hierarchical approach. This clustering algorithm depends mainly on the Gaussian kernel used to define the neighbourhoods of pixels considered, that in practice defines the number of clusters. Once the image has been segmented, it is necessary to perturb the image to generate the training set for the surrogate model by removing superpixels randomly. Next, the definition of the proximity measure Π_x should also be chosen carefully to select the neighbourhood of perturbed images. Current implementations of LIME use an exponential smoothing kernel where the kernel width defines how close an instance must be to influence the local model.

Finally, the interpretable surrogate model used by LIME is linear regression, corresponding to the $\Omega(g)$ function in Eq. 1. Here, the user has to define the number of the top superpixels being considered. The lower top superpixels, the

Table 1. Variables used to configure the LIME method.

Clusters size	C	This parameter defines the width of the Gaussian kernel used to define the neighbourhoods of pixels considered
Number of perturbations	P	Number of perturbed images generated through the random removal of parts from the original image
Proximity measure	Π	Width of the exponential kernel that defines how close a perturbation must be to be included in the linear regression model
Number of features	F	Number of superpixels being considered by the linear regression model, representing to the $\Omega(g)$ function in Eq. 1

easier it is to interpret the model. A higher value potentially produces models with higher fidelity.

The use of linear regression makes LIME unable to explain the model correctly on some scenarios where simple perturbations are not enough. Ideally, the perturbations would be driven by the variation that is observed in the dataset. The same authors proposed a new way to perform model interpretation which is Anchors [15]. Anchor is also a local model-agnostic explanation algorithm that explains individual predictions, i.e., only captures the behaviour of the model on a local region of the input space. However, it improves the construction of the perturbation data set around the query. Instead of adding noise to continuous features, hiding parts of the image, to learn a boundary line (or slope) associated to the prediction of the query instance, Anchors improves LIME using a "local region" instead of a slope. Nevertheless, it also uses a generic configuration for every image.

Once we have described LIME and its limitations, the next section introduces the CBR-LIME method that improves its configuration through a case-based reasoning process.

4 The CBR-LIME Method

As explained in the previous section, instead of using the default LIME setup, its configuration can be optimized in order to achieve higher performance. Here, an image-specific configuration of these parameters is critical in order to obtain good explanations. In our approach, we will consider the parameters to configure the LIME method listed in Table 1. In this table we have selected those parameters with a higher impact in the final explanation after a preliminary evaluation based on the results obtained by the LIME implementation provided by the authors[1]. Figure 1 illustrates the impact of these parameters, showing the resulting explanations for a given image when applying different LIME configurations. In this case, the underlying neural network classifier identifies the

[1] https://github.com/marcotcr/lime.

image as "ski". However, the visual explanations provided by LIME change significantly depending on its setup. As we can observe, the explanation generated using the default parameters (top-left pair) is not a proper choice to explain the outcome of the classifier.

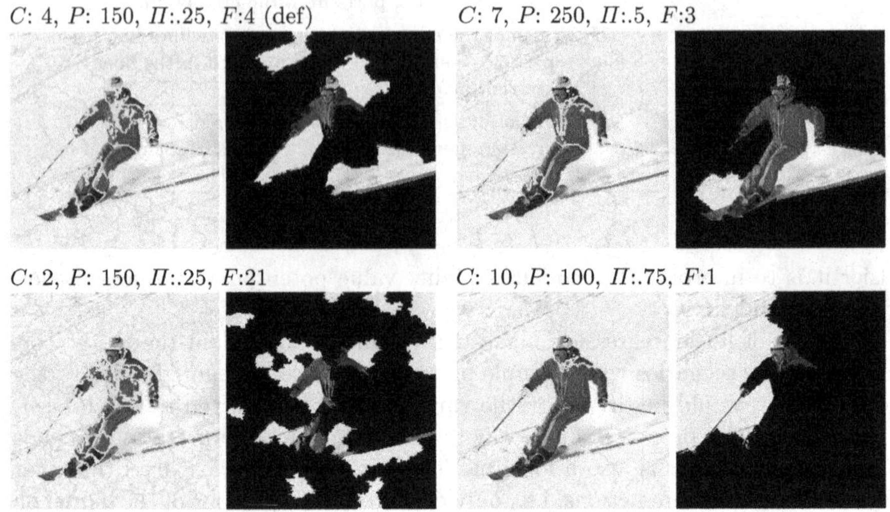

Fig. 1. Examples of LIME explanations for the same image using different setups. Each pair shows the image segmentation on the left and the explanation generated according to the parameters above. Top-left pair corresponds to the default values of the LIME implementation.

A straightforward solution is to adjust these parameters according to the predicted instance. However, as explanations depend on their utility to the user, it is not possible to find an algorithmic solution to compute the best setup. Therefore, we propose the use of a CBR approach where a case base of instances and their most suitable configuration for LIME is collected and reused to provide explanations.

4.1 Case Base Elicitation

To ease the evaluation of explanation cases with users, we have focused on the LIME method for images. The case base of images has been obtained from the dataset provided by the Visual Genome project [7]. We selected 200 images that were confidently classified by Google's Inception deep convolutional neural network architecture [21] with a predominant class (*precision* > 95%). For every image, we generated eight different explanations through the heterogeneous configuration of the variables in Table 1, plus the default configuration of LIME. Then, these nine explanations were presented to users, that could select the most suitable explanatory image, as illustrated in Fig. 2. Explanations were randomly shuffled, and the corresponding LIME configuration is not displayed to the user. Each time the user selects an explanation, a new image and its corresponding explanations are shown until the 200 images have been voted. Concretely, users were asked to select the most specific explanation, meaning that, in case of two similar images, they should choose the one with less image area.

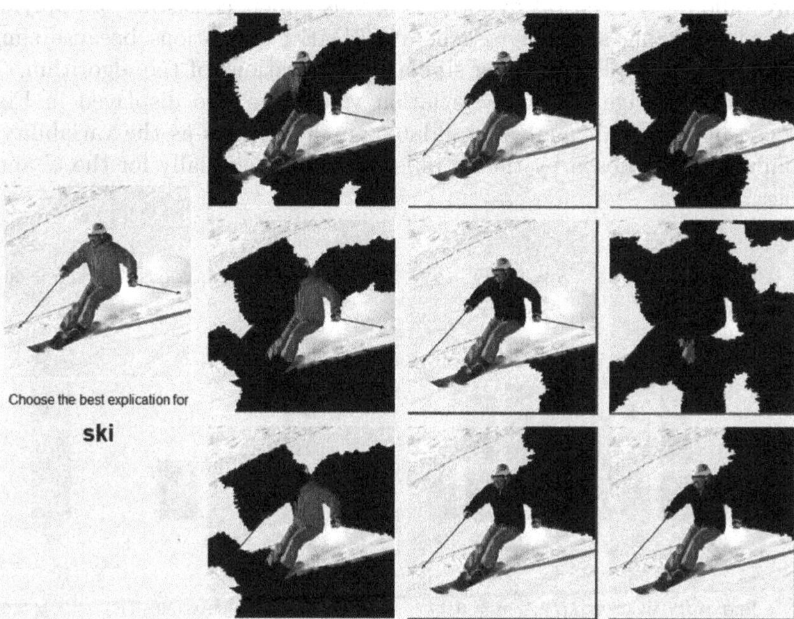

Fig. 2. Application used to vote for the best explanation and generate the case base. The original image and the majoritarian predicted class is shown on the left. Images on the right are generated through 8 random configurations of LIME plus the default setup.

After repeating this process with 15 users we collected a total of 3.000 votes (15 per image) that were used to generate the case base. The description of each case is the image itself (its pixel matrix) plus the feature's vector returned by the classifier. Then, the solution of each case is the average of the values for C, P, Π and F from the LIME configurations chosen by the users. This representation of cases can be formalized as:

$$\begin{aligned} &Case = \langle D, S \rangle \\ &where \\ &\quad D = \langle image, \boldsymbol{f} \rangle \\ &\quad S = \langle C, P, \Pi, F \rangle \end{aligned} \tag{2}$$

The analysis of the configurations voted by the users confirmed our initial hypothesis stating that the default configuration of LIME is not suitable for a general-purpose explanation. As Fig. 3 shows, the default configuration values for each parameter (red columns) are not predominant, and there is significant heterogeneity. This conclusion is also contrasted by the analysis of the variability on the user's choices. If we compute the standard deviation of the configuration values chosen for every image, we can study if users tend to select a similar configuration for LIME as the best explanation. Through this analysis, we collaterally validate the central hypothesis of this paper, consisting of applying a case-based reasoning solution to generate LIME explanations because similar images should be explained using similar configurations of the algorithm. The corresponding average standard deviation values are also displayed in Fig. 3. As we can observe, this analysis validates our hypothesis as the variability on the configurations chosen by the users is quite low, especially for the C and F variables.

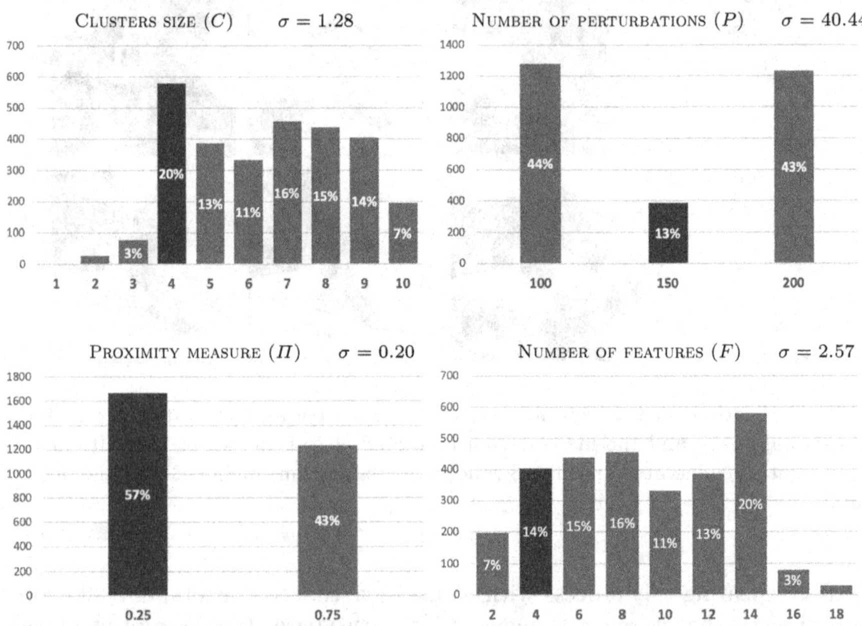

Fig. 3. Histograms describing the values (x-axis) chosen by users when voting for the best explanation. Red columns highlight the default values in LIME. Numbers inside columns reflect the percentage of explanations chosen by users that were configured with the corresponding value in the x-axis. σ values correspond to the average of the standard deviation for each image. (Color figure online)

4.2 Case-Based Explanation

Once the case base has been generated, we can define the CBR process used to find the most suitable configuration for LIME given an instance and its corresponding classification by the global model. The first step is the retrieval of similar images (and their corresponding LIME configurations) from the case base. A straightforward method to retrieve similar images is the comparison of the pixel matrix. However, in practice, this approach is not a good choice because we must focus on the objects in the image that were identified by the global model. Therefore, we have defined the retrieval process as the comparison of the feature vectors $\boldsymbol{f}$ given by the global model. This way, once we have the classification of the query image (q), we can compare its feature vector with the vectors describing the cases simply by applying a distance metric such as the Euclidean distance.

$$sim(D_q, D_x) = Eucl\_Dist(\boldsymbol{f_q}, \boldsymbol{f_x}) \tag{3}$$

Then, the k most similar images can be selected. This retrieval process is illustrated in Fig. 4, where the three most similar images (yellow border) to the query (blue border) are displayed together with their feature vectors $\boldsymbol{f}$. Here we can observe that the feature-based similarity achieves our goal of retrieving related images and avoids problems associated with pixel-based comparisons such as colour or image contrast.

Fig. 4. Application used display the similarity between images using the features identified by the global model (Eq. 3). (Color figure online)

The following step in the CBR cycle is adaptation. Here, the final configuration for the LIME algorithm is calculated as the average of the configurations of the k most similar cases. This way, we are reusing the user's experience to generate the explanation instead of applying a setup by default.

$$S_q = \underset{x \in \text{kNN}(q)}{\forall} \langle \overline{C_x}, \overline{P_x}, \overline{\Pi_x}, \overline{F_x} \rangle \tag{4}$$

Then, the generated explanation is presented to the user that can revise the configuration values in order to adjust its quality. Finally, the user can store the new generated case into the case base to close the CBR cycle. Figure 5 shows a capture of the CBR application that implements this process.

5 Evaluation

In order to demonstrate the benefits of CBR-LIME we have conducted two complementary evaluations. Firstly, an offline evaluation compares the explanatory images generated by the default LIME setup and our case-based approach using cross-validation. Secondly, we implemented an online evaluation with users similar to the experiment described in Sect. 4.1. This time, explanatory cases are shown, and users must vote the most suitable explanation. Both offline and online evaluations are presented next.

Fig. 5. Application implementing the full CBR cycle. It shows the original image, its associated perturbation and the resulting explanatory image given by the configuration obtained by CBR-LIME (Eq. 4). This configuration can be revised by the user, that also can store the generated new case into the case base.

5.1 Offline Evaluation

The goal of the offline evaluation is to compare, using an image similarity metric, the explanatory images generated by the default LIME setup and different configurations of our CBR-LIME method. Given any image in a case of our case base, we can compute the "optimal" explanatory image (according to the users' votes) through the configuration stored in its solution. Then, other explanatory images generated with different configurations of LIME can be compared to this optimal explanation in order to measure their quality. If we repeat this process throughout the whole case base using a leave-one-out approach we can evaluate the performance of the default LIME setup in contrast to the configurations provided by our CBR-LIME method (with different k values: 1NN, 3NN, etc.).

A key element in this evaluation is the similarity metric used to compare the explanatory images. There is an extensive catalogue of such metrics in the field of Image Quality Assessment (IQA) that must be carefully chosen depending on the nature of the image and the type of comparison that is required [18]. In our case, we need to compare variations of the same original image where some parts have been removed. Therefore, we need a metric that is able to compare the structural changes in the image, such as the Structural SIMilarity (SSIM) index. This metric that has demonstrated good agreement with human observers in image comparison using reference images [25]. The SSIM index can be viewed as a quality measure of one of the images being compared, provided the other image is regarded as of perfect quality. It combines three comparison measurements between the samples of x and y: luminance, contrast and structure. In our evaluation, the explanation generated with the (average) configuration chosen by the users is the image of perfect quality to compare with. In contrast, the explanations generated with other configurations of LIME (default, 1NN, 3NN, ...) are the variations that we need to find out their comparative quality.

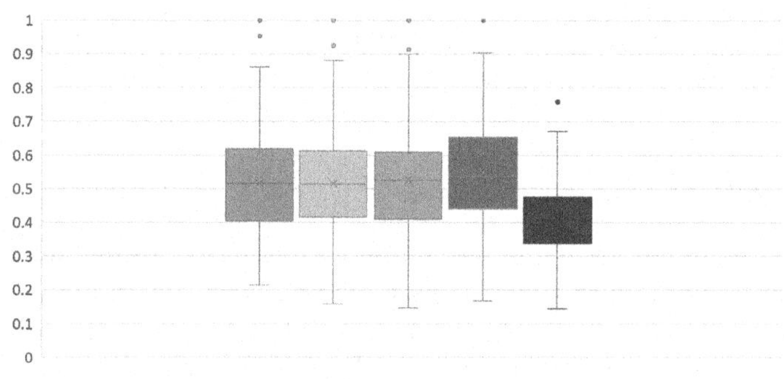

	LIME default	CBR-LIME 1NN	3NN	5NN	7NN
$\overline{SSIM}$	0.42	.51	.51	.53	.55

Fig. 6. Boxplot (top) and average SSIM values (bottom) obtained when comparing explanatory images generated with different LIME configurations.

Results are summarized in Fig. 6 that shows a boxplot (top) and the average (bottom) of the SSIM values obtained by the explanatory examples generated with different configurations. We can observe that the SSIM index is higher using the CBR-LIME method. As we have computed the SSIM index for the 200 images in the case base we can contrast the resulting series in order to validate this improvement statistically. Therefore, we have run a two-pair Wilcoxon signed-rank test comparing the SSIM indexes obtained by the default LIME setup and the values from the CBR-LIME configurations. In all cases, the improvement was statistically significant at $p < 0.05$. However, there is a little improvement when increasing the k parameter of the CBR-LIME method, finding only statistical evidence between $k = 7$ and $k = 1, 3$.

These series comparisons are graphically presented in Fig. 7 that plots the difference between the SSIM values obtained by the kNN configurations and the default LIME setup. As we can observe, the positive area (on the right side of the y-axis) is much larger than the negative, indicating that the explanations generated by CBR-LIME are more similar to the optimal explanatory image.

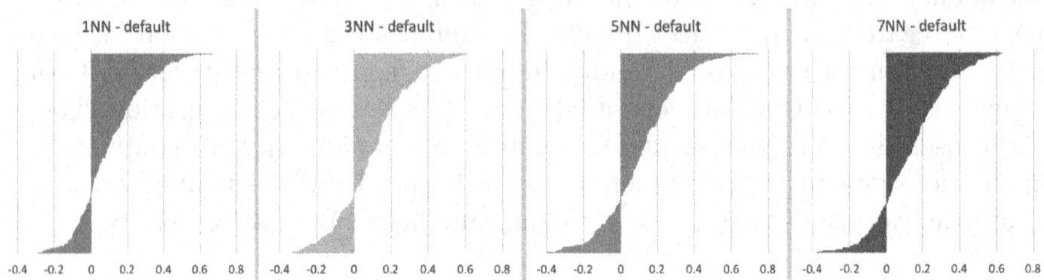

Fig. 7. Plots of the differences between the SSIM index obtained by the k-NN configurations minus the default LIME setup for every image.

5.2 Online Evaluation with Users

We have also conducted an online evaluation with users to corroborate the results of the offline analysis. In this case, users had to choose between two explanatory images: one is generated with the default LIME setup, and the other generated from the configuration obtained by CBR-LIME[2]. The application used to conduct this evaluation (Fig. 8 left) shows the original image, the classification

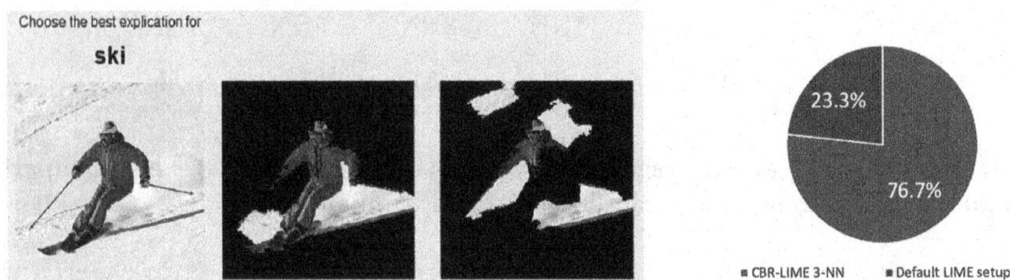

Fig. 8. (left) Application used in the online evaluation where users have to vote for the best explanation comparing the images generated by the default LIME setup and the CBR-LIME configuration. (right) Percentage of votes given by the users to each alternative (1600 total votes).

[2] Explanations were generated using 3-NN as there are no significant changes with other k values.

given by the global model, and the two explanatory images. One more time, this application shuffles the images to avoid any kind of bias in the users' choices, and the voting process must be repeated for all the images in the case base.

After collecting 1600 votes, results corroborate the benefits of CBR-LIME, as 76.7% of the images selected by the users as the best explanation were generated using the configuration provided by our method.

6 Conclusions and Future Work

This paper presents a Case-based reasoning method that takes advantage of human knowledge to generate explanations. Concretely, we have defined and evaluated a CBR solution to the problem of configuring the well-known LIME algorithm for images. This algorithm attempts to understand a global black-box classification model by perturbing the input of data samples. However, this method applies a generic setup for any image, that leads to inadequate explanations as demonstrated in this paper through an evaluation performed with 200 images and 15 users. This evaluation let us collect a case base of images and their associated "optimal" LIME configurations according to the users. From this case base, we can implement a CBR-LIME method where, given a new query image, similar images are retrieved, and their corresponding configurations are reused to generate an explanation through the LIME algorithm.

To validate CBR-LIME, we have conducted two complementary evaluations. The offline evaluation compares through cross-validation the explanatory images generated by the default LIME setup and the configurations obtained by CBR-LIME to the "optimal" explanation according to the users. To compare the images, we use the SSIM image comparison index, that is a reference method in image quality assessment, able to compare variations of the original image. The results of the offline evaluation demonstrated that CBR-LIME improves up to 13% the similarity of the generated images with the optimal explanation. Then, we conducted an online evaluation with real users in order to corroborate these results. In this case, users had to choose between two explanations for the same image, one generated with the default LIME setup, and the other with CBR-LIME. Again, the results confirmed the benefits of the later as it obtained 76% of the votes.

This paper leaves many open lines for future work. Firstly, we would like to explore the impact of other configuration parameters of LIME that were considered initially as less relevant to generate the explanation. For example, the is a ratio threshold in the Quisckshift algorithm that defines the trade-off between colour importance and spatial importance to create image clusters. This parameter was not included in CBR-LIME because initial evaluations did not demonstrate a significant impact on the performance of the method. However, this must be methodologically validated.

The combination of these parameters as the solution of the cases also requires further evaluation. Obviously, during the case base elicitation process, users did not choose the same best explanation for a particular image. We, therefore, obtained several LIME configurations for each image, that were averaged to compute the final solution of the case. Thus, other alternatives may be considered and evaluated, i.e., the median value or just selecting the most voted configuration.

We must also analyze the impact of the case base quality in the explanation process regarding cold-start scenarios where no similar images are available in order to find out the minimum similarity threshold and class distributions required to provide good explanations. Also, our evaluation only includes images that are confidently classified by the neural network, so we need to evaluate the impact of incorrect or ambiguously classified images. Additionally, the impact of user bias in the case base elicitation and evaluation must be carefully analyzed too.

Another relevant line of future work is the improvement of the similarity metric. Equation 3 does not take into consideration the pixel matrix of the image to retrieve similar cases. However, it was our initial idea, and we tested the SSIM index and other feature matching methods like FLANN [20] as similarity metrics. Unfortunately, results were disappointing due to the variability of the images in the case base. So we discarded the pixel matrix comparison and focused on the similarity of the image features. Nevertheless, further research is required in order to enhance the similarity metric by including pixel-based comparisons.

An open implementation of CBR-LIME in Phyton is available at:
https://github.com/UCM-GAIA/CBR-LIME.

References

1. Breiman, L.: Random forests. Mach. Learn. **45**(1), 5–32 (2001). https://doi.org/10.1023/A:1010933404324
2. Doyle, D., Cunningham, P., Bridge, D.G., Rahman, Y.: Explanation oriented retrieval. In: Funk, P., González-Calero, P.A. (eds.) Advances in Case-Based Reasoning, ECCBR 2004. Lecture Notes in Computer Science, vol. 3155, pp. 157–168. Springer, Heidelberg (2004). https://doi.org/10.1007/978-3-540-28631-8_13
3. Friedman, J.H.: Greedy function approximation: A gradient boosting machine. Ann. Statist. **29**(5), 1189–1232 (2001). https://doi.org/10.1214/aos/1013203451
4. Gates, L., Kisby, C., Leake, D.: CBR confidence as a basis for confidence in black box systems. In: Bach, K., Marling, C. (eds.) Case-Based Reasoning Research and Development, ICCBR 2019. Lecture Notes in Computer Science, vol. 11680, pp. 95–109. Springer, Cham (2019). https://doi.org/10.1007/978-3-030-29249-2_7
5. Goldstein, A., Kapelner, A., Bleich, J., Pitkin, E.: Peeking inside the black box: visualizing statistical learning with plots of individual conditional expectation. J. Computat. Graph. Stat. **24**(1), 44–65 (2015). https://doi.org/10.1080/10618600.2014.907095
6. Keane, M.T., Kenny, E.M.: How case-based reasoning explains neural networks: A theoretical analysis of XAI using post-hoc explanation-by-example from a survey of ANN-CBR twin-systems. In: Bach, K., Marling, C. (eds.) Case-Based Reasoning Research and Development, ICCBR 2019. Lecture Notes in Computer Science, vol. 11680, pp. 155–171. Springer, Heidelberg (2019). https://doi.org/10.1007/978-3-030-29249-2_11

7. Krishna, R., et al.: Visual genome: connecting language and vision using crowdsourced dense image annotations (2016). https://arxiv.org/abs/1602.07332
8. Leake, D.B., McSherry, D.: Introduction to the special issue on explanation in case-based reasoning. Artif. Intell. Rev. **24**(2), 103–108 (2005). https://doi.org/10.1007/s10462-005-4606-8
9. Li, O., Liu, H., Chen, C., Rudin, C.: Deep learning for case-based reasoning through prototypes: a neural network that explains its predictions. In: McIlraith, S.A., Weinberger, K.Q. (eds.) Proceedings of the Thirty-Second AAAI Conference on Artificial Intelligence, AAAI-18. pp. 3530–3537. AAAI Press (2018)
10. Lipton, Z.C.: The mythos of model interpretability. Commun. ACM **61**(10), 36–43 (2018). https://doi.org/10.1145/3233231
11. Lundberg, S.M., Lee, S.I.: A unified approach to interpreting model predictions. In: Guyon, I., Luxburg, U.V., Bengio, S., Wallach, H., Fergus, R., Vishwanathan, S., Garnett, R. (eds.) Advances in neural information processing systems, **30**, pp. 4765–4774. Curran Associates, Inc. (2017)
12. Miller, T.: Explanation in artificial intelligence: Insights from the social sciences. CoRR abs/1706.07269 (2017). http://arxiv.org/abs/1706.07269
13. Molnar, C.: Interpretable Machine Learning (2019). https://christophm.github.io/interpretable-ml-book/
14. Ribeiro, M.T., Singh, S., Guestrin, C.: "why should i trust you?": explaining the predictions of any classifier. In: Proceedings of the 22nd ACM SIGKDD International Conference on Knowledge Discovery and Data Mining, pp. 1135–1144. Association for Computing Machinery, New York, NY, USA (2016). https://doi.org/10.1145/2939672.2939778
15. Ribeiro, M.T., Singh, S., Guestrin, C.: Anchors: High-precision model-agnostic explanations. In: McIlraith, S.A., Weinberger, K.Q. (eds.) Proceedings of the Thirty-Second AAAI Conference on Artificial Intelligence, AAAI-2018, pp. 1527–1535. AAAI Press (2018). https://www.aaai.org/ocs/index.php/AAAI/AAAI18/paper/view/16982
16. Roth-Berghofer, T., Richter, M.M.: On explanation. Künstliche Intelligenz KI **22**(2), 5–7 (2008)
17. Sanchez-Ruiz, A.A., Ontanon, S.: Structural plan similarity based on refinements in the space of partial plans. Computat. Intell. **33**(4), 926–947 (2017). https://doi.org/10.1111/coin.12131
18. Sheikh, H.R., Sabir, M.F., Bovik, A.C.: A statistical evaluation of recent full reference image quality assessment algorithms. IEEE Trans. Image Process. **15**(11), 3440–3451 (2006). https://doi.org/10.1109/TIP.2006.881959
19. Sørmo, F., Cassens, J., Aamodt, A.: Explanation in case-based reasoning-perspectives and goals. Artif. Intell. Rev. **24**(2), 109–143 (2005). https://doi.org/10.1007/s10462-005-4607-7
20. Suju, D.A., Jose, H.: Flann: Fast approximate nearest neighbour search algorithm for elucidating human-wildlife conflicts in forest areas. In: 2017 Fourth International Conference on Signal Processing, Communication and Networking (ICSCN), pp. 1–6, March 2017. https://doi.org/10.1109/ICSCN.2017.8085676
21. Szegedy, C., et al.: Going deeper with convolutions. In: Computer Vision and Pattern Recognition (CVPR) (2015). http://arxiv.org/abs/1409.4842
22. Vedaldi, A., Soatto, S.: Quick shift and kernel methods for mode seeking. In: Forsyth, D., Torr, P., Zisserman, A. (eds.) Computer Vision - ECCV 2008, pp. 705–718. Springer, Heidelberg (2008)

23. Weber, R.O., Johs, A.J., Li, J., Huang, K.: Investigating textual case-based XAI. In: Cox, M.T., Funk, P., Begum, S. (eds.) Case-Based Reasoning Research and Development, ICCBR 2018, Proceedings. Lecture Notes in Computer Science, vol. 11156, pp. 431–447. Springer, Cham (2018). https://doi.org/10.1007/978-3-030-01081-2_29
24. Weld, D.S., Bansal, G.: The challenge of crafting intelligible intelligence. Commun. ACM **62**(6), 70–79 (2019). https://doi.org/10.1145/3282486
25. Zhou, W., Bovik, A.C., Sheikh, H.R., Simoncelli, E.P.: Image quality assessment: from error visibility to structural similarity. IEEE Trans. Image Process. **13**(4), 600–612 (2004). https://doi.org/10.1109/TIP.2003.819861

A User-Centric Evaluation to Generate Case-Based Explanations Using Formal Concept Analysis

Jose Luis Jorro-Aragoneses(✉), Marta Caro-Martínez(✉), Belén Díaz-Agudo(✉), and Juan A. Recio-García(✉)

Department of Software Engineering and Artificial Intelligence, Instituto de Tecnologías del Conocimiento, Universidad Complutense de Madrid, Madrid, Spain
{jljorro,martcaro,belend,jareciog}@ucm.es

Abstract. Recommender systems are useful to find relevant products for a certain user. Some recommender techniques based on models, for example, Matrix Factorization, act as a black box for users. Explanations for recommender systems are useful to make recommendations more effective and help the users to trust the system and understand why certain items have been recommended. In this paper, we propose a post-hoc model-agnostic explanation system for MF recommendations based on Case-Based Reasoning and Formal Concept Analysis. We have conducted an experimental evaluation with real users to define what are the most useful explanation features that allow users a better understanding of the system recommendation.

Keywords: Explainable Artificial Intelligence · Case-based explanations · Recommender systems · Formal Concept Analysis

1 Introduction

In recent years, there has been an increasing interest in *Explainable Artificial Intelligence* (XAI) [1,9,14,18] to make AI algorithms comprehensible for the final user. Explanations in recommender systems have also been an area of active research [2]. Explanations in RS improve users' trust in the recommended products [3,21,23,27]. Besides, explanations can persuade users to buy a recommended product [13,29]. Content-based recommenders are more transparent, or understandable for users, as they can make use of explanations based on the user profile or the products with similar features [17]. However, collaborative filtering techniques are considered as black-boxes as they are based on training models with the user ratings [25] that are not easily interpretable.

Supported by the UCM (Research Group 921330), the Spanish Committee of Economy and Competitiveness (TIN2017-87330-R) and the fundings provided by Banco Santander in UCM (CT17/17-CT17/18) and (CT42/18-CT43/18).

I. Watson and R. Weber (Eds.): ICCBR 2020, LNAI 12311, pp. 195–210, 2020.
https://doi.org/10.1007/978-3-030-58342-2_13

The research conducted in this paper is related to our previous work [16]. In our previous work, we demonstrated that the latent factors obtained from the matrix factorization process are useful as properties to build a case base of items that are related to the recommended item. This methodology takes into account the users' experiences. The latent factors are obtained from the ratings the users made. Furthermore, the case base is only built with the items with which the target user has interacted. From this case base, using the cosine similarity metric, we retrieve a set of *explanatory items* for the final user. However, the latent factors are not interpretable, and it is not so understandable why the explanatory items are similar to the recommended one. We observed that these items usually have not got similar features at first sight. For instance, with our system, we got two movies that are not very similar: Star Wars and The Shawshank Redemption. In the current paper, we aim to build more informative explanations and propose an approach based on Formal Concept Analysis (FCA) to build a property-based explanation. We use the general approach described in [6], where FCA is used to capture explanation knowledge from a set of objects and attributes. In this paper, to explain why the explanatory items obtained with matrix factorization support the recommendation, we apply FCA to get the maximal common groupings among the set of explanatory items. FCA is an approach typically used to explain data employing lattice theory [11]. In the past, our research group has also used FCA to enrich the CBR processes [7,8].

In this analysis, we want to demonstrate the following hypotheses:

H1 Users prefer explanations where they can see the most specific common features between the recommended item and the explanatory items. These specific features are the discriminating ones that describe the items accurately.

H2 Grouping items to explain a recommendation using the most discriminating features increases users' understanding of the recommended item. The grouping helps users to relate the common features among them.

The verification of the hypotheses is related to users' opinions. Therefore, we have made a questionnaire with real users where they select the most understandable explanations for a recommendation. This questionnaire allows us to determine the essential features to show to users and design the final explanation system. Furthermore, this questionnaire will help us to achieve a more effective, transparent, and trustworthy explanation system.

The rest of this paper is organized as follows. Section 2 reviews related work about explanations for recommender systems. Next, Sect. 3 describes the recommender system and how to generate explanations for a recommendation using a two-step process: retrieve explanatory items from the matrix factorization knowledge and create and travel the FCA lattice to create comprehensive explanations. Section 4 explains the experiment to determine which is the type of explanation more attractive for users. Finally, Sect. 5 concludes the paper and describes some lines of future work.

2 Related Work

Currently, there is an active research line to generate explanations in recommender systems. In the state-of-the-art, we can encounter several works that have studied this problem. The work presented in [29] contains a survey about explanation properties and aims in recommender systems, for example, transparency and effectiveness. Based on these aims, we find some studies that propose different visualization modes to improve the explanations [12,15]. Taking into account the transparency in recommender systems, we can divide them in *white-box* and *black-box* conceptual models [15]. The white-box models are transparent to users; therefore, the explanations can be generated focusing on the process of recommender technique used. An example is [28], which proposes an explanation system using the similarity functions from the recommender system.

However, the most challenging task in XAI is to generate explanations for black-box models [22]. The black-box models cannot convey the recommendation process to users. In these situations, it is necessary to generate explanations independently of the model. One of the most studied black-box techniques in recommender systems is collaborative-filtering based on models, like matrix factorization. For example, [30] uses matrix factorization and sentiment analysis on user reviews to make explanations in recommendations. In [32], the authors describe an explanation proposal for matrix factorization that takes into account the most critical items in the prediction of the ratings and the users' opinions. In the work [31], we can find an explanation approach that uses the latent factors as the knowledge source. Our current work proposes using information from latent factors to build a CBR system that retrieves explanatory items. Many examples use CBR systems to generate explanations. In [20], we observe a CBR system proposal to explain recommendations, using reviews from users and user profiles to build the case base. Other related work from our research group is [5], where we proposed a CBR system to explain black-box recommendations using interaction graphs to get the explanatory items. Another example is [24], where we described an approach to visualize explanations for group recommendations using social information.

As we have introduced, this paper extends previous research [16], where we studied how to explain the recommendation results for the *Non-Negative Matrix Factorization* (NMF) [10] algorithm. We proposed an item-based explanation system to obtain a set of items from the NMF model. Using the latent factors for each user and her ratings, we build a case base with the description of each item.

3 Explanation System

In Artificial Intelligence, the so-called *black-box* techniques, such us Neural-Networks, are not interpretable for users. Some recommender techniques, like the models obtained by the matrix factorization algorithm, are also considered

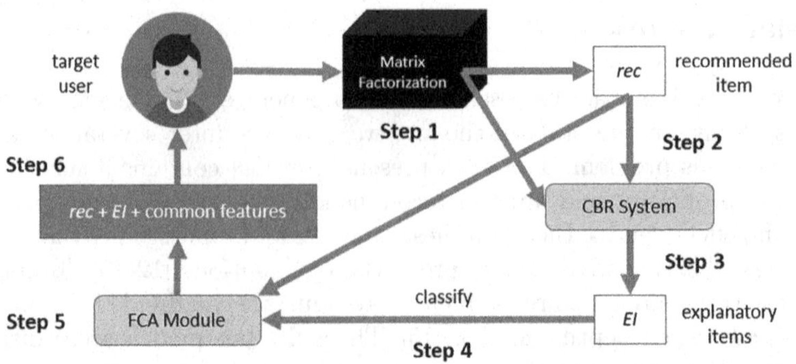

Fig. 1. General overview of the case-based explanation approach using FCA

as black-boxes because it is difficult to understand the reasons behind a recommendation, and what is the meaning of matrices values used to generate the recommendation.

Taking into account that the model is a black-box, we propose an item-based explanation to justify a recommendation. Using CBR, it chooses a set of items that have similar conditions, based on the matrix factorization model, to the recommended item and uses them as explanatory items. Our method is a post-hoc model-agnostic explanation system since we used introspective knowledge: we use the recommendation model to justify the recommendation [4,19]. Moreover, the use of CBR relates with the knowledge from the user experience: the latent factors used to describe the cases in our case base are obtained from the previous experiences that are reflected in the user ratings. On the other hand, we build the set of items, or case base, with the description of the items with which the target user has interacted. In Fig. 1, we show an overview of our proposal, that can be structured according to the following steps:

Step 1 MF algorithm recommends the item *rec* for the target user.
Step 2 Build the case base using the latent factors, which reflects the user experience in terms of ratings and interactions.
Step 3 Retrieve a set of explanatory items EI using the cosine similarity measure.
Step 4 Build the FCA lattice using $G{=}\{rec \cup EI\}$ and a subset of attributes M. The lattice built is unique for a recommendation because it contains *rec* and EI. We classify *rec* in the lattice, so we can know its features.
Step 5 Travel the lattice to get different explanations from the concepts and dependencies, getting common features between *rec* and EI. Travel the lattice means that we traverse the lattice from the top to the bottom to explore the common nodes (attributes) that join two items.
Step 6 Show the explanation to the target user.

Next, we detail how our system works to retrieve all the possible explanations, using CBR and FCA. In Sect. 3.1, we describe our system Step 1. Next, we detail the Steps 2 and 3 in Sect. 3.2. Later, we depict the Steps 4 and 5 in Sect. 3.3. Finally, what we have to show in Step 6 to design our system is the goal of this work and is verified in the user-centric evaluation in Sect. 4.

3.1 Matrix Factorization Recommender System

In collaborative filtering recommender systems, one of the main problems is the sparsity in the set of ratings. It means that, usually, users only rate a small set of items. Therefore we do not have got information about a large number of users and items. One of the most popular methods to resolve this problem is the matrix factorization model [10], which is based on the use of latent factors to predict the unknown ratings. The main goal of this algorithm is to complete the matrix $R \in \mathbb{R}^{U \times I}$ that contains the ratings that users (U) have made on items (I). It defines two new matrices: $P \in \mathbb{R}^{U \times N}$, which relates each user in U to a set of latent factors of N dimensionality, and $Q \in \mathbb{R}^{N \times I}$, that relates the items in I to the same latent factors. The dot product of both matrices returns the $R' = PQ^T$ matrix, which contains the rating estimation for each user and each item. The values in P and Q are learned by the approach of *stochastic gradient descent*. In this approach, the algorithm calculates the error between the known ratings ($r_{ui} \in R$) and its prediction ($r'_{ui} \in R'$). Then, it modifies the value in P and Q in the opposite direction of the gradient. When this error is minor than bias, the algorithm finishes, and we can use both matrices to suggest recommendations.

The main problem in this algorithm is its opacity, i.e., it is difficult to understand the meaning of the latent factors. We have used them to select a set of items that can explain a recommendation for a specific user. The next section describes the CBR system that uses the information in P and Q to retrieve the explanatory items. Next, we apply the FCA method to generate the final explanations.

3.2 Retrieving Explanatory Items

As we have mentioned, in previous work, we proposed a methodology that uses dimensions from matrix factorization latent factors to obtain a set of explanatory examples for a recommendation [16].

As we described before, P relates users (U) to N-dimension of latent factors. Values in P may be considered as the user preferences for each dimension. It occurs similarly in Q, which relates the N-dimension to items (I). In this case, values in Q could be considered as to how items are represented in each dimension. Our methodology consisted of building new descriptions for the items using the information calculated in both matrices. To do that, we created the matrix Q^u for each user. It transforms the values in Q into a collection of vectors $Q^u = \{q^u_1, \ldots, q^u_M\}$ where each $q^u_i = p_u q_i$ represents the description of an item multiplied by the user preferences.

These vectors represent the features of each item based on preferences from a specified user and constitute the case base for our system. Therefore, explanations are personalized: the case base is an item description from the point of view of this user.

It is not possible to understand the meaning of these values; however, we can use the information saved in Q^u to define a similarity metric to obtain items with a similar description. We proposed applying the cosine similarity function to compare the items using the Q^u description. The main advantage of this function is that it does not take into account the vector magnitude, and we do not need to study the meaning of the values in each dimension. Then, the function defined to search the similar items from a recommendation is as follow:

$$sim^{Q^u}(i, rec) = cos(q_i^u, q_{rec}^u) = \frac{q_i^u \cdot q_{rec}^u}{|q_i^u| \cdot |q_{rec}^u|} \tag{1}$$

It selects the most similar items from the items rated by the user in the past. The result is the explanatory item set (EI). The next step is to apply the FCA methodology to obtain all possible features in common between EI, and the item recommended (rec). It allows us to generate all possible explanations for the recommended item.

3.3 Generating Explanations Using FCA

In [6], we proposed the use of *Formal Concept Analysis* (FCA) as a general methodology to generate explanations for recommender systems based on different ways to build and travel the concept lattice. FCA extracts the formal concepts that relate the items according to the shared properties. There are three elements in a formal concept $< G, M, I >$ where G is the set of objects, M is the set of attributes of objects, and I is the relation between objects and attributes. The use of FCA helps in finding the knowledge structure and we demonstrated how this knowledge is useful as the explanation knowledge applied to different sets of items and properties. Note that the sense of the term explanation here refers to *justification*. The explanation system based on FCA attempts to make comprehensible the result of a black-box recommender system. Our previous work was oriented to explanations of collaborative filtering approaches that recommend items based on users' past behavior and ratings. We proposed different approaches that vary in the way we build and travel the lattice. For example, we create the *user profile lattice*, building a lattice using the set of the user personal best-rated items. This lattice can be used itself to explain the user profile and the diversity of her preferences and let her refine her ratings or understand why a particular item has been recommended. The explanation lattice is computed for each user, and it can be reused to generate personalized explanations for different recommendation processes. Besides, we also explore how the dependencies between attributes and the maximal groups of items are useful as explanation knowledge in different ways: *item-style*, *property-style* and *dependency style*. The *FCA-based explanation algorithm* (see Algorithm 1) allows us to organize the knowledge on the user preferences and obtain the vocabulary to explain the user profile. According to this profile, we are able to justify why an item has been recommended using either the *item-style* explanation, which includes the similar items rated by the user; the *property-style* explanation, which describes the properties of the formal concepts regarding the common attributes; and the *dependency-style* explanation, that includes the description of the association rules elicited by the FCA. The general process runs as follow:

Step 1 Select the M_u (attributes) and G_u (items) sets used to build the lattice.
Step 2 Apply FCA and evaluate and refine the resulting lattice.
Step 3 Choose between explaining the user profile or explain a specific recommendation (rec), so we classify rec to generate more specific explanations.
Step 4 Generate explanations from textual templates filled with the corresponding elements obtained while travelling the lattice *item-style, property-style, dependency-style.*

Algorithm 1: Travelling the lattice to build Explanations

Input: G_u, M_u, I_u, rec, sel_g, sel_m
Output: *Expl-item, Expl-property, Expl-dependency*

$G_u{}' = sel_g(G_u)$
$M_u{}' = sel_m(M_u)$
$Ret = FCA(G_u{}', M_u{}', I_u)$
$C_r \leftarrow Ret.classify(rec) \parallel TOP$
Expl-item $\leftarrow \{traverseLevels(C_r.extent)\ \}$
Expl-property $\leftarrow \{traverseLevels(C_r.intent)\ )\ \}$
Expl-dependency $\leftarrow$ {obtainRules(Ret) }

In this paper, we build the FCA lattice using $G = rec \cup EI$, i.e., the recommended item and the set of explanatory items, and M, the set of attributes with at least two common attributes between rec and EI. We propose to classify rec in the formal concept lattice and using a *property style* explanation based on those common attributes. The next section describes our experiment with users to find out which relations in I are the most useful to explain a recommended item. Figure 2 shows an example, where rec is the movie entitled "E.T" and EI is the set of explanatory items obtained from latent factors of the MF algorithm. The table includes explanations for the recommendation following the Algorithm 1.

4 User-Centric Evaluation

As we have described in the previous sections, the explanation system proposed has two foundations: the explanatory items found by the CBR system and their common attributes with the recommended item that the FCA obtains. The problem here is to select those attributes that are more useful to explain the

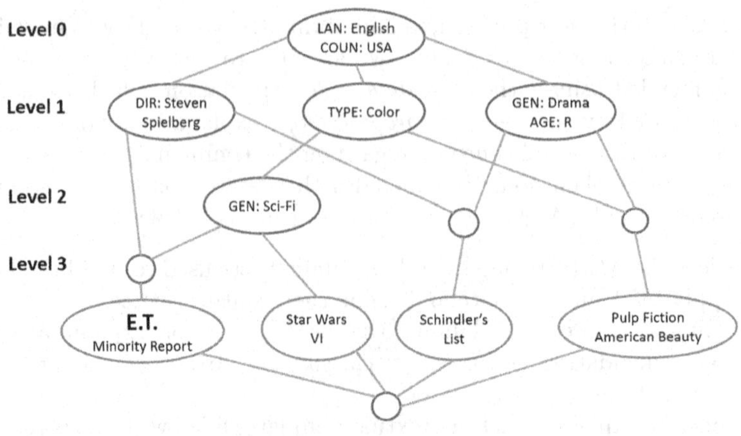

	"The system recommends you ***E.T.*** *because..."*
Level 0	*"...share LAN:English, COUN:USA with* ***Star Wars VI, Schindler's List, Pulp Fiction, American Beauty*** *and* ***Minority Report.****"*
Level 1	*"...share DIR:Steven Spielberg with* ***Minority Report*** *and* ***Schindler's List****"* *"...share TYPE:Color with* ***Minority Report, Star Wars VI, Pulp Fiction*** *and* ***American Beauty****"*
Level 2	*"...share GEN:Sci-Fi with* ***Minority Report, Star Wars VI****"*
Level 3	*"...share DIR:Steven Spielberg, GEN:Sci-Fi with* ***Minority Report****"*

Fig. 2. Example of the lattice built with $rec = \{E.T.\}$ and $EI = \{$*Minority Report, Star Wars VI, Schindler's list, Pulp Fiction, American Beauty*$\}$ to get their common features. In the table, we show the *Property-style* explanations extracted from lattice.

outcome of the recommender system. We hypothesize that the most specific common attributes will be the most effective. It will provide effectiveness to our system because it will help users to find the most interesting items, as stated in previous results [29]. Moreover, users may prefer a short explanation with a few specific attributes or a detailed one with a larger number of attributes.

The goal of this evaluation is to check whether this hypothesis is correct, taking into account the users' opinions. Eventually, we should be able to decide which is the best way to travel the lattice. Therefore, the experimental setup carried out was an online evaluation, i. e. with real users, to know the real opinions from users about the different FCA-based explanatory strategies that we can generate with our approach. Through the analysis of this feedback, we will be able to optimize our final explanation system with the most suitable strategy according to the users' preferences and the lattice's features. In consequence, we have designed a test where we showed a movie recommendation to the users, and we presented all the possible explanations that we can retrieve with our FCA-based explanation system. These explanations consist of explanatory items and the common attributes between them.

Here below, we describe the dataset used to generate the recommendations and the explanations. Later, we detail the experimental setup in Sect. 4.2. Finally, we analyze the results in Sect. 4.3.

4.1 Data

In recommender systems, one of the most popular domains is movie recommendation. Previously, we have demonstrated our recommendation methods in the movie domain [6,16], and therefore, this choice follows this line of work.

We have required two datasets: the 100K MovieLens dataset[1] and the IMDB[2] dataset. On the one hand, we need the MovieLens dataset because it includes information about the ratings provided by the users to different movies. This information was necessary to train the CBR system based on the latent factors obtained by the matrix factorization. On the other hand, the IMDB dataset was required in order to build the lattice and find the common attributes among movies.

4.2 Experimental Setup

As we explained before, the main goal in our evaluation is to select explanations that allow users to better understand a recommendation. Therefore, it is necessary to conduct an online evaluation with real users. To do that, we decided to make an online questionnaire. In most of the literature about explanations in recommender systems, authors use this type of evaluation to test their proposals [15,26]. These evaluations are more reliable than offline evaluations, allow us to reach a larger population, and are suitable instruments to measure dimensions such as transparency or trust.

The questionnaire was designed to include five recommendations where users can select multiple explanations (Fig. 3). These five recommendations were selected, trying to represent heterogeneous use cases regarding the features of the FCA lattice that the recommendation comes from. This way, we generated two small lattices with a low number of nodes (less than 5), two regular lattices (5 to 10 nodes), and a large lattice (more than 11 nodes) that is more unusual but feasible.

For each recommendation, presented as a question, we showed the recommended item and all the possible explanations obtained by our system from the corresponding lattice. Explanations contain a set of explanatory items and a sentence that describes the common attributes between them and the recommended item. Therefore, there are as many explanations as to the possible combination of nodes in the lattice that are superconcepts of the recommended item. Moreover, each explanation is presented through the enumeration of the attributes included in the considered nodes.

[1] https://grouplens.org/datasets/movielens/100k/.

[2] https://www.imdb.com/.

Fig. 3. Question 1 from the questionnaire filled in our user study.

For example, Fig. 3 presents different explanations for the recommended movie: "E.T.", obtained from the lattice we have already described in Fig. 2. This way, users have to select which explanations help them to better understand the recommendation. After distributing the online questionnaire, we collected answers from 111 users and analyzed them according to five features: depth of the top-level concept and closest concept (most specific ancestor); total concepts included in the explanation; and the total number of attributes and objects from these concepts that are shown to the user.

In the next section, we present the results obtained through this evaluation and analyze them in order to find the best explanation strategy for our FCA-based method.

4.3 Results

Results are graphically analyzed in Fig. 4. It is organized in three subfigures corresponding to (a) small lattices, (b) regular lattices, and (c) large lattice and legend. For each lattice, built for a particular recommendation, we include a table on the right with the number of votes for each explanation, highlighting

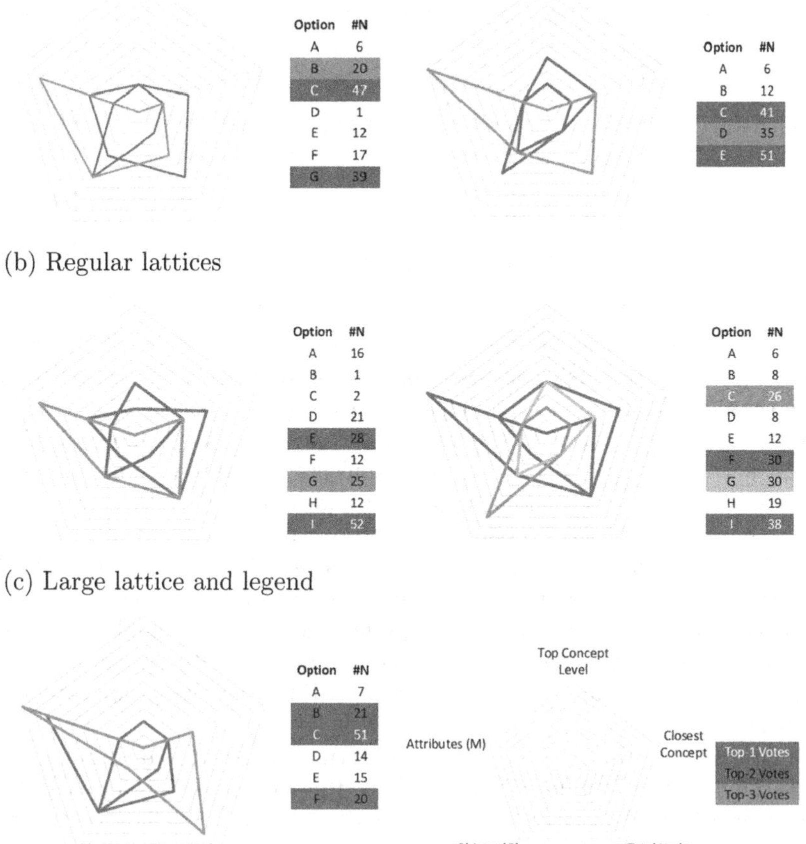

Fig. 4. Spider charts analysing the features of the most voted explanatory examples according to size the lattice: small (a), regular (b) and large (c). (Color figure online)

the three top-voted answers (top-1 blue, top-2 green, and top-3 orange). We analyzed each one of these top-3 explanations in the corresponding spider chart on the left according to the five features of the lattice (top, closest and total nodes, number of attributes, and objects), where the line color represents the number of votes obtained by the explanation.

These charts show interesting patterns that are later averaged in Fig. 5. For the small lattices (Fig. 4.a), we can see an analogous structure for the top-1 (blue) explanations, whose average is presented in Fig. 5.a. They are explanations with a large number of objects (explanatory items) but low values for the other dimensions. As small lattices correlate to explanatory objects with com-

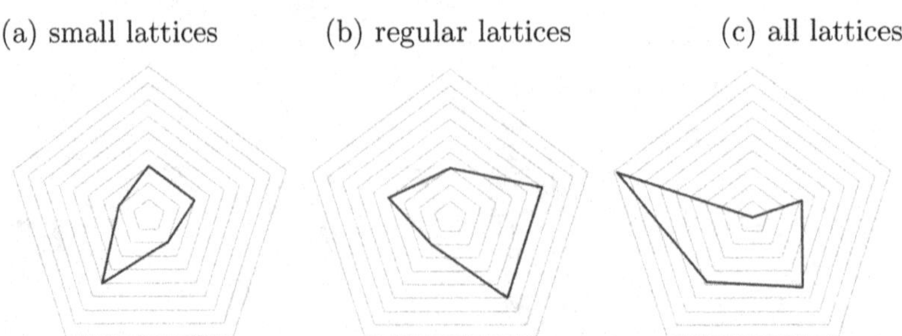

Fig. 5. Average common patterns found for small, regular and all lattices. (Color figure online)

mon features, this a consistent result because it represents that users tend to choose those explanations with similar examples.

However, the structure of the regular lattices (Fig. 4.b) follows a slightly different pattern, where the top-1 explanations are biased to include more specific/closest concepts and a larger number of nodes. This pattern is averaged in Fig. 5.b. Interpretation is clear and confirms our preliminary hypothesis: when the explanatory items are more heterogeneous, users prefer explanations that point out the common attributes captured by the most specific concepts.

Lattice in Fig. 4 also remarks on the preference for a high number of objects. However, this is an extreme case with a large number of objects and attributes it is not possible to obtain a clear correlation, and further evaluation is required, as presented in Sect. 5.

Finally, we can observe a remarkable pattern that is repeated throughout the 5 cases. This pattern is followed by one of the top-3 explanations for each lattice and is biased towards a large number of attributes and to include the top-level concept. This pattern is averaged in Fig. 5.c and should be considered as an explanation strategy "by default" that is a good option, although not optimal, if the system could not infer the properties of the lattice.

In order to validate the conclusions drawn from the evaluation of the lattices, we have conducted a complementary evaluation using linear regression analysis. The goal is to estimate the relationship between the five lattice features that describe each explanation and the votes that the explanation received from the users. This way, the number of votes is the dependent variable, and the features of the explanation are the independent variables whose relevance we want to estimate. Results are shown in Fig. 6, where we can observe the relationship between including very specific concepts in the explanation and the votes received from the users. This result validates the hypothesis of this paper and our previous analysis of the top-3 spider charts. Moreover, in the case of small lattices, the linear regression analysis also validates our conclusion regarding the importance of including a large number of explanatory items.

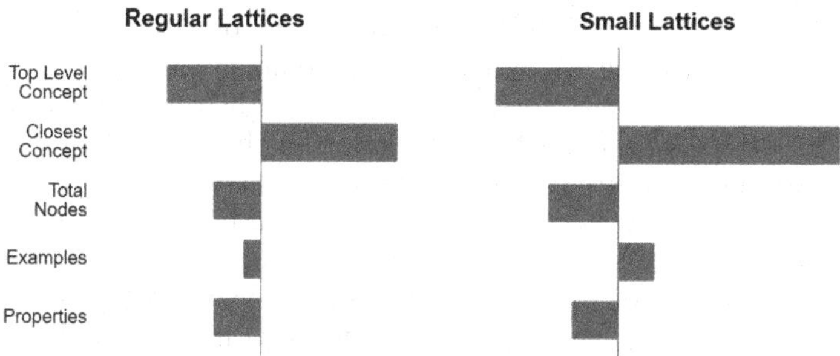

Fig. 6. Results of the linear regression analysis that relates the features of the explanations and the number of votes received from the users. X-axis represents negative (left) or positive (right) correlation.

5 Conclusions and Future Work

Nowadays, recommender systems are one of the most useful tools on the Internet. However, users do not trust the recommendations provided because they do not know how the systems work. Explanations in recommender systems are necessary to justify to users why an item is interesting for them. Therefore, the users' trust rises, and the recommendations become more effective.

In our previous works, we proposed two explanations approaches for black-box recommender systems. In the first one [16], we proposed an explanation system based on CBR that uses the latent factors from NMF as the knowledge source. As a result, we get some retrieved items that we want to present to the users as explanatory items. The problem in this solution is that we need to increase the information we present within the explanatory items because some of them could not be understood. In the second work [6], we describe a general methodology that uses FCA to show different modes of explaining a recommendation taking into account the shared properties between the items in the lattice. The goal of the current work is to apply the methodology proposed in [6] to solve the problem that we have encountered in [16]. As a consequence, we want to support the explanatory items obtained from the CBR system using the FCA methodology to make the explanation more understandable. However, using the proposed FCA methodology, we can traverse the lattice variously. We had two hypotheses to verify in the current work. Users prefer explanations with the most specific attributes that we can get from the lattice (**H1**), and grouping the explanatory items using these specific common features is effective (**H2**). Therefore, we have conducted an online evaluation to know which are the most successful strategies to generate the best explanations according to users' opinions.

Experimental evaluation shows that the strategy to travel the lattice and generate the explanation depends on its features. For small lattices corresponding to explanatory items with common features, users prefer explanations that include many examples. However, in regular lattices where explanatory items are more heterogeneous, users prefer explanations based on the most specific parent nodes. Additionally, the evaluation shows a common pattern for any kind of lattice that is not optimal but good enough that can be considered as a default strategy. This strategy is focused on presenting to the user a large number of attributes from the most specific parent nodes.

As future work, further analysis of the correlation between the properties of the lattices and the explanations chosen by users must be extended to include more use cases. Mainly, we must focus on the analysis of large lattices that are too heterogeneous to draw significant conclusions without an in-depth ad-hoc evaluation. Additionally, we plan to explore other types of FCA-based explanations such us the *item-style* and the *dependency-style* that are presented in this paper.

References

1. Adadi, A., Berrada, M.: Peeking Inside the Black-box: A Survey on Explainable Artificial Intelligence (XAI). IEEE Access **6**, 52138–52160 (2018)
2. Recommender Systems. Springer, Cham (2016). https://doi.org/10.1007/978-3-319-29659-3_9
3. Berkovsky, S., Taib, R., Conway, D.: How to Recommend?: User Trust Factors in Movie Recommender Systems. In: Proceedings of the 22nd International Conference on Intelligent User Interfaces. pp. 287–300. ACM (2017)
4. Caro-Martinez, M., Jimenez-Diaz, G., Recio-Garcia, J.A.: A Theoretical Model of Explanations in Recommender Systems. ICCBR **2018**, 52 (2018)
5. Caro-Martinez, M., Recio-Garcia, J.A., Jimenez-Diaz, G.: An algorithm independent case-based explanation approach for recommender systems using interaction graphs. In: Bach, K., Marling, C. (eds.) ICCBR 2019. LNCS (LNAI), vol. 11680, pp. 17–32. Springer, Cham (2019). https://doi.org/10.1007/978-3-030-29249-2_2
6. Diaz-Agudo, B., Caro-Martinez, M., Recio-Garcia, J.A., Jorro-Aragoneses, J., Jimenez-Diaz, G.: Explanation of recommenders using formal concept analysis. In: Bach, K., Marling, C. (eds.) ICCBR 2019. LNCS (LNAI), vol. 11680, pp. 33–48. Springer, Cham (2019). https://doi.org/10.1007/978-3-030-29249-2_3
7. Díaz-Agudo, B., González-Calero, P.A.: Classification based retrieval using formal concept analysis. In: Aha, D.W., Watson, I. (eds.) ICCBR 2001. LNCS (LNAI), vol. 2080, pp. 173–188. Springer, Heidelberg (2001). https://doi.org/10.1007/3-540-44593-5_13
8. Díaz-Agudo, B., González-Calero, P.A.: Formal concept analysis as a support technique for CBR. Knowl.-Based Syst. **14**(3–4), 163–171 (2001)
9. Došilović, F.K., Brčić, M., Hlupić, N.: Explainable artificial intelligence: a survey. In: 2018 41st International Convention On Information and Communication Technology, Electronics and Microelectronics (MIPRO), pp. 0210–0215. IEEE (2018)
10. Funk, S.: Netflix Update: Try This at Home (2006)
11. Ganter, B., Rudolph, S., Stumme, G.: Explaining data with formal concept analysis. In: Krötzsch, M., Stepanova, D. (eds.) Reasoning Web. Explainable Artificial Intelligence. LNCS, vol. 11810, pp. 153–195. Springer, Cham (2019). https://doi.org/10.1007/978-3-030-31423-1_5
12. Gedikli, F., Jannach, D., Ge, M.: How should i explain? a comparison of different explanation types for recommender systems. Int. J. Hum. Comput. Stud. **72**(4), 367–382 (2014)

13. Gkika, S., Lekakos, G.: The persuasive role of explanations in recommender systems. In: 2nd International Workshop on Behavior Change Support Systems (BCSS 2014), vol. 1153, pp. 59–68 (2014)
14. Gunning, D., Aha, D.W.: DARPA's explainable artificial intelligence program. AI Magazine **40**(2), 44–58 (2019)
15. Herlocker, J.L., Konstan, J.A., Terveen, L.G., Riedl, J.T.: Evaluating collaborative filtering recommender systems. ACM Trans. Inf. Syst. (TOIS) **22**(1), 5–53 (2004)
16. Jorro-Aragoneses, J., Caro-Martinez, M., Recio-Garcia, J.A., Diaz-Agudo, B., Jimenez-Diaz, G.: Personalized case-based explanation of matrix factorization recommendations. In: Bach, K., Marling, C. (eds.) ICCBR 2019. LNCS (LNAI), vol. 11680, pp. 140–154. Springer, Cham (2019). https://doi.org/10.1007/978-3-030-29249-2_10
17. Lops, P., de Gemmis, M., Semeraro, G.: Content-based recommender systems: state of the art and trends. In: Ricci, F., Rokach, L., Shapira, B., Kantor, P.B. (eds.) Recommender Systems Handbook, pp. 73–105. Springer, Boston (2011). https://doi.org/10.1007/978-0-387-85820-3_3
18. Miller, T.: Explanation in artificial intelligence: insights from the social sciences. Artif. Intell. **267**, 1–38 (2019)
19. Molnar, C.: Interpretable Machine Learning. Lulu. com (2019)
20. Muhammad, K.I., Lawlor, A., Smyth, B.: A Live-USER study of opinionated explanations for recommender systems. In: Proceedings of the 21st International Conference on Intelligent User Interfaces, pp. 256–260 (2016)
21. O'Donovan, J., Smyth, B.: Trust in recommender systems. In: Proceedings of the 10th International Conference on Intelligent User Interfaces, pp. 167–174 (2005)
22. Papadimitriou, A., Symeonidis, P., Manolopoulos, Y.: A generalized taxonomy of explanations styles for traditional and social recommender systems. Data Min. Knowl. Disc. **24**(3), 555–583 (2012)
23. Pu, P., Chen, L.: Trust-inspiring explanation interfaces for recommender systems. Knowledge-Based Systems **20**(6), 542–556 (2007), Special Issue On Intelligent User Interfaces
24. Quijano-Sanchez, L., Sauer, C., Recio-Garcia, J.A., Diaz-Agudo, B.: Make it personal: a social explanation system applied to group recommendations. Expert Syst. Appl. **76**, 36–48 (2017)
25. Schafer, J.B., Frankowski, D., Herlocker, J., Sen, S.: Collaborative filtering recommender systems. In: Brusilovsky, P., Kobsa, A., Nejdl, W. (eds.) The Adaptive Web. LNCS, vol. 4321, pp. 291–324. Springer, Heidelberg (2007). https://doi.org/10.1007/978-3-540-72079-9_9
26. Shani, G., Gunawardana, A.: Evaluating recommendation systems. In: Ricci, F., Rokach, L., Shapira, B., Kantor, P.B. (eds.) Recommender Systems Handbook. LNCS, pp. 257–297. Springer, Boston, MA (2011). https://doi.org/10.1007/978-0-387-85820-3_8
27. Sharma, R., Ray, S.: Explanations in recommender systems: an overview. Int. J. Bus. Inf. Syst. **23**(2), 248–262 (2016)
28. Symeonidis, P., Nanopoulos, A., Manolopoulos, Y.: MoviExplain: a recommender system with explanations. In: RecSys 2009 - Proceedings of the 3rd ACM Conference on Recommender Systems, pp. 317–320 (2009)
29. Tintarev, N., Masthoff, J.: A survey of explanations in recommender systems. In: 2007 IEEE 23rd International Conference on Data Engineering Workshop, pp. 801–810. IEEE (2007)

30. Wang, H., Fi, Q., Liu, L., Song, W.: A probabilistic rating prediction and explanation inference model for recommender systems. China Commun. **13**(2), 79–94 (2016)
31. Wang, X., He, X., Feng, F., Nie, L., Chua, T.S.: TEM: tree-enhanced embedding model for explainable recommendation. In: Proceedings of the 2018 World Wide Web Conference, pp. 1543–1552 (2018)
32. Zhang, Y., Lai, G., Zhang, M., Zhang, Y., Liu, Y., Ma, S.: Explicit factor models for explainable recommendation based on phrase-level sentiment analysis. In: The 37th International ACM SIGIR 2014, pp. 83–92 (2014)

Technical Session: Deep learning

Improved and Visually Enhanced Case-Based Retrieval of Room Configurations for Assistance in Architectural Design Education

Viktor Eisenstadt[1,2](✉), Christoph Langenhan[3], Klaus-Dieter Althoff[1,2], and Andreas Dengel[1]

[1] German Research Center for Artificial Intelligence (DFKI), Trippstadter Strasse 122, 67663 Kaiserslautern, Germany
{viktor.eisenstadt,klaus-dieter.althoff,andreas.dengel}@dfki.de

[2] Institute of Computer Science, University of Hildesheim, Samelsonplatz 1, 31141 Hildesheim, Germany

[3] Chair of Architectural Informatics, Technical University of Munich, Arcisstrasse 21, 80333 Munich, Germany
langenhan@tum.de

Abstract. This paper presents a system for case-based retrieval of architectural designs in the form of graph-based room configurations by means of applying a case preselection process using a convolutional neural network and the subsequent graph and subgraph matching on the preselected cases. An integral part of the system is its specific user interface that visualizes the architectural concepts of the system in the way familiar for the target user group. The goal of the system is to support higher architectural education with digital assistance methods by providing a tool that can be used to enhance early design phases. The evaluation showed that the system outperforms its predecessor and is suitable for use in education. The approach was developed in context of a bigger framework, however, the research can be considered self-contained and the methods transferred to the domains other than architecture.

Keywords: Case-based design · Convolutional neural network · Architecture · Room configuration · Education · Contextualization

1 Introduction

Architectural design process is a multi-faceted discipline that combines many creative phases and iterative decision-making stages in order to create the architectural unit (e.g. a floor plan or 3D model) that satisfies the requirements of the client or the teaching supervisor. Common to all kinds of the architectural design process is that they usually start with an *early conceptual design* phase during which the first design ideas are created and elaborated, for example in

I. Watson and R. Weber (Eds.): ICCBR 2020, LNAI 12311, pp. 213–228, 2020.
https://doi.org/10.1007/978-3-030-58342-2_14

the form of pen-drawn sketches that represent differently layouted variations of the architectural design that has to be detailed out in the later design phases.

Considering this early design phase essential for setting up the design direction, future space layout, and utilization of the building, many designers use past design references from digital or printed collections to find inspiration or take a look at how the current design variation is used in similar contexts. While every architect is familiar with this process, as the search for similar references has proven itself over the years as a robust tool in early as well as in later phases, it is still an absolute exception that *digital assistance methods* are used to perform this search replacing the currently usual method of manual search.

One of the reasons that using digital assistance tools is still not considered a standard procedure for early design phases is their absence in higher architectural education. Currently, the architecture students are taught to make use of pen and paper for sketching their ideas and manually search for similar design references in the digital or printed collections. A digital assistance tool, however, can speed up the search process providing methods for standardized digital sketching of architectural designs and contextualized search with semantic parameters defined by the user and/or derived by the system through analysis of the different design variations for which the references should be found.

In this work, we present a *combined digital system for support and assistance during the early design phases*, aimed specifically at *architects in academia*, i.e. architecture students, teaching personnel, and researchers from the domain of computer-aided architectural design (CAAD). The system consists of a design retrieval component, that is based on the artificial intelligence (AI) methods *convolutional neural networks* (CNN) and *case-based reasoning* (CBR), and a visual component in the form of a user interface (UI) that uses standardized methods of architectural design description to digitally configure and modify a room layout and display the retrieval results in the user-friendly way.

The goal of the research work behind the system is to help to establish AI-based digital assistance as the method of choice for designing of initial versions of floor plans among designers in academia and so help to prepare the students for digitization of early conceptual phases in the industry. The future of architectural design was already linked with the AI-based digitization [5]. The system is a result of research for the CAAD+AI projects *Metis-I* and *Metis-II*[1] and is the successor to the other design retrieval approaches of the projects.

2 Concepts and Foundations of the System

2.1 Artificial Intelligence Methods

Case-based reasoning is a methodology for analogy-driven search and adaptation of a suitable solution for the given problem. CBR is known for its robustness when dealing with feature-rich data. Data in CBR is organized in *cases* – knowledge units that are kept in a *case base*. CBR-based systems mostly implement the

[1] Funded by German Research Foundation (Deutsche Forschungsgemeinschaft, DFG).

4R CBR cycle [1] whose steps *Retrieve*, *Reuse*, *Revise*, and *Retain* are responsible for finding the most similar case, adapting its solution to the current problem and recording the new case based on evaluation of the solution.

The ability to handle knowledge-intensive data organized in particular units, makes CBR a logical choice for retrieval approaches for support of architectural design, as the knowledge base of such approaches consists of structurized architectural data entities, e.g. floor plans. Approaches, such as ARCHIE [21], PRECEDENTS [16], CBArch [7], or VAT [14] can be named as some of the essential representatives of this research direction. These approaches provided a number of foundational concepts as well as insightful experimental paradigms.

In the Metis-I project, different approaches for case-based retrieval of floor plans in the form of graphs or attribute-value-based cases, were developed and evaluated with the target user group [3,18]. The combined retrieval + UI system presented in this paper is the continuation of this CBR research direction in the Metis-II project and the evolution of the systems named above.

Convolutional Neural Networks are the sub-type of artificial neural networks, whose showcase application is image classification using machine learning (ML) methods of image convolution on multiple layers. CNNs were already applied for the architectural design and related domains as well [2,19].

2.2 Room Configuration

In the early design phases, architectural building designs are represented by abstract floor plan sketches that contain the essential space layout information only, for example, which types of rooms are available and how they are connected to each other. Shapes of the planned rooms are available in very abstract forms only (e.g. as simple rectangles or bubbles), room connections are usually represented by dashes (number of dashes stands for the type of connection). This type of representation is also known as *room configuration* or *spatial configuration* and is one of the core concepts of the early conceptual phases. In computational terms, room configuration is a graph and can be formalized using Definition 1.

Definition 1. *Room configuration is an undirected graph $G = (R, C)$ where the set of vertices $R \neq \varnothing$ represents the rooms available in the floor plan, and the set of edges $C \neq \varnothing$ represents the connections between the rooms. Each room $r \in R$ possesses at least one connection $c \in C$ to another room of the configuration.*

For the definition above, a number of room types were defined during the Metis-I project, some examples are `LIVING`, `SLEEPING`, `WORKING`, `BATH`, `CORRIDOR`, or `KITCHEN`. To complement them, a number of connection types were defined as well, e.g. `DOOR`, `WALL`, `PASSAGE`, or `ENTRANCE`. These types are based on the established architectural space description language *Space Syntax*. In Fig. 1, an example of a room configuration graph derived from an early sketch is shown.

Closely related to room configuration is the concept of *semantic fingerprints of architecture* [12], a collection of graph-based patterns for representation of semantic spatial features. Based on established topological concepts such as

Accessibility or *Adjacency* of rooms, the fingerprints (FP) can be applied as semantic search patterns during retrieval of floor plan references, acting as a similarity measure template between the query and the reference.

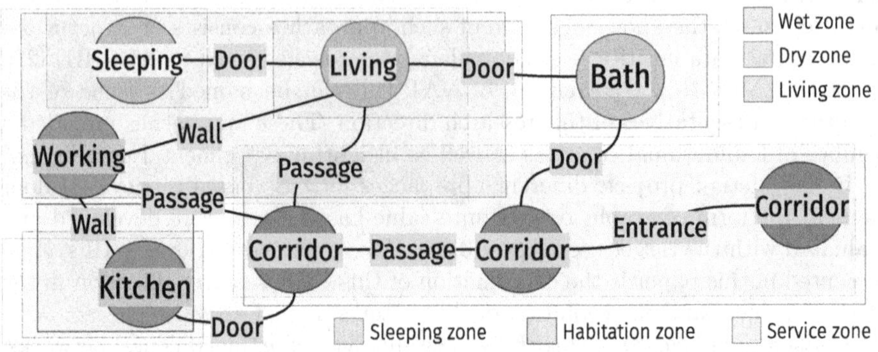

Fig. 1. An example of a room configuration graph and ARZ assignment.

2.3 Architectural Room Zones

Another essential concept that is used throughout the system presented in this paper is the paradigm of *architectural room zones* (ARZ) introduced as an extensible taxonomy for housing architecture [13]. Each such zone represents a building functionality and contains a selection of room types typical for this zone. Room types (see Sect. 2.2) were assigned to the zones, such that each room type is in at least one and maximum three ARZs. In a spatial configuration, zones can overlap, that is, each room can be part of multiple zones.

The ARZ taxonomy (see Table 1) was conceptualized for modern housing development in Germany, however, it can be extended for use in other architectural disciplines and cultural contexts. Figure 1 shows an example of zone assignment to the room types in the room configuration, including the overlapping of zones.

While room configuration and semantic FPs are established foundations for almost all approaches of the Metis projects, the concept of ARZs *was never implemented before* and makes its debut in the system presented in this paper.

2.4 Zoned Connection Map

The room configuration data for use in CBR methods is usually represented in the form of attribute-value-based cases. To extend the research range and use the room configuration cases in hybrid ML+CBR methods and so make them available for application in the modern machine learning frameworks, such as *Keras*, it is required to represent them as *numerical tensor data.* Different

Table 1. Architectural room zones with the corresponding room types.

ARZ name	Description	Room types
Wet zone	Frequent contact to water	KITCHEN, TOILET, BATH
Dry zone	No frequent contact to water	LIVING, SLEEPING, WORKING CORRIDOR, CHILDREN
Living zone	Social + free time activities	LIVING, KITCHEN
Sleeping zone	Rest + relax activities	SLEEPING
Habitation zone	Frequent human contact	LIVING, SLEEPING, WORKING KITCHEN, CHILDREN, EXTERIOR
Service zone	Rare presence of humans	CORRIDOR, TOILET, BATH STORAGE, PARKING, BUILDINGSERVICES

methods were examined by us to convert the room configuration graphs into tensors. In the end, a 2D-matrix-based data structure, the *connection map* (also: *ConnMap*), was created. It is partially inspired by the concept of *architectural morphospaces* [20] and related to the geometry-based *connectivity maps* [15].

A ConnMap is a modified adjacency matrix of the graph that replaces the relation indicators and weights with specific numerical *connection codes* that encode relations between the rooms available in the room configuration. Each code provides information about which room types are connected to each other and by which connection type. To each room and edge type, a specific number was assigned. For example, the connection code `542` represents the room types `KITCHEN` (5) and `CORRIDOR` (4) connected by a `PASSAGE` (2). The ConnMap data is then converted to a grayscale image and can be used, for example, in CNNs.

The original version of the case-to-map conversion was already used in our approach for ML+CBR-based evolution of room configurations [9]. However, the crucial issue with this version is that the ConnMap data produced by it does not allow for versatile use in ML methods as many connection codes repeat.

Therefore, to allow for manifoldly differentiable ConnMaps, it was decided to include the ARZ data in the tensor, producing the *Z-ConnMap* (zoned connection map) that adds information about zones of the connected rooms to the code. For example, the connection code `51422` represents the room types `KITCHEN` (`5`) from the *Wet zone* (`1`) and `CORRIDOR` (4) from the *Dry zone* (`2`) connected by a `PASSAGE` (2). In Fig. 2, an example of a zoned connection map can be seen.

3 Combined Retrieval + UI System

This section contains the detailed description of the combined retrieval + UI approach for digital assistance during the early phases of architectural design. The system is part of the digital assistance framework *MetisCBR*[2], it is the *next version of the retrieval component* of the framework. The crucial factor for

[2] http://veisen.de/metiscbr.

examination and implementation of methods for the next version were the results of the user study [3] (referred further as the *coordinator study*), in which the previous version of the retrieval component was evaluated against the rule-based retrieval coordination system that uses graph matching to find similar references. In the next sections, the components of the new retrieval + UI system will be presented in detail describing their mode of operation and available features. The complete graphical overview of the approach is shown in Fig. 2.

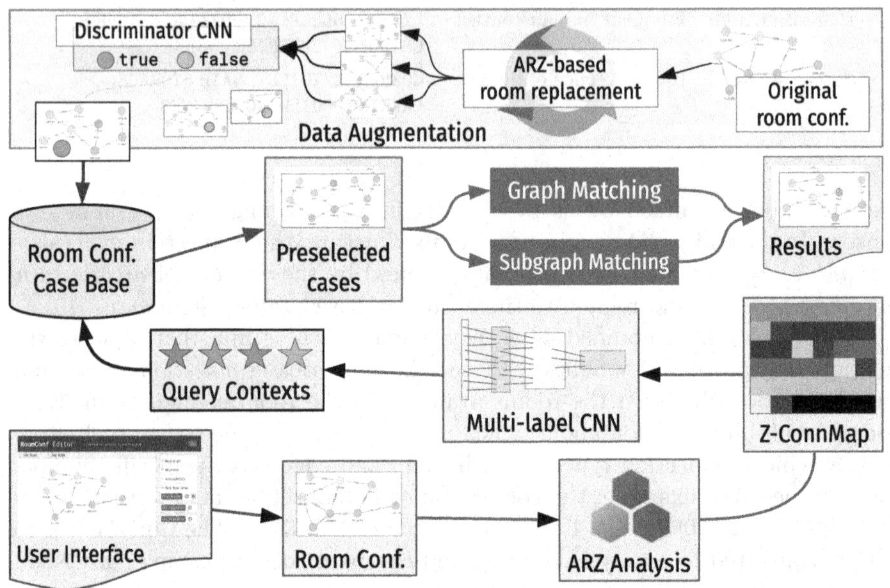

Fig. 2. Overview of the retrieval process of the combined system.

3.1 Data Augmentation

During the coordinator study as well as other evaluations of Metis-related approaches, one of the main issues was the insufficient amount of room configuration data. This precluded the systems from working with diversified references and so increasing the inspiration space. In many search scenarios, the same references were provided. Additionally, the quantitative performance tests could not be performed on big datasets. That is, for the retrieval component of the combined system, one of the foremost tasks was to examine and implement methods for *data augmentation* of cases in the room configuration case base.

To solve this task, it was decided to apply the currently widely used approach GAN (Generative Adversarial Nets) [11]. In combination with CBR, GAN was already used for the previously mentioned design evolution approach and showed good results for this task [9]. This approach consisted of three modules:

application of the *room-replacement-based* merge of query configuration with the feature-wise most similar case configurations *(Generator module)*, decision on how strong the merge should be *(Classificator)*, and rating if the results of the merge can be considered a real evolution of the configuration *(Discriminator)*.

For data augmentation, the design evolution GAN was reworked and adapted for the requirements of the combined system. While the evolution version used the non-zoned connection maps for the conversion of room configurations and training of the Discriminator CNN, the data augmentation approach makes use of the Z-ConnMaps (see Sect. 2.4) to convert graphs and train the CNN and decide if the produced design can be considered real. Additionally, the room replacement method was reworked: the classification step was skipped so that the *merge level remained constant* for all augmentations, and the room replacement method was modified in the way that a room in the query could be replaced with the room from case *only if they are in the same ARZ* (see Sect. 2.3).

We assumed that the modifications will allow for generation of a sufficiently large and diverse but at the same time structurally close to the original dataset of room configurations that can be used in the comprehensive system evaluations.

3.2 Context-Based Preselection of Cases

A paramount task for all retrieval systems is to provide the most relevant results that satisfy the expectation of the user. Especially in our case, it is also important to decrease the retrieval time as much as possible, because the graph-based cases are known for the complexity of knowledge they contain. I.e. our search strategy should return *the most relevant case references in the least possible time.*

In MetisCBR's previous retrieval component a case preselection method based on MAC/FAC [10] was used to select the most relevant references: for each query floor plan, the system looked for a certain amount of the most similar rooms and edges in the case base and then filtered out all *non-paired* floorplans, i.e. those whose elements were represented only by one entity type (i.e. either rooms or edges). The remained cases were considered relevant and ordered by the *room type distance* measure building the final result set. While this preselection method worked quite fast for a small amount of cases, there were reasonable doubts that it will take too long for a bigger amount (see Sect. 3.1).

To improve the selection of the most relevant cases, it was decided to use the Z-ConnMaps of query and cases. Using a multi-label classifier in the form of a specifically configured CNN, the system analyzes the query's Z-ConnMap and assigns labels to it, and then selects the cases from the case base that have the same labels. It can be configured how many labels should match between query and case to add the case to the set of relevant cases. The labels represent different *design contexts* that correspond to *structural*, *temporal* or *typological* properties of the room layout (see Table 2). The contexts were either defined during the Metis-II project or represent the well-known architectural concepts.

In order to train the multi-label CNN on room configuration cases in the case base, structural contexts are initially assigned to these cases using a histogram

Table 2. Currently implemented design contexts.

Type	Contexts	Explanation	×
Structural	`SparseConnections` `RoomTypeDominance`	*Number of edges < number of rooms A room type dominates the configuration*	`OR`
Temporal	`PreDesign` `FullDesign`	*Different states of the room configuration during the early design phases*	`XOR`
Typological	`SocialHousing` `StandaloneHousing` `UnknownHousing`	*Housing category of the room configuration*	`XOR`

of the room configuration's room types for the `RoomTypeDominance` context and comparing the room and edge counts for `SparseConnections`.

However, for the more important temporal and typological contexts, no heuristics could guarantee correct labels, except the labels are explicitly available in the meta data of the floor plan. If they are not available, these contexts are assigned manually by a CAAD expert and/or MetisCBR system designer.

3.3 Graph Matching

After the cases were preselected using the Z-ConnMap-based contexting, the search for similar room configurations continues with the actual similarity assessment between the query and cases in the case base using *graph matching* (also known as *graph isomorphism*). This method was selected as a superior one to the distance-measure-based sorting of cases used in the previous retrieval component (see Sect. 3.2), because it provides possibilities to match exact as well as inexact and complete as well as partial (also known as *subgraph*) structures between the graphs providing a wide range of reference recommendations.

In the combined retrieval system two different graph matching algorithms are currently used: *VF2* [8] and *Color Refinement Isomorphism (CRI)* [6]. VF2 showed the best performance in a previous evaluation [18] and was migrated to MetisCBR with extension of its tasks (e.g. inexact subgraph matching was added). CRI was tested afterwards as an alternative and showed a faster performance on the important task of pure structure matching (*without preselection*, as identical structures are very rare). The algorithms were assigned to the semantic fingerprints (see Sect. 2.2) used in the system as shown in Table 3.

At this point it should be explained in detail what we mean with the term 'inexact matching'. While exact matching matches *the structure and semantic data in the case exactly as provided in the query* (i.e. room and edge semantics as well as structure should be fully identical), the inexact type of matching applies the so-called *replacement rules* if the structure could be matched exactly but the semantics could not. In this case, room for room and connection for connection in the matched structure, the system looks if the currently compared rooms are in the same ARZ (see Sect. 2.3) and if the connections have certain type relationships. Such rooms and edges are considered *interchangeable*. The ARZ-based replacement is the new inexact matching method, while the edge replacement was already used in a similar manner in the coordinator study.

For example, `LIVING` and `SLEEPING` are interchangeable as both of them are members of the habitation zone and the dry zone, while `LIVING` and `BATH` are not interchangeable. `DOOR` and `PASSAGE` are interchangeable as both of them provide an open connection to another room, while `WALL` is a closed connection and not interchangeable with `DOOR` or `PASSAGE`. *All rooms and edges in the case should provide either exact or inexact match to be included in the final result set.*

Table 3. Currently implemented graph matching methods and semantic FPs.

Sem. Fingerprint	Algo.	Matching types	Features
`Room Graph`	CRI	Exact graphs w/o preselection	*Matches exact structure only* All semantics are ignored
`Adjacency`	VF2	Exact and inexact graphs and subgraphs	Semantics of edges are ignored *Matches rooms semantics only*
`Accessibility`	VF2	Exact and inexact graphs and subgraphs	Semantics of rooms are ignored *Matches edges semantics only*
`Full Room Graph`	VF2	Exact and inexact graphs and subgraphs	*Matches rooms as well as edges semantics*

3.4 User Interface: RoomConf Editor

Richter [17] published a seminal work that examined CBR in architecture. While Richter's main conclusion was that for architects it is not native to use AI/CBR-based digital assistance tools, our experience during the Metis projects suggests that the missing link between the architects as user group and such systems is the proper UI that visualizes relevant architectural concepts and knowledge available in the room configuration cases in designer-friendly and intuitive way.

As a basis for this hypothesis, the coordinator study [3] revealed the improper visualization of the results. Mainly, it was criticized that it was hardly possible to examine similarity between query and result/case. According to the participants of that study, this was a major issue, because architects, as the user group, are interested in the effortless examination of similarity between the current design and the reference. The participants suggested to implement a *mapping view* that shows which rooms provide the highest similarity between query and result.

To provide a solution to the knowledge visualization problem, a specific UI *RoomConf Editor*[3] was developed for MetisCBR. The editor is the successor and further development of the other UIs developed for the Metis projects, e.g. Metis-WebUI [4]. In contrast to these other UIs, but also to the room layout editors of the established architecture modeling software, an explicit goal of RoomConf

[3] Source code and live version: https://github.com/cenetp/roomconf-editor.

Editor is not to mimic the sketching of a full floor plan (i.e. incl. geometry or detailed light conditions). Instead, the editor was developed to digitize the process of creation of an abstract spatial configuration using native digital user interaction methods such as clicking and dragging and to be fully compatible to MetisCBR (incl. its other functionalities such as design process autocompletion).

The user can quickly create a graph-based room configuration with a couple of clicks using *Add Room* and *Add Edge* functions. Rooms and edges can be edited after addition and enriched with type (see Sect. 2.2) and feature data (area, label etc.). It is possible to send a request to MetisCBR for search for similar references using the semantic FPs shown in Table 3. Before retrieval, the user can select if the system should use all case graphs or just the Z-ConnMap-preselected set and examine and manipulate zones to influence the *Smallest Degree Last Coloring* algorithm-based initial ARZ analysis that delivers basis for the Z-ConnMap (see Fig. 3 and Fig. 2). After receiving the results, similarity between query and case can be examined using the mapping view (see Fig. 3).

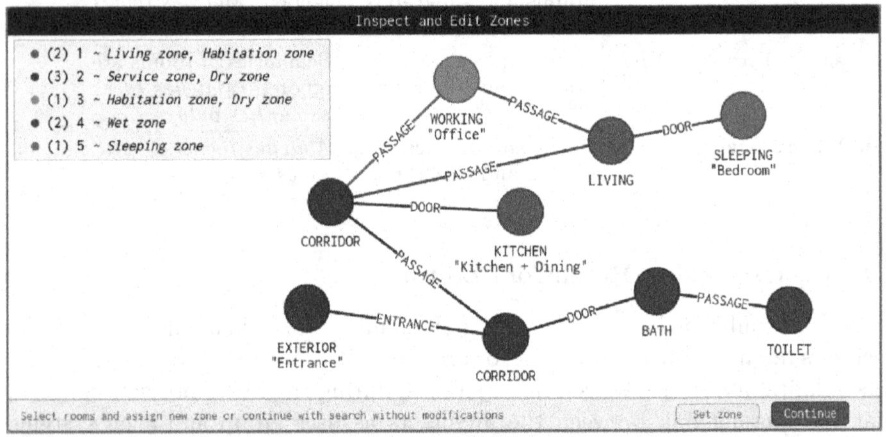

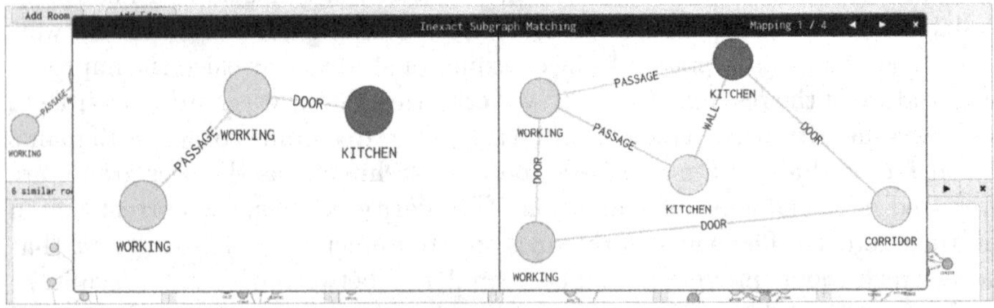

Fig. 3. RoomConf Editor. *Above:* Pre-search zone modification window. *Below:* The mapping between query (left) and case (right), where the room color codes indicate matched rooms and the edge colors show the connection direction. The user can click through different exact and inexact mappings. These are the mapping differences to Metis-WebUI that used arrows for rooms and the per-FP visualization. In the background, the query and the search results can be seen. (Color figure online)

4 Evaluation

To evaluate the combined retrieval system, a two-phase experiment was conducted that should confirm that the retrieval process was indeed improved by applying ARZs and zoned connection maps for context-based preselection in combination with exact and inexact (sub)graph matching as well as with the RoomConf Editor UI. It should also be revealed if the system can be used in the architectural design education as assistance tool for the early design phases.

Both phases of the experiment were performed on 2852 room configuration references in the case base, from which 250 were manually created ones and the rest was generated using data augmentation (see Sect. 3.1). For the context-based preselection of cases, the corresponding CNN was initially trained using the Keras framework's own data augmentator on the manual 250 cases to label the generated cases, and then the second time on the labeled generated cases.

4.1 Quantitative Analysis

In the first phase of the evaluation, the automated comparative analysis should reveal if the new system can outperform the old one in terms of performance on a set of differently complex room configuration queries. 20 queries of different complexity were used, the complexity value for each query was calculated as $|R| * |C|$ (see Definition 1). Min. complexity value was 2 and max. was 56.

Preselection Results. First of all, we were interested if the new preselection process is better than the previous one. The previous, CBR-based, process was

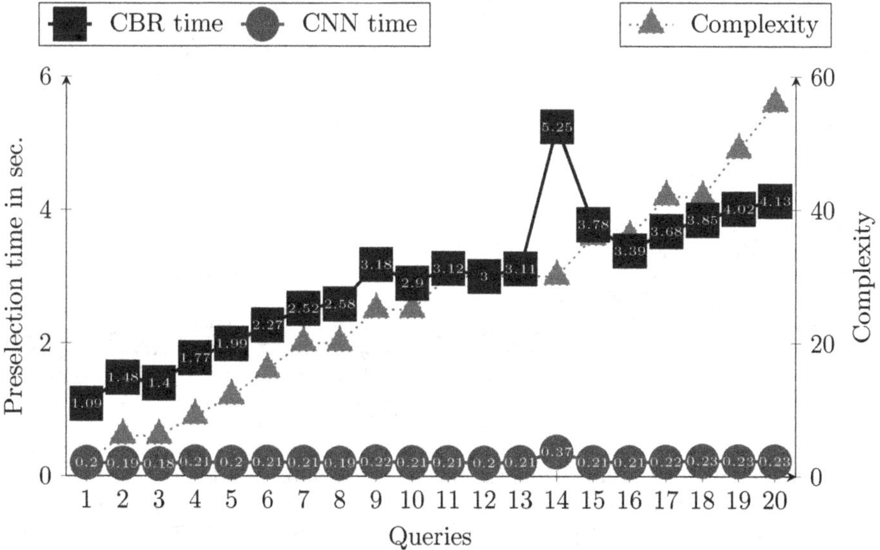

Fig. 4. Results of the preselection evaluation.

set up to use 2900 elements for both rooms and edges (i.e. at least one room and edge per case in order to ensure a chance for pairing for every floor plan). The new preselection classifier CNN was configured with 3 Conv2D layers, 3 Dropouts, and 2 MaxPoolings. Figure 4 shows the preselection evaluation results.

The results (see Fig. 4) showed that the CNN-based preselection clearly beats the CBR-based. The new preselection method remained almost constantly under 0.3 s regardless of complexity, while the old one needed more than 2 s for the majority of queries and its time increased with complexity (the times for the old method would be even higher with a higher number of pairing candidates).

Graph Matching Results. Additionally to the preselection phase, we were interested in how long the (sub)graph matching would take for the sets of relevant cases produced by both preselection methods and how many graphs will be

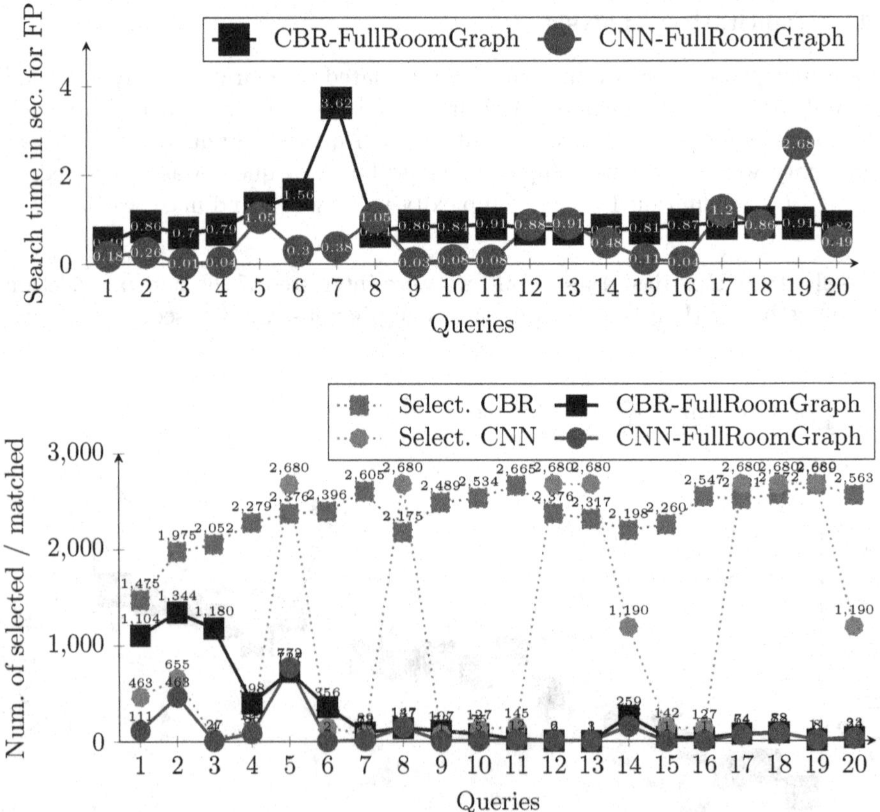

Fig. 5. Graph matching results. Upper graph shows a comparison between search times for CBR- and ARZ-preselected cases. Bottom graph shows amounts of matched graphs in relation to the amounts of preselected graphs. The semantic FP `Full Room Graph` stands representative for all tested FPs as the one with the most restrictive handling of semantics (results for other FPs are similar).

eventually matched. The time and matches were counted per semantic FP. As for `RoomGraph` no preselection is used, only VF2-based FPs were evaluated.

The results (see Fig. 5) revealed that in this phase of the quantitative evaluation, the new retrieval method showed the better performance as well. Regarding graph matching times, searching for (sub)graphs in the sets produced by the CNN-based preselection method required less time in a clear majority of queries. Similar results were achieved regarding relation of preselected/matched graphs.

All things considered, the results achieved during the quantitative experiment delivered multiple numerical evidences that the new retrieval component clearly outperforms the old one and can be safely used for the subsequent user study.

4.2 User Study

In the second part of the evaluation, a user study at the Technical University of Munich was conducted to collect feedback on potential of the new retrieval system for use in early design phases education. Eight representatives of the target group of the system, i.e. architects in academia, agreed to take part in the study. Among them were graduates and undergraduates (for example, master students with major in architecture), PhD candidates who work on their own CAAD projects but also have teaching responsibilities, and the industry partners that offer internship programs for students with CAAD-related research projects.

The participants were required to create a room configuration using the RoomConf Editor UI, initiate search processes with the CNN-based preselection and zone modification for similar references using arbitrary semantic FPs, and rate the relevance of the results using the similarity examination with the mapping view (see Fig. 3). Afterwards they should tell if they would consider to use the system for the education process of the early design phases.

The user study was performed as a free exploration session using the *thinking aloud* method. That is, the participants explained comprehensively what they do and why and how they feel about the user experience of the combined system. We used this method to provide the closest possible setup to the real-world use. *For this part of the experiment, the manually created and validated results were put before the data-augmented ones in the final result set in the user interface.*

4.3 General Results

Regarding the general pre-search use of the system, all participants provided a satisfactory feedback, RoomConf Editor was considered user-friendly, all visible concepts, such as room configuration or room and edge attributes, were recognized. An exception were the FPs, that were unknown to the industry partners. The participants were explicitly not explained what the system does and had to figure it out, all of them eventually found out the purpose of the system.

However, for improvement of the system's user experience, the participants made some suggestions. For example, it was suggested to implement multiple weighted connections and set the bubble size in relation to the area of the room.

The initial ARZ assignment by the system resulted in satisfactory feedback as well, but some of the participants wished for more explanation on the ARZ concept to the new users. Most of the participants also edited the zones to see if they can influence the retrieval process and get other results.

The system managed to leave a good impression on the assignment of design contexts as well. To evaluate this assignment, some participants tried to create untypical, non-housing, room configurations. In some of such cases, the system was irritated first, but then corrected itself when the room configuration was slightly adapted. An example is the case where the floor plan was on purpose designed as part of office building, was mistakenly classified as `StandaloneHousing` first, but then correctly classified as `UnknownHousing` after the zones were edited.

Likewise for the mapping view, the overall impression was good and the functionality was perceived as user-friendly and worthwhile for the retrieval process. Some users wished for functionality of a complete transfer of the result design to the main design area in order to continue with it and not the own design.

The relevance of the delivered results was considered good as well, placing the manually created and validated floor plans before the data-augmented ones was considered a good decision. The data-augmented results were also the main issue named by every participant: some of these results had structural problems, e.g. the room that replaced the old one did not fit to the current position.

4.4 Feedback on Use in Education

To find out if the system has potential to be used in architectural design education, the participants were explicitly asked if they would use it for their teaching and learning activities. The answers can be seen, overall, as positive, ranging from complete acceptance and wish to use the digital assistance tools in everyday academia life (for example, to accomplish homework assignments), to more moderate and critical reactions stating that the system needs to step-by-step fix the issues named above first. None of the participants declined the use of the system. Overall, it can be concluded that the combined system reached its goal.

5 Conclusion and Future Work

We presented and evaluated an AI-based digital assistance system developed for architectural design education in the area of the early conceptual design phases. A specific user interface is an inseparable part of the system and integrates deeply into its concepts visualizing them for the user. The system uses convolutional neural networks and graph matching to find similar references in a case base of room configuration graphs. The system was evaluated with a quantitative experiment and a user study. For the future, it is planned to use the feedback of the user study to improve the system and evaluate it by professional architects.

References

1. Aamodt, A., Plaza, E.: Case-based reasoning: foundational issues, methodological variations, and system approaches. AI Commun. **7**(1), 39–59 (1994)
2. Zhang, Y., Grignard, A., Aubuchon, A., Lyons, K., Larson, K.: Machine learning for real-time urban metrics and design recommendations. In: Proceedings of the 38th Annual Conference of the Association for Computer Aided Design in Architecture (ACADIA), ACADIA 2018: Recalibration. On imprecisionand infidelity, Mexico City, Mexico 18–20 October, 2018, pp. 196–205 (2018). ISBN 978-0-692-17729-7
3. Ayzenshtadt, V., et al.: Comparative evaluation of rule-based and case-based retrieval coordination for search of architectural building designs. In: Goel, A., Díaz-Agudo, M.B., Roth-Berghofer, T. (eds.) ICCBR 2016. LNCS (LNAI), vol. 9969, pp. 16–31. Springer, Cham (2016). https://doi.org/10.1007/978-3-319-47096-2_2
4. Bayer, J., et al.: Migrating the classical pen-and-paper based conceptual sketching of architecture plans towards computer tools - prototype design and evaluation. In: 11th IAPR International Workshop on Graphics Recognition - GREC 2015, Nancy, France (2015)
5. Belém, C., Santos, L., Leitão, A.: On the impact of machine learning, architecture without architects? CAAD Futures 2019: Hello Culture (2019)
6. Berkholz, C., Bonsma, P., Grohe, M.: Tight lower and upper bounds for the complexity of canonical colour refinement. Theory Comput. Syst. **60**(4), 581–614 (2017)
7. Cavieres, A., Bhatia, U., Joshi, P., Zhao, F., Ram, A.: CBArch: a case-based reasoning framework for conceptual design of commercial buildings. In: Artificial Intelligence and Sustainable Design - Papers from the AAAI 2011 Spring Symposium (SS-11-02) pp. 19–25 (2011)
8. Cordella, L.P., Foggia, P., Sansone, C., Vento, M.: A (sub) graph isomorphism algorithm for matching large graphs. IEEE Trans. Pattern Anal. Mach. Intell. **26**(10), 1367–1372 (2004)
9. Eisenstadt, V., Langenhan, C., Althoff, K.D.: Generation of floor plan variations with convolutional neural networks and case-based reasoning-an approach for transformative adaptation of room configurations within a framework for support of early conceptual design phases (2019)
10. Gentner, D., Forbus, K.D.: MAC/FAC: a model of similarity-based retrieval. In: Proceedings of the Thirteenth Annual Conference of the Cognitive Science Society, vol. 504, p. 509. Citeseer (1991)
11. Goodfellow, I., et al.: Generative adversarial nets. In: Advances in Neural Information Processing Systems, pp. 2672–2680 (2014)
12. Langenhan, C., Petzold, F.: The fingerprint of architecture-sketch-based design methods for researching building layouts through the semantic fingerprinting of floor plans. Int. Electr. Sci. Educ. J. Archit. Modern Inf. Technol. **4**, 13 (2010)
13. Langenhan, C.: Data Management in Architecture. Investigating the organisation of design information in IT infrastructures and identifying potential uses in knowledge-based systems. Dissertation, Technical University of Munich, Munich (2017)
14. Lin, C.J.: Visual architectural topology. In: Open Systems: Proceedings of the 18th International Conference on Computer-Aided Architectural Design Research in Asia, pp. 3–12 (2013)
15. de Miguel, J., Villafañe, M.E., Piškorec, L., Sancho-Caparrini, F.: Deep form finding using variational autoencoders for deep form finding of structural typologies. In: eCAADe 37 / Sigradi 23, pp. 71–80. CumInCAD (2019)

16. Oxman, R., Oxman, R.: Precedents: memory structure in design case libraries. CAAD Fut. **93**, 273–287 (1993)
17. Richter, K.: Augmenting Designers' Memory: Case Based Reasoning in Architecture. Logos Verlag Berlin GmbH (2011)
18. Sabri, Q.U., Bayer, J., Ayzenshtadt, V., Bukhari, S.S., Althoff, K.D., Dengel, A.: Semantic pattern-based retrieval of architectural floor plans with case-based and graph-based searching techniques and their evaluation and visualization. In: ICPRAM 2017, February 24–26, Porto, Portugal (2017)
19. Silvestre, J., Ikeda, Y., Guéna, F.: Artificial imagination of architecture with deep convolutional neural network. laissez-faire: loss of control in the esquisse phase. In: CAADRIA 2016, pp. 881–890. The Association for Computer-Aided Architectural Design Research in Asia (2016)
20. Steadman, P., Mitchell, L.J.: Architectural morphospace: mapping worlds of built forms. Environ. Plan. **37**(2), 197–220 (2010)
21. Pearce, M., Goel, A.K., Kolodner, I.L., Zimring, C., Sentosa, L., Billington, R.: Case-based design support: a case study in architectural design. IEEE Expert **7**(5), 14–20 (1992)

Using Siamese Graph Neural Networks for Similarity-Based Retrieval in Process-Oriented Case-Based Reasoning

Maximilian Hoffmann[1(✉)], Lukas Malburg[1], Patrick Klein[1], and Ralph Bergmann[1,2]

[1] Business Information Systems II, University of Trier, 54296 Trier, Germany
{hoffmannm,malburgl,kleinp,bergmann}@uni-trier.de
[2] German Research Center for Artificial Intelligence (DFKI), Branch University of Trier, Behringstraße 21, 54296 Trier, Germany
ralph.bergmann@dfki.de
http://www.wi2.uni-trier.de

Abstract. Similarity-based retrieval of semantic graphs is widely used in real-world scenarios, e. g., in the domain of business workflows. To tackle the problem of complex and time-consuming graph similarity computations during retrieval, the *MAC/FAC* approach is used in *Process-Oriented Case-Based Reasoning* (POCBR), where similar graphs are extracted from a preselected set of candidate graphs. These graphs result from a similarity computation with a computationally inexpensive similarity measure. The contribution of this paper is a novel similarity measure where vector space embeddings generated by two siamese *Graph Neural Networks* (GNNs) are used to approximate the similarities of a precise but therefore computationally complex graph similarity measure. Our approach includes a specific encoding scheme for semantic graphs that enables their usage in neural networks. The evaluation examines the quality and performance of these models in preselecting retrieval candidates and in approximating the ground-truth similarities of the graph similarity measure for two workflow domains. The results show great potential of the approach for being used in a MAC/FAC scenario, either as a preselection model or as an approximation of the graph similarity measure.

Keywords: Process-Oriented Case-Based Reasoning · MAC/FAC Retrieval · Graph embeddings · Siamese Graph Neural Networks

1 Introduction

Nowadays, cases represented as semantic graphs are increasingly used in several domains, e. g., as cooking recipes in the form of simple business workflows [19], as scientific workflows to represent data mining tasks [28], or as argument graphs for case-based argumentation [14]. The problem-solving paradigm

I. Watson and R. Weber (Eds.): ICCBR 2020, LNAI 12311, pp. 229–244, 2020.
https://doi.org/10.1007/978-3-030-58342-2_15

of *Process-Oriented Case-Based Reasoning* (POCBR) [3,16] focused on these semantic graphs to represent workflows in scenarios of similarity-based retrieval and reuse of procedural experiential knowledge. Especially in retrieval situations, the main influencing factor on user experience is its runtime to retrieve useful cases. However, due to the need for computing multiple pairwise semantic graph similarities throughout a single retrieval, an increasing size and complexity of the used graphs has a strong influence on the overall retrieval time, which in turn results in slow and unresponsive applications for relatively large graphs. The *MAC/FAC* ("Many are called, but few are chosen") approach introduced by Forbus et al. [9] can be used to counteract the previously mentioned problem of slow retrieval times. To solve this, a two-phased retrieval is applied: The first phase (MAC) utilizes a simplified and often knowledge-poor similarity measure for a fast preselection of similar cases w. r. t. the query. The second phase (FAC) then applies the computationally intensive graph-based similarity measure to the results of the MAC phase. The strategy reveals the importance of a well-chosen MAC similarity measure because the preselection of candidates must not disregard highly similar workflows to maintain an appropriate retrieval quality.

Our previous work to design MAC similarity measures shifted the focus from manually-modeled approaches [5] to approaches based on machine learning techniques [13,18]. Recently, Klein et al. [13] embedded semantic graphs into a low-dimensional vector space using the general-purpose unsupervised embedding framework *StarSpace* [26]. In this approach, the graph similarity is determined by applying a standard vector similarity measure on the generated graph embeddings. However, semantic annotations and the graph structure are not considered at all, although this is indispensable in certain domains [14,28]. In this paper, we continue to pursue the idea of automatically learned low-dimensional graph representation vectors to speed-up retrieval. We investigate two novel siamese *Graph Neural Networks* (GNNs) specifically tailored for graph structures introduced by Li et al. [15], for generating more expressive graph embeddings. We propose a generic approach to modify those GNNs to fully include semantic annotations and the workflow structure into the embedding process.

In the following section, previous work on POCBR including representation of semantic workflows, similarity assessment between these workflows, and different MAC/FAC approaches is presented. Our concept for assessing the similarity of semantic graphs with the help of GNNs is introduced in Sect. 3. Next, we apply our developed concept to cooking recipes and evaluate it. Finally, Sect. 5 concludes the results and discusses future work.

2 Foundations and Previous Work

Research on *Process-Oriented Case-Based Reasoning* (POCBR) [3,16] deals with the integration of CBR and *Process-Aware Information Systems* (PAISs) such as workflow management systems [8]. For instance, the effectiveness of POCBR has been demonstrated by Müller [19] for assisting workflow designers during the task of workflow modeling with best-practice workflows from a case base.

Thus, POCBR supports the development of workflows as an experience-based activity [3,16]. Therefore, an appropriate case representation for workflows as well as a similarity measure that assesses the suitability of a workflow w. r. t. a new problem situation is important in POCBR.

2.1 Semantic Workflow Representation

For the representation of workflows, we use semantically annotated directed graphs referred to as *NEST* graphs introduced by Bergmann and Gil [3]. More specifically, a *NEST* graph is a quadruple $W = (N, E, S, T)$ that is composed of a set of nodes N and a set of edges $E \subseteq N \times N$. Each node and each edge has a specific type from Ω that is indicated by the function $T : N \cup E \rightarrow \Omega$. Additionally, the function $S : N \cup E \rightarrow \Sigma$ assigns a *semantic description* from Σ (*semantic metadata language*, e. g., an ontology) to nodes and edges. Whereas nodes and edges are used to build the structure of each workflow, types and semantic descriptions are additionally used to model semantic information. Hence, each node and each edge can have a semantic description.

To demonstrate the introduced representation and as part of the experimental evaluation, we use cooking recipes represented as workflows. Each workflow consists of tasks that represent cooking steps and data nodes that represent the ingredients that belong to the corresponding cooking steps. In the cooking domain, the semantic metadata language is defined by taxonomic ontologies, one for ingredients and one for cooking steps. Figure 1 shows a simple example of a *NEST* graph that represents a cooking recipe for making a sandwich. The cooking workflow contains two task nodes (`coat` and `layer`) as well as four data nodes (`mayo`, `baguette`, `sandwich dish`, and `gouda`). Task nodes are connected by control-flow edges that define the order in which tasks are executed. Furthermore, dataflow edges are used to connect task nodes with data nodes in order

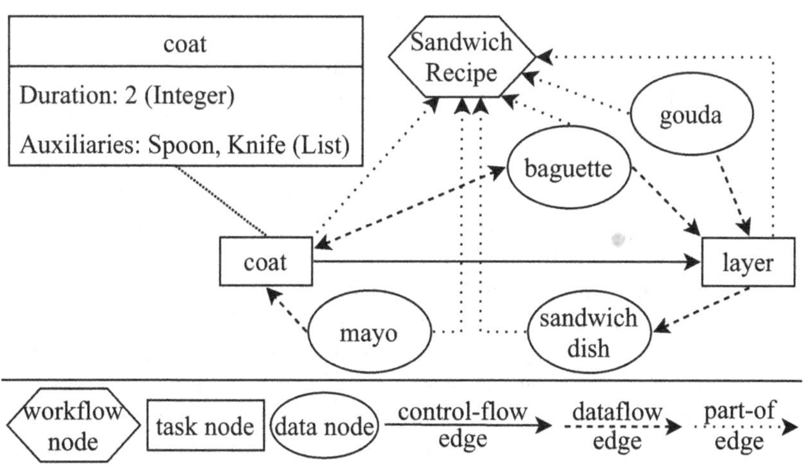

Fig. 1. Exemplary Cooking Recipe represented as NEST Graph

to model that a task consumes inputs and produces outputs. For instance, the dataflow edge between `coat` and `layer` indicates that baguette has an interaction with the task `coat` and is consumed by the task `layer`. Semantic descriptions of task nodes and data nodes are used to further specify semantic information belonging to the workflow components in an attribute-value way. Figure 1 shows an example of the semantic description of the task node `coat`. The provided information is used to describe the task more precisely. In this case, a spoon and a baguette knife is needed to execute the task (`Auxiliaries`) and the estimated time that the task takes is two minutes (`Duration`).

2.2 Similarity Assessment

Determining the similarity between two *NEST* graphs, i.e., a query workflow QW and a case workflow CW, requires a similarity measure that assesses the link structure of nodes and edges as well as the semantic descriptions and types of these components. Bergmann and Gil [3] propose a semantic similarity measure that determines a similarity based on the local-global principle [21]. A global similarity, i.e., the similarity between two graphs, is composed of local similarities, i.e., the pairwise similarities of nodes and edges. The similarity between two nodes with identical types is defined as the similarity of the semantic descriptions of these nodes. The similarity between two edges with identical types does not only consider the similarity of the semantic descriptions of the edges, but in addition the similarity of the connected nodes as well. In order to put together a global similarity by aggregating local similarities, the domain's similarity model has to define similarity measures for all components of the semantic description, i.e., $sim_\Sigma : \Sigma \times \Sigma \rightarrow [0,1]$. The global similarity of the two workflows $sim(QW, CW)$ is finally calculated by finding an injective partial mapping m that maximizes $sim_m(QW, CW)$.

$$sim(QW, CW) = max\,\{sim_m(QW, CW) \mid \text{admissible mapping } m\} \qquad (1)$$

The process of finding the mapping that maximizes the global similarity between a query QW and a single case CW is very complex due to the high number of possible mappings and thus requires solving an optimization problem. Bergmann and Gil [3] developed a parallelized version of the A^* search algorithm that can be used for finding a mapping solution by utilizing search heuristics and an adjustable A^* maximum queue size. The queue size defines the maximum number of not expanded solutions to store and influences the trade-off between quality of the mappings and time required for finding them, i.e., reducing the queue size results in solutions with worse quality at a lower computation time and vice versa. Only a queue of infinite length could deterministically find the optimal solution. Even when using the A^* search with a suitable heuristic, solving the problem to find the best-possible mapping is still very complex w.r.t. time and memory consumption (see [20] for more details). That mainly motivates this paper.

2.3 MAC/FAC Retrieval for POCBR

In contrast to Zeyen and Bergmann [27] who tackled the aforementioned problems by optimizing the A^* search and its underlying heuristic, we used the approach of a two-phase retrieval procedure, referred to as MAC/FAC [9], to face long retrieval times [5,11,18]. It aims to decrease computation time by pre-filtering the case base in order to reduce the number of cases that have to be evaluated by an often computationally complex similarity measure. The major difficulty with MAC/FAC retrieval in general is the definition of the filter condition of the MAC stage, as it has a great impact on the overall retrieval quality and performance.

Prior work of Bergmann and Stromer [5] addressed this issue by utilizing a feature-based domain specific case representation of workflows and an appropriately modeled similarity measure in the MAC stage. In order to avoid additional modeling effort, Müller and Bergmann [18] developed a MAC/FAC approach that uses a hierarchically partitioned cluster tree that can be traversed for finding clusters with cases similar to the query. This algorithm shows acceptable performance if the case base has a strong cluster structure. However, it has not reached quality and retrieval speed of the feature-based MAC/FAC approach. Our recent work [13] applied the general-purpose embedding framework StarSpace [26] to POCBR. Therefore, the authors learned vector representations in an unsupervised manner based on structural properties of workflow graphs, e. g., relation between task, data, and workflow nodes. The resulting embeddings allow to efficiently compute the similarity between a given query and a workflow from the case base by vector similarity measures, without any consideration of knowledge-intensive manually-modeled similarity measures. The approach achieves a nearly comparable performance to the feature-based MAC/FAC retrieval w. r. t. retrieval time and quality. Since the embedding-based approach does not adequately consider semantic descriptions or the graph structure that are relevant for the semantic similarity assessment, we consider this weakness as a starting point for improvements.

3 Similarity Learning for Workflow Graphs with Siamese Graph Neural Networks

This section presents our approach for generating pairwise similarities of semantic graphs by using neural networks. Since semantic labels of nodes and edges contain valuable information for similarity assessment, it is necessary to provide these semantics in combination with the workflow structure as input data for the neural networks. To the best of our knowledge, the encoding of such semantic information for learning graph similarities is a rather unexplored research area (see [20] for an overview) also in POCBR. Consequently, we present our method for encoding semantic graphs to be used as input data of neural networks (see Sect. 3.1). Additionally, we show how this data can be used to determine graph similarities with neural networks. Therefore, two graph neural networks developed by Li et al. [15] are adjusted in order to generate these similarities (see Sect. 3.2) and to enable usage in retrieval scenarios (see Sect. 3.3).

3.1 Encoding Semantic Graphs for Similarity Learning

Our encoding scheme for *NEST* graphs creates numeric vector space encodings that can be fed into neural networks for similarity assessment. To the best of our knowledge, encoding the semantic annotations of nodes and edges is often not considered as a main aspect in papers that present novel neural network structures (e. g., [2,15]) for processing graphs. However, for semantic graphs like *NEST* graphs, the semantic annotations at nodes and edges reflect domain-specific knowledge that has a great impact on the global similarity. Thus, it is crucial that the encoding methods can transform this knowledge to vector encodings. This leads to individually created encoding schemes for node and edge *types* and their *semantic annotations.*

Encoding Node and Edge Types. Properly encoding node and edge types is important because, during similarity assessment, only nodes and edges with identical types are mapped (see Sect. 2.2). The types are encoded separately for nodes and edges by *one-hot encodings.* One-hot encoding vectors encode information in binary form by setting a single element as a 1 while all other vector elements are set to 0. This way, a single one-hot encoding vector can only have as many different value allocations as it has vector elements. For *NEST* graphs, there are four different one-hot encodings of node types and edge types each (see Fig. 2). The main advantage is that all encodings are clearly distinguishable by a neural network that allows suitable processing of these vectors.

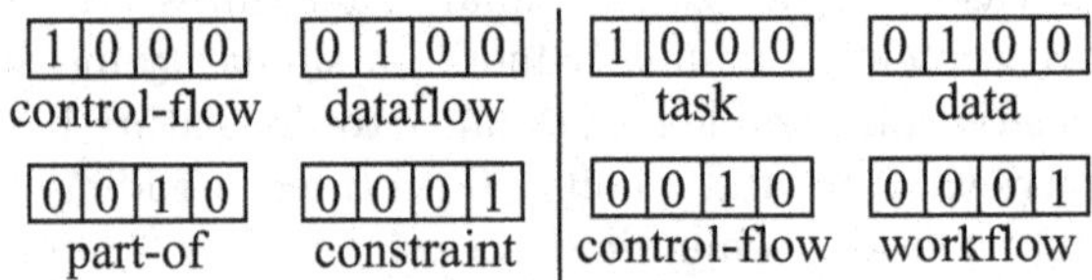

Fig. 2. One-Hot Encodings of Edge Types (left) and Node Types (right)

Encoding Semantic Descriptions. Encoding the semantic descriptions of nodes and edges requires the transformation of several data types and complex data relations. The data types that can be used inside of a semantic description are not specified in detail according to the *NEST* graph publication [3]. Referring to the ProCAKE framework[1] [4] that fully supports *NEST* graphs, a semantic description is composed of *atomic data types* and *composite data types*: Atomic types comprise *integer*, *double*, *boolean*, *string*, *void*, and *time* and composite data types consist of *list*, *set*, and *attribute-value pairs.* Each of these data types requires an individual encoding approach in order to map the semantics of the data to the encoding vectors as fully as possible. We implemented these individual encoding algorithms but due to space restrictions in this paper, only the general encoding approach of atomic and composite types is presented.

[1] https://procake.uni-trier.de.

Each atomic type is encoded to a single encoding vector with length α that is part of the vector space $\mathbb{R}^\alpha$. Thereby, these encoding vectors are made up of two subvectors, where the first one encodes the atomic data type (e. g., string, boolean, double) and the second one encodes the actual value to encode (e. g., "Hello World", *true*, 1.0). The additional encoding of the used atomic data type serves as further semantic information for the neural networks that process the encoding vectors. By that, encodings of semantic description entries of different types can be distinguished more easily although they are mapped to a common vector space. Encoding composite types is not as straightforward as encoding atomic types due to the complexity of semantic descriptions. The task node `coat` from Fig. 1, for instance, is made up of composite attribute-value pairs with three entries. The entry `Duration` is an atomic type and the entry `Auxiliaries` is a list of atomic strings (composite type) that is nested inside of the attribute-value pair. This arrangement of composite types nesting other atomic or composite types can be visualized as a *tree structure* (see Fig. 3a). Regarding the transformation of these semantic descriptions to numeric vectors, this means that the encoding of a composite type aggregates the encodings of the nested types. However, using tree-structured data in a neural network requires the definition of complex layers and very special additional encoding schemes (e. g., [22,24]). In order to simplify the tree structures to encode, each composite type is redefined as a *sequence of atomic types* (see Fig. 3b). In case a composite type contains another composite type (e. g., the tree structure in Fig. 3a), the encoding sequences of parent type and child type are computed recursively and put together to a single sequence. Converting tree structures to sequences is in particular motivated by techniques that are used in natural language processing (e. g., [7,23]), where a word or a sentence is often represented as a sequence of encoding vectors. Similar to the previously mentioned approaches, we also use *Recurrent Neural Networks* (RNNs) to process these sequences, which is described in the next section.

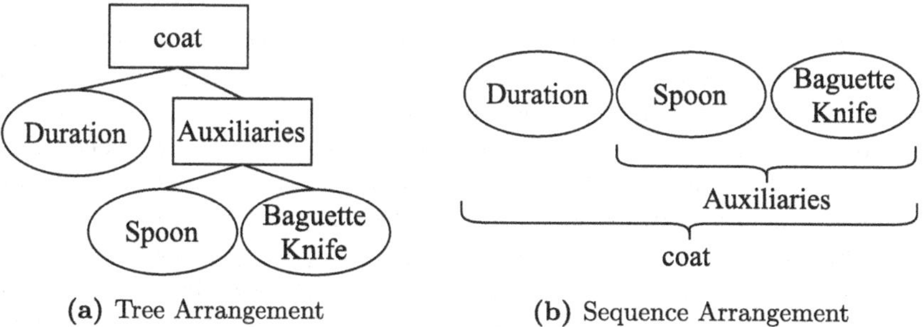

(a) Tree Arrangement **(b)** Sequence Arrangement

Fig. 3. Tree and sequence arrangement of semantic description components

3.2 Similarity Learning for Workflow Graphs

The neural networks that are used for graph retrieval are based on the *Graph Embedding Model* (GEM) and the *Graph Matching Network* (GMN) introduced by Li et al. [15]. In their work, they present two neural networks that are capable of learning to assess the similarity of graphs. Both neural networks compute compact vector representations of graphs that can be eventually compared using a vector similarity measure. Thereby, the GEM is designed to enable a lightweight, fast similarity assessment, whereas the GMN is optimized to learn more expressive similarity patterns on the pairwise graph features. Both neural networks feature three main components (see Fig. 4): the *encoder*, the *propagation layer*, and the *aggregator*. We completely reuse the propagation layer of both networks from the original implementation of Li et al.[2] and adjusted the encoder and the final graph similarity for our application scenario.

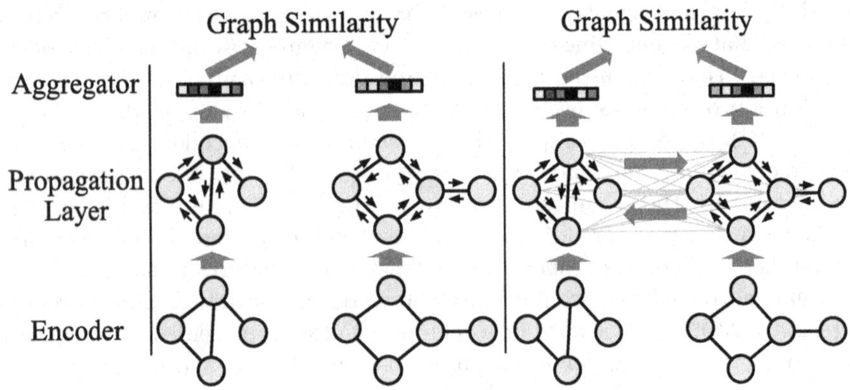

Fig. 4. GEM (left) and GMN (right) (based on [15])

The *encoder* transforms the raw graph input data into a first embedding of all nodes and edges. The components that are embedded in this process cover the semantic descriptions and types allocated to each node and edge (see Sect. 2). These components are embedded independent of each other and concatenated afterwards to a single embedding vector for each node and edge of the graph. This way, separate neural network structures can be adequately trained to generate suitable embeddings. Whereas the embeddings of the types are generated by using separate feed-forward networks for node and edge types, the embedding procedure of the semantic descriptions utilizes an RNN [7]. An RNN is specifically designed to handle sequences of inputs as they are present in the encodings of semantic descriptions. Please note that the influence of both parts of the embedding vector can be controlled by manipulating the respective vector lengths.

[2] https://github.com/deepmind/deepmind-research/tree/master/graph_matching_networks.

The *propagation layer* iteratively combines the node embeddings according to the edge structure of the graph in order to capture information on the local neighborhood in each node's embedding. Therefore, an iterative process is used that updates the node embeddings in multiple steps. In each step, the embedding of a single node is updated by merging the node's embedding with the embeddings of nodes that are connected via an edge. This enables information to be distributed by the node embeddings across the propagation steps. The definition of a node's neighborhood is the main difference of the propagation approach present in GEM and GMN. As depicted in Fig. 4, the GEM only propagates information within a single graph. This means that a node's embedding vector is updated according to all nodes that are connected via an edge that only allows information flow within a single graph. In contrast, the GMN also accumulates information across both graphs during the similarity assessment by using an attention-based matching component. This enables information to distribute between both graphs in an early state of similarity computation that contributes to the increased expressiveness of GMN compared to GEM.

After iteratively propagating information within the graphs, the *aggregator* merges the final node embeddings of all graph nodes to form an embedding for the whole graph. The embeddings of each of the two graphs are then used to determine a *graph similarity* value in [0, 1]. Therefore, we use cosine similarity for the GEM and a feed-forward neural network layer for the GMN. Given two graph embedding vectors, the cosine similarity is defined to be the dot product of these two vectors, divided by the product of the Euclidian vector length of both vectors. This leads to a computationally inexpensive way of generating the final graph similarity value. The feed-forward neural network that is used to compute the final similarity for the GMN can be trained in order to learn the characteristics of the whole-graph embedding vectors resulting from the aggregator. Thus, this process is more expressive than using a vector similarity measure, at the expense of a higher computation effort.

The *training* procedure for both networks utilizes the gradient-descent-based optimizer Adam [12] in a mini-batch setup. Each training graph pair from the batch of training examples is labeled with the ground truth similarity value that is determined using the semantic similarity measure *sim* introduced in Sect. 2.2. This data is used to compute the *Mean Squared Error* (MSE) that serves as a differentiable loss function. The MSE sums up all squared differences of the similarity predicted by the neural network and the labeled similarity, and then divides by the amount of all batched training examples to get the average deviation.

3.3 Siamese GNN-Based Workflow Retrieval

In a workflow retrieval, the k-most similar cases CW are retrieved from the case base CB, according to the similarity to a query workflow QW, i.e., $sim(QW, CW)$. The neural networks can be integrated into this process as the similarity measure for generating the pairwise graph similarities, i.e., $fsim(QW, CW)$. Therefore, the query workflow and all cases from the case base have to be encoded to a numerical vector format first (see Sect. 3.1). After that, an offline training session can be started that trains the neural networks GEM and GMN for predicting the similarities of all cases from the case base. The machine learning framework *Tensorflow*[3] [1] is utilized for this purpose. Given the encoded graphs and the trained neural networks, either GEM or GMN can be used to determine the pairwise similarities for the query and all cases from the case base, i. e., $sim(QW, CW)$ is approximated by $fsim(QW, CW)$. Eventually, the retrieval result is finalized by putting together the k-most similar workflows according to the similarity computed by the neural network.

4 Experimental Evaluation

To evaluate our approach, we measure performance and quality of GEM and GMN in different retrieval scenarios. Thereby, both neural networks are compared to the feature-based retriever by Bergmann and Stromer [5] (FBR), to the latest embedding-based retriever by Klein et al. [13] (EBR), and to the A^*-retriever by Bergmann and Gil [3] (A*R). We investigate the following hypotheses in two experiments:

H1 Using GEM and GMN as a MAC retriever of a MAC/FAC retrieval leads to better retrieval results than using EBR as MAC retriever.

H2 The GMN retriever is able to approximate the ground-truth graph similarities better than A*R, using parameter settings such that the retrieval time of both retrievers is comparable.

The first experiment examines the retrievers in a MAC/FAC setup, where the focus is put on the suitability of GEM and GMN as a MAC similarity measure (see H1). The second experiment examines to which degree the retrievers are capable of approximating the ground-truth A^*-similarities (see H2).

4.1 Experimental Setup

In the evaluation, workflows representing cooking recipes [4] and workflows representing Data Mining processes from RapidMiner[4] [28] are examined, with a training and a testing case base for each domain. The cooking workflows (CB-I) are derived from 40 manually-modeled cooking recipes that are extended to 800 workflows by previously developed adaptation methods [19], resulting in 680 training cases and 120 testing cases. The workflows of the Data Mining domain (CB-II) are built from sample processes that are delivered with RapidMiner, resulting in 529 training cases and 80 testing cases. We build these different case bases in order to investigate if our approach performs differently regarding the complexity of the workflow domains. Therefore, we evaluate on the cooking workflows with rather simple semantic descriptions and on the RapidMiner workflows with more complex semantic descriptions.

[3] https://tensorflow.org/.
[4] https://rapidminer.com/.

The metrics that are used to evaluate our approach cover performance and quality. The performance is measured by taking the retrieval time in seconds. The quality of the results to evaluate RL_{eval} is measured by comparing them to the ground-truth retrieval results RL_{true} in terms of Mean Absolute Error (MAE), correctness (see [6] for more details), and k-NN quality (see [13] and [18] for more details). The MAE (ranged between 0 and 1) expresses the average similarity error between all pairs of query workflow and case workflow in RL_{true} and the same pairs in RL_{eval}. The correctness (ranged between -1 and 1) describes the conformity of the ranking positions of the workflow pairs in RL_{eval} according to RL_{true}. Given two arbitrary workflow pairs $WP_1 = (QW, CW_1)$ and $WP_2 = (QW, CW_2)$, the correctness is decreased if WP_1 is ranked before WP_2 in RL_{eval} although WP_2 is ranked before WP_1 in RL_{true} or vice versa. The k-NN quality (ranged between 0 and 1) quantifies to which degree highly similar cases according to RL_{true} are present in RL_{eval}. Therefore, the $|RL_{\text{eval}}|$ most-similar cases from RL_{true} are compared with RL_{eval}. Each case from the most-similar cases that is missing in RL_{eval} decreases the quality, with highly relevant cases affecting the quality stronger than less relevant cases.

All experiments are computed on a PC with an Intel i7 6700 CPU (4 cores, 8 threads) and an NVIDIA GTX 1080 GPU with 16 GB RAM, running Windows 10 64-bit. The retrievers (EBR, GEM, and GMN) that require an offline training phase are trained with the two training case bases, resulting in two models per retriever, i. e., one for each domain. The training time for GEM on both case bases is approx. 12 h, for GMN approx. 18 h, and for EBR approx. 6 min. Each retriever uses all processing cores of CPU or GPU for calculating the similarities. A retrieval is always conducted with a query from the testing case base and with the cases from the training case base. To produce meaningful performance and quality values, the results of the retrieval runs of all query cases from a single domain are averaged.

4.2 Experimental Results

The first experiment evaluates our neural networks as retrievers in a scenario of MAC/FAC retrieval. Table 1 shows the results (k-NN quality and retrieval time) as compared with FBR and EBR, since these two retrievers are specifically designed for MAC/FAC applications. For CB-I, FBR outperforms all other retrievers w. r. t. quality for all combinations of FS and k. EBR and GMN have quality values in a similar range, with both consistently outperforming the quality values of GEM.

When only considering the time, EBR and GEM clearly outperform all other retrievers. For CB-II, the quality values of GMN outperform those of EBR and are in a similar range as those of FBR. The quality values of GEM surpass those of EBR with comparable retrieval times. The results show that the suitability of GEM and GMN increases for retrieval situations with more complex semantic descriptions of task and data nodes, as present in CB-II. The performance of GEM and GMN for retrieving graphs from a rather simple domain, such as those of CB-I, is respectable but does not lead to a replacement of current approaches

Table 1. Evaluation results of MAC/FAC experiment

			GMN		GEM		FBR		EBR	
	FS	k	Quality	Time	Quality	Time	Quality	Time	Quality	Time
CB-I	5	5	0.534	07.91	0.521	00.27	0.598	00.86	0.552	00.29
	50	5	0.564	10.31	0.535	02.52	0.704	03.22	0.639	02.55
	10	10	0.581	08.19	0.550	00.53	0.647	01.11	0.599	00.56
	80	10	0.641	11.81	0.572	03.99	0.749	04.76	0.697	03.98
	25	25	0.649	09.02	0.600	01.31	0.721	01.92	0.658	01.34
	100	25	0.727	12.83	0.628	04.95	0.814	05.82	0.748	04.91
CB-II	5	5	0.584	08.48	0.356	00.19	0.659	00.43	0.348	00.13
	50	5	0.861	10.78	0.508	02.54	0.909	02.10	0.483	01.80
	10	10	0.625	08.60	0.408	00.42	0.658	00.57	0.384	00.25
	80	10	0.875	12.69	0.550	03.99	0.916	03.85	0.550	03.60
	25	25	0.718	08.00	0.474	01.13	0.696	01.10	0.450	00.97
	100	25	0.895	14.14	0.602	04.62	0.887	05.13	0.585	04.60

(EBR and FBR). Anyhow, the FBR with its manually-modeled similarity measure still performs best for both case bases, taking into account the combination of quality and time. When only looking at the automatically-learned retrievers in the results for CB-II, i. e., GEM, GMN, and EBR, GEM is the most suitable for a MAC/FAC scenario since it shows a good combination of very low retrieval times and high quality values. Thus, H1 is partly confirmed due to different results for the two case bases. The results for CB-I do not confirm H1 since EBR outperforms GEM in terms of quality and even though GMN shows better quality results than EBR, it has infeasible retrieval times for a MAC/FAC setup. For CB-II, H1 can be clearly accepted due to higher quality values with approximately equal retrieval times, when comparing GEM and EBR.

The second experiment examines to which degree GEM, GMN, EBR, and FBR are able to approximate the ground-truth graph similarities. Since GMN and GEM are evaluated as MAC retrievers in the first experiment, the second experiment focuses more on the suitability as FAC retrievers by measuring the prediction errors (see Table 2). Therefore, we compare all previously mentioned retrievers to a variant of the A*R with an adjusted queue size (see Sect. 2.2) so that the retrieval time of A*R is approx. equal to that of GMN. Aligning the retrieval times of A*R and GMN enables a fair comparison of the resulting MAE and correctness.

For CB-I, GMN has the lowest MAE and A*R has the highest correctness. FBR achieves a high level of correctness but lags behind in terms of MAE. When comparing the results of CB-I and CB-II, it becomes apparent that GMN still has the lowest MAE and now also has the highest value of correctness. This leads to the assumption that the suitability of GMN increases with more complex cases. The reason for that might be the different levels of computational complexity of both retrievers, i. e., exponential complexity for A*R and quadratic complexity for GMN. GMN outperforming A*R in terms of MAE is even more

Table 2. Evaluation results of A-Star approximation experiment

	Retriever	MAE	Correctness	Time
CB-I	A*R	0.054	0.753	8.203
	GMN	0.049	0.479	7.612
	GEM	0.123	0.231	0.008
	FBR	0.187	0.646	0.539
	EBR	0.354	0.190	0.006
CB-II	A*R	0.040	0.778	9.520
	GMN	0.021	0.797	8.444
	GEM	0.170	0.064	0.006
	FBR	0.199	0.580	0.350
	EBR	0.404	0.064	0.004

remarkable when considering that GMN learns to assess the similarity of graphs without knowing the original algorithmic context, e. g., similarities of semantic descriptions or node and edge mappings. Additionally, this experiment shows that FBR and EBR are not suitable for generating similarities that are close to the ground-truth similarities. The reason for this could be the inadequate processing of semantic annotations and the workflow structure. Thus, we clearly accept H2 for CB-II and partly accept this hypothesis for CB-I.

5 Conclusion and Future Work

This paper examines the potential of using two siamese GNNs in a retrieval scenario in POCBR. Therefore, an encoding scheme is presented that covers the workflow structure, the types of nodes and edges, and their semantic descriptions. The encoded workflows are furthermore processed by two neural networks GEM and GMN that are adjusted and optimized for being used in retrieval scenarios. The evaluation of both neural networks investigates how both approaches perform in being used in a MAC/FAC setup and in approximating the ground-truth similarities of the graph similarity measure. Compared to previous retriever approaches, the results show great potential: GEM is suitable for a MAC/FAC setup, due to its fast similarity computation and reasonable retrieval quality. Furthermore, GMN shows great potential in approximating the ground-truth graph similarities.

A focus of future research should be on optimizing the presented approach of a GNN-based retrieval. This optimization ranges from aspects of parameterization to adjustments of the data encoding scheme and the usage of different neural network structures. The neural network structures could be optimized to better process other graph domains, e. g., argument graphs [14], or even other types of complex similarity measures [17]. Two more optimizations could be, for instance, using a differentiable ranking loss function that optimizes according to the ground-truth ordering of the retrieval results (e. g., [25]) or considering the relationships between different graphs from a case base during training (e. g., Neural Structured Learning[5]). Furthermore, the neural networks that are used in this work are not capable of explaining the results they produce, i. e., black boxes. In current research (also in the CBR community, e. g., [10]), this lack of explainability is tackled in the context of Explainable Artificial Intelligence (XAI). Future research should address this issue by investigating which methods are suitable for increasing the explainability of the presented neural networks.

Acknowledgments. This work is funded by the German Research Foundation (DFG) under grant No. BE 1373/3-3 and grant No. 375342983.

References

1. Abadi, M., et al.: TensorFlow: large-scale machine learning on heterogeneous distributed systems. CoRR abs/1603.04467 (2016)
2. Bai, Y., et al.: SimGNN: a neural network approach to fast graph similarity computation. In: Culpepper, J.S., Moffat, A., Bennett, P.N., Lerman, K. (eds.) Proceedings of the 12th ACM International Conference on Web Search and Data Mining 2019, Australia, pp. 384–392. ACM (2019)
3. Bergmann, R., Gil, Y.: Similarity assessment and efficient retrieval of semantic workflows. Inf. Syst. **40**, 115–127 (2014)
4. Bergmann, R., Grumbach, L., Malburg, L., Zeyen, C.: ProCAKE: a process-oriented case-based reasoning framework. In: Kapetanakis, S., Borck, H. (eds.) Workshops Proceedings for the 27th International Conference on Case-Based Reason. Research and Deviation. CEUR Workshop Proceedings, vol. 2567, pp. 156–161. CEUR-WS.org (2019)
5. Bergmann, R., Stromer, A.: MAC/FAC retrieval of semantic workflows. In: Boonthum-Denecke, C., Youngblood, G.M. (eds.) Proceedings of the 26th International Florida Artificial Intelligent Research Society Conference on AAAI Press (2013)
6. Cheng, W., Rademaker, M., De Baets, B., Hüllermeier, E.: Predicting partial orders: ranking with abstention. In: Balcázar, J.L., Bonchi, F., Gionis, A., Sebag, M. (eds.) ECML PKDD 2010. LNCS (LNAI), vol. 6321, pp. 215–230. Springer, Heidelberg (2010). https://doi.org/10.1007/978-3-642-15880-3_20
7. Cho, K., et al.: Learning phrase representations using RNN encoder-decoder for statistical machine translation. In: Moschitti, A., Pang, B., Daelemans, W. (eds.) Proceedings of the Conference on Empirical Methods in Natural Language Processing, EMNLP 2014, Qatar. pp. 1724–1734. ACL (2014)
8. Dumas, M., van de Aalst, W.M.P., ter Hofstede, A.H.M.: Process-Aware Information Systems: Bridging People and Software Through Process Technology. Wiley, New York (2005)
9. Forbus, K.D., Gentner, D., Law, K.: MAC/FAC: a model of similarity-based retrieval. Cogn. Sci. **19**(2), 141–205 (1995)
10. Keane, M.T., Kenny, E.M.: How case-based reasoning explains neural networks: a theoretical analysis of XAI using *Post-Hoc* explanation-by-example from a survey of ANN-CBR twin-systems. In: Bach, K., Marling, C. (eds.) ICCBR 2019. LNCS (LNAI), vol. 11680, pp. 155–171. Springer, Cham (2019). https://doi.org/10.1007/978-3-030-29249-2_11

[5] https://www.tensorflow.org/neural_structured_learning.

11. Kendall-Morwick, J., Leake, D.B.: A study of two-phase retrieval for process-oriented case-based reasoning. In: Montani, S., Jain, L. (eds.) Successful Case-based Reasoning Applications-2, pp. 7–27. Springer, Heidelberg (2014). https://doi.org/10.1007/978-3-642-38736-4_2
12. Kingma, D.P., Ba, J.: Adam: A Method for Stochastic Optimization. In: Bengio, Y., LeCun, Y. (eds.) 3rd International Conference on Learning Representations, ICLR, USA, p. 2015. Track Proceedings Conference (2015)
13. Klein, P., Malburg, L., Bergmann, R.: Learning workflow embeddings to improve the performance of similarity-based retrieval for process-oriented case-based reasoning. In: Bach, K., Marling, C. (eds.) ICCBR 2019. LNCS (LNAI), vol. 11680, pp. 188–203. Springer, Cham (2019). https://doi.org/10.1007/978-3-030-29249-2_13
14. Lenz, M., Ollinger, S., Sahitaj, P., Bergmann, R.: Semantic textual similarity measures for case-based retrieval of argument graphs. In: Bach, K., Marling, C. (eds.) ICCBR 2019. LNCS (LNAI), vol. 11680, pp. 219–234. Springer, Cham (2019). https://doi.org/10.1007/978-3-030-29249-2_15
15. Li, Y., Gu, C., Dullien, T., Vinyals, O., Kohli, P.: Graph matching networks for learning the similarity of graph structured objects. In: Chaudhuri, K., Salakhutdinov, R. (eds.) Proceedings of the 36th International Conf. on Machine Learning, ICML 2019, USA. Proceedings of Machine Learning Research, vol. 97, pp. 3835–3845. PMLR (2019)
16. Minor, M., Montani, S., Recio-García, J.A.: Process-oriented case-based Reasoning. Inf. Syst. **40**, 103–105 (2014)
17. Mougouie, B., Bergmann, R.: Similarity assessment for generalizied cases by optimization methods. In: Craw, S., Preece, A. (eds.) ECCBR 2002. LNCS (LNAI), vol. 2416, pp. 249–263. Springer, Heidelberg (2002). https://doi.org/10.1007/3-540-46119-1_19
18. Müller, G., Bergmann, R.: A cluster-based approach to improve similarity-based retrieval for process-oriented case-based reasoning. In: Schaub, T., Friedrich, G., O'Sullivan, B. (eds.) ECAI 2014–21st European Conference on Artificial Intelligence, pp. 639–644. IOS Press (2014)
19. Müller, G.: Workflow Modeling Assistance by Case-based Reasoning. Springer, Wiesbaden (2018). https://doi.org/10.1007/978-3-658-23559-8
20. Ontañón, S.: An overview of distance and similarity functions for structured data. Artif. Intell. Rev. pp. 1–43 (2020). https://doi.org/10.1007/s10462-020-09821-w
21. Richter, M.M.: Foundations of similarity and utility. In: Wilson, D., Sutcliffe, G. (eds.) Proceedings of the 20th International Florida Artificial Intelligent Research Society Conference, pp. 30–37. AAAI Press (2007)
22. Socher, R., Lin, C.C., Ng, A.Y., Manning, C.D.: Parsing natural scenes and natural language with recursive neural networks. In: Getoor, L., Scheffer, T. (eds.) Proceedings of the 28th International Conference on Machine Learning, ICML 2011, USA, pp. 129–136. Omnipress (2011)
23. Sutskever, I., Vinyals, O., Le, Q.V.: Sequence to sequence learning with neural networks. Adv. Neural Inf. Process. Syst. **27**, 3104–3112 (2014)
24. Tai, K.S., Socher, R., Manning, C.D.: Improved Semantic Representations From Tree-Structured Long Short-Term Memory Networks. In: Proceedings of the 53rd Annual Meeting of the Assoc. for Computer Linguist. and the 7th International Joint Conference on NLP of the Asian Federation, pp. 1556–1566. The Association for Computer Linguistics (2015)

25. Taylor, M.J., Guiver, J., Robertson, S., Minka, T.: SoftRank: optimizing non-smooth rank metrics. In: Najork, M., Broder, A.Z., Chakrabarti, S. (eds.) Proceedings of the International Conference on Web Search and Web Data Mining, WSDM 2008, USA, pp. 77–86. ACM (2008)
26. Wu, L.Y., Fisch, A., Chopra, S., Adams, K., Bordes, A., Weston, J.: StarSpace: Embed All The Things! In: McIlraith, S.A., Weinberger, K.Q. (eds.) Proceedings of the 32nd AAAI Conference on Artifical Intelligent, USA, 2018, pp. 5569–5577. AAAI Press (2018)
27. Zeyen, C., Bergmann, R.: A*-based similarity assessment of semantic graphs. In: Watson, I., Weber, R. (eds.) ICCBR 2020, LNAI 12311, pp. 3–18. Springer, Cham (2020)
28. Zeyen, C., Malburg, L., Bergmann, R.: Adaptation of scientific workflows by means of process-oriented case-based reasoning. In: Bach, K., Marling, C. (eds.) ICCBR 2019. LNCS (LNAI), vol. 11680, pp. 388–403. Springer, Cham (2019). https://doi.org/10.1007/978-3-030-29249-2_26

Applying Class-to-Class Siamese Networks to Explain Classifications with Supportive and Contrastive Cases

Xiaomeng Ye(✉), David Leake, William Huibregtse, and Mehmet Dalkilic

Luddy School of Informatics, Computing, and Engineering,
Indiana University, Bloomington, IN 47408, USA
{xiaye,leake,whuibreg,dalkilic}@iu.edu

Abstract. Case-based classification is normally based on similarity between a query and class members in the case base. This paper proposes a difference-based approach, *class-to-class siamese network* (C2C-SN) classification, in which classification is based on learning patterns of both similarity and difference between classes. A C2C-SN learns patterns from one class C_i to another class C_j. The network can then be used, given two cases, to determine whether their similarity and difference conform to the learned patterns. If they do, it provides evidence for their belonging to the corresponding classes. We demonstrate the use of C2C-SNs for classification, explanation, and prototypical case finding. We demonstrate that C2C-SN classification can achieve good accuracy for case pairs, with the benefit of one-shot learning inherited from siamese networks.

Keywords: Case-based reasoning · Classification · Inter-class pattern · Class-to-class · Difference measure · Prototypical cases · Siamese network · Similarity

1 Introduction

The success of neural networks in deep learning has underlined both their capabilities and limitations. As they are applied in safety-critical task domains, such as for autonomous and semi-autonomous vehicles, there has been much effort to exploit their capabilities while providing explainability (e.g., [8]), as well as interest in harnessing their capabilities while requiring fewer training examples. This has prompted interest in the case-based reasoning (CBR) [16] community in integrations of network methods with CBR (e.g., [10]). For example, case-based reasoning, paired with a "black box" system, can provide explanations based on similar cases [12].

Case-based classification is normally based on similarity between a query and an already-classified case—not on the differences between the query and cases from other classes. Interestingly, learning the difference between classes has been

I. Watson and R. Weber (Eds.): ICCBR 2020, LNAI 12311, pp. 245–260, 2020.
https://doi.org/10.1007/978-3-030-58342-2_16

considered an essential part of human cognition [22]. For example, in counseling psychology, both schizophrenia and delusional disorder are psychoses. To learn to classify instances of the two illnesses, a counselor may put the cases of the two classes side-by-side and focus on the differences: schizophrenia causes functional impairment, while delusional disorder may not; furthermore, schizophrenia is associate with hallucination, while delusional disorder may cause "non-bizarre" delusions—that is, perceptions that might ordinarily occur.

Early research on case-based interpretation focused extensively on both similarities and differences, through processes such as "compare and contrast" [1] and the use of differences for indexing, to replace a retrieved case with a nearby alternative [2]. Automated classification methods for learning similarity have made impressive progress, including the use of deep learning—in particular, applying siamese networks [3]—to learn similarity [18,19]. However, such work generally focuses on capturing similarity, with difference captured implicitly.

This paper presents an approach that uses *inter-class patterns*, the patterns of similarity and difference between two classes, in case-based classification. Specifically, it applies a class-to-class (C2C) approach for learning to distinguish inputs that belong to different classes, implemented with siamese networks, to create what we call a class-to-class siamese network (C2C-SN). This work can be considered as a counter part of [19].

The proposed C2C-SN method is a knowledge-light approach that can make and explain classification decisions using inter-class patterns. We demonstrate that it can support classification tasks, one-shot learning, an enriched form of explanation by cases, and prototype finding. For explanation, as in standard case-based reasoning (CBR) systems, a system using C2C-SN can explain classifications by retrieving a case similar to the query ("The patient Q has delusional disorder because a similar patient A also has delusional disorder"). However, a C2C-SN can also offer explanations for negative conclusions by providing a contrastive argument ("The patient Q does not have schizophrenia. Although both Q and schizophrenia patient B have delusions, Q's delusion is far less bizarre").

The paper is organized as follows. First, we present background, briefly describing the class-to-class approach to classification, siamese networks, and explanation by presentation of cases. We next describe the C2C-SN approach and an evaluation of its performance for classification and one-shot learning. We then illustrate its value for providing explanations for classifications and for generating prototypical cases, which can in turn be used for classification. We close with conclusions and future directions.

2 Background

2.1 The Class-to-Class (C2C) Approach

The C2C approach is based on the assumption that there exist consistent similarity and difference patterns between different classes. Such inter-class patterns can be learned and reused for various purposes.

The C2C approach was initially tested as a feature weighting method (C2C weighting) for a k-nearest neighbors classification algorithm. In general, the traditional weighting methods assume that similar cases share similar (non)important features [17,23]. C2C weighting adds another assumption: that cases of different classes differ from each other, with respect to certain features, in a consistent manner. Unlike traditional weighting methods, which focus on finding the pattern of features within a class, C2C weighting aims to learn the patterns between pairs of classes and to apply these patterns as an additional information source for classification [24,25]. C2C weighting can be used in classification, case retrieval, and explanation. However, C2C weighting has limitations as well, such as poor classification accuracy when the inter-class patterns involve hidden relations between features. The approach presented here does not use C2C weighting.

2.2 Siamese Networks

Siamese networks (SN) were introduced in the 1990's by Bromely *et al.* [3]. A siamese network consists of a pair of identical networks, each receiving different input vectors, but joined together at a distance measure layer, which outputs a result value. The twin networks share the same weights and configuration and, therefore, perform identical feature extraction on each of the two inputs. At the distance layer, the distance between the extracted features is computed and transformed to a value between 0 and 1 using a sigmoid function [4]. A siamese network can be used for classification, similarity assessment, as well as feature extraction in CBR [18,19].

In contrast to a neural network that learns to directly classify input cases into classes, a siamese network learns a similarity function between cases. While a neural network for classification needs many samples from every class, a siamese network may even require only a single instance of a new class to achieve one-shot learning ability [13].

An important benefit of siamese networks for learning from limited data is that training is based on pairs of cases, rather than single cases [13]. If there are n cases in a case base, a neural network for classification can train on n input cases and their expected classifications, while a SN can train on $n \times n$ pairs of input cases and their expected similarities (which, in the absence of other information, can correspond to 0 if they belong to different classes and 1 if they belong to the same class). When given a single case from a new class, a neural network for classification can only train once for the new class, while a siamese network can train on $n+1$ pairs of cases involving the new case, by pairing the new case with n old cases and itself. This enables much more rapid training.

2.3 Explanation by Cases in CBR

From the early days of CBR, the ability to explain the outputs of CBR systems by presenting the cases on which they are based has been an important benefit of case-based reasoning [14]. The value of such explanations has received experimental support [6]. A recent focus is explaining black-box systems such as neural networks by "twinning" them with CBR systems [11]. In the twin system, the artificial neural network (ANN) component is expected to produce high-quality predictions while the CBR component provides explanations for the ANN's outputs. The explainability provided by the CBR system is post-hoc, meaning that the CBR system provides explanation of the ANN's output after the ANN makes the prediction. Displaying the conclusion along with the retrieved case is expected to boost the user's confidence compared to simply displaying the solution or displaying a rule used in finding the solution [6].

For explaining classifications based on cases, multiple approaches have been advanced for providing convincing evidences. Doyle et al. [7] suggest that cases between the query and the class boundary are more convincing support than the nearest neighbor of the query. By using a metric based on explanation utility rather than on similarity, their CBR system retrieves cases to best explain the class prediction. To aid users of a design feasibility assessment system in assessing the severity of design problems, Leake et al. [15] use *bracketing cases* (the most similar cases and without the problem) to illustrate the limits of the problem. Nugent et al. [20] illustrate an example of *a fortiori* arguments: A child pleading to her parent to see the movie Harry Potter will use the example of a much younger child who has seen the movie, instead of the example of a similar-age child, based on the assumption that "the older you are, the more likely you are allowed to see the movie." The authors frame this in terms of the concept of nearest unlike neighbor (NUN), the nearest neighbor of a different class. If the difference between NUN and the query case is large, this contrastive evidence suggests that the query is far from the class boundary and the prediction is thus convincing.

3 Class-to-Class Siamese Networks

To combine C2C weighting with siamese networks for case-based classification, we propose a new network approach, the *class-to-class siamese network* (C2C-SN). The general structure of a C2C-SN is shown in Fig. 1. The network is trained by pairs of cases to extract features that can be used to characterize a pattern between two specific classes. The twin networks extract features from the input cases. The difference between the extracted features is passed to a neural network learning the inter-class pattern, which outputs a number between 0 and 1 indicating the extent to which the extracted feature difference matches with the target pattern.

A premise of the approach is that, because the pattern between every pair of classes is unique, so is the feature extraction procedure for this pattern. For example, considering classifying psychotic diagnoses such as schizophrenia, delusional disorder, and schizotypal personality disorder: The difference between schizophrenia and delusional disorder may be focused on functional impairment; while the difference between schizophrenia and schizotypal personality disorder may be on delusions and illusions.

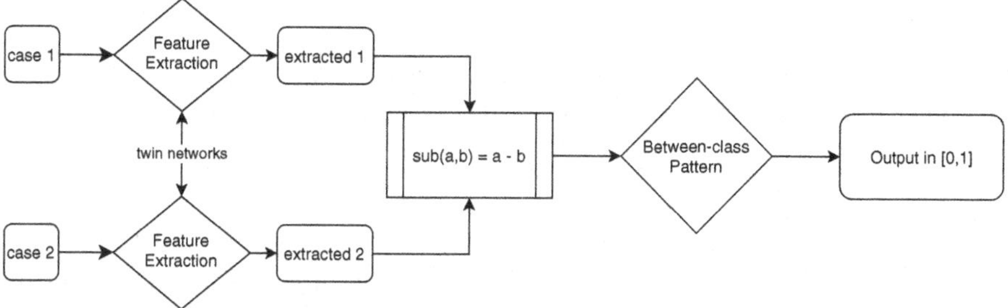

Fig. 1. The Structure of a C2C-SN

In the following, a C2C-SN learning the pattern from a class C_i to a class C_j will be denoted as a $C_i - C_j$ SN. When $i = j$, the corresponding siamese network $C_i - C_i$ SN learns the similarity pattern within the class C_i.

Each $C_i - C_j$ SN can be trained by back propagation. The features of a pair of cases $(case_1, case_2)$ are the input. A pair of cases is a positive pair (with output label 1) if the $case_1$ is an element of C_i and $case_2$ is an element of C_j. All other pairs of cases are negative pairs (with output label 0). If there are m classes, then there can be a family of up to m^2 C2C-SNs as there are m^2 pairs of classes. If the inter-class patterns are symmetric, then the number of patterns and networks is reduced by half.

3.1 Benefits of the C2C-SN Approach

A C2C-SN combines benefits from both the C2C approach and neural network learning. The C2C approach enables explaining membership in a class C_i by the fact that the input case is different from C_j cases in a way that existing C_i cases are different from C_j cases, as shown in the C2C weighting [24]. In other words, C2C-SN can offer a supportive/contrastive explanation by providing a case of the same class or a different class.

The use of a siamese network provides several benefits beyond prior work on the C2C approach: (1) Hidden Features and Relationships: Prior work on C2C weighting assigns weightings to surface features to reflect inter-class patterns. Use of the network in C2C-SN enables learning patterns in both surface features and implicit features. (2) Flexible Patterns: A major flaw of C2C weighting is that one weighting can only capture one pattern. If there exist multiple patterns between two classes, multiple weightings are needed and training convergence is more difficult. The ability of networks to represent rich concepts enables the C2C-SN approach to capture complex relationships between two classes with one network. (3) Difference Direction and Magnitude: C2C weighting learns the direction of a inter-class pattern. In addition to the direction, C2C-SN also learns the magnitude of an inter-class pattern. (4) Lastly, inherited from siamese networks, a C2C-SN has one-shot learning ability.

3.2 Building a C2C-SN

Given a working SN for a task domain, a C2C-SN learning the $C_i - C_j$ pattern can be generated by converting the existing SN with following steps.

Assemble the network:

1. Reuse the upper layers of the network: If the SN performs well (as a classification tool or a similarity measure), then the upper layers are powerful enough to extract hidden features for the task domain. The same configuration (layers and connections) for the upper layers of the SN can be used in a C2C-SN, however the trained weights and biases will be different.
2. Reconfigure the lower layers of the network: A SN's lower layers are used to calculate the distance between two extracted features, while a C2C-SN's lower layers are used to learn the pattern between the two extracted features. Therefore the lower layers of the SN need to be replaced. Because the interclass pattern might be hidden, a dense network is recommended.

Train the network:

1. Assemble and relabel training/testing pairs: Collect pairs of cases for training and testing. If the first case of the pair is of class C_i and the second case is of class C_j, then the pair label is 1, otherwise 0.
2. Retrain: Train the network weightings using back-propagation.

4 Experiments

This section illustrates and tests the performance of a C2C-SN for classification, one-shot learning, explanation, and prototypical case finding. Most experiments were conducted on the MNIST dataset. The dataset contains 60,000 training cases and 10,000 testing cases. Each case is a 28×28 image of a handwritten numerical digit, with each digit considered a class, providing ten classes labeled C_0 through C_9 for digits 0 through 9. Each digit appears in roughly the same number of cases.

The standard SNs and C2C-SNs were trained and tested on pairs of cases. Training pairs were assembled from the training set and testing pairs from the testing set.

We modified an existing SN implementation for classification in MNIST [5] to build C2C-SNs. In its original form, the upper layers first extract features from two cases, and the lower layer is a distance layer that computes the Euclidean distance between extracted feature vectors. The feature extraction layers are optimized by contrastive loss. This SN is referred to as the standard SN.

We reused the same initial configuration for the upper layers because the standard SN proved to be capable of extracting feature vectors for the classification task. The lower layers, however, are replaced with a subtraction layer, calculating the element-wise difference between two hidden vectors, followed by

Table 1. Pair accuracies for the MNIST dataset

i =	0	1	2	3	4	5	6	7	8
$C_i - C_i$ SN	0.991	0.994	0.982	0.981	0.985	0.985	0.987	0.978	0.978
$C_i - C_{i+1}$ SN	0.992	0.987	0.982	0.981	0.984	0.985	0.980	0.978	0.969

four fully connected ReLU (rectified linear unit) layers of 128 nodes, and a final output layer with a single node using sigmoid activation.

For a C2C-SN learning the $C_i - C_j$ pattern, we assembled $C_i - C_j$ pairs as the positive examples (labeled 1), and $C_x - C_y (x \neq i$ **or** $y \neq j)$ pairs as negative examples (labeled 0). Note that a $C_i - C_y$ pair and a $C_x - C_j$ pair are both negative examples. Lastly, we retrained the network using contrastive loss [9].

4.1 Classification Accuracy of Pairs

Pair accuracy is defined as the percentage of correctly identified labels for positive and negative pairs. To illustrate the classification performance, we tested the classification accuracies of multiple C2C-SNs. The $C_i - C_i$ SNs illustrate the capability of C2C-SNs that learn the similarity patterns within each class, while the $C_i - C_{i+1}$ SNs illustrate the capability of C2C-SNs that learn inter-class patterns.

For both training and testing, 5,000 positive and 5,000 negatives pairs were used. For a $C_i - C_j$ SN, all of the 5,000 positive pairs were $C_i - C_j$ pairs. Of negative pairs, 35% pairs were $C_i - C_y$ pairs, 35% were $C_x - C_j$ pairs, and the remaining 30% were $C_x - C_y$ pairs, where $x \neq i$ and $y \neq j$. The breakdown of negative pairs is intended to emphasize pairs that partially mismatch. Table 1 shows the performance of the best validation run chosen among 20 epochs.

In comparison, the original implementation of the standard SN (from which we derived our C2C-SNs) achieved a pair accuracy of 97.2% after 20 epochs, each epoch with 60,000 positive pairs and 60,000 negative pairs [5]. Note that the meanings of accuracy are different for a standard SN and a C2C-SN, therefore they are not directly comparable: (1) For the standard SN, a positive pair is a pair of cases in the same class C_i, where i is unspecified (2) For a $C_i - C_j$ SN, a positive pair is of $C_i - C_j$, where i and j are determined.

4.2 One-Shot Learning

We tested the one-shot learning ability of C2C-SNs in comparison with SNs. One-shot learning ability is the ability to learn when a minimum number of training cases for a certain class are presented.

In this experiment, we restricted the number of C_5 cases, n_5, in the training set, and compared the performance of the standard SN, the $C_5 - C_5$ SN, and the $C_5 - C_6$ SN. The number of C_5 training cases n_5 is set to 1, 10, 100, and 1,000, for four different experiments.

To ensure fairness and consistency in the comparison, each network was trained with 1,000 positive pairs and 1,000 negative pairs. The pairs were different for different networks. For the standard SN and the $C_5 - C_5$ SN: the positive pairs were 1,000 $C_5 - C_5$ pairs (which may include repeated pairs because C_5 cases are limited); the negative pairs were 350 $C_5 - C_j (j \neq 5)$ pairs, 350 $C_i - C_5 (i \neq 5)$ pairs, and 300 $C_i - C_j (i \neq 5 \text{ and } j \neq 5)$ pairs. For the $C_5 - C_6$ SN: the positive pairs were 1,000 $C_5 - C_6$ pairs; the negative pairs were 350 $C_5 - C_j (j \neq 6)$ pairs, 350 $C_i - C_6 (i \neq 5)$ pairs, and 300 $C_i - C_j (i \neq 5 \text{ and } j \neq 6)$ pairs.

Additionally, the standard SN received 100 $C_i - C_i$ training pairs for every i except when $i = 5$. The extra training pairs were available only for the standard SN but not for C2C-SNs, because the standard SN learns a distance measure across all classes. We tested the performance of the standard SN with and without the extra training pairs.

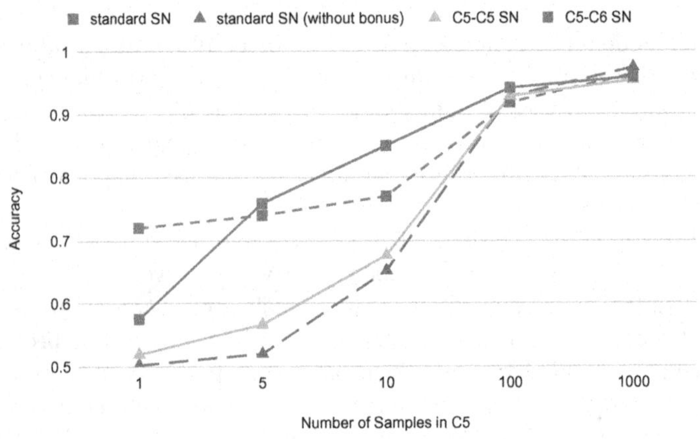

Fig. 2. The accuracies of networks under different one-shot learning constraint

After training, each SN was tested with 1,000 positive pairs and 1,000 negative pairs assembled from the testing dataset, in which the number of C_5 cases was not restricted. We recorded the highest validation accuracy across 20 epochs of training and testing. The experiment was run 10 times and the average was used as the final results. The results are shown in Fig. 2. We observe:

- The standard SN benefits strongly from the extra training pairs. A distance measure trained for all classes rather than only for C_5, giving additional data, benefits performance on C_5 as well. This contributes to the standard SN being superior when a minimum number of C_5 cases is available.
- The $C_5 - C_6$ SN performs better than the $C_5 - C_5$ SN. The positive examples for the $C_5 - C_5$ SN are pairs of few C_5 cases. Both sides of the $C_5 - C_5$ pairs have few cases and the knowledge available to exploit is minimal.

On the other hand, the positive examples for the $C_5 - C_6$ SN are $C_5 - C_6$ pairs. While C_5 cases are limited, C_6 cases are abundant, leading to more variety of training pairs and thus more knowledge to exploit.

- The $C_5 - C_6$ SN has the fastest accuracy growth throughout the multiple experiments. As more C_5 cases are available, the first case of $C_5 - C_6$ pairs is no longer restricted to a single case, and the $C_5 - C_6$ pattern becomes easier to learn. In Fig. 2, when $n_5 = 5$ and $n_5 = 10$, the $C_5 - C_6$ SN achieves superior accuracy, even in comparison to the standard SN with bonus training pairs.

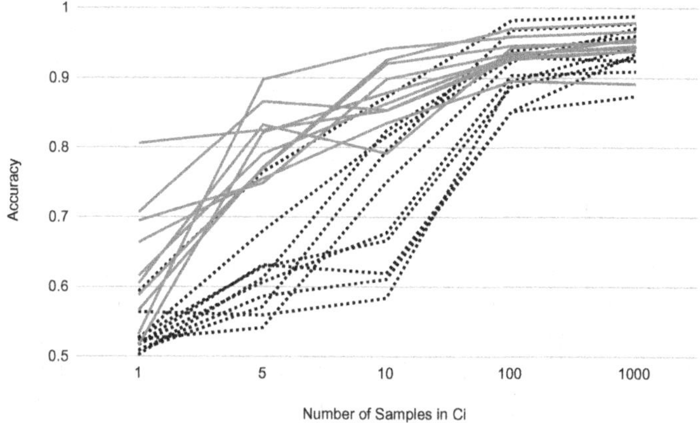

Fig. 3. The accuracy of C2C-SNs under different one-shot learning constraints. Dashed lines are $C_i - C_i$ SNs and solid lines are $C_i - C_{i+1}$ SNs

A second experiment was conducted using the same settings but for 10 $C_i - C_i$ SNs and 10 $C_i - C_{i+1}$ SNs where $0 \leq i \leq 9$. The highest validation accuracy across 10 training epochs was recorded for each SN. As shown in Fig. 3, $C_i - C_{i+1}$ SNs generally outperformed $C_i - C_i$ SNs in one-shot learning settings, and they eventually converged to similar accuracy when more cases were available.

4.3 Explanation by Cases

Here we illustrate the ability of C2C-SNs to support explanation. We start with showing conventional CBR explanation (by presenting a similar case), followed by explaining contrastively (by presenting a relevant different case from a non-target class). Finally, we demonstrate its ability to find prototypical cases.

Explanation by a Similar Case in the Target Class: Given a query q, we can pair it with C_i cases to form $q - C_i$ pairs for each i, then apply a $C_i - C_i$ SN to the pairs. The highest activation achieved by a $q - C_i$ pair indicates q is of class C_i. The second case of the $q - C_i$ pair is a similar case of class C_i,

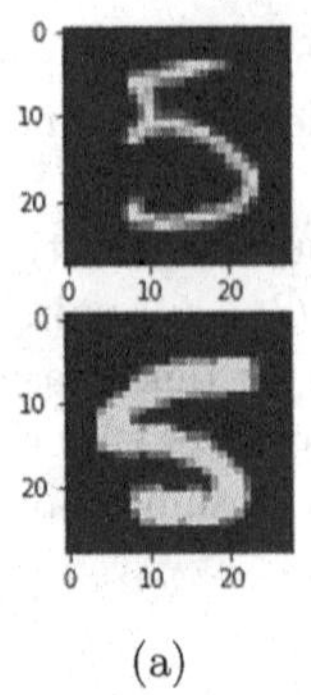

(a)

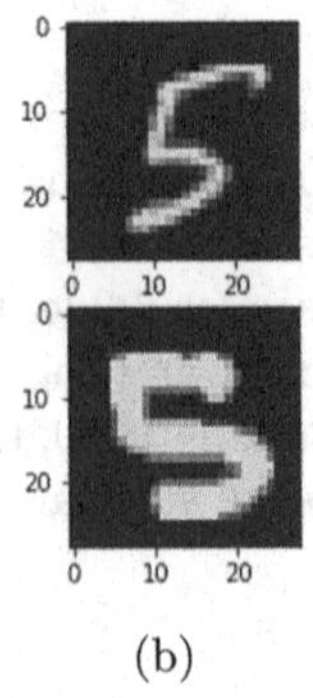

(b)

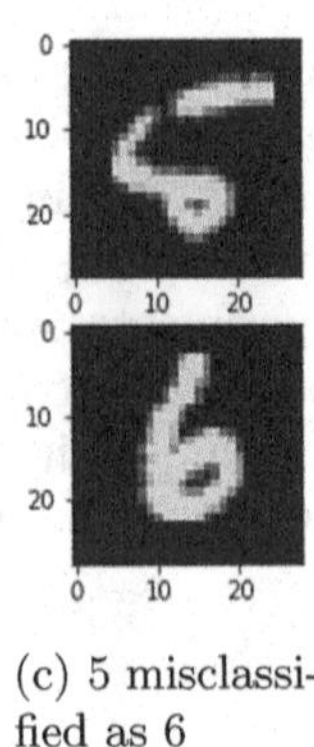

(c) 5 misclassified as 6

Fig. 4. The images of different 5s (top), and their paired cases (bottom) achieving highest activation in $C_i - C_i$ SNs

thus offering an explanation by a similar case in the target class. This follows the usage standard SNs for classification.

Figure 4a and Fig. 4b show examples of explanation by a similar case. Figure 4c shows a misclassification where a badly written digit 5 was misclassified as 6. In this experiment, when the activation threshold was lowered to 0.9, there were 4,998 instances of digit 5s and 5,824 instances of digit 6s achieving the activation threshold. This shows that although classification by C2C-SN is not perfect, it has the potential to indicate the query case as an outlier which is difficult to classify.

Note that the $C_5 - C_5$ pairs were not selected based on their similarity, but based on the extent of which the pattern matches an average pattern between two digit 5s. The second cases of $C_5 - C_5$ pairs in Fig. 4a and 4b were not necessarily the most similar cases in terms of surface features.

Explanation by a Different Case in the Non-target Class: Given a query q, for each i and j ($i \neq j$), we can pair q with C_j cases to form $q - C_j$ pairs, and then use a $C_i - C_j$ SN on the pairs. The highest activation of a $C_i - C_j$ SN achieved by a $q - C_j$ pair suggests q is of class C_i. In this scenario, the second case of the $q - C_j$ pair is not a similar case, because it is of class C_j instead of class C_i. Each $q - C_j$ pair provides an explanation with a contrastive argument.

In this experiment, the top row of Fig. 5 shows the query q, a digit 5. The bottom row of Fig. 5 shows the paired cases in digit 3s, 6s, and 8s achieving the highest activation.

The second cases of the high-activation $q - C_j$ pairs are often not the most standard C_j cases, but rather the C_j cases that magnify the difference between C_i and C_j *when they are compared to the query* q. For example: (1) In Fig. 5a, the digit 3 has a large upper curve in the top right portion; (2) In Fig. 5b, the digit 6 has no horizontal bar in the top portion and no sharp turn in the top left portion; (3) In Fig. 5c, the digit 8 is large in the upper portion but small in

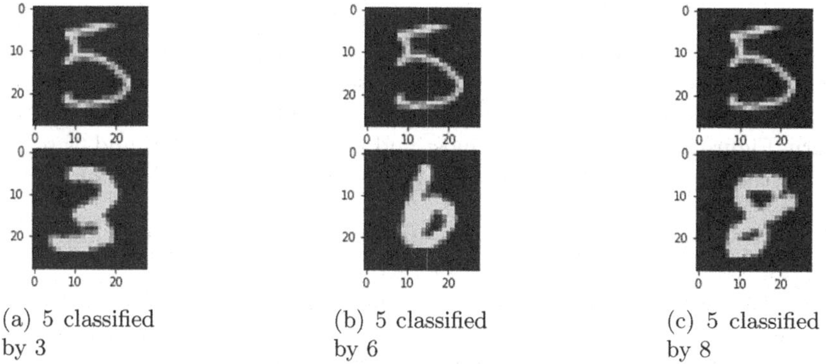

(a) 5 classified by 3 (b) 5 classified by 6 (c) 5 classified by 8

Fig. 5. The images of a single 5 (top), and its paired cases (bottom) achieving highest activation in $C_i - C_j$ SNs

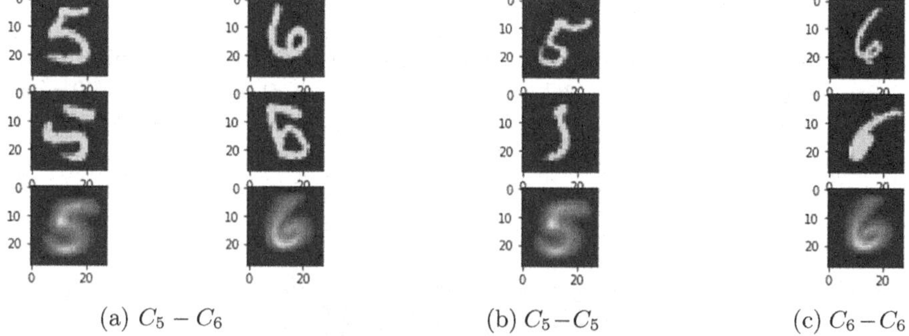

(a) $C_5 - C_6$ (b) $C_5 - C_5$ (c) $C_6 - C_6$

Fig. 6. The most and least prototypical cases found from C2C-SNs. Top: prototypical cases; middle: least prototypical cases; bottom: average of cases

the lower portion. These features are observable in $C_j (j = 3, 6, 8)$ but not usual in C_5. These features are also not present in the specific digit 5 in the pairs. Therefore the $C_5 - C_j$ pairs exemplify the $C_5 - C_j$ patterns.

4.4 Finding Prototypical Cases

A prototypical case is a case that best represents a class. Traditional machine learning methods find a prototypical case by clustering algorithms that find the center, or the average of cases of a class.

A $C_i - C_i$ SN can find a prototypical case a_i in C_i by finding the case with the highest average score in all $C_i - C_i$ pairs. A prototypical case of class C_i thus represents the center of the intra-class pattern of class C_i. In addition, a $C_i - C_j$ SN can find a prototypical case b_i in C_i by finding the case with the highest average score in all $C_i - C_j$ pairs. The prototypical case b_i represents the inter-class pattern of $C_i - C_j$, instead of the intra-class pattern of class C_i.

A $C_i - C_j$ SN can also be used to find the least prototypical case, the case achieving the lowest average score in all $C_i - C_j$ pairs.

Figure 6 illustrates the prototypical cases found in multiple C2C-SNs. Figure 6a shows the most and the least prototypical 5s and 6s in the $C_5 - C_6$ pattern. Figure 6b and 6c show the most and least prototypical 5s and 6s respectively in the $C_5 - C_5$ pattern and the $C_6 - C_6$ pattern. We observe:

- A prototypical case in a intra-class pattern is not necessarily close to the average case, as shown in Fig. 6b and 6c.
- The least prototypical cases are outliers that do not conform to a C2C pattern. In the $C_5 - C_6$ pattern, intuitively, a distinctive feature is the upper left of the digit being a sharp bend (for digit 5s) or a curve (for digit 6s). Figure 6a shows that the least prototypical 5 and 6 lack the corresponding features.
- The prototypical cases for the same class found from different C2C-SNs are not necessarily alike, because they are representing prototypes in different patterns. The same applies to the least prototypical cases.

To further illustrate the last point above, Fig. 7 shows the prototypical cases in every class found from all C2C patterns. For reasons of efficiency, 1,000 samples from every class were used to assemble the case pairs. An entry on ith row and jth column shows the prototypical C_i case in the $C_i - C_j$ pattern. The diagonals are intra-class prototypes while the rest are inter-class prototypes.

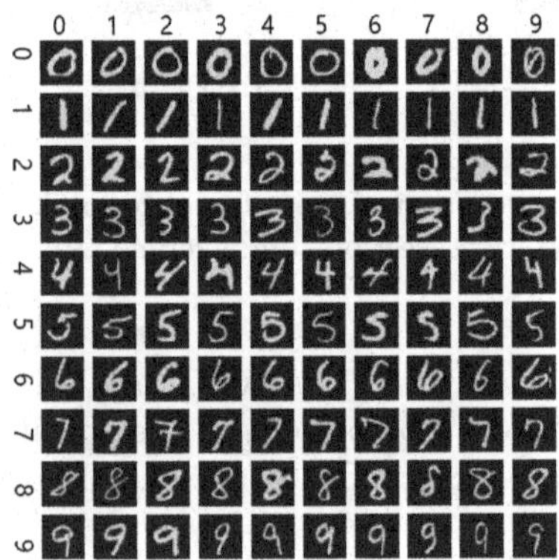

Fig. 7. The prototype matrix. A entry at (i, j) indicates the prototypical C_i case in the $C_i - C_j$ pattern

4.5 Using Prototypical Cases in Classification of a Case

A $C_i - C_j$ SN has two prototypical cases, one for C_i and one for C_j. Instead of pairing the query with each case, the CBR system can classify a query case by pairing the query with prototypical cases of C2C-SNs and finding the highest activation pairs.

For reasons of efficiency, a prototypical case for C_i in the $C_i - C_j$ pattern is found among pairs made from n C_i cases and n C_j cases. When $n = 300$, the number of pairs for training one C2C-SN is $n^2 = 90,000$. A query q is paired with the prototypical C_i case of the $C_i - C_j$ pattern, for every i and j. The $C_i - q$ pair with the highest activation is used for classification. The C2C-SN achieved an accuracy of 92.6%.

Table 2. Pair accuracy for the fashion MNIST dataset

i =	0	1	2	3	4	5	6	7	8
$C_i - C_i$ SN	0.931	0.976	0.894	0.954	0.895	0.958	0.839	0.979	0.975
$C_i - C_{i+1}$ SN	0.954	0.934	0.922	0.923	0.943	0.799	0.903	0.976	0.971

In Sect. 4.3, a digit 5 misclassified as a digit 6 is shown in Fig. 4c. This pair actually achieved the highest activation possible, 1.0, in the $C_6 - C_6$ SN. Even though the correct classification pairs achieved high scores, a certain misclassification pair achieved the maximum score. To remediate this issue, instead of finding the maximum activation pair, we changed the algorithm to have the pairs vote, where each $C_i - q$ pair for the $C_i - C_j$ pattern with activation >0.5 counts as one vote for the class C_j. This algorithm improved the accuracy to 94.23%. In addition, 98.37% of the test cases' true labels were within the top two votes.

Note that the classification accuracy for cases is different from the pair accuracy from Sect. 4.1. In comparison, the standard SN performing case classification by finding the highest activation pair achieves an accuracy of 96.9%; A neural network using the same structure of the upper layers of the C2C-SN and a final classification layer achieved an accuracy of 98.31%.

Last, we note that we built C2C-SN on a simple SN implementation with only dense layers. Preprocessing techniques such as deskewing, noise removal, blurring, and other layers like convolutional layers and pooling layers may be easily applied and could further improve performance. However, such refinements are not the focus of this paper.

5 Additional Results and Future Directions

To assess the performances of the models on a second dataset, experiments were conducted on the Fashion MNIST dataset, which contains images of 10 types of clothing [21]. On this dataset the standard SN achieves pair accuracy of 91.6% and case accuracy of 87.4%. The C2C-SNs pair accuracies are shown in Table 2. Using prototype voting the C2C-SNs achieve case accuracy of 84.2%, and 95.0% within top two votes.

The C2C-SN approach achieves good accuracy in the classification of pairs, and offers a new perspective for explanations and prototypical cases. However, its classification accuracy for cases does not equal existing techniques. It would be interesting to explore ensemble methods to unify all C2C-SNs for the purpose of case classification.

One future direction concerns applying C2C-SNs for outlier detection. When the C2C-SNs agree with each other, the prediction is of a single class. However, when C2C-SNs disagree, the result is a set of votes for multiple classes. Such disagreements may suggest outliers. Moreover, the votes may be used as attributes to describe unseen classes for zero-shot learning.

6 Conclusion

Traditional classification methods focus on learning and reasoning from information about the hidden patterns within a class, in the context of all classes, or rely on similarities between individual cases. Similarity is a well studied topic, with difference often simply defined as the complement of a similarity measure. However, differences between classes can be exploited in novel ways. This paper has argued for the potential of learning about inter-class patterns for classification. In service of this goal, it has shown how a standard siamese network design can be converted into a C2C-SN, by replacing the lower layers and re-purposing the network towards learning inter-class patterns. Experiments illustrated how the C2C-SN approach provides a novel method for classification, one-shot learning, explanation by contrastive cases, and finding prototypes.

Acknowledgment. This material is based upon work supported in part by the Department of the Navy, Office of Naval Research under award number N00014-19-1-2655.

References

1. Ashley, K., Rissland, E.: Compare and contrast, a test of expertise. In: Proceedings of the Sixth Annual National Conference on Artificial Intelligence, AAAI, pp. 273–284. Morgan Kaufmann, San Mateo (1987)
2. Bareiss, R.: Exemplar-Based Knowledge Acquisition: A Unified Approach to Concept Representation, Classification, and Learning. Academic Press, San Diego (1989)
3. Bromley, J., et al.: Signature verification using a siamese time delay neural network. Int. J. Pattern Recogn. Artif. Intell. **7**(04), 669–688 (1993)
4. Bromley, J., Guyon, I., LeCun, Y., Säckinger, E., Shah, R.: Signature verification using a "siamese" time delay neural network. In: Proceedings of the 6th International Conference on Neural Information Processing Systems, NIPS 1993, pp. 737–744. Morgan Kaufmann Publishers Inc., San Francisco (1993)
5. Chollet, F., et al.: MNIST siamese (2015), code retrieved from keras.io. https://keras.io/examples/mnist_siamese/
6. Cunningham, P., Doyle, D., Loughrey, J.: An evaluation of the usefulness of case-based explanation. In: Ashley, K.D., Bridge, D.G. (eds.) ICCBR 2003. LNCS (LNAI), vol. 2689, pp. 122–130. Springer, Heidelberg (2003). https://doi.org/10.1007/3-540-45006-8_12

7. Doyle, D., Cunningham, P., Bridge, D., Rahman, Y.: Explanation oriented retrieval. In: Funk, P., González Calero, P.A. (eds.) ECCBR 2004. LNCS (LNAI), vol. 3155, pp. 157–168. Springer, Heidelberg (2004). https://doi.org/10.1007/978-3-540-28631-8_13
8. Gunning, D., Aha, D.W.: DARPA's explainable artificial intelligence program. AI Mag. **40**(2), 44–58 (2019)
9. Hadsell, R., Chopra, S., LeCun, Y.: Dimensionality reduction by learning an invariant mapping. In: Proceedings of the 2006 IEEE Computer Society Conference on Computer Vision and Pattern Recognition, CVPR 2006, vol. 2, p. 17351742. IEEE Computer Society, USA (2006)
10. Kapetanakis, S., Martin, K., Wijekoon, A., Amin, K., Massie, S. (eds.): Proceedings of the ICCBR-19 Case Based Reasoning and Deep Learning Workshop CBRDL-19 (2019)
11. Bach, K., Marling, C. (eds.): ICCBR 2019. LNCS (LNAI), vol. 11680. Springer, Cham (2019). https://doi.org/10.1007/978-3-030-29249-2
12. Keane, M.T., Kenny, E.M.: How case based reasoning explained neural networks: an XAI survey of post-hoc explanation-by-example in ANN-CBR twins. CoRR arxiv:1905.07186 (2019)
13. Koch, G., Zemel, R., Salakhutdinov, R.: Siamese neural networks for one-shot image recognition. In: ICML 2015 Deep Learning Workshop (2015)
14. Leake, D.: CBR in context: the present and future. In: Leake, D. (ed.) Case-Based Reasoning: Experiences, Lessons, and Future Directions, pp. 3–30. AAAI Press, Menlo Park (1996)
15. Leake, D., Birnbaum, L., Hammond, K., Marlow, C., Yang, H.: An integrated interface for proactive, experience-based design support. In: Proceedings of the 2001 International Conference on Intelligent User Interfaces, pp. 101–108 (2001)
16. de Mántaras, R.L., et al.: Retrieval, reuse, revision, and retention in CBR. Knowl. Eng. Rev. **20**(3), 215–240 (2005)
17. Marchiori, E.: Class dependent feature weighting and k-nearest neighbor classification. In: Ngom, A., Formenti, E., Hao, J.-K., Zhao, X.-M., van Laarhoven, T. (eds.) PRIB 2013. LNCS, vol. 7986, pp. 69–78. Springer, Heidelberg (2013). https://doi.org/10.1007/978-3-642-39159-0_7
18. Martin, K., Wiratunga, N., Sani, S., Massie, S., Clos, J.: A convolutional siamese network for developing similarity knowledge in the selfback dataset. In: ICCBR (Workshops) (2017)
19. Mathisen, B.M., Aamodt, A., Bach, K., Langseth, H.: Learning similarity measures from data. Prog. Artif. Intell. **9**(2), 129–143 (2019). https://doi.org/10.1007/s13748-019-00201-2
20. Nugent, C., Doyle, D., Cunningham, P.: Gaining insight through case-based explanation. J. Intell. Inf. Syst. **32**, 267–295 (2009)
21. Research, Z.: Fashion MNIST (2020), data retrieved from Kaggle. https://www.kaggle.com/zalando-research/fashionmnist
22. Tversky, A.: Features of similarity. Psychol. Rev. **84**(4), 327–352 (1977)
23. Wettschereck, D., Aha, D., Mohri, T.: A review and empirical evaluation of feature-weighting methods for a class of lazy learning algorithms. Artif. Intell. Rev. **11**(1–5), 273–314 (1997)

24. Ye, X.: The enemy of my enemy is my friend: class-to-class weighting in k-nearest neighbors algorithm. In: Proceedings of the Thirty-First International Florida Artificial Intelligence Research Society Conference, FLAIRS, vol. 2018, pp. 389–394 (2018)
25. Ye, X.: C2C trace retrieval: fast classification using class-to-class weighting. In: Proceedings of the Thirty-Second International Florida Artificial Intelligence Research Society Conference, FLAIRS, vol. 2019, pp. 353–358 (2019)

Technical Session: Applications

Building Non-player Character Behaviors By Imitation Using Interactive Case-Based Reasoning

Maximiliano Miranda(✉), Antonio A. Sánchez-Ruiz, and Federico Peinado

Departamento de Ingeniería del Software e Inteligencia Artificial, Universidad Complutense de Madrid, c/ Profesor José García Santesmases 9, 28040 Madrid, Spain
{m.miranda,antsanch}@ucm.es, email@federicopeinado.com
https://www.narratech.com

Abstract. The creation of believable characters is one of the most challenging problems in the interactive entertainment industry. Although there are different tools available for designers and programmers to define the behavior of non-player characters, it remains a complex and error prone process that requires a high level of technical knowledge. Learning from Demonstration is a promising field that studies how to build intelligent agents that are able to replicate behaviors, learning from demonstration of human experts. This approach is interesting for developers who do not have a computer science background, alleviating the need of representing tasks and knowledge in a formal way. In this work we present an online and case-based reasoning agent that learns how to imitate real players of Pac-Man using an interactive approach in which both the human player and the computational agent take turns controlling the main character. In our previous work, the agent was in complete control of the learning process so it decided when to give up or regain control of the character. Now the system have been improved so the player can also regain control of the character and go back in time to correct improper behaviors manifested by the agent whenever they are detected. We also present an evaluation of the system performed by three professional video game designers, followed by the main insights we have gained.

Keywords: Interactive online learning · Learning from Demonstration · Human behavior imitation · Interactive entertainment

1 Introduction

The creation of believable characters in video games is currently one of the most challenging problems in the game industry. There is a widespread assumption that the game experience generally improves when the non-player characters

This work has been partially supported by the Spanish Committee of Economy and Competitiveness (TIN2017-87330-R) and the UCM (Group 921330).

I. Watson and R. Weber (Eds.): ICCBR 2020, LNAI 12311, pp. 263–278, 2020.
https://doi.org/10.1007/978-3-030-58342-2_17

(NPCs) interact with the player in a more "human" way. These type of interactions make the players perceive the game to be less predictable, more replayable, and more challenging than when the bots are hand-coded [18]. For this reason, player modeling in video games has been an increasingly important field of study, not only for academics but for professional developers as well [22], and several competitions on developing believable characters have emerged during the last decade [6].

There are different tools available for game programmers and designers in the game industry to define the behavior of NPCs[1,2], and most of them are based on two underlying technologies for decision-making: finite state machines and behavior trees [1]. Although these tools are much more friendly nowadays than they used to be and provide visual interfaces, the definition of complex behaviors in different and changing scenarios is a difficult task. Unfortunately, the creation of these behaviors remains a complex and error prone process that requires a high level of technical knowledge and many hours of trial and error.

Learning from demonstration (LfD), on the other hand, studies the design of agents that learn to behave and solve problems just from the imitation of human experts. This approach is much more interesting for domain experts who do not have a background in knowledge engineering, since it alleviates to a great extend the need to represent problem solving knowledge in a formal representation. We believe LfD might be an interesting and promising approach for game designers to define the complex character behaviors required in modern video games.

Obviously, LfD also faces important challenges that must be solved before it can be used in the game industry. For example, Machine Learning (ML) classical techniques do not work well to learn behaviors from static datasets of games traces because this setup violates the *independent, identically distributed* (i.i.d.) data assumption of supervised learning, since the training data (states visited by the players who train the agent) and test data (states reached by the agent when it plays) does not come from the same distribution.

To overcome this kind of limitations, we presented an online case-based reasoning (CBR) agent that learned to imitate a human player to some extend using an interactive approach in which both the human demonstrator and the CBR agent took turns controlling the main character in a Pac-Man game [11]. This intelligent agent was in complete control of the learning process and it decided when to give up or regain control of the character.

In this work we improve our system so that the human expert can also regain control of the character to correct improper behaviors of the CBR agent whenever they are detected. Note that this is an essential feature for game designers: they must be able to overwrite or refine behaviors learned by the CBR agent when they are not correct. Moreover, we have evaluated the system with three professional video game designers and collected their impressions and thoughts regarding the use of LfD to train video game characters.

---

[1] Unity, https://unity.com.

[2] Unreal Engine, https://www.unrealengine.com.

The rest of the paper is structured as follows: the next two sections summarize the related work in the field and introduces the video game used in our experiments. Section 4 describes our interactive and online CBR agent and how the control changes between the human expert and the CBR agent. Next, Sects. 5 and 6 explain the evaluation with three game designers and discuss their impressions and thoughts. Finally, we close the paper with some conclusions and future lines of research.

2 Related Work

There are several works regarding the imitation of behavior in video games in the scientific literature, for imitating human players and even other script-driven characters. The behavior of an agent can be characterized by studying its reactions to sequences of events over a period of time, but achieving that involves a significant amount of effort and technical knowledge [21] in the best case. ML techniques can be used to automate the problem of learning how to play a video game either progressively using players' game traces as input, in direct imitation approaches, or using some form of optimization technique such as Evolutionary Computation or Reinforcement Learning to develop a fitness function that, for instance, "measures" the human likeness of an agent's playing style [19].

ML approaches like ANNs and Naive Bayes classifiers, have been used for modeling human-like players in first-person shooter games by using sets of examples [5]. Other techniques based on indirect imitation like dynamic scripting and Neuroevolution achieved better results in Super Mario Bros than direct imitation techniques [12].

CBR has been used successfully for training RoboCup soccer players, observing the behavior of other players and using traces taken from the game, without requiring much human intervention [4]. In this context, Floyd *et al.* [2] also noted that when working in a setting with time constraints, it is very important to study what characteristics of the cases really impact the precision of the system and when it is better to increase the size of the case base while simplifying the cases. Furthermore, they described how applying preprocessing techniques to a case base can increase the performance of a CBR system by increasing the diversity of the case base.

About how the case base is obtained, we follow a similar approach as the described by Lam *et al.* [8], as the cases are generated in an automated manner by recording traces of the player that will be imitated as pairs of *scene* state (representation of the player's point of view) and player's outputs. Floyd and Esfandiari [3] incorporated active learning with learning by observation studying how to create sequences of problems to show to the expert. Finally, Lamontagne *et al.* [9] also studied how the cases could be built from sequential traces during game demonstrations in Pac-Man.

The problem of violating the i.i.d. assumption in LfD has been addressed before with no regret algorithms in online learning settings, resulting in

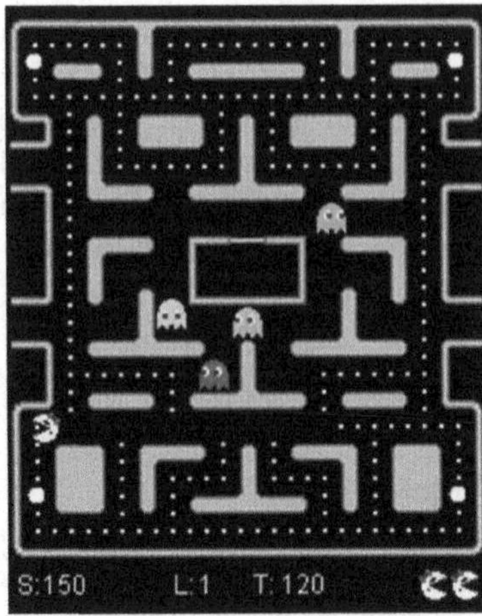

Fig. 1. A screenshot of the first maze of Ms. Pac-Man vs. Ghosts

algorithms like SMILe and DAGGER proposed by Ross *et al.* [16,17] which outperform previous approaches like SEARN [7] in the Super Tux Kart and Super Mario Bros video games. However, these methods have limitations when the demonstrator is a human player. Because of this, Packard and Ontañón presented *SALT*, which main idea is to let the learning agent play until it has moved out of the space for which it has training data, giving the control to the expert at this point to show the agent how to get back into this space, turning the learning process into an i.i.d. task allowing the use of supervised learning algorithms [13]. Further on, they extended this approach studying its efficiency in environments where the amount of training data the learning agent is allowed to request from the expert is limited [14]. These methods inspired the interactive CBR system used in this work [11].

Finally, about the use of Pac-Man as test bed for imitation learning, it should be noticed that, during decades, it has been considered a promising platform for research due to its many characteristics that make it stand out from other games. Thus, there have been nearly 100 different approaches covering a wide selection of techniques used to develop controllers for Pac-Man or the ghosts, including rule-based and finite state machines, tree search and Monte Carlo, evolutionary algorithms, neural networks, neuro-evolution and reinforcement learning [15].

3 Ms. Pac-Man vs. Ghosts

Pac-Man is an arcade video game produced by Namco in 1980. In this game, the player has direct control over Pac-Man (a small yellow character), pointing the direction it will follow in each game step. The level is a simple maze full of white pills, called Pac-Dots, that Pac-Man eats gaining points. There are four ghosts with different behaviors trying to capture Pac-Man, causing it to lose one live.

Pac-Man initially has three lives and the game ends when the player looses all of them. In the maze there are also four special pills, bigger than the normal ones and named Power Pellets or Energizers, which make the ghosts to be "edible" during a short period of time. Every time Pac-Man eats one of the ghosts during this period, the player is rewarded with several points.

Ms. Pac-Man vs Ghosts (see Fig. 1) is a new version of the classical video game designed to develop bots to control both the protagonist and the ghosts. This framework has been used in several academic competitions during the recent years [15,20] to compare different AI techniques.

It is interesting to note that even a classic arcade game such as Pac-Man hides a very high dimensional feature space that is a challenge for ML algorithms. The full state representation of the game contains 256 different parameters and the player can perform 5 possible actions at each game step (move left, right, up, down or neutral). Typically, an averaged-skill human player needs between 1200 to 1800 game steps to complete one level of the game, so the trace of a game contains thousand of *state-action* pairs.

4 An Online and Interactive CBR Agent

The CBR agent uses a case base in which each case is a pair (state, action) where the state is an abstract representation of the real game state and the action is the direction chosen by the player in that moment. The representation of the state is based on a set of distances in each one of the 4 possible directions to the closest Pac-Dot, Power Pellet and ghost, the time the nearest ghost will remain edible in each direction, and the direction chosen by the player in the previous game step. We compute the similarity between cases as the similarity between states, and the states are compared using a linear combination of the similarities between features. Finally, the similarities between features are computed using the inverse of the euclidean distances [10]. Given the current game state, the agent selects the action to execute using k Nearest Neighbor with k = 3.

The agent learns from the human player using an interactive approach in which both the agent and the human demonstrator take turns controlling the main character in Pac-Man [11]. In our previous work, the CBR agent was in complete control of the learning process and it decided when to give up or regain control of the character by following policies based on the similarities of the last cases retrieved using a time window (i.e. considering the mean value and the coefficient of the linear regression). The human demonstrator played for a while until the game states were similar to the ones in the case base again, and then the CBR agent regained control of the game. The intuitive idea is that when the agent makes mistakes and reaches unknown areas of the state space, the human demonstrator must teach the agent how to correct its mistakes and go back to known scenarios. In order to avoid too many changes regarding who is in control of Pac-Man, there are some minimum time intervals between control changes. Finally, the CBR agent only learns new cases when the human demonstration is playing the game.

The new contribution of this work is that now the human demonstrator can also interrupt the CBR agent and correct incorrect or strange behaviors whenever they are detected. This way, game designers can teach to the agent specific behaviors for specific situations or even to change the way the agent plays towards a different style of playing. This interaction is different from the previous one in which the game was paused a few seconds just to give time to the human demonstrator to take control of the game. In this interaction, the human demonstrator needs to be able to go back in time a few seconds to replay that part of the game and teach the agent what to do. Note that we can only know that the agent has made a mistake after the mistake is made, and in order to correct it we might need to change some previous decisions that led to that error. Currently, the human demonstrator can decide how many seconds to go back in time interactively, watching the characters of the game undo their movements.

From the point of view of the CBR agent, there are basically two approaches to correct a behavior: we can add new cases to the case base or delete old cases. The first approach is preferred when the agent has learned a correct behavior for some past situation but the current scenario is slightly different and requires a different strategy. We are basically teaching more specific strategies to the agent and refining its domain knowledge. However, we could also want to correct some behavior that was learned because the human player made a mistake in some previous game that the agent is replicating. In this situation we would like to remove those cases from the case base. Unfortunately, from the perspective of the human demonstrator is not easy to distinguish between these two situations. Besides, removing those cases can lead to leave unreachable cases in the memory of the agent or even to break more complex strategies. In our current approach, we only add new cases when the human demonstrator takes control of the game.

5 Experimental Setup

We have performed an experiment with three professional game designers who are used to define the behaviors of NPCs in different types of video games. Their goal during the experiment was to create a Pac-Man agent with some specific style of play using our system. It is important to remark that the goal was not necessarily to train an agent for obtaining a high score but to play in some specific way, described in a human way, so we expect the agent to make errors as long as those errors are coherent with that style of play.

At the beginning of the experiment the game designers filled in a questionnaire regarding their skills as video game players and more specifically as Pac-Man players, and their thoughts about the use of LfD techniques to define behaviors in video games.

Then each designer was asked to describe the type of agent they wanted to create and, therefore, how they were going to play:

- Designer *A* wanted to create a *fierce* agent. His main goal was to maximize the score eating several ghost in a row using the Power Pellets (each consecutive

ghost eaten provides many more points than the previous one). In order to do it, the player stays close to the Power Pellets waiting for the ghosts to come close. This strategy can produce very high scores but it is also dangerous because there are only 4 Power Pellets in the maze and the ghosts can corner the player in different parts of the level. Ending the level is not a primary goal for this player and he will only try to eat the Pac-Dots of the level when there are no more Power Pellets available.
- Designer B wanted to create a *conservative* agent. His main goal was to survive and complete the level. This player will try to eat the Pac-Dots unless there are ghosts close in which case he will run away. This player will only eat edible ghosts if they are on its way or very close but he will not chase them through the maze.
- Designer C wanted to create a *moderate* agent. He will try to complete the maze and maximize the score so he will combine eating Pac-Dots as fast as possible with eating ghosts whenever possible.

Next, each player played 5 games using the style of play chosen. Each game ends when the player finishes the maze by eating all the Pac-Dots and Power Pellets, or when the player loses his 4 lives. We use these games to compute some high level metrics to characterize their playing style. In addition, during those games we also gather the traces to train an offline CBR system. We play 100 games with the offline CBR system to compute the same high level metrics. Then we show 4 random games to the designer and ask him to answer some questions about how well the agent is replicating his style of play.

In the second part of the experiment we use the interactive CBR agent described in the previous section, but we do not allow the expert to correct the agent (the designer only controls Pac-Man when the agent decides so). The designer and the CBR agent take turns to control Pac-Man during 10 games. Then we play 100 games with the interactive CBR agent to compute the same high level metrics and show 4 random games to the designer to answer the same questions regarding the imitation skills of the resulting agent.

In the third part of the experiment we use the last interactive CBR agent and explain to the designer that he can correct unexpected behaviors stopping the game at any time, go back in time, and replaying parts of the game. This last part of the experiment ends when the designer is pleased with the behavior of the agent or when he is bored to teach the agent. Then we evaluate the agent in the same way, computing the high level metrics and showing 4 random games to the designer.

Finally the experiment ends with a closing questionnaire to evaluate the interactive online CBR system as a tool for building agents during a video game development, including a free text section so that the designers can express their conclusions and thoughts.

This way, we evaluate each one of the 3 agents using two different approaches: (1) a phenomenological evaluation using a questionnaire with Likert scale questions, and (2) comparing some high level metrics automatically extracted from the game traces to characterize different ways to play the game. These metrics, that are listed next, were detailed in previous works [10,11]:

Table 1. High level parameters obtained by the human designer A during his 5 complete games and the CBR agent after the first (iCBR1) and second (iCBR2) stages of the interactive CBR experiment (average values after 100 games).

HL param	Player A (fierce)	iCBR1	iCBR1 diff	iCBR2	iCBR2 diff
Time	1,846.43	1,264.85	31.50%	1,486.37	19.50%
Score	7,194.29	4,288.00	40.40%	4,111.00	42.86%
Restlessness	1.25	0.96	23.42%	1.10	12.14%
Recklessness	42.71	49.52	13.75%	46.56	8.26%
Aggressiveness	9.43	5.69	39.65%	5.51	41.56%
Clumsiness	24.86	99.92	75.12%	28.48	12.72%
Survival	0.57	0	40.40%	0.02	96.50%
Craving	38.58	63.83	39.55%	42.25	8.67%
Hungry	641.10	451.63	29.55%	523.41	18.36%

- *Time*, duration of the game in game steps.
- *Score*, number of points gained at the end of the game.
- *Restlessness*, number of direction changes per second.
- *Recklessness*, average distance to the closest ghost.
- *Aggressiveness*, number of ghosts eaten.
- *Clumsiness*, number of game steps in which the player is stuck.
- *Survival*, number of lives left when the player completes the level.
- *Craving*, average time elapsed between a Power Pellet is eaten and the first edible ghost is eaten.
- *Hungry*, average time between two eaten Power Pellets.

6 Results and Discussion

When analyzing the human games the desired style of play of each designer is clearly represented on the high level parameters obtained. This can be seen on the second column of Tables 1, 2 and 3. For example, designer *A* is the one who obtained the highest scores but he has the lowest *Survival* value, which is just what was expected as the designer's main objective was to maximize the score by eating ghosts, not paying attention in finishing the maze. Moreover he has the highest *Aggressiveness* by far, lowest *Recklessness* and *Craving* and even the highest *Clumsiness* as he is the player who spends more time in corners waiting for the ghosts to come closer.

About the designer *B* playing style, is the one who faster ends the level by eating all the Pac-Dots, he is also the one who spends less time waiting

Table 2. High level parameters obtained by the human designer B during his 5 complete games and the CBR agent after the first (iCBR1) and second (iCBR2) stages of the interactive CBR experiment (average values after 100 games).

HL param	Player B (conserv.)	iCBR1	iCBR1 diff	iCBR2	iCBR2 diff
Time	1,152.20	1,163.80	1.00%	1,245.78	7.51%
Score	3,344.00	3,440.00	2.79%	3,298.67	1.36%
Restlessness	1.17	0.98	16.34%	1.10	6.66%
Recklessness	49.75	54.49	8.72%	52.87	5.90%
Aggressiveness	3.80	4.38	13.24%	3.62	4.68%
Clumsiness	0.40	47.72	99.16%	8.76	95.43%
Survival	1.40	0	100.00%	1.09	22.22%
Craving	105.93	111.10	4.65%	119.81	11.58%
Hungry	428.17	418.68	2.22%	418.12	2.35%

Table 3. High level parameters obtained by the human designer C during his 5 complete games and the CBR agent after the first (iCBR1) and second (iCBR2) stages of the interactive CBR experiment (average values after 100 games).

HL param	Player C (moderate)	iCBR1	iCBR1 diff	iCBR2	iCBR2 diff
Time	1,287.57	1,342.48	4.09%	1,386.13	7.11%
Score	3,561.43	4,046.20	11.98%	3,799.50	6.27%
Restlessness	1.09	1.00	8.14%	0.99	8.98%
Recklessness	47.14	47.72	1.22%	50.81	7.23%
Aggressiveness	3.71	5.00	25.71%	4.57	18.72%
Clumsiness	4.29	0.36	91.60%	3.90	9.00%
Survival	1.86	0.56	69.85%	0.10	94.62%
Craving	120.71	93.12	22.86%	96.99	19.65%
Hungry	464.04	421.84	9.09%	422.08	9.04%

(lowest *Clumsiness* value). On the order hand, designer C has some mixed values, he takes a little longer to complete the maze but achieve a score slightly better than B with similar number of ghost eaten, this is because designer C manages to eat more ghosts in a row after eating a Power Pellet.

These tables also display the high level parameters obtained by the resulting bots of the interactive CBR experiment. Column *iCBR1* corresponds to 100 new games of the agent after the second part of the experiment in which the bot and the human player take turns. And column *iCBR2* corresponds to 100 new games at the end of the last part in which the designer can regain control of the game at any moment and go back in time to correct specific mistakes of the bot.

Looking at the values obtained by the bot after each stage, we can see that column *iCBR2* displays, on average, better results. Although some measures

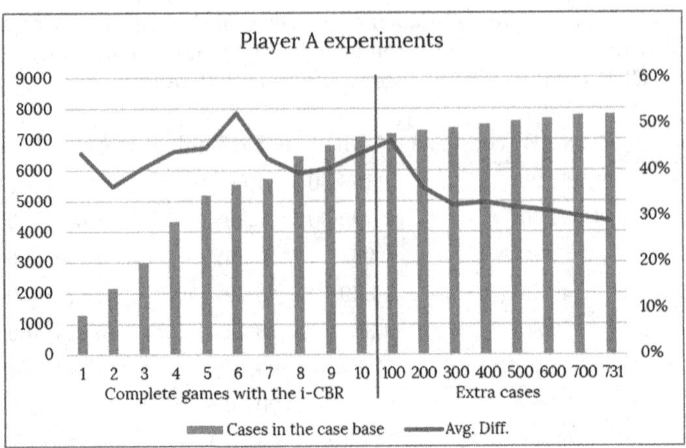

Fig. 2. Evolution of the case base during the experiment and the average percentage difference between the high level parameters obtained by the designer A and the ones obtained by the CBR agent every game finished (on the left side) and every 100 extra cases learned (on the right side). (Color figure online)

are slightly worse, the average difference between these parameters with the ones obtained by the designer (first column) decreases. Revealing that the new feature that gives the designers the ability to stop the bot at any time, go back in time, and correct specific sections tested in the last part of the experiment, seems to have an important impact by improving the results of the interactive online CBR by adding a few new cases.

This is more clearly visible on Figs. 2, 3 and 4 where the red lines display the evolution of the average percentage difference between the high level metrics obtained by the human designer in the 5 initial full games and the values obtained by the CBR agent after each training game (labeled with the percentage values on the right y-axis). This figures also show the evolution of the case base size throughout the experiment (displayed using blue bars and labeled with the numbers of the left y-axis).

It is important to note that each graph is divided in two sides corresponding to the second and the third part of the experiment. The left side corresponds to the first stage of the interactive CBR experiment when the bot is tested with the case base exported every game finished (x-axis is divided in complete games). And the right side corresponds to the second stage of the interactive CBR experiment in which the player can regain control at any time, where the case base is exported and tested every 100 new cases (so in this side the x-axis values increase every 100 new cases).

Looking at the evolution of the average difference (red lines), we have mixed outcomes. As expected, Figs. 3 and 4 show how the resulting bots of the designers B and C decrease their differences with the style of play of the designers remaining almost constant throughout the experiments.

On the other hand, this is not so evident in the experiment of designer A (Fig. 2), where the average difference is quite fluctuating, undergoing noticeable ups and downs. We think this is due to two different, but related, facts. Firstly, the style of play of this designer (described in Sect. 5) is the one that entails the greatest difficulty when playing and, consequently, to imitate. For example, the action of waiting for the ghosts, stuck in a corner, close to a Power-Pellet, and then, when ghost are close enough, eat the pill and go towards them seems to be very difficult to generalize in cases, as this move can be planed in many positions of the maze and involves many variables (e.g. having the four ghosts very close and having a Power-Pellet close but in opposite direction). Secondly the course of the experiment was quite irregular in terms of the evolution of the player himself throughout the games, making a lot of mistakes and nonsense

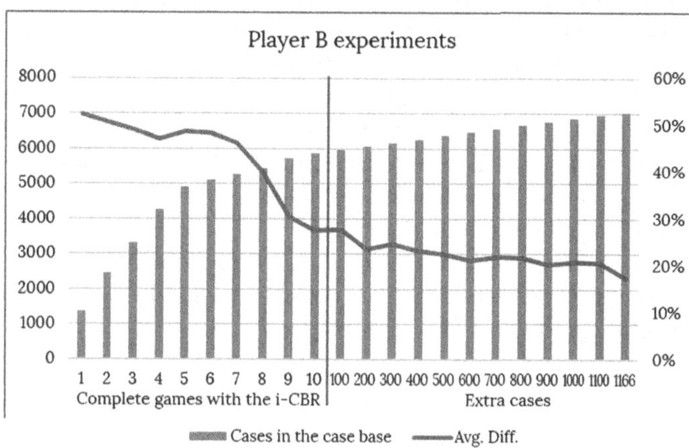

Fig. 3. Evolution of the case base during the experiment and the average percentage difference between the high level parameters obtained by the designer B and the ones obtained by the CBR agent every game finished (on the left side) and every 100 extra cases learned (on the right side). (Color figure online)

Table 4. Metrics taken during the last section of the experiment (interactive CBR going back in time) of the three designers.

Metrics	Player A	Player B	Player C
Number of corrections	38	58	42
Average bot steps per correction	266.61	407.21	325.05
Minimum bot steps per correction	16	19	15
Maximum bot steps per correction	2,061	3,274	1,362
Avg. game steps rewound per correction	38.03	21.29	19.05
Min game steps rewound per correction	15	7	7
Max game steps rewound per correction	62	70	59

movements. However, as we will see in the designer evaluation, the resulting bot was quite convincing (considering the irregularity of the evolution of the experiment).

Focusing at the performance of the bots at the end of the experiment, and comparing with the results after stage 1 of the interactive CBR experiment, we can see that designer *A* (Fig. 2) achieve an improvement from 43.66% to 28.95% by adding 731 new cases (9.35% of the total), designer *B* (Fig. 3) advance from 27.57% to 17.52% by adding 1166 new cases (16.57% of the total) and the designer *C* (Fig. 4) decrease from 27.17% to 20.07% with 840 new cases (10.59% of the total).

The actions of the experts during the third part of the experiment can be seen on Table 4. Designer *B* is the one who made more corrections although he let the bot play for longer periods of time. Designer *A* made fewer corrections and, in average, took more time in realizing that the bot should be corrected (as he has the highest value in game steps rewound per correction). On the other hand, designer *C* seems to be the most agile in detecting errors in the bot.

Regarding the questionnaires answered by the experts before the experiment (collected in Table 5), we can highlight some interesting ideas: they agree in pointing that, during the development process of video games, the development of intelligent agents represents an important amount of time. Although they remind quite sceptical about the existence of LfD tools in real video game development they believe that, if it existed, it would be a great help during the development process. The three designers consider themselves expert video game players (in general), and good Pac-Man players.

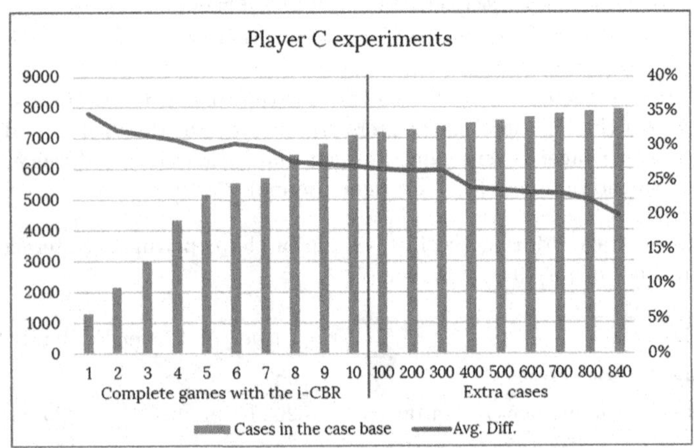

Fig. 4. Evolution of the case base during the experiment and the average percentage difference between the high level parameters obtained by the designer *C* and the ones obtained by the CBR agent every game finished (on the left side) and every 100 extra cases learned (on the right side). (Color figure online)

When evaluating the CBR agent after every step of the experiment, all the experts point an improvement in the agent's behavior, although they agree that the bot is trying to imitate their movements since the first step (4 points), at the question "the resulting bot plays as I though it should play" their score goes from 2 at the end of the first step, to 4, an finally 4.66. There is also a clear sense of progress throughout the experiment, marked at the end in the answers to "The bot has improved during this part of the experiment comparing with the previous one" with a score of 4.66, to "I think that the bot was really learning from my gameplay" 4.66 after step two and three, and to "If this bot were the final result of the system I would use it as a tool" 2.33 points after the first part, 4 after the second and 4.66 at the end.

The results of the questionnaire after the last stage (see Table 6) deliver other positive results. The designers do not find the system tedious (2.3 points) and they clearly see that the bot needs less expert intervention over time (4 points).

Finally, they all agree in pointing a promising evaluation of the system as a tool: the questions "The Learning from Demonstration system is a good idea" and "I find it easier to make a bot this way that programming its logic by scripting" obtained 5 points each.

Some other comments point ideas to improve the system: "I would like to be able to correct errors in the game made by me", "I think there are still some very specific situations that hasn't arise during the experiment, so the bot would probably confront wrongly". Others point to specific characteristics of the resulting bots: "There are some errors that make it clear that the player is not a scripted bot", "It nails the openings".

Table 5. Results of the questionnaires after stage 1 and 2, questions are evaluated using a Likert-type scale ranged from 1 to 5.

Question	A	B	C	Avg.
1. During the development process of video games, the creation of intelligent agents represents an important amount of time	5	5	5	5
2. A tool for developing AIs for agents by imitating the playing style of designers is possible nowadays	3	3	3	3
3. If this tool existed, it would be of great use during the development process	5	5	5	5
4. I am an expert video game player	5	5	5	5
5. I am an expert Pac-Man player	4	3	4	3.66
6. (Stage 1) The resulting bot seems to try to imitate my movements	5	3	4	4
7. (Stage 1) The resulting bot plays as I though it should play	3	1	2	2
8. (Stage 1) If this bot were the final result of the system I would use it as a tool	3	2	2	2.33
9. (Stage 2) The bot has improved during this part of the experiment comparing with the previous one	4	5	5	4.66
10. (Stage 2) The resulting bot seems to try to imitate my movements	5	3	5	4.33
11. (Stage 2) The resulting bot plays as I though it should play	4	4	4	4
12. (Stage 2) If this bot were the final result of the system I would use it as a tool	3	4	5	4

Table 6. Results of the questionnaires at the end of the experiment, questions are evaluated using a Likert-type scale ranged from 1 to 5.

Question	A	B	C	Avg.
13. (Stage 3) The bot has improved during this part of the experiment comparing with the previous one	4	5	5	4.66
14. (Stage 3) The resulting bot seems to try to imitate my movements	4	5	5	4.66
15. (Stage 3) The resulting bot plays as I though it should play	4	5	5	4.66
16. (Stage 3) If this bot were the final result of the system I would use it as a tool	4	5	5	4.66
17. (Stage 3) I have found this system tedious	3	2	2	2.33
18. (Stage 3) Each time I had to correct the bot less	3	5	4	4
19. The Learning from Demonstration system is a good idea	5	5	5	5
20. I find it easier to make a bot this way that programming its logic by scripting	5	5	5	5

7 Conclusions

During this work we have presented an experiment to test an interactive and online case-based reasoning system firstly introduced in [11] in which a bot using CBR gives control to a human player when it reaches unknown game states. There are some new improvements in the system like the feature of giving the human player full control to take control whenever a wrong action by the bot is detected, and go back in time to that specific moment and correct it. During the experiment, three different video games designers play a Pac-Man game in order to teach a bot to play with a specific style.

The results show that the system allows human designers to create virtual players with distinctly behaviors, that are capable, to some extend, to imitate the style of play of human experts without needing large amounts of training data.

Compared to previous approaches [10,11] the resulting bots are capable of achieving a better level of imitation when the experts are able to correct specific errors adding a few more cases into the case base.

Furthermore, the phenomenological evaluation given by the video game designers during the experiments allow us to be reasonably optimistic regarding the use of the system as a tool for building NPCs, moreover considering that this was the first time the system was expose to these video game designers. However, the resulting bots are not perfect and there is still room for improvement.

As part of the future work we would like to address the problem of deleting specific cases from the case base to forget wrong behaviors, and better understand the impact of those deletions, as during the experiment we saw that unwanted errors during the training produce behaviors in the bot from which it is very difficult to recover. Furthermore, we would like to explore the idea of using our interactive approach to modify a collection of standard behaviors and adapt them, instead of training a new agent from scratch. We think that having such a library of behaviours could help game designers to test their ideas faster.

Finally, we would like to improve our system from the perspective of the user experience. Designer tools need to provide a powerful and intuitive interface so that users can focus on the creative problems and test different solutions fast.

References

1. Colledanchise, M., Ögren, P.: Behavior trees in robotics and AI: an introduction (2017)
2. Floyd, M.W., Davoust, A., Esfandiari, B.: Considerations for real-time spatially-aware case-based reasoning: a case study in robotic soccer imitation. In: Althoff, K.-D., Bergmann, R., Minor, M., Hanft, A. (eds.) ECCBR 2008. LNCS (LNAI), vol. 5239, pp. 195–209. Springer, Heidelberg (2008). https://doi.org/10.1007/978-3-540-85502-6_13
3. Floyd, M.W., Esfandiari, B.: An active approach to automatic case generation. In: McGinty, L., Wilson, D.C. (eds.) ICCBR 2009. LNCS (LNAI), vol. 5650, pp. 150–164. Springer, Heidelberg (2009). https://doi.org/10.1007/978-3-642-02998-1_12
4. Floyd, M.W., Esfandiari, B., Lam, K.: A case-based reasoning approach to imitating RoboCup players. In: Proceedings of the Twenty-First International Florida Artificial Intelligence Research Society Conference, 15–17 May, 2008, Coconut Grove, Florida, USA, pp. 251–256 (2008)
5. Geisler, B.: An empirical study of machine learning algorithms applied to modeling player behavior in a "first person shooter" video game. Ph.D. thesis, Citeseer (2002)
6. Hingston, P.: A new design for a turing test for bots. In: Proceedings of the 2010 IEEE Conference on Computational Intelligence and Games, CIG 2010, Copenhagen, Denmark, 18–21 August, 2010, pp. 345–350 (2010)
7. Daumé, H., Langford, J., Marcu, D.: Search-based structured prediction. Mach. Learn. **75**(3), 297–325 (2009)
8. Lam, K., Esfandiari, B., Tudino, D.: A scene-based imitation framework for RoboCup clients. MOO-Modeling Other Agents from Observations (2006)
9. Lamontagne, L., Rugamba, F., Mineau, G.: Acquisition of cases in sequential games using conditional entropy. In: ICCBR 2012 Workshop on TRUE: Traces for Reusing Users' Experience (2012)
10. Miranda, M., Sánchez-Ruiz, A.A., Peinado, F.: A CBR approach for imitating human playing style in Ms. Pac-Man video game. In: Cox, M.T., Funk, P., Begum, S. (eds.) ICCBR 2018. LNCS (LNAI), vol. 11156, pp. 292–308. Springer, Cham (2018). https://doi.org/10.1007/978-3-030-01081-2_20
11. Miranda, M., Sánchez-Ruiz, A.A., Peinado, F.: Towards human-like bots using online interactive case-based reasoning. In: Bach, K., Marling, C. (eds.) ICCBR 2019. LNCS (LNAI), vol. 11680, pp. 314–328. Springer, Cham (2019). https://doi.org/10.1007/978-3-030-29249-2_21
12. Ortega, J., Shaker, N., Togelius, J., Yannakakis, G.N.: Imitating human playing styles in super mario bros. Entertain. Comput. **4**(2), 93–104 (2013)
13. Packard, B., Ontañón, S.: Policies for active learning from demonstration. In: 2017 AAAI Spring Symposia, Stanford University, Palo Alto, California, USA, March 27–29, 2017 (2017)
14. Packard, B., Ontañón, S.: Learning behavior from limited demonstrations in the context of games. In: Proceedings of the Thirty-First International Florida Artificial Intelligence Research Society Conference, FLAIRS 2018, Melbourne, Florida, USA, May 21–23, 2018, pp. 86–91 (2018)

15. Rohlfshagen, P., Liu, J., Pérez-Liébana, D., Lucas, S.M.: Pac-Man conquers academia: two decades of research using a classic arcade game. IEEE Trans. Games **10**, 233–256 (2018)
16. Ross, S., Bagnell, D.: Efficient reductions for imitation learning. In: Proceedings of the Thirteenth International Conference on Artificial Intelligence and Statistics, AISTATS 2010, Sardinia, Italy, May 13–15, 2010, pp. 661–668 (2010)
17. Ross, S., Gordon, G.J., Bagnell, D.: A reduction of imitation learning and structured prediction to no-regret online learning. In: Proceedings of the Fourteenth International Conference on Artificial Intelligence and Statistics, AISTATS 2011, Fort Lauderdale, USA, April 11–13, 2011, pp. 627–635 (2011)
18. Soni, B., Hingston, P.: Bots trained to play like a human are more fun. In: 2008 IEEE International Joint Conference on Neural Networks (IEEE World Congress on Computational Intelligence), pp. 363–369 (2008)
19. Togelius, J., Nardi, R.D., Lucas, S.M.: Towards automatic personalised content creation for racing games. In: 2007 IEEE Symposium on Computational Intelligence and Games, pp. 252–259 (2007)
20. Williams, P.R., Liebana, D.P., Lucas, S.M.: Ms. Pac-Man versus ghost team CIG 2016 competition. In: IEEE Conference on Computational Intelligence and Games, CIG 2016, Santorini, Greece, September 20–23, 2016, pp. 1–8 (2016)
21. Wooldridge, M.: Introduction to multiagent systems. Cell **757**(239), 8573 (2002)
22. Yannakakis, G.N., Maragoudakis, M.: Player modeling impact on player's entertainment in computer games. In: Ardissono, L., Brna, P., Mitrovic, A. (eds.) UM 2005. LNCS (LNAI), vol. 3538, pp. 74–78. Springer, Heidelberg (2005). https://doi.org/10.1007/11527886_11

Case-Based Approach to Automated Natural Language Generation for Obituaries

Ashish Upadhyay[1](✉), Stewart Massie[1], and Sean Clogher[2]

[1] Robert Gordon University, Aberdeen, UK
{a.upadhyay,s.massie}@rgu.ac.uk
[2] The Obituary Company, Aberdeen, UK
theobituarycompany.contact@gmail.com

Abstract. Automated generation of human readable text from structured information is challenging because grammatical rules are complex making good quality outputs difficult to achieve. Textual Case-Based Reasoning provides one approach in which the text from previously solved examples with similar inputs is reused as a template solution to generate text for the current problem. Natural Language Generation also poses a challenge when evaluating the quality of the text generated due to the high cost of human labelling and the variety in potential good quality solutions. In this paper, we propose two case-based approaches for reusing text to automatically generate an obituary from a set of input attribute-value pairs. The case-base is acquired by crawling and then tagging existing solutions published on the web to create cases as problem-solution pairs. We evaluate the quality of the text generation system with a novel unsupervised case alignment metric using normalised discounted cumulative gain which is compared to a supervised approach and human evaluation. Initial results show that our proposed evaluation measure is effective and correlates well with average attribute error evaluation which is a crude surrogate to human feedback. The system is being deployed in a real-world application with a startup company in Aberdeen to produce automated obituaries.

Keywords: Natural Language Generation · Textual Case-Based Reasoning · Text evaluation

1 Introduction

Text generation from structured information is a common requirement for problem solving in variety of tasks and domains, such as compiling incident reports, writing customer reviews, and presenting weather forecasts [4,9,12]. These use-case examples typically have a common problem representation in that the generated text is the combination of the structured data (a set of pre-defined attribute values) and textual content, required to improve human readability. In this paper

I. Watson and R. Weber (Eds.): ICCBR 2020, LNAI 12311, pp. 279–294, 2020.
https://doi.org/10.1007/978-3-030-58342-2_18

we address a similar task in which a text generation system is required to automatically generate an obituary based on information about the deceased's life. The information typically includes: personal details; relationships, such as next-to-kin, spouse, children, friends; and details about funeral arrangements for the funeral or memorial.

The effectiveness of text generation system depend on the quality of the text produced, in terms of accuracy and readability, as well as the diversity of texts generated from the system. One approach is to use a standard abstract template with all the pre-defined attributes available as slots to be filled. But having a single template for every problem are difficult to construct for complex scenarios and result in very repetitive text outputs. Textual Case Based Reasoning (TCBR) gives an opportunity to develop dynamic templates with diverse text by re-using previous experiences.

In general, a TCBR system has a case-base containing information about previous experiences as its central knowledge source, which is used together with other key knowledge sources: the case representation and similarity knowledge [14]. In combination these knowledge sources enable the retrieval of similar cases from the case-base, providing a mechanism to re-use knowledge captured in previous examples to solve a new problem. Thus TCBR, as with CBR more generally, relies on the basic principle that "similar problems have similar solutions" [1]. Supervised Machine Learning approaches take advantage of this principle to learn more tailored representation or retrieval knowledge in order to improve some evaluation metric e.g. accuracy. However, in TCBR learning from labelled solutions is difficult because each solution tends to be unique and so simple feedback metrics are not so easily available to either refine or evaluate developing systems. We introduce a novel approach to evaluation that measures the extent to which similar problems have similar solutions by investigating the alignment between local neighbourhoods in the problem and solution space. This approach reduces the requirement for human evaluations.

In this work we generate a case-base by crawling the web to extract obituaries from Funeral Notices websites[1]. The information extracted from the website is plain text and needs pre-processing for building the case-base. In particular generating a structured representation in a knowledge rich manner. By manually analysing the processed obituaries, relevant attributes are identified to provide alternative representations for the problem component of the cases. An unsupervised evaluation technique is developed to evaluate the alternatives.

The main contributions of the work are as follows:

1. developing a real world system based on a TCBR approach for automatically generating obituaries which is being deployed by a start-up company;
2. a novel technique for evaluation of text generation with TCBR employing a case alignment approach using normalised discounted cumulative gain; and
3. demonstrating the effectiveness of the approach with experiments and comparison of results with other baselines and an average attribute error as a crude surrogate to human feedback.

[1] https://funeral-notices.co.uk/.

The rest of the paper is organised as follows. The problem domain is discussed in more detail in Sect. 2 before relevant related works are highlighted in the Sect. 3. The proposed case-based methodology for generation of textual obituaries identifies our alternative approaches to representation and similarity measuring in Sect. 4. The experimental design is discussed in Sect. 5, where we also introduce our novel evaluation method. In the Sect. 6, we discuss the results obtained from our experiments, before concluding the paper and looking at future works in Sect. 7.

2 Obituary Generation

An obituary is a written announcement of someone's death which is traditionally published in a local newspaper to inform the wider community about the death. It generally outlines the life and personality of the deceased person and provides the details of the funeral arrangements and memorials. In the growing digital era, people are tending towards using digital website to publish the obituaries instead of local newspapers to expand the audience from a local community to the wider world on the internet.

There are approximately 57,000 deaths in Scotland each year, of these two sites are providing obituaries notices currently. The main site captures only 10% of all death notices. There is an opportunity to improve the service provided and to integrate the latest AI technologies to support Funeral Directors to help the next of kin with the creation of digital public obituary notices.

Our commercial partner is in the process of providing a publication platform for obituary generation that focuses on supporting a sympathetic acknowledgement of the recently departed as a digitisation of the traditional print obituaries. In this paper, we investigated utilising a TCBR approach to generate dynamic and individual obituaries that help the next of kin prepare their tribute. The aim is to achieve a two-minute publication timeline, through an intuitive form that will lead to the generation of five bespoke obituary options, the undertaker and family can select the appropriate option with the ability to edit as required. New solutions generated on the system can be retained to increase the case-base size and diversity of solutions available.

A large number (around 100k) of obituaries, dating back to the year 2000, have been crawled and extracted from the web. As initial pre-processing, 30k obituaries created after 2015 are selected and out of these, the top 1000 notices based on those with higher word count is selected. After analysing this data an obituary can be divided into at least three distinct components: the personal information component; the relationships component; and funeral component.

1. **Personal Information**: this component gives the personal details of the deceased person, e.g. name, age, date and place of death, and cause of death. It can also include the information about the person's home town or previous working places, as well their hobbies.

2. **Relations**: this component presents the relatives' details, e.g., spouse, children, grand children, or in-laws. This component may also contain an emotional message about the family & friends and how the person is going to be missed by all who knew them.
3. **Funeral**: this component provides the details of funeral arrangements and will typically have the date, time and place for the memorial service. The component will also provide the information about the delivery of flowers and the potential guest list. For example, flowers may only be welcome from family members but all the friends and relatives are welcome to join at the memorial service. Options for donations and charity name can also be provided in this section in the lieu of flowers.

The main task for this project is to generate five diverse textual messages (obituary) based on the features given by the user. A simple message can be generated using an abstract template but then there will be no diversity in the generations and all the obituaries will become monotonous. The challenge is to generate human readable natural text which includes (almost) every feature to the generation and is diverse in nature as well.

3 Related Works

Automated generation of human readable text from structured data has been studied in various domains [6,9,13]. The studies mainly focus on the difficulties of mapping unstructured text from previous experience to a structured representation, measuring semantic or synaptic similarity for the retrieval & reuse of previous cases and automated evaluation of the generated text.

3.1 Text Generation

In [2], the author proposed a CBR system to generate weather forecast texts using examples from previous cases with similar weather states. For the retrieval of similar cases it is necessary to have same number of weather states in the retrieved one and the input query. The system fails to return a result if there's any mismatch in the number of states in input query and previous similar data. The system uses NIST5 score for evaluation requiring substantial reference texts for better performance. In [5] the textual summary of time series were generated using an end-to-end CBR system. The summary generation involved two steps where first an abstraction of time series is generated which in turns help the system to generate the textual summary of that abstraction. The system generated text was evaluated using a modified version of the edit distance measure [10] which heavily relies on the domain specifications. This is a custom evaluation approach that is difficult to use across different TCBR domains.

3.2 Case Alignment

There have been several approaches to measuring the performance of unsupervised CBR systems which focus on measuring the extent to which the problem-side space and solution-side space of case representation align with each other. In [7], authors proposed a case cohesion alignment to evaluate the performance of a CBR system which measures the level of overlap in retrieval set. However, the method requires a trial and error approach to set up a threshold for selecting the number of nearest neighbours in both the sets. A mechanism of case alignment was presented in [9] where the alignment was measured by taking the average solution similarity of its neighbours weighted by their problem-side similarities. Authors in [17] modified the case alignment measure by utilising the case ranking of similar cases in problem and solution sets by using a modified version of Kendall tau distance. Although the method works well in several CBR problems, it fails to scale in a TCBR scenario [17].

In this work, previous examples are marked up to act as dynamic templates which can be populated with structured data to generate good quality, diverse natural text. Alternative representations and similarity measures are compared. We also evaluate the quality of the generated text with a problem-solution alignment measure but propose a novel, domain independent metric taken from information retrieval.

4 Case-Based Methodology

Central to developing a CBR system is the availability of experiential knowledge that can provide previously solved successful examples for reusing to solve new problems. The crawled examples from the web provide a suitable source of past examples. However as obituaries in natural language they provide a case solution example but not with separate problem and solution representations required for CBR systems. The first task in developing a TCBR system is to create a case representation to effectively capture case knowledge as associated problem and solution components. The second stage is to develop a similarity metric utilising the problem representation to support retrieval.

4.1 Case Representation

In TCBR, cases are generally represented in two parts: problem and solution component. The problem representation comprises a set of attributes whose values can either be extracted from the crawled obituaries or are known for a new problem. The solution representation is the natural language text of the obituary but may be considered as a template with the associated problem attribute values identifed and replaced by mark-up tags.

For example given an obituary: "*OLIVIA WILSON, Peacefully on the 14th May 2019 at home, Olivia of Patna. Beloved wife to the late James Wilson, much loved mum to Jack and partner Emily, gran to Ava, Lucy and Logan, loving aunt, sister and a friend to all. Funeral service will be help at Patna Kirk, Patna on Monday 26th May, 2019 at 11.00am and thereafter to Patna Cemetery to which all friends are respectfully invited. Donations if desired to Cancer Research UK and Strathcarron Hospice.*", Fig. 1 shows the case representation marked-up with attribute-value pairs in XML format.


```xml
<obit>
    <personal_info_component>
        <name>OLIVIA WILSON</name>,
        <demise_how>Peacefully</demise_how> on the
        <demise_date>14th May 2019</demise_date> at
        <demise_place>home</demise_place>,
        <nick_name>Olivia</nick_name> of
        <home_town>Patna</home_town>.
    </personal_info_component>
    <relations_component>
        Beloved
        <spouse_gender>wife</spouse_gender> to
        <spouse_name>the late James Wilson</spouse_name>, much loved
        <parent_gender>mum</parent_gender> to
        <children_name>Jack</children_name> and partner
        <children_in_law_name>Emily</children_in_law_name>,
        <grandparent_gender>gran</grandparent_gender> to
        <grandchildren_name>Ava, Lucy and Logan</grandchildren_name>, loving
        <other_relations_types>aunt</other_relations_types>,
        <siblings_gender>sister</siblings_gender> and a friend to all.
    </relations_component>
    <funerla_component>
        Funeral service will be help at
        <funeral_place>Patna Kirk, Patna</funeral_place> on
        <funeral_date>Monday 26th June, 2017</funeral_date> at
        <funeral_time>11.00am</funeral_time> and thereafter to
        <cemetery_place>Patna Cemetery</cemetery_place> to which
        <guests_list>all friends</guests_list> are respectfully invited. Donations if desired to
        <charity_name>Cancer Research UK and Strathcarron Hospice</charity_name>.
    </funerla_component>
</obit>
```


Fig. 1. Representation of a case marked-up in XML format.

Hence, an obituary contains information, as attribute values, on the different people, relationships, places, organisations, etc involved, and can be used to build an effective case representation that will be helpful for identifying similar cases to new problems. Around 40 relevant attributes have been selected to represent an obituary as a case in the case-base, as shown in Fig. 2 [2]. From the example obituary, we can see that the first sentence talks about the personal details of the deceased person, followed by relatives in second sentence and funeral information in the last sentence. This is a typical paragraph construction, so we can divide all the extracted obituaries into three components and annotate them with the identified attributes.

The attributes identified for annotations are set to be gender independent. For example, in Fig. 1 we have taken "*mum*" as a value for attribute "*parent_gender*". That means, the deceased person was parent (in this case mother)

[2] For the columns marked M/O: Mandatory/Optional, '-': Attribute value filled automatically based on the deceased's gender.

to "*Jack*" ("*children_name*"). So if we have a target problem with "*parent_gender* → *father*", the case in fig. 1 can still be re-used as a possible solution. An initial case-base has been created to seed the system by manually annotating 100 samples.

Attribute Name	Identifier Tag	Attribute Type	M/O	Comment
Name	$< name >$	String	M	
Gender	$< gender >$	Binary	M	Male (1) or Female (2)
Age	$< age >$	Number	O	Numbers in range 110
Demise Date	$< demise\_date >$	Date	M	
Demise Place	$< demise\_place >$	String	O	
Demise How	$< demise\_how >$	3 Category	O	Peacefully (1), Suddenly (2), Peacefully but suddenly (3)
Demise Reason	$< demise\_reason >$	Dropdown List	O	Name of any specific illness or accident
Home Town	$< home\_town >$	String	O	Deceased Person Home Town
Nick Name	$< nick\_name >$	String	O	
Occupation	$< occupation >$	String	O	Most recent job
Previous Works	$< previous\_works >$	String	O	any previous achievements/-works

(a) Personal Information

Attribute Name	Identifier Tag	Att. Type	M/O	Comment
Spouse Name	$< spouse\_name >$	String	O	
Spouse Gender	$< spouse\_gender >$	Binary	-	Husband or Wife
Children Name	$< children\_name >$	Array	O	
Parent Gender	$< parent\_gender >$	String	-	Father or Mother
Grandchildren Name	$< grandchildren\_name >$	Array	O	
Grandparent gender	$< grandparent\_gender >$	String	-	Grandpa or Grandmother
Siblings Name	$< siblings\_name >$	Array	O	
Siblings gender	$< siblings\_gender >$	String	-	Brother or sister
Children-in-law Name	$< children\_in\_law\_name >$	Array	O	
Parent-in-law gender	$< parent\_in\_law\_gender >$	String	-	Father or Mother in law
Siblings-in-law Name	$< siblings\_in\_law\_name >$	Array	O	
Siblings-in-law gender	$< siblings\_in\_law\_gender >$	String	-	Brother or sister in law
Other Relations	$< other\_relations\_names >$	Array	O	
Friends Name	$< friends\_name >$	Array	O	Name of the friends

(b) Relations Details

Attribute Name	Identifier Tag	Attribute Type	M/O	Comment
Funeral Place	$< funeral\_place >$	String	M	
Funeral Date	$< funeral\_date >$	Date	M	
Funeral Time	$< funeral\_time >$	Time	M	
Cemetery Place	$< cemetery\_place >$	String	O	
Cemetery Time	$< cemetery\_time >$	Time	O	
Funeral Flowers	$< flowers >$	Binary	M	Family flowers only or welcome from all
Guests List	$< guests\_list >$	Category	M	Public or private
Attire Request	$< funeral\_attire >$	String	O	Any specific kind of attire
Donation	$< charity\_name >$	String	O	Charity name for any donation
Associated Message	$< funeral\_message >$	String	O	If the user wants to drop some message

(c) Funeral Details

Fig. 2. Attributes used for representation of obituaries.

4.2 Similarity Measure for Retrieval

We investigate two variants of similarity measure for retrieval of similar cases for a target problem. The first approach is straight-forward, where we match the number of features in the target problem with number of features in each case from the case-base. The first similarity measure ($sim1$) is defined by Eq. (1).

$$sim1 = |q \cap c| \tag{1}$$

where q is the list of attributes in target problem and c is the list of attributes in each case from case-base.

There can be a problem with Eq. (1) where the target case has fewer features than the case retrieved from the case-base. Let's take an example where the target case has only 10 attributes out of a possible 40. In that scenario, cases with more than the 10 attributes will also have the same similarity score as cases with the exact 10 features. To counter this problem, we use a different similarity measure ($sim2$), which is the Jaccard Similarity Coefficient (J) described in Eq. (2).

$$sim2 = J(q, c) = \frac{|q \cap c|}{|q \cup c|} \tag{2}$$

4.3 Text Reuse

In the previous section we observed that there can be problems in situations where there is a misalignment in the number of attribute values. We used a different similarity measure to address this problem in Eq. (2). However, this method can also lead to a problem. The set of retrieved cases for a target problem with very less attributes might have same number of attributes but have different attribute types. For example, for a target problem with only "*spouse name*" in "*relation section*" and "*funeral place/time*" in "*funeral section*" along with all the attributes from "*personal info section*", the retrieved cases might contain only "*name*" and "*home town*" of the deceased person along with all the attributes from "*funeral section*". In that way the number of attributes may be the same giving a high similarity score for the retrieved case but in practice, it is not a good example of a similar case for re-use.

To address this problem, we investigate an alternative case representation where the case-base is broken down into three components, namely: *personal info component*; *relations component*; and *funeral component*. In this way, we can leverage our data and to find good retrieval examples with fewer cases. These components can also be broken down further into different sub-components such as: *relations component* could be separated in *spouse component*, *parent component*, and *grandparent component*. But this further breaking will reduce the attribute count in each sub-component and hence resulting into non-diverse case retrieval for every target problem, which will lead into generation of similar kind of text from the system every time. Thus, we need to find a balanced number of components for breaking the obituary representations.

With these insights, we propose two kinds of case retrievals for text reuse:

- **Basic**: retrieving whole obituary as an one entity; and
- **Component**: retrieving cases as 3 different components.

In Fig. 1, we can see that the three components are marked-up with separate "*component tags*". For *basic retrieval*, whole obituary is retrieved as one entity thus ignoring the component tags while for *component retrieval*, all three components are retrieved separately. Then the retrieved case's text is reused by replacing the each attribute's value with the attribute's value from the target problem. The new modified text is the solution generated by CBR system. In case of component retrieval, we combine the texts generated for each component separately to propose the final solution.

4.4 Solution Adaptation

The proposed solution may contain some general mistakes such as: referring to the deceased person with male pronoun even if the gender of the person is female or vice-versa; or adding an attribute which is not given in the target problem. These kinds of error occur because of the fact that the proposed solution is generated only by simply reusing the text from solution-side of the retrieved case after replacing the attributes' values.

To tackle the gender problem, we apply a rule-based adaptation process where each generated text is checked against the gender of the deceased person. If a pronoun with different gender is found in the text, it is replaced with the same pronoun of the deceased person's gender. For the extra attributes problem, we simply replace the attribute's value with a blank for any attribute which is not given in the target problem.

5 Experimental Evaluation

Evaluation of our TCBR system is a challenging task. It is difficult to automatically measure the effectiveness of a system due to the diversity found in the natural language output. Human evaluation is an alternative which, while effective is expensive and very time consuming. Traditional machine translation and summarising metrics such as BLEU [11] and ROUGE [8] scores are unlikely to work well because these metrics are based on the overlap of n-grams of the generated text with an original reference text and so only consider lexical similarity. Also, they require a lot of reference text to measure the quality of generation which is very costly to get. To overcome these challenges we propose a problem-solution alignment metric as an unsupervised evaluation measure.

5.1 Case Alignment

A key principle of CBR is that "*similar problems have similar solutions*". The extent to which this principle holds true can be assessed by measuring the alignment between the problem-side and solution-side space. It is surmised that a good system design will have better alignment [9]. In this evaluation, we employ a novel approach to measuring case alignment by using normalised discounted cumulative gain to assess the correlation between problem-side and solution-side nearest neighbours. If the alignment is good then for a given problem-solution pair, the k nearest cases on problem-side must be similar as the k nearest-cases on the solution side.

For a given case-base C containing all the cases $\{c_1, c_2, \cdots, c_n\}$. Cases in C consist of problem−solution pairs, such that $c_i = \{p_i, s_i\}$, where $p_i \in P$ (problem set) and $s_i \in S$ (solution set). A target problem t represented using the case knowledge, we will retrieve two lists *pl* & *sl* which are sorted in order to the most similar cases both from the problem (*pl*) and the solution (*sl*) set respectively. On the solution side, BERT [3] is used to encode the sentences and then cosine similarity [15] between the test sample and other samples is used to generate the ordered list of similar cases. For the problem side the ordered list is created using the retrieval methods discussed in Sect. 4. Both the lists will have $n-1$ items, where n is the size of the case-base.

From the list *pl*, we shall create a new list of weighted scores for the problem-side. We call it problem list weighted or *plw*. The weighting is done as follows:

$$plw(i) = \begin{cases} (k+1) - i, & \text{if } i \leq k \\ 1, & \text{otherwise} \end{cases} \tag{3}$$

where k is the number of neighbours considered for retrieval and i is the index of each element from the *pl*. Similarly the cases in *sl* are weighted according to their *pl* counter-part and creating a solution list weighted or *slw*.

For example, if we have 10 cases in the case-base and for a given case c_i, with $k=3$ the *sl* and *pl* are as follows:

$$pl = [8, 5, 6, 1, 4, 2, 3, 7, 0]$$
$$sl = [5, 6, 2, 4, 3, 7, 8, 1, 0]$$

These are the indices of the cases from both the sets. According to the Eq. (3), weighted lists *plw* and *slw* are given as follows:

$$plw = [4, 3, 2, 1, 1, 1, 1, 1, 1]$$
$$slw = [3, 2, 1, 1, 1, 1, 4, 1, 1]$$

For an ideal case, both of the list should have same ranking order as they are retrieved for the same case. To measure the alignment of a target case t we can use the *"normalised Discounted Cumulative Gain" (nDCG)* [16] using the following formula:

$$nDCG(t) = \frac{DCG_{(slw)}}{DCG_{(plw)}} \tag{4}$$

where, *slw* and *plw* are the weighted lists for the target case while *DCG* is the *"Discounted Cumulative Gain"*, defined for some list *lw* as:

$$DCG(lw) = \sum_{i=1}^{|lw|} \frac{lw(i)}{\log_2(i+1)} \tag{5}$$

where, *lw* is some weighted list (e.g., *plw* or *slw*) and $|lw|$ is the size of that list. The value of nDCG $\in (0, 1]$.

The alignment of whole case-base can be the average of nDCG score of all the cases in the case-base (CB).

$$AlignScore(CB) = \sum_{i=1}^{n} \frac{nDCG(i)}{n}, \forall i \in CB \tag{6}$$

where, n is the size of case-base. For component retrieval method, the total alignment score would be the average of *AlignScore* of all the components. In our experiments, we take the value of $k=5$ because of the fact that we need to show 5 options of automatically generated obituaries to the user.

Table 1. Nomenclature of different methods.

	Basic	Component
*sim*1	**BS1**	**CS1**
*sim*2	**BS2**	**CS2**

5.2 Other Evaluations

In addition to the case alignment, we use BLEU score and cosine similarity for the evaluation of our system. BLEU score counts the average of overlapped n-grams from generated text with the reference texts. Cosine similarity on other hand measures the cosine angle between the projection of vectors in multi-dimensional space. For the vector representation of a sentence, we used BERT encoder to produce a contextual embedding for each sentence.

5.3 Average Attribute Errors

We define a reference metric as the number of missed attributes in the generated text as one measure of the competence of the evaluation metrics. In our scenario, where the pre-defined attributes play an important role in the retrieval and reuse of cases, it is important to measure the inclusion of these attributes in the generated text. In the absence of a human evaluation, we employ **Average Attribute Error (AAE)** as a crude surrogate for human feedback.

The average attribute error is defined as the average number of missed attributes from the top 5 generated texts from our system. Again, top 5 cases are chosen because of the fact that the system needs to provide 5 optional texts to the user for a given input. For a target problem t, if we have na number of attributes and the $G = \{g_1, \cdots, g_5\}$ as the set of top 5 generated texts from one of the methods defined in Table 1. The average attribute error e would be:

$$e(t) = \frac{\sum_{i=1}^{5} ||(na - |g_i|)||}{5} \tag{7}$$

where, $|g_i|$ is the number of attributes included in the ith generation. The average of every sample's attribute error in a case-base will be the average attribute error for the case-base.

6 Results and Discussion

Our case-base contains 100 seed cases manually annotated to identify problem and solution components. We use a leave-one-out experiment for both representations described in Sect. 4.3 (Basic and Component) with both similarity measures described in Sect. 4.2 (*sim*1 and *sim*2). Hence, We have four system combinations to evaluate as named in Table 1.

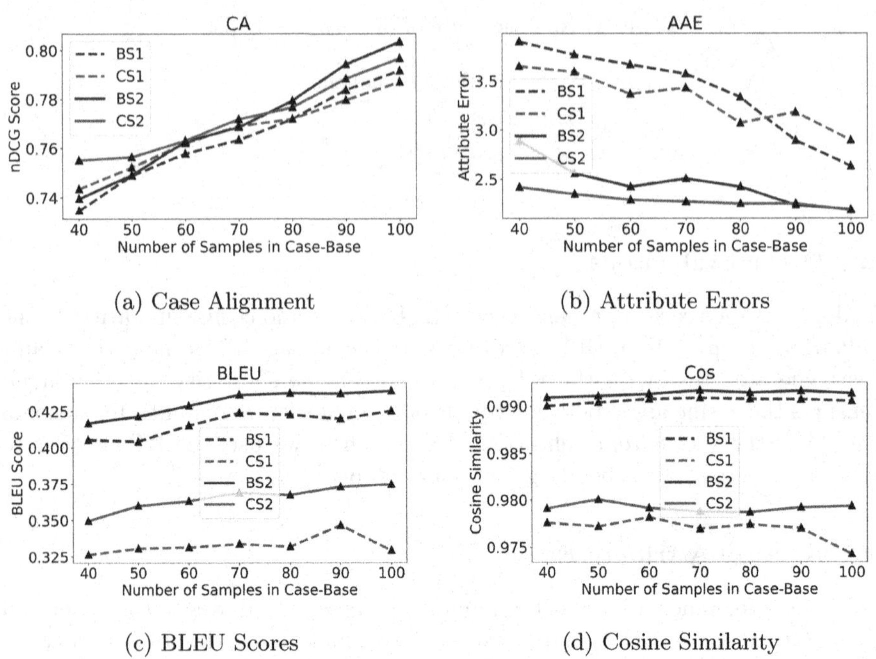

(a) Case Alignment

(b) Attribute Errors

(c) BLEU Scores

(d) Cosine Similarity

Fig. 3. Various results from leave-one-out-experiment

6.1 Different Evaluations

The results from applying the 4 evaluation metrics to the retrieval sets obtained when employing the 4 system combinations are shown in Fig. 3. We start our experiments with 40 cases initially, chosen to reflect the 40 attributes present in the problem representation. We repeat the experiments with increasing number of samples until we reach 100, i.e., the maximum number of seed cases available.

Case Alignment (CA) results are shown in Fig. 3a, where we plot the change in case alignment score with respect to the number of cases used for experiment. For a given value on the x-axis, the corresponding value on the y-axis represent the average case alignment score of all the cases from the leave-one-out experiment. We can see that with the number of samples increasing, the case alignment is also improving. Which means with more data used for experiment we are continuing to achieve improved results and do not appear to have reached a plateau.

We can also observe that before 70 cases the alignment is better for *component retrieval* compared to *basic retrieval* while after 70 samples, the *basic retrieval* for both *similarity measures* gets better alignment than the *component retrieval.* This indicates that after sufficient case data is available there may be no need to break down the obituary representation into several components because with more labelled cases, diversity in the case base is increased allowing sufficiently similar cases to be retrieved.

Table 2. Pearson coefficient score for correlation

	Case alignment	BLEU score	Cosine similarity
Pearson Score	−0.9238	−0.7019	−0.0296

Results from the **Average Attribute Error (AAE)** evaluation metric is shown in Fig. 3b. Here we can see that with the change in number of cases used for experiment, the average count of missing attributes is reducing for all the four system combinations. Also, before 80 cases, the performance for *component* is better, while after 80 *basic* for both *similarity measures* gives improved results. This further supports the idea that with more cases available, there is no need to split obituaries into components.

In Figs. 3c and 3d we show results for **BLEU score (BLEU)** and **cosine similarity (Cos)** between the generated text and reference text. Both the metrics show little variations in score with respect to the change in number of cases available. The BLEU score for BS1 and BS2 is always around 0.40 to 0.44 while for CS1 and CS2 is 0.33 to 0.37. Similarly for cosine similarity, the average is almost 0.99 for BS1 and BS2 during all the number of samples while the score for CS1 and CS2 is around 0.975 go 0.98. This may be because these metrics only consider lexical similarity while ignoring the measure of attributes inclusion for generation.

6.2 Correlation of Metrics

We calculate the pearson correlation coefficient between average attribute error and the other three automated evaluation metrics which is shown in Table 2. Here, we can observe that our proposed case alignment metric is highly correlated to the average attribute error. BLEU score is ranked second while the cosine similarity is third and is much less correlated. This demonstrates that our case alignment measure is an effective evaluation metric for the TCBR system.

6.3 Generated Texts

Some texts generated from the CBR system are shown in Fig. 4, one for each method from Table 1. The texts shown here are generated from the case-base with all 100 samples stored. It can be observed that the generations from *sim*2 measure are quite accurate and include most of the information correctly. On the other hand, it can be observed that the generations from *sim*1 measure have more tendency of making attribute's related errors such as: in BS1, the two major attributes, *age* and *charity_name* are missing; while in CS1, the retrieved case has some extra attributes which are not present in the target case, observe the sentence "Cherished to and a dear of the family". Here after *cherished to*, an extra attribute value is present in the retrieved case which is absent in the target problem and hence during the adaptation process, the value of that attribute is replaced with a blank.

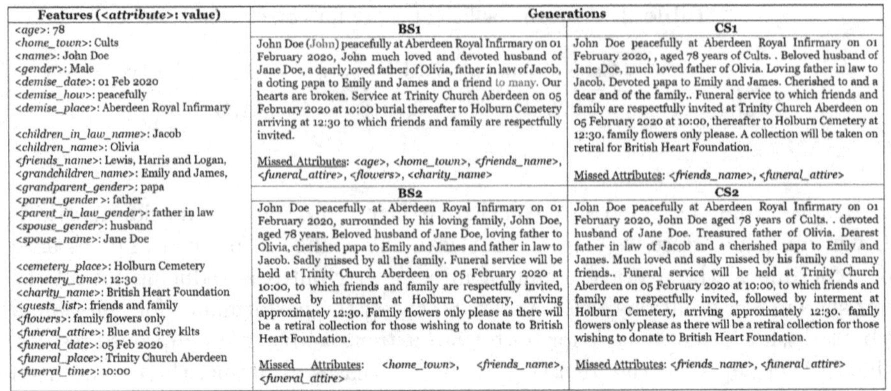

<table>
<tr><th rowspan="2">Features (<<i>attribute</i>>: value)</th><th colspan="2">Generations</th></tr>
<tr><th>BS1</th><th>CS1</th></tr>
<tr><td rowspan="3"><<i>age</i>>: 78
<<i>home_town</i>>: Cults
<<i>name</i>>: John Doe
<<i>gender</i>>: Male
<<i>demise_date</i>>: 01 Feb 2020
<<i>demise_how</i>>: peacefully
<<i>demise_place</i>>: Aberdeen Royal Infirmary

<<i>children_in_law_name</i>>: Jacob
<<i>children_name</i>>: Olivia
<<i>friends_name</i>>: Lewis, Harris and Logan,
<<i>grandchildren_name</i>>: Emily and James,
<<i>grandparent_gender</i>>: papa
<<i>parent_gender</i> >: father
<<i>parent_in_law_gender</i>>: father in law
<<i>spouse_gender</i>>: husband
<<i>spouse_name</i>>: Jane Doe

<<i>cemetery_place</i>>: Holburn Cemetery
<<i>cemetery_time</i>>: 12:30
<<i>charity_name</i>>: British Heart Foundation
<<i>guests_list</i>>: friends and family
<<i>flowers</i>>: family flowers only
<<i>funeral_attire</i>>: Blue and Grey kilts
<<i>funeral_date</i>>: 05 Feb 2020
<<i>funeral_place</i>>: Trinity Church Aberdeen
<<i>funeral_time</i>>: 10:00</td>
<td>John Doe (John) peacefully at Aberdeen Royal Infirmary on 01 February 2020, John much loved and devoted husband of Jane Doe, a dearly loved father of Olivia, father in law of Jacob, a doting papa to Emily and James and a friend to many. Our hearts are broken. Service at Trinity Church Aberdeen on 05 February 2020 at 10:00 burial thereafter to Holburn Cemetery arriving at 12:30 to which friends and family are respectfully invited.

<u>Missed Attributes</u>: <<i>age</i>>, <<i>home_town</i>>, <<i>friends_name</i>>, <<i>funeral_attire</i>>, <<i>flowers</i>>, <<i>charity_name</i>></td>
<td>John Doe peacefully at Aberdeen Royal Infirmary on 01 February 2020, , aged 78 years of Cults. . Beloved husband of Jane Doe, much loved father of Olivia. Loving father in law to Jacob. Devoted papa to Emily and James. Cherished to and a dear and of the family.. Funeral service to which friends and family are respectfully invited at Trinity Church Aberdeen on 05 February 2020 at 10:00, thereafter to Holburn Cemetery at 12:30. family flowers only please. A collection will be taken on retiral for British Heart Foundation.

<u>Missed Attributes</u>: <<i>friends_name</i>>, <<i>funeral_attire</i>></td></tr>
<tr><th>BS2</th><th>CS2</th></tr>
<tr><td>John Doe peacefully at Aberdeen Royal Infirmary on 01 February 2020, surrounded by his loving family, John Doe, aged 78 years. Beloved husband of Jane Doe, loving father to Olivia, cherished papa to Emily and James and father in law to Jacob. Sadly missed by all the family. Funeral service will be held at Trinity Church Aberdeen on 05 February 2020 at 10:00, to which friends and family are respectfully invited, followed by interment at Holburn Cemetery, arriving approximately 12:30. Family flowers only please as there will be a retiral collection for those wishing to donate to British Heart Foundation.

<u>Missed Attributes</u>: <<i>home_town</i>>, <<i>friends_name</i>>, <<i>funeral_attire</i>></td>
<td>John Doe peacefully at Aberdeen Royal Infirmary on 01 February 2020, John Doe aged 78 years of Cults. . devoted husband of Jane Doe. Treasured father of Olivia. Dearest father in law of Jacob and a cherished papa to Emily and James. Much loved and sadly missed by his family and many friends.. Funeral service will be held at Trinity Church Aberdeen on 05 February 2020 at 10:00, to which friends and family are respectfully invited, followed by interment at Holburn Cemetery, arriving approximately 12:30. family flowers only please as there will be a retiral collection for those wishing to donate to British Heart Foundation.

<u>Missed Attributes</u>: <<i>friends_name</i>>, <<i>funeral_attire</i>></td></tr>
</table>

Fig. 4. Text generations from the TCBR system. Errors are shown in red. (Color figure online)

It is also noted that missing the $< friends\_name >$ and $< funeral\_attire >$ attributes is common for all the four generations. We can also observe that the component retrieval method is also prone to different punctuation errors such as: ending the sentence with two full stops; or starting a sentence with small-caps letter. This may be due to the mix and match property of text generated from component retrieval methods.

7 Conclusion and Future Work

In this paper we presented a TCBR system developed for the automated generation of natural language obituaries from a large set of structured input attributes. The paper introduced two alternative case representation approaches, along with two different measures of similarity used for the retrieval of similar cases from the case-base.

The performance of our methods is evaluated using a novel unsupervised case alignment metric employing normalised discounted cumulative gain to compare problem-side and solution-side retrieval sets. Extensive experiments are conducted with an increasing number of seed cases available in a leave-one-out experiment. The proposed case alignment evaluation metric is compared with other commonly used supervised metrics as well as with average attribute error score, a simple surrogate for human feedback. The experiment results show that our unsupervised evaluation metric better correlates to the average attribute error compared to BLEU score and cosine similarity. Our evaluation metric is also domain independent and can be applied to different kinds of TCBR systems.

In future work for this project the intention is to measure and introduce more diversity into the set of generated obituaries and to automate the process of marking-up the data to ease the case-base creation process.

Acknowledgements. This work was part funded by The Scottish Funding Council via The Innovation Voucher Scheme.

References

1. Aamodt, A., Plaza, E.: Case-based reasoning: foundational issues, methodological variations, and system approaches. AI Commun. **7**(1), 39–59 (1994)
2. Adeyanju, I.: Generating weather forecast texts with case based reasoning. arXiv preprint arXiv:1509.01023 (2015)
3. Devlin, J., Chang, M.W., Lee, K., Toutanova, K.: Bert: pre-training of deep bidirectional transformers for language understanding. arXiv preprint arXiv:1810.04805 (2018)
4. Dong, R., Schaal, M., O'Mahony, M.P., McCarthy, K., Smyth, B.: Harnessing the experience web to support user-generated product reviews. In: Agudo, B.D., Watson, I. (eds.) ICCBR 2012. LNCS (LNAI), vol. 7466, pp. 62–76. Springer, Heidelberg (2012). https://doi.org/10.1007/978-3-642-32986-9_7
5. Dubey, N., Chakraborti, S., Khemani, D.: Textual summarization of time series using case-based reasoning: a case study. In: Workshop on Reasoning about Time in CBR-RATIC 2018. Workshop at the 26th International Conference on Case-Based Reasoning (ICCBR 2018), pp. 164–174 (2018)
6. Hüske-Kraus, D.: Text generation in clinical medicine - a review. Methods Inf. Med. **42**(1), 51–60 (2003)
7. Lamontagne, L.: Textual CBR authoring using case cohesion. In: Proceedings of 3rd Textual Case-Based Reasoning Workshop at the 8th European Conference on CBR, pp. 33–43 (2006)
8. Lin, C.Y.: ROUGE: a package for automatic evaluation of summaries. In: Text Summarization Branches Out, pp. 74–81. Association for Computational Linguistics, Barcelona, Spain, July 2004. https://www.aclweb.org/anthology/W04-1013
9. Massie, S., Wiratunga, N., Craw, S., Donati, A., Vicari, E.: From anomaly reports to cases. In: International Conference on Case-Based Reasoning, pp. 359–373 (2007)
10. Miura, N., Takagi, T.: WSL: sentence similarity using semantic distance between words. In: Proceedings of the 9th International Workshop on Semantic Evaluation (SemEval 2015), pp. 128–131 (2015)
11. Papineni, K., Roukos, S., Ward, T., Zhu, W.J.: Bleu: a method for automatic evaluation of machine translation. In: Proceedings of the 40th annual meeting on association for computational linguistics. pp. 311–318. Association for Computational Linguistics (2002)
12. Ramos-Soto, B.: Barro, Taboada: linguistic descriptions for automatic generation of textual short-term weather forecasts on real prediction data. IEEE Trans. Fuzzy Syst. **23**(1), 44–57 (2015)
13. Recio-Garcıa, J.A., Dıaz-Agudo, B., González-Calero, P.A.: Textual CBR in JCOLIBRI: from retrieval to reuse. In: Proceedings of the ICCBR 2007 Workshop on Textual Case-Based Reasoning: Beyond Retrieval, pp. 217–226 (2007)
14. Richter, M.M.: Knowledge containers. In: Readings in Case-Based Reasoning (2003)
15. Singhal, A., et al.: Modern information retrieval: a brief overview. IEEE Data Eng. Bull. **24**(4), 35–43 (2001)

16. Wang, Y., Wang, L., Li, Y., He, D., Liu, T.Y.: A theoretical analysis of NDCG type ranking measures. In: Conference on Learning Theory, pp. 25–54 (2013)
17. Zhou, X., Shi, Z., Zhao, H.: Reexamination of CBR hypothesis. In: Bichindaritz, I., Montani, S. (eds.) ICCBR 2010. LNCS (LNAI), vol. 6176, pp. 332–345. Springer, Heidelberg (2010). https://doi.org/10.1007/978-3-642-14274-1_25

Case-Based Gesture Interface for Multiagent Formation Control

Divya Srivastava[1], Daniel M. Lofaro[2], Tristan Schuler[2], Donald Sofge[2(✉)], and David W. Aha[2]

[1] Department of Mechanical Engineering, Georgia Institute of Technology, Atlanta, Georgia, USA
divya.srivastava@gatech.edu

[2] Navy Center for Applied Research in Artificial Intelligence, Naval Research Laboratory, Washington, D.C., USA
{daniel.lofaro,tristan.schuler,donald.sofge, david.aha}@nrl.navy.mil

Abstract. Current multiagent systems require human operators to communicate in real-time with one another. A better option would be to have a single human operator control a swarm of agents using a natural interface, such as something worn by the operator. This includes being able to control the shape and movement of the agents in a dynamically shifting environment using an intuitive interface. Prior research has focused on moving the collective of agents as a whole, and has not used a case-based approach for this purpose. We show that a swarm can be shaped into different formations via a case-based gesture control strategy using a wearable (smart watch) interface. This approach enables a swarm to complete a task by taking high-level commands from an operator/user. We describe our approach, our initial results and demonstrations, and discuss next steps.

Keywords: Human-computer interface · Human-in-the-loop · Gesture recognition · Case-based reasoning · Multiagent systems · Swarm · Smart watch

1 Introduction

We address the limitations of current approaches for controlling multiagent systems and describe how a wearable device (a smart watch) and gesture recognition can be used to control the movement and formation of swarms. Our method for gesture recognition uses a simple case-based approach to match a human operator's gesture with a library of gestures known to the agents/robots in the swarm.

There are two schools of thought when it comes to multiagent systems that involve human and robotic agents. The first is that a robot is a tool to complete a task. The second is that a robot is a teammate that humans can work with to complete a task. This distinction is important because the overall goal of our work is to create a seamless human-swarm collaborative team. In this scenario, the human operator should be able to robustly control the agents to change their goals or adapt their behavior to the circumstance at hand. This

I. Watson and R. Weber (Eds.): ICCBR 2020, LNAI 12311, pp. 295–306, 2020.
https://doi.org/10.1007/978-3-030-58342-2_19

is useful for navigating dynamically shifting domains, such as those addressed in goal reasoning research (Jaidee et al. 2013; Aha 2018).

Previous research on swarm control has focused on moving individual agents or a swarm from one location to another. To the best of our knowledge, this is the first attempt at manipulating the shape of a swarm with gesture-based controls. Changing the shape is important; if you are in a geometrically constrained environment, have complex tasks to complete, or have limited sensing, assistance from an external observer (the operator/user) in adjusting the swarm's shape can help it navigate, complete a task, and otherwise make decisions using input from the external observer to make up for its limited sensing.

Prior research on case-based robotics has not addressed this specific task. Work exists on using case-based (or *memory*-based) approaches to control multiple robots, such as for RoboCup Soccer (Ros et al. 2007; Altaf et al. 2016), or in simulation, such as for controlling agents in games (Jaidee et al. 2013; O'Connor et al. 2018). Case-based reasoning (CBR) approaches have also been used for several other robotics tasks (e.g., diagnosis (Olsson et al. 2004), learning reactive control strategies (Peula et al. 2009), the interpretation of skill demonstrations (Fitzgerald et al. 2015), or other control tasks (Atkeson et al. 1997). Finally, while some work exists on case-based gesture recognition for robotic control, such as for recognizing hand gestures (Deng et al. 2007), we believe ours is the first application of case-based reasoning for gesture recognition in the context of swarm control.

Section 2 provides context for the task we address. We then describe our methodology in Sect. 3, and report on initial demonstrations in Sect. 4. Our key finding is that a case-based recognition approach works well for our relatively simple swarm control task. In Sect. 5 we conclude and discuss some future work objectives.

2 Background

There are multiple ways to approach human-swarm research where the human user is in the same workspace as the robotic agents. These include: (1) designing the swarms to function as independently as possible (increasing autonomy), and (2) designing them to collaborate closely with human operators (human-agent teaming (HAT)). In previous work, the majority of the focus has been on making agents function completely autonomously so that they do not require a human operator. We instead focus here on HAT scenarios.

For these situations, where the human operator is in the same workspace as the robotic agents, we aim to increase teamwork efficiency by greatly decreasing the number of human operators required to control a swarm. This is known as the *conductor-orchestra paradigm* (Secchi et al. 2015). In previous research the level of human interaction with the system varied depending on the teaming requirements and the system's capabilities. For example, there are HAT scenarios involving pre-programmed flight plans or trajectories in which the role of the human operator is limited to only starting the program. In this case, goals are assumed to be static and unmalleable. However, if the environment or situation changes, the whole path plan may become obsolete. Often when goals need to be changed, the human operator must stop the program/action, make changes, and then restart the program. Common human-computer interfaces for changing the program include computers, tablets, smartphones, joysticks, and other like devices. Typical feedback includes light, sound, and touch (haptic). Secchi et al. (2015) describe a novel bilateral control architecture for teleoperating a group of mobile robots. This method is useful but the physical haptic interface is inherently not portable and thus does not allow the user to operate in the same workspace as the robotic agents. Such haptic devices provide feedback to the user in the form of vibrations and force feedback. These devices improve situational awareness, but can be limited in executable control (e.g., joysticks are limited to executing forward, backward, right, and left commands). Gioioso et al. (2014) created a system to control a swarm that uses the fingertips of the user (as tracked by an RGB-D camera) to command the contact points between multiple aerial agents and an object. Like the previous example, this system can control multiple agents but requires the user to be in a separate workspace than the swarm due to the finger tracking mechanism. Alternative methods of finger tracking for controlling these agents will be examined in future work. Finally, Villani et al. (2017) show that using smart watches to control agents can increase performance metrics and improve the human-robot interaction experience. Their device allows the human operator to be in the field with the agents and capitalize on the operator's ability to adapt to new situations and goals. Villani et al. show that using a smart watch interface to control an agent produces better task performance than teleoperating the aerial vehicle with a joystick. Knowing this, we show that it is possible to use a smart watch interface to control the shape of the swarm, which we speculate can produce even better results in task performance than simply moving the collective swarm through some non-gestural interface.

3 Methodology

3.1 System Architecture

To control the swarm, the human operator makes a recognizable gesture by using the wearable device. The wearable device we use is a Samsung Gear S3 smart watch, which we also used in our prior swarm research to provide feedback to the user about the swarm's formation (Lofaro et al. 2018). We used the inertial measurement unit (IMU) on the smart watch to recognize gestures. Currently the raw IMU data is sent to the swarm server over a wireless network. IMU data is sent to the server every 50 ms (20 Hz). The time that data is delivered is more important than if the data is delivered; thus, we use the User Datagram Protocol (UDP) as the transmission protocol. Currently gesture recognition is performed on the swarm server, but in future implementations, gesture recognition will occur on the smart watch itself. Lofaro and Sofge (2018) provide further detail about these methods for gesture recognition.

Lofaro and Sofge (2018) developed and described a smart watch control interface for the lighter-than-air (LTA) agents. They used a control input method based on the Android Robot Controller (ARC) and Wearable Robot Controller (WRC) message type standard by Lofaro et al. (2017). This method sends a human readable string type message over UDP to the controller of the robots. In this instance, the string included $\langle x, y \rangle$ joystick values and a button press message. The joystick commands control the translation of the robot. The button press is a signal to stop. All of the latter messages are sent over UDP to reduce latency and to simplify robot sensing abilities. Figure 1 shows a picture of the smart watch WRC.

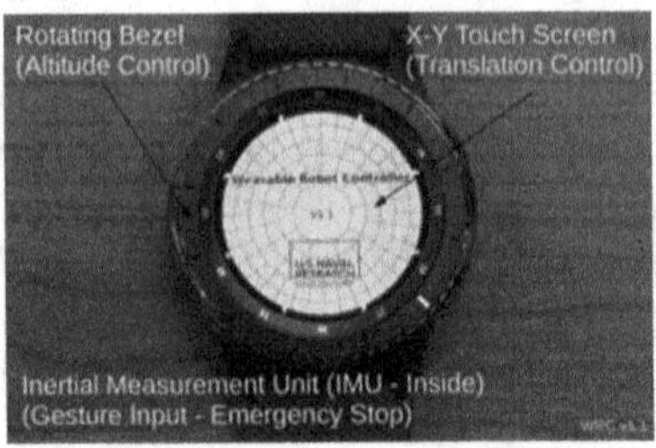

Fig. 1. The Samsung Gear S3 Frontier smart watch Wearable Robot Controller (WRC).

The LTA platforms are controlled by sending commands to the motors on the vehicles. We define the normalized power parameters P_L and P_R as:

$$P_L = \frac{x}{x_{max}} + \frac{y}{y_{max}} \quad P_R = \frac{x}{x_{max}} - \frac{y}{y_{max}}$$

where: P_L and P_R are normalized power (± 1.0) commands to the left and right propellers respectively; x_{max} and y_{max} are the maximum values that the x or the y command inputs can be; and x and y are the inputs from the watch. The left and right normalized motor power commands P_L and P_R are applied to the left and right propellers and held as a zero-order-hold between updated commands from the WRC interface.

When controlling the LTA agents the user might encounter situations where a robot needs to be stopped. For this reason, a hand gesture is used to stop the robot. In this instance, a raising of the hand is used as the stop command. When the stop command is issued P_L and P_R are set to 0.0 and the altitude set point is set to its current altitude. The addition of this stopping mechanism allows a user to naturally stop the LTA agent. Note that for this effort no button press was used to halt the agents; only a recognized *Freeze* gesture was used. The agents may be controlled to perform other maneuvers by adjusting the control outputs of the motors as desired based upon receipt and recognition of gestures as described below.

Once the swarm server determines the gesture, the appropriate control commands are sent to the agents. Currently recognized gestures and formation pairs are:

- **Gesture *Up***: Vertical formation command; it tells the agents to go to the same x and y location while being separated by 1.5 m in z.
- **Gesture *Right***: Horizontal formation command gesture; it tells the agents to go to the same altitude and form a straight line with one another.
- **Gesture *Freeze***: Agents stop their current action and station keep until further instructed.
- **Gesture *Null***: No gesture is found in the case library.

We define the mapping from gesture to formation methodology in Sect. 3.3. Figure 2 shows an example in which a user performs the *Up* gesture to the agents and their real-time response.

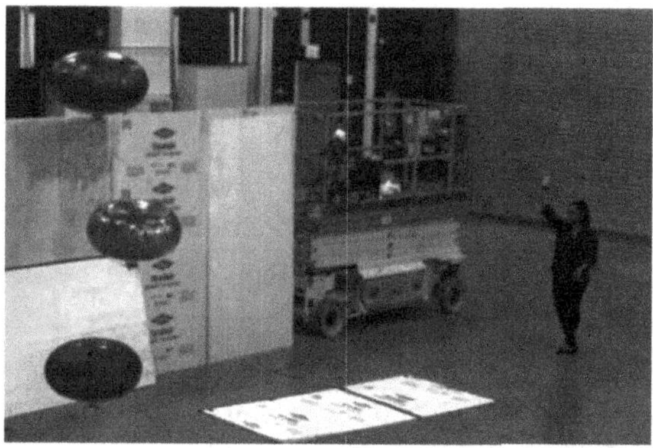

Fig. 2. A user makes the *Up* gesture, which is the vertical formation command gesture. This tells the agents to go to the same x and y location but be separated in altitude (z) by 1.5 m between each agent.

We use a motion capture system to receive world frame position and orientation information from each agent. Future implementations will remove the motion capture system and replace it with a local-frame localization system we developed called LPS (Local Positioning System) (Lofaro 2017). Currently, the feedback to the user is visual. Future iterations of the system will include auditory and haptic feedback from the smart watch. This feedback will aid the user in recognizing when the agents believe that they have completed their task, the agents' physical interaction state, and other pertinent information. Figure 3 depicts the complete system to control multiple agents via the smart watch interface and the message types sent and received throughout the system.

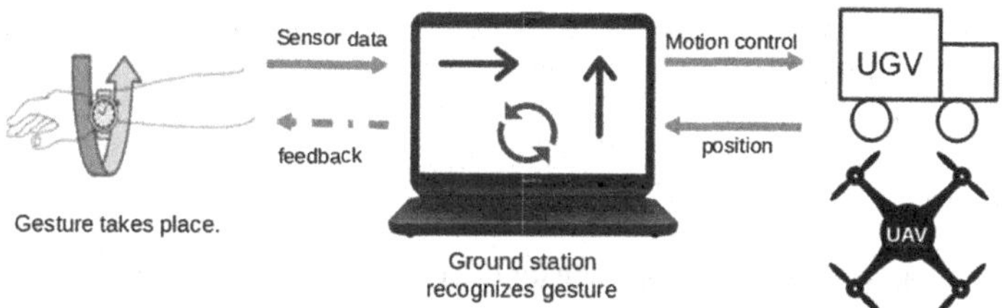

Fig. 3. System diagram of using a wearable to control the formation of a multiagent/swarm system using gesture control.

3.2 Gesture Creation, Recognition, and Validation

Creating gestures for users involves getting raw sensor data from the smart watch (as explained in Sect. 3.1). We utilize the gesture training templates from Villani et al. (2017) as a starting point for our work. To create the templates, we recorded 40 repetitions for each of three gestures (*Up, Right,* and *Freeze*) from one user, for 120 total templates. We

Table 1. Confusion matrix for gesture recognition using correlation coefficients. *Up* is the vertical formation command; it tells the agents to go to the same x and y location while being separated by 1.5 m in z. *Right* is the horizontal formation command gesture; it tells the agents to go to the same altitude and form a straight line with one another. The *null* notation means that no gesture is input. All values are percentages.

Actual \ Recognized	Up	Right	null
Up	96.6	0	3.4
Right	0	96.0	4.0
null	0	0	100.0

then used these to train a Hidden Markov Model (HMM) for each gesture.[1] We chose to use Hidden Markov Models (one per gesture) rather than Dynamic Time Warping for this research due to time constraints. HMMs use observations to provide likelihoods of a hidden state. We provided each HMM with 40 templates, or 40 sets of observed sensor data, to train the model to recognize and classify the pattern of a gesture. Each HMM then produced an ideal template of what observed sensor data should look like for a specific gesture. These templates serve as cases for each gesture (i.e., there are only three cases in our case library, one per gesture, where each case was generated by a trained HMM for that gesture). We used a sliding window queue to view 50 real-time data points at a time. The data-sampling period is 50 ms (20 Hz); the sliding window size is 2.5 s in temporal duration. We chose this window length experimentally. Our algorithm's case similarity function compares the queue to each stored case by computing a Pearson Product Moment Correlation Coefficient:

$$r = \frac{(\Sigma xy) - (\Sigma x)(\Sigma y)}{\sqrt{([\Sigma x^2 - (\Sigma x)^2][\Sigma y^2 - (\Sigma y)^2])}}$$

In the above equation, x is the queued sensor data, and y is the template of what observed sensor data should look like for a specific gesture. If there is a correlation of over 60% to a stored case, then we deem a gesture to be recognized (i.e., it matches one of the stored cases). We selected this value for the correlation coefficient to reduce the amount of false positives and determined it experimentally. Correlation coefficients higher than that threshold resulted in higher precision but lower recall for the *Up* and *Right* gestures, and higher recall but lower precision for the *null* gesture. In future iterations, more sensor data will be used to create cases for the gestures, at which point we will increase the correlation coefficient to account for more complex gestures. Table 1 depicts the gesture recognition accuracy of the *Up*, *Right*, and *null* (i.e., meaning that no matching gesture

[1] We leave as future work a comparison of this method vs. an alternative case-based method in which the repetitions themselves, or a filtered subset of them, are stored and used as cases, where each is compared with the queue during gesture recognition.

was found) gestures using our approach. As shown, this simple case-based strategy has relatively high gesture recognition accuracy.

3.3 Mapping Gestures to Formations

Controlling a specific swarm activity, such as creating formations or clustering, involves: (1) polling each agent's location; (2) allocating desired targets for the swarm; and (3) planning the path for each agent to take to achieve the formation. Because we are using a world-frame motion capturing system, we can obtain accurate position data for each agent in the system. In this work, formation requires an *anchor* agent, which acts as the local-frame origin for the formation. In addition, gestures are mapped to movements that seem "natural" to the user. This means that it is transparent to the user as to why the agents move into a specific formation once a gesture is made. For example, a sharp upward movement (gesture *Up*) is mapped to the agents forming a vertical line, while a sharp rightward movement (gesture *Right*) is mapped to a horizontal line. In future work we plan to use a larger case library of gestures, drawing inspiration from standard human/team collaborative hand signals.

4 Demonstrations

In this section we describe the system and platform that we use in our demonstrations, and then the demonstrations themselves.

4.1 System and Platform

The smart watch interface can be used to control any multiagent system of homogeneous and/or heterogeneous types of agents. In this study we used several Miniature Autonomous Blimps (Cho et al. 2017; Lofaro and Sofge 2018) to demonstrate our smart watch interface. We used the Samsung Gear S3 Frontier smart watch; the sensor data were 3-axis accelerometer readings. We based the smart watch interface on Lofaro et al.'s (2017) work on controlling static robotic/automated devices. We described the communications and computation structure in Sect. 3.1, the gesture recognition methodology in Sect. 3.2, and the mapping of the gestures to formations in Sect. 3.3.

4.2 Demonstration 1: Gesture-Action Mapping

Our first objective was to demonstrate that one of our agents can follow a human operator until they perform a *Freeze* gesture. For this demonstration, we used a miniature autonomous blimp, as shown in Fig. 4. When the demonstration begins, the blimp follows the operator autonomously, which is its default action when no gestures are given (Fig. 4, top).

Alternatively, the operator can perform a *Freeze* gesture, which is the common hand signal of the same name, by making a sharp upward hand movement (Fig. 4, lower left). Upon gesture recognition, the agent stops following the operator and hovers as the operator freely moves to another location. While continuing to make the *Freeze* gesture, the operator can continue to move without the agent following (Fig. 4, bottom). This gesture maps to the agent stopping in place and holding its current position (station keeping) until further instructions are provided. This is a natural and intuitive gesture, as the agent performs the same freezing movement as humans do upon observing this gesture.

Once the operator stops making this gesture (not pictured), the agent enters the *null* gesture state, and resumes its task of operator following. In summary, this demonstration shows that gesturing using a smart watch can be used to control an autonomous blimp's movement, and how a gesture can map intuitively to agent movement.

Fig. 4. Single agent responding to a gesture command. Default action is to *follow* the operator. Gesture enabled action is to *Freeze* (i.e., to stop following the operator). **Top**: Single agent following the operator (no *Freeze* gesture detected). **Bottom**: Single agent detects the *Freeze* gesture and stops following the operator. All frames are in time sequence from left to right.

4.3 Demonstration 2: Shaping the Swarm

Our second demonstration involved shaping a swarm using gesture control, in which the human operator interacted with three aerial agents. (For this demonstration, the golden-colored agent is the *anchor* agent as described in Sect. 3.3.) The agents start in their station-keeping mode. If the human operator makes the *Up* gesture (i.e., the vertical formation command gesture) then, upon recognition, the agents form a vertical line, with a pre-defined distance (1.5 m) between neighboring agents. If the human operator performs the *Right* gesture (i.e., the horizontal formation command gesture) the agents form a horizontal line at a defined altitude (2 m) and distance between neighboring agents (1.5 m). If no recognized gesture occurs, then the system will return to the *null* state and the agents will return to station-keeping mode. The agents' reactions to the *Up, Right*, and *null* gesture states can be seen in Fig. 5 (top, bottom, and middle, respectively). We validate the locations of the agents using the feedback from the motion-capture system to ensure that the agents performed as intended upon each gesture command. These gestures are intuitive and natural to the operator as it is clear to them what each gesture does and how it maps to the agents' formation. This shows that it is possible to control the shape of a swarm using a form of case-based gesture recognition via a wearable interface, in this case a smart watch.

Fig. 5. Multiple agents responding to gesture commands in real-time. **Top**: A user performs the *Up* gesture. This gesture is the vertical formation command gesture. The vertical formation command gesture tells the agents to go to the same x and y location but be separated in altitude (z) by 1.5 m between each agent. **Middle**: The user does not make a recognized gesture, the multiagent system falls into the *null* state, and the agents station-keep together. **Bottom**: The user performs the *Right* gesture. This gesture is the horizontal formation command gesture. The horizontal formation command gesture tells the agents to go to the same altitude and form a straight line with one another.

5 Conclusion

In this paper we presented a novel application of case-based reasoning in which an operator used a wearable device (a smart watch) to control a multiagent system of lighter-than-air miniature autonomous blimps. We described the limitations of current control interfaces of multiagent systems. We then described how our approach: (1) learns a Hidden Markov Model (HMM) for each gesture; (2) generates an ideal sample (a temporal sequence of 50 data points) from each HMM to serve as a case; and (3) uses this small case library in an attempt to match a human operator's gesture. If that gesture is sufficiently correlated with one of the stored cases (we use the Pearson Product Moment Correlation Coefficient for case similarity, and assess a match exists if the correlation exceeds 60%), then it is recognized as such and the agents respond accordingly (here, by aligning themselves horizontally, vertically, or by holding steady in their respective locations). Our demonstrations, in which the operator wore a smart watch to communicate her gestures, showed that we can attain high accuracy for gesture recognition, though we have trained our system for only a small number of gestures. However, our demonstrations showed that this approach works in our laboratory environment, and there have been comparatively few prior studies on using gestures to control swarm formations. Indeed, we are not aware of any prior efforts that use case-based reasoning techniques for this task.

Future work will include creating more gesture templates (i.e., cases) to increase the number of formations that the swarm can make. As the library of gestures expands, we anticipate that similar, multiple gestures could simultaneously meet the correlation coefficient. To mitigate the chance of a false positive recognition, we plan to (1) incorporate sensor data beyond IMU data to create more unique gestures, and (2) determine the desired gesture by taking into account the sequential context of previously given gestures. To accomplish this, we will train our system on patterns of gestures that traditionally occur sequentially, so that if multiple gestures meet the correlation coefficient, the gesture predicted to be the next logical step in the pattern will be recognized. The human operator reacts to the scenario in front of her to best guide the shape and movement of the swarm. Accounting for the current sequential context would further provide a way for the swarm to adapt to the specific environment at that instant.

To date we have made a key simplifying assumption: only one case is required per gesture. In future work, we will test this assumption. In particular, our future work will include multiple human operators communicating gestures under varying conditions (e.g., distances, arm movement speeds, agent/blimp altitudes, relative locations, and movements). Thus, we will examine an alternative of our approach that selectively generates, stores, and uses multiple cases (per gesture) for gesture recognition. We will also compare our approach with one that does not train a set of HMMs to produce ideal cases, but instead stores user repetitions of gestures as cases (i.e., a lazy case-based reasoning strategy). For both alternative approaches, selectively generating, storing, and using multiple cases (per gesture) for gesture recognition may increase gesture recognition accuracy and yield more robust performance under a variety of scenarios.

Finally, for both these eager and lazy approaches we will examine the role of case adaptation, in which the agents' responses may vary depending on environment context (e.g., due to the presence of obstacles or other agents), and we will compare our case-based approaches vs. others for swarm formation control (e.g., Nagavalli et al. 2017) to better assess the unique contributions of CBR approaches for this interesting and important robotics task.

Acknowledgements. Thanks to ONR for supporting this research. The first author conducted the research described in this paper while working as a student employee at NRL. She is currently pursuing her PhD at the Georgia Institute of Technology and can be contacted at divya.srivastava@gatech.edu.

References

Aha, D.W.: Goal reasoning: foundations, emerging applications, and prospects. AI Mag. **39**(2), 3–24 (2018)

Altaf, M.M., Elbagoury, B.M., Alraddady, F., Roushdy, M.: Extended case-based behavior control for multi-humanoid robots. Int. J. Humanoid Robot. **13**(2), 1550035 (2016)

Atkeson, C.G., Moore, A.W., Schaal, S.: Locally weighted learning for control. Artif. Intell. Rev. **11**(1–5), 75–113 (1997)

Cho, S., et al.: Autopilot design for a class of miniature autonomous blimps. In: Proceedings of the Conference on Control Technology and Applications, pp. 841–846. IEEE Press, Kohala Coast (2017)

Deng, L.Y., Lee, D.L., Liu, Y.J., Tang, N.C.: Human computer interaction based on hand gesture ontology. In: Proceedings of the Eleventh WSEAS International Conference on Computers, pp. 26–31. ACM Press, Crete Island (2007)

Fitzgerald, T., McGreggor, K., Akgun, B., Thomaz, A., Goel, A.: Visual case retrieval for interpreting skill demonstrations. In: Hüllermeier, E., Minor, M. (eds.) ICCBR 2015. LNCS (LNAI), vol. 9343, pp. 119–133. Springer, Cham (2015). https://doi.org/10.1007/978-3-319-24586-7_9

Gioioso, G., Franchi, A., Salvietti, G., Scheggi, S., Prattichizzo, D.: The flying hand: a formation of UAVs for cooperative aerial tele-manipulation. In: Proceedings of the International Conference on Robotics and Automation, pp. 4335–4341. IEEE Press, Hong Kong (2014)

Jaidee, U., Muñoz-Avila, H., Aha, D.W.: Case-based goal-driven coordination of multiple learning agents. In: Delany, S.J., Ontañón, S. (eds.) ICCBR 2013. LNCS (LNAI), vol. 7969, pp. 164–178. Springer, Heidelberg (2013). https://doi.org/10.1007/978-3-642-39056-2_12

Lofaro, D.: Utilizing the Android robot controller for robots, wearable apps, and the hotel room of the future. In: Proceedings of the Fourteenth International Conference on Ubiquitous Robots and Ambient Intelligence, pp. 570–575. IEEE Press, Jeju (2017)

Lofaro, D., Sofge, D.: Multimodal control of lighter-than-air agents. In: Proceedings of the Twentieth International Conference on Multimodal Interaction, pp. 555–556. ACM Press, Boulder (2018)

Lofaro, D., Taylor, C., Tse, R., Sofge, D.: Wearable interactive display for the local positioning system (LPS). In: Proceedings of the Nineteenth International Conference on Multimodal Interaction, pp. 522–523. ACM Press, Glasgow (2017)

Nagavalli, S., Chandarana, M., Sycara, K., Lewis, M.: Multi-operator gesture control of robotic swarms using wearable devices. In: Proceedings of the Tenth International Conference on Advances in Computer-Human Interactions. IARIA, Nice (2017)

O'Connor, D., Kapetanakis, S., Samakovitis, G., Floyd, M., Ontañon, S., Petridis, M.: Autonomous swarm agents using case-based reasoning. In: Bramer, M., Petridis, M. (eds.) SGAI 2018. LNCS (LNAI), vol. 11311, pp. 210–216. Springer, Cham (2018). https://doi.org/10.1007/978-3-030-04191-5_20

Olsson, E., Funk, P., Bengtsson, M.: Fault diagnosis of industrial robots using acoustic signals and case-based reasoning. In: Funk, P., González Calero, P.A. (eds.) ECCBR 2004. LNCS (LNAI), vol. 3155, pp. 686–701. Springer, Heidelberg (2004). https://doi.org/10.1007/978-3-540-28631-8_50

Peula, J.M., Urdiales, C., Herrero, I., Sánchez-Tato, I., Sandoval, F.: Pure reactive behavior learning using case based reasoning for a vision based 4-legged robot. Robot. Auton. Syst. **57**(6–7), 688–699 (2009)

Ros, R., López de Màntaras, R., Arcos, J.L., Veloso, M.: Team playing behavior in robot soccer: a case-based reasoning approach. In: Weber, Rosina O., Richter, Michael M. (eds.) ICCBR 2007. LNCS (LNAI), vol. 4626, pp. 46–60. Springer, Heidelberg (2007). https://doi.org/10.1007/978-3-540-74141-1_4

Secchi, C., Sabattini, L, Fantuzzi, C.: Conducting multirobot systems: gestures for the passive teleoperation of multiple slaves. In: Proceedings of the International Conference on Intelligent Robots and Systems, pp. 2803–2808. IEEE Press, Hamburg (2015)
Villani, V., Sabattini, L., Riggio, G., Secchi, C., Minelli, M., Fantuzzi, C.: A natural infrastructure-less human–robot interaction system. Robot, Autom. Lett. **2**(3), 1640–1647 (2017)

Technical Session: Retrieval and Adaptation

The French Correction: When Retrieval Is Harder to Specify than Adaptation

Yves Lepage[1], Jean Lieber[2], Isabelle Mornard[2,3], Emmanuel Nauer[2(✉)], Julien Romary[2], and Reynault Sies[2]

[1] Waseda University, IPS, 2-7 Hibikino, Kitakyushu 808-0135, Japan
yves.lepage@waseda.jp

[2] Université de Lorraine, CNRS, Inria, LORIA, 54000 Nancy, France
{jean.lieber,isabelle.mornard,emmanuel.nauer,julien.romary, reynault.sies}@loria.fr

[3] Université Jean Monnet, Université de Lyon, Saint-Étienne, France
isabelle.mornard@etu.univ-st-etienne.fr

Abstract. A common idea in the field of case-based reasoning is that the retrieval step can be specified by the use of some similarity measure: the retrieved cases maximize the similarity to the target problem and, then, the adaptation step has to take into account the mismatches between the retrieved cases and the target problem in order to this latter. The use of this methodological schema for the application described in this paper has proven to be non efficient. Indeed, designing a retrieval procedure without the precise knowledge of the adaptation procedure has not been possible. The domain of this application is the correction of French sentences: a problem is an incorrect sentence and a valid solution is a correction of this problem. Adaptation consists in solving an analogical equation that enables to execute the correction of the retrieved case on the target problem. Thus, retrieval has to ensure that this application is feasible. The first version of such a retrieval procedure is described and evaluated: it is a knowledge-light procedure that does not use linguistic knowledge about French.

Keywords: Case-based reasoning · Retrieval · Analogy · Sentence correction

1 Introduction

Case-based reasoning (CBR [8]) aims at solving a problem with the help of a case base, where a case is the representation of a problem-solving episode. It is often decomposed in several steps including its inference steps, retrieval and adaptation. Retrieval consists in selecting one or several case(s) from the

The authors wish to thank Bruno Guillaume who has given us some valuable remarks for this project and Nicolas Lasolle who has helped us for its evaluation.
(The authors are listed alphabetically according to their second names).

I. Watson and R. Weber (Eds.): ICCBR 2020, LNAI 12311, pp. 309–324, 2020.
https://doi.org/10.1007/978-3-030-58342-2_20

case base that is/are similar to the target problem (i.e., the problem to be solved). Adaptation consists in modifying this/these retrieved case(s) in order to obtain a plausible solution to the target problem. For many CBR applications, the specification of retrieval is quite simple and amounts to choose a similarity metric or a distance function on the problem space. Then, the main difficulty of retrieval is algorithmic: how to design a program that efficiently implements this specification. By contrast, adaptation is often considered as more difficult to specify within a given application: the issue of its efficient implementation comes only in a second time.

The CBR application presented in this paper contrasts with this viewpoint: the adaptation has been rather simple to specify, whereas the first version of retrieval giving some relevant results has not. This CBR application aims at correcting linguistic errors in French sentences: its input is an incorrect sentence, its output is a correction of this sentence. For the sake of readability, the examples in this paper are in English. It is noteworthy that the correction is only at the grammatical level: the corrected sentence is expected to be orthographically and syntactically correct but there are no expected correction at the semantic level. For example, consider the following example:

Input: *Tomatoes grows outdoors in winter.*
Output: *Tomatoes grow outdoors in winter.*

The output sentence is orthographically and syntactically correct, but no correction is made at the semantic level (that would consist, for example, in substituting *winter* with *summer*).

The system presented in this paper is called *The French Correction* (abbreviated in TFC) and has several features that are worth mentioning. First, this first version of TFC is intentionally knowledge-light: almost all its knowledge lies in the case base (very little domain knowledge). Therefore, the system should give similar results in another alphabetic language using spaces for separating words. Indeed, it works at the character level (letters and punctuation marks). Second, TFC is *not* meant to be competitive with other correcting systems that are currently used in, e.g., word processing systems. By contrast, TFC's main goal is to provide a playground for CBR research.

This paper is organized as follows. Section 2 presents some preliminaries: the main assumptions and notations on CBR that are considered in this paper and some notions related to strings and to analogies. Section 3 informally specifies the TFC system. Building a CBR system requires the acquisition of a case base: case authoring is described in Sect. 4. The case-based inference is described in Sects. 5 and 6: adaptation first and then retrieval. Indeed, the TFC retrieval module must be adaptation-guided for this application, hence this unusual order in the presentation. Section 7 presents the evaluation of TFC. Section 8 discusses the design of this system and, in particular, its originality with respect to the respective design of the retrieval and adaptation phases. Finally, Sect. 9 concludes this article with some research directions around *The French Correction.*

Main Objective of this Paper. This paper presents a problem that is easy to understand but not so easy to solve, together with a first baseline solution. Such a problem could be a challenge for the CBR community, or even a benchmark. The authors agree to distribute the case base and the test base for this purpose.

2 Preliminaries

This section recalls some notions related to CBR, strings and analogies. These notions are used in particular to define the adaptation step of TFC which relies on analogies on strings.

2.1 Preliminaries: Assumptions and Notations About CBR

Let $\mathcal{P}$ and $\mathcal{S}$ be two sets respectively called the *problem space* and *the solution space.* A *problem* $\mathtt{x}$ (resp., a solution $\mathtt{y}$) is by definition an element of $\mathcal{P}$ (resp., $\mathcal{S}$). Let $\rightsquigarrow$ be a relation on $\mathcal{P} \times \mathcal{S}$. For $(\mathtt{x}, \mathtt{y}) \in \mathcal{P} \times \mathcal{S}$, $\mathtt{x} \rightsquigarrow \mathtt{y}$ is read "$\mathtt{x}$ has for solution $\mathtt{y}$" or "$\mathtt{y}$ solves $\mathtt{x}$". The relation $\rightsquigarrow$ is in general incompletely known, though it is known to hold for a finite set of pairs $(\mathtt{x}^s, \mathtt{y}^s)$. This finite set is called the *case base*, denoted by $\mathtt{CB}$, and every $(\mathtt{x}^s, \mathtt{y}^s) \in \mathtt{CB}$ is called a *source case.*

CBR aims at solving a new problem, called the *target problem* and denoted by $\mathtt{x}^{\mathtt{tgt}}$, with the help of $\mathtt{CB}$.

The process model of CBR consists (1) in selecting k source cases similar to the target problem, (2) in inferring from these k source cases a candidate solution $\mathtt{y}^{\mathtt{tgt}}$ of $\mathtt{x}^{\mathtt{tgt}}$, (3) in confronting the hypothetical case $(\mathtt{x}^{\mathtt{tgt}}, \mathtt{y}^{\mathtt{tgt}})$ to, e.g., a human that validate it as a case if $\mathtt{x}^{\mathtt{tgt}} \rightsquigarrow \mathtt{y}^{\mathtt{tgt}}$ or correct $\mathtt{y}^{\mathtt{tgt}}$ otherwise, (4) in storing the validated and potentially corrected case $(\mathtt{x}^{\mathtt{tgt}}, \mathtt{y}^{\mathtt{tgt}})$ in $\mathtt{CB}$ if this storage is deemed useful. These steps are called (1) retrieval, (2) adaptation, (3) validation and repair, and (4) storage (aka as retrieve, reuse, revise and retain in the 4 R's model of [1]). In many applications, as the one described in this paper, $k = 1$: only one source case is retrieved and adapted to solve the target problem. For some of these applications, adaptation consists in reusing as such the solution of the retrieved case (i.e., $\mathtt{y}^{\mathtt{tgt}} = \mathtt{y}^s$): this is called *adaptation by copy.*

Case retrieval is often performed thanks to a distance function $\mathtt{dist}$ on $\mathcal{P}$: the selected case(s) $(\mathtt{x}^s, \mathtt{y}^s)$ being the one(s) that minimize(s) $\mathtt{dist}(\mathtt{x}^s, \mathtt{x}^{\mathtt{tgt}})$.[1] Thus, $\mathtt{dist}$ induces a ranking $\prec^{\mathtt{dist}}_{\mathtt{x}^{\mathtt{tgt}}}$ between problems defined by $\mathtt{x}^s \prec^{\mathtt{dist}}_{\mathtt{x}^{\mathtt{tgt}}} \mathtt{x}^u$ ("$\mathtt{x}^s$ is more similar to $\mathtt{x}^{\mathtt{tgt}}$ than $\mathtt{x}^u$ according to $\mathtt{dist}$") if $\mathtt{dist}(\mathtt{x}^s, \mathtt{x}^{\mathtt{tgt}}) < \mathtt{dist}(\mathtt{x}^u, \mathtt{x}^{\mathtt{tgt}})$.

The knowledge model of CBR consists in four knowledge containers: the case base $\mathtt{CB}$, the domain knowledge $\mathtt{DK}$, the retrieval knowledge $\mathtt{RK}$ and the adaptation knowledge $\mathtt{AK}$ [7]. $\mathtt{DK}$ is also known as the domain ontology and serves two purposes: giving a vocabulary for describing the cases and some integrity constraints, i.e., some *necessary* conditions for a pair $(\mathtt{x}, \mathtt{y})$ to be a case

[1] This can be equivalently defined by the maximization of the similarity measure $\mathtt{sim}$ defined by $\mathtt{sim}(\mathtt{x}^1, \mathtt{x}^2) = \frac{1}{1+\mathtt{dist}(\mathtt{x}^1, \mathtt{x}^2)}$.

(i.e., $\mathtt{x} \rightsquigarrow \mathtt{y}$). RK and AK contain the application-dependent knowledge for, respectively, performing retrieval and adaptation. A CBR system is qualified as *knowledge light* if most of the knowledge lies in CB.

2.2 Strings

Let $\mathcal{A}$ be a finite set; a *character* c is an element of $\mathcal{A}$. Let $\mathcal{A}^*$ be the set of strings on $\mathcal{A}$. The empty string is denoted by ϵ. The concatenation of two strings S and T is denoted by the juxtaposition ST. For $S, T \in \mathcal{A}^*$, S is a *substring* of T if there exist $X, Y \in \mathcal{A}^*$ such that $T = XSY$.

The length of a string $S \in \mathcal{A}^*$ is denoted by $|S|$. For instance, $|\epsilon| = 0$. For $c \in \mathcal{A}$ and $S \in \mathcal{A}^*$, $\#\mathtt{occ}(c, S)$ is the number of occurrences of c in S, e.g., $\#\mathtt{occ}(\text{'}t\text{'}, \mathit{tomato}) = 2$.

Given $S \in \mathcal{A}^*$, a *subsequence* of S is a string that can be obtained by removing 0 to $|S|$ characters from S. For example, *toto* is a subsequence of *tomato*. Given two strings S and T, an LCS (longest common subsequence) of S and T is a string L that is a subsequence of both S and T of maximum length (it exists, but it is not necessarily unique, though all LCSs of S and T have the same length). For example, an LCS of *tomato* and *toad* is *toa*.

For $S, T \in \mathcal{A}^*$, $\mathtt{dist}_{\mathrm{LCS}}(S, T)$ is the LCS distance from S to T defined by

$$\mathtt{dist}_{\mathrm{LCS}}(S, T) = |S| + |T| - 2\,|L|$$

where L is an LCS of S and T. It can be equivalently defined as the edit distance with the "delete a character" and "add a character" edit operations with the same cost of 1. For example, $\mathtt{dist}_{\mathrm{LCS}}(\mathit{tomato}, \mathit{toad}) = 6 + 4 - 2 \times 3 = 4$.

2.3 Analogies

An *analogy* on a set $\mathcal{U}$ is a quaternary relation on $\mathcal{U}$ denoted, for $(A, B, C, D) \in \mathcal{U}^4$, by $A{:}B::C{:}D$, and read "A is to B as C is to D" that satisfies the following postulates (for any $A, B, C, D \in \mathcal{U}$): (1) $A{:}B::A{:}B$, (2) if $A{:}B::C{:}D$ then $C{:}D::A{:}B$, and (3) if $A{:}B::C{:}D$ then $A{:}C::B{:}D$.

An *analogical equation* is an expression of the form $A{:}B::C{:}x$ where $A, B, C \in \mathcal{U}$ and x is a symbol called the unknown of the analogical equation. Solving $A{:}B::C{:}x$ aims at finding the set of $D \in \mathcal{U}$ such $A{:}B::C{:}D$. An analogical equation may have 0, 1 or several solutions, depending on the analogy.

For analogies on sentences, an analogy can be built at the string level (i.e., without taking into account linguistic knowledge neither on the lexical level nor on the syntactic level) and it has been introduced for the purpose of machine translation [4]. It is defined as follows, for $A, B, C, D \in \mathcal{A}^*$:

$$A{:}B::C{:}D \quad \text{if} \quad \#\mathtt{occ}(c, B) - \#\mathtt{occ}(c, A) = \#\mathtt{occ}(c, D) - \#\mathtt{occ}(c, C), \quad (\text{for any } c \in \mathcal{A})$$

$$\mathtt{dist}_{\mathrm{LCS}}(A, B) = \mathtt{dist}_{\mathrm{LCS}}(C, D) \quad \text{and} \quad \mathtt{dist}_{\mathrm{LCS}}(A, C) = \mathtt{dist}_{\mathrm{LCS}}(B, D)$$

For example:

You don't say! : *He does not say it.* :: *You don't know!* : *He does not know it.*

Now, a quaternary relation $\mathcal{R}$ can be defined on $\mathcal{A}^*$ that constitutes a subrelation of this analogical relation: if $\mathcal{R}(A, B, C, D)$ then $A{:}B::C{:}D$, for $A, B, C, D \in \mathcal{A}^*$. This relation is useful for the purpose of the presentation of most examples in the paper as it appears to be at the same time simpler to apprehend and sufficient for many examples. It is also used in the retrieval procedure to make it more efficient. For $A, B, C, D \in \mathcal{A}^*$, $\mathcal{R}(A, B, C, D)$ holds if there exists a substring S common to A and C and a substring T common to B and D such that B (resp., D) is obtained by a string replacement of S with T in A (resp., in C). Formally, $\mathcal{R}(A, B, C, D)$ if there exist $S, T, X, Y, X', Y' \in \mathcal{A}^*$ such that $A = XSY$, $B = XTY$, $C = X'SY'$ and $D = X'TY'$. For example (with the occurrences of S and T underlined),

$$\text{if}\left|\begin{array}{ll} A = \textit{Do you want some } \underline{\textit{coffee}}\textit{?} & C = \textit{This } \underline{\textit{coffee}} \textit{ is hot!} \\ B = \textit{Do you want some } \underline{\textit{tea}}\textit{?} & D = \textit{This } \underline{\textit{tea}} \textit{ is hot!} \end{array}\right.$$

then $\mathcal{R}(A, B, C, D)$ and, thus, $A{:}B::C{:}D$.

It can be noted that $\mathcal{R}$ is not an analogical relation (it satisfies the first and second postulates, but not the third one).

3 Goals of the TFC System

TFC is a CBR system that takes as input a sentence $\mathtt{x}^{\mathtt{tgt}}$ that is supposed to be incorrect and gives as output a sentence $\mathtt{y}^{\mathtt{tgt}}$ with the following objective: $\mathtt{y}^{\mathtt{tgt}}$ is a correction of $\mathtt{x}^{\mathtt{tgt}}$ at the language level. For a source case $(\mathtt{x}^s, \mathtt{y}^s)$, $\mathtt{x}^s$ is an incorrect sentence and $\mathtt{y}^s$ is a sentence obtained by correcting $\mathtt{x}^s$.

It is practical, in particular for further explanations, to consider special types of cases, called SR cases (SR stands for String Replacement). An SR case $(\mathtt{x}, \mathtt{y})$ is such that $\mathtt{y}$ is obtained by a single string replacement of a substring S of $\mathtt{x}$ by a string T where S and T contain no space (i.e., the modification lies within a single word). For example, $(\mathtt{x}^s, \mathtt{y}^s)$ defined below is an SR source case (with $S = es$ and $T = \epsilon$):

$$\mathtt{x}^s = \textit{They goes to the beach.} \qquad \mathtt{y}^s = \textit{They go to the beach}$$

The TFC case base in its current version contains only French sentences, though most of the ideas developed in this paper can be considered in another alphabetical language. Let $\mathcal{A}$ be the set of characters in such a language (letters, letters with diacritics, punctuation marks, space, etc.). Therefore, every problem $\mathtt{x}$ and every solution $\mathtt{y}$ belongs to $\mathcal{A}^*$, therefore $\mathcal{P} = \mathcal{S} = \mathcal{A}^*$. It is noteworthy that, in TFC, the problems and solutions belong to a common space (i.e., from an algorithmic viewpoint, they have the same type), which is not the general case in CBR.

4 Case Authoring

Since TFC, at least in the version presented in this paper, is a knowledge-light CBR system, the acquisition of its case base is crucial. For this purpose, two approaches have been considered: a manual one and a semi-automatic one.

The manual case authoring approach has consisted in searching for documents about French grammar, frequent mistakes, etc., and in defining cases reflecting such errors. For example, in English, the case $(\mathbf{x}^s, \mathbf{y}^s)$ can be found with:[2]

$$\mathbf{x}^s = \textit{You like dance with me?} \qquad \mathbf{y}^s = \textit{Would you like to dance with me?}$$

The irregular forms in the language can be used to define cases. For example, the verb *to meet* is irregular: its preterit is *met* (and not *meeted*), hence the following case:

$$\mathbf{x}^s = \textit{He meeted her yesterday.} \qquad \mathbf{y}^s = \textit{He met her yesterday.}$$

Then, other cases were added by various contributors. The case base built that way is rather small (300 cases at the time of submission of this article), and the source cases are chosen to cover frequent common mistakes. Of course, when TFC fails to correctly solve a problem, the last steps of the CBR process (repair and storage) leads to an enrichment of the case base. This aspect of the system has not been studied in depth yet, but it is operational.

The semi-automatic case authoring approach uses WiCoPaCo [3] which is a collection of sentence (or text) pairs $(\mathtt{x}, \mathtt{y}) \in \mathcal{A}^{*2}$ taken from the Wikipedia French pages, where $\mathtt{x}$ is a sentence written by an editor and $\mathtt{y}$ is a sentence replacing it (in a next edition of the same article). WiCoPaCo comes with some markups explaining some of the changes.

However, using WiCoPaCo as such for a TFC case base has appeared to be inefficient. Indeed, a WiCoPaCo pair $(\mathtt{x}, \mathtt{y})$ is not necessarily a valid case, for example, $\mathtt{y}$ may contain an error, or $\mathtt{y}$ corrects $\mathtt{x}$ at a semantic level, or corresponds to an information update. Since WiCoPaCo contains hundreds of thousands pairs, a manual selection of such pairs that could be used as TFC cases would be too tedious for the project. Some automatic filters have been defined for deleting some irrelevant pairs, but they are not currently sufficient to obtain a TFC case base with a low level of noise. That is why, for this work, it has been decided to use a small case base containing 300 well-formed cases collected from several persons whose native language is French.

[2] https://www.engvid.com/english-resource/50-common-grammar-mistakes-in-english/.

5 Adaptation

A single case adaptation is used in TFC. Consider first an example of adaptation problem, with $(\mathtt{x}^s, \mathtt{y}^s)$ the retrieved case and $\mathtt{x}^{\mathtt{tgt}}$, the problem to be solved:

$\mathtt{x}^s =$ *David would not eating his soup.* $\mathtt{y}^s =$ *David would not eat his soup.*
$\mathtt{x}^{\mathtt{tgt}} =$ *Cindy will going to Nancy.*

In this example, the error corrected in $(\mathtt{x}^s, \mathtt{y}^s)$ corresponds to the inappropriate *-ing* form at the end of the verb. The same error occurs in $\mathtt{x}^{\mathtt{tgt}}$, thus the transformation from $\mathtt{x}^s$ to $\mathtt{y}^s$ can be suggested as correction:

$$\mathtt{y}^{\mathtt{tgt}} = \textit{Cindy will go to Nancy.}$$

Therefore, with the analogy on strings defined in Sect. 2.3, $\mathtt{y}^{\mathtt{tgt}}$ is a solution of the following analogical equation with unknown y:

$$\mathtt{x}^s{:}\mathtt{y}^s :: \mathtt{x}^{\mathtt{tgt}}{:}y \tag{1}$$

More generally, the adaptation of TFC consists in solving the analogical Eq. (1). When this equation has no solution, adaptation fails. When it has several solutions, TFC's adaptation proposes all of them if there is no way to make a preference among them: this issue is considered again in the next section.

In practice, if $(\mathtt{x}^s, \mathtt{y}^s)$ is an SR source case, solving $\mathtt{x}^s{:}\mathtt{y}^s :: \mathtt{x}^{\mathtt{tgt}}{:}y$ consists, in such a situation, in solving $\mathcal{R}(\mathtt{x}^s, \mathtt{y}^s, \mathtt{x}^{\mathtt{tgt}}, y)$. This occurs for the above example: $\mathtt{y}^{\mathtt{tgt}}$ is obtained by substituting *ing* with ϵ in $\mathtt{x}^{\mathtt{tgt}}$.

Sometimes, there are several retrieved cases, when the retrieval procedure cannot distinguish them. When this occurs, the adaptation is performed on all these cases and this provides a multiset of solutions. The final result is an element of this multiset with the highest multiplicity.

What makes this adaptation rather simple to define is first that it is based on a previous work on analogy on strings [4] and second the fact that the problem and solution spaces coincide for this application. Moreover, although it is defined at a character level (since it only relies on the analogical relation defined on strings, without any linguistic knowledge), it gives results that are quite convincing for the correction of sentences, provided that an appropriate correction case exists in the case base, which is the role of the case authoring process, and provided that such an appropriate case has been selected, which is the role of case retrieval.

6 Retrieval

Retrieval aims at selecting a source case to be adapted. Given a target problem $\mathtt{x}^{\mathtt{tgt}}$ and two source cases $(\mathtt{x}^1, \mathtt{y}^1)$ and $(\mathtt{x}^2, \mathtt{y}^2)$, which one, if any, should be preferred? Following the principle of adaptation-guided retrieval (AGR [9]), it should be a case that is adaptable (i.e., the adaptation function returns a candidate solution to $\mathtt{x}^{\mathtt{tgt}}$, given this case and $\mathtt{x}^{\mathtt{tgt}}$). For comparing two cases $(\mathtt{x}^1, \mathtt{y}^1)$

and $(\mathrm{x}^2, \mathrm{y}^2)$ that both can be adapted in candidate solutions $\mathrm{y}^{1,\mathtt{tgt}}$ and $\mathrm{y}^{2,\mathtt{tgt}}$ to the target problem $\mathrm{x}^{\mathtt{tgt}}$, an ideal retrieval function will choose $(\mathrm{x}^1, \mathrm{y}^1)$ if the candidate solution $\mathrm{y}^{1,\mathtt{tgt}}$ is better than $\mathrm{y}^{2,\mathtt{tgt}}$ (e.g., $\mathrm{y}^{1,\mathtt{tgt}}$ is a correct solution of $\mathrm{x}^{\mathtt{tgt}}$ while $\mathrm{y}^{2,\mathtt{tgt}}$ is not).

This principle of AGR adapted to the retrieval problem of TFC is considered via an example. Then, the description of the knowledge-light retrieval approach of the first version of TFC is presented.

6.1 Example

Consider the following target problem:

$$\mathrm{x}^{\mathtt{tgt}} = \textit{George has read this books.}$$

and the three source cases $(\mathrm{x}^s, \mathrm{y}^s)$ $(s \in \{1, 2, 3\})$:

x^1 = *George have read this book.* y^1 = *George has read this book.*
x^2 = *You has read this book.* y^2 = *You have read this book.*
x^3 = *Put it on the tables, please.* y^3 = *Put it on the table, please.*

Now, consider someone who is agnostic to the task to be performed by the TFC system and who does not know the solutions y^1, y^2 and y^3. This person is asked to rank x^1, x^2 and x^3 according to their similarity to $\mathrm{x}^{\mathtt{tgt}}$, without any precision on what "similar" means. It is likely that he/she would give the ranking $\mathrm{x}^1 \prec_{\mathrm{x}^{\mathtt{tgt}}} \mathrm{x}^2 \prec_{\mathrm{x}^{\mathtt{tgt}}} \mathrm{x}^3$ where $\prec_{\mathrm{x}^{\mathtt{tgt}}}$ is read "is strictly more similar to $\mathrm{x}^{\mathtt{tgt}}$ than". This ranking is consistent with the one that is induced by, e.g., the LCS distance function:

$$\mathtt{dist}_{\mathrm{LCS}}(\mathrm{x}^1, \mathrm{x}^{\mathtt{tgt}}) \;<\; \mathtt{dist}_{\mathrm{LCS}}(\mathrm{x}^2, \mathrm{x}^{\mathtt{tgt}}) \;<\; \mathtt{dist}_{\mathrm{LCS}}(\mathrm{x}^3, \mathrm{x}^{\mathtt{tgt}})$$

Now, it is argued that the ranking of these three cases with respect to the target problem should be the reverse order, according to the defined adaptation process and to the English language correctness.

First, the source case $(\mathrm{x}^1, \mathrm{y}^1)$ is simply *not* adaptable to solve $\mathrm{x}^{\mathtt{tgt}}$: the analogical equation $\mathrm{x}^1{:}\mathrm{y}^1 {::} \mathrm{x}^{\mathtt{tgt}}{:}y$ has no solution. Indeed, if y was a solution, $\#\mathtt{occ}(\text{'}v\text{'}, \mathrm{y}^1) - \#\mathtt{occ}(\text{'}v\text{'}, \mathrm{x}^1) = \#\mathtt{occ}(\text{'}v\text{'}, y) - \#\mathtt{occ}(\text{'}v\text{'}, \mathrm{x}^{\mathtt{tgt}})$, thus $\#\mathtt{occ}(\text{'}v\text{'}, y) = 0 - 1 + 0 = -1$, which is not possible.

The source case $(\mathrm{x}^2, \mathrm{y}^2)$ is adaptable to solve $\mathrm{x}^{\mathtt{tgt}}$: the analogical equation $\mathrm{x}^2{:}\mathrm{y}^2 {::} \mathrm{x}^{\mathtt{tgt}}{:}y$ is solvable and its solutions are:

y = *George ha<u>ve</u> read this books.* y = *George has read thi<u>ve</u> books.*

and y = *George has read this book<u>ve</u>.*

Unfortunately, both solutions are incorrect solutions of $\mathrm{x}^{\mathtt{tgt}}$, since these two sentences violate the English language.

The source case $(\mathrm{x}^3, \mathrm{y}^3)$ is also adaptable to solve $\mathrm{x}^{\mathtt{tgt}}$, thus, according to the adaptation-guided principle, both $(\mathrm{x}^2, \mathrm{y}^2)$ and $(\mathrm{x}^3, \mathrm{y}^3)$ are preferred to $(\mathrm{x}^1, \mathrm{y}^1)$, given the target problem $\mathrm{x}^{\mathtt{tgt}}$. The solutions of $\mathrm{x}^3 : \mathrm{y}^3 :: \mathrm{x}^{\mathtt{tgt}} : y$ are:

$y =$ *George ha read this books.* $y =$ *George has read thi books.*

and $y =$ *George has read this book.*

The third solution is a correct correction of $\mathrm{x}^{\mathtt{tgt}}$, therefore $(\mathrm{x}^3, \mathrm{y}^3)$ is preferred to $(\mathrm{x}^2, \mathrm{y}^2)$ according to an *a posteriori* help from a domain expert (i.e., someone who can say which sentence is correct in English and which is not). The design of retrieval aims at finding a way of *predicting* which cases are the most likely to provide a correct solution to $\mathrm{x}^{\mathtt{tgt}}$.

What this third example shows is that, even with a retrieved case such that adaptation gives a correct solution, it may give other solutions that are not: among the 3 values for y proposed above, only the third one is correct. Therefore, an interesting byproduct of retrieval would be to have some relevant information in order to discriminate among these solutions.

With a sufficient level in English linguistic knowledge, retrieval could consist in finding the error in $\mathrm{x}^{\mathtt{tgt}}$ and then in finding a source case that represents the correction of the same error (at the character level). Now, a challenge is to design a retrieval process that uses no linguistic knowledge. The retrieval process presented in the next section is a first attempt to meet this challenge.

6.2 Proposed Retrieval Procedure

The retrieval procedure described below is knowledge-light. In particular, it uses no linguistic knowledge about French, except for the fact that sentences can be split in words.

The filter phase aims at discarding cases that are not adaptable to solve the target problem $\mathrm{x}^{\mathtt{tgt}}$ such as the case $(\mathrm{x}^1, \mathrm{y}^1)$ in the example. More generally, a source case $(\mathrm{x}^s, \mathrm{y}^s)$ is filtered if the analogical equation $\mathrm{x}^s : \mathrm{y}^s :: \mathrm{x}^{\mathtt{tgt}} : y$ has no solution, which can be easily tested.

This filter can be efficiently implemented by considering necessary conditions and sufficient conditions for $(\mathrm{x}^s, \mathrm{y}^s)$ to be adaptable to solve $\mathrm{x}^{\mathtt{tgt}}$ (i.e., the analogical equation $\mathrm{x}^s : \mathrm{y}^s :: \mathrm{x}^{\mathtt{tgt}} : y$ has at least one solution). If a necessary condition does not hold, then the case is not adaptable and must be filtered. If a sufficient condition holds, then the case is adaptable (no more testing is needed at this phase of retrieval for this case). Examples of such conditions are presented below.

A *necessary condition* based on the definition of the analogy on strings is related to the character count. Indeed, if y is a solution of $\mathrm{x}^s : \mathrm{y}^s :: \mathrm{x}^{\mathtt{tgt}} : y$, then, for every character c,

$$\#\mathtt{occ}(c, y) = \underbrace{\#\mathtt{occ}(c, \mathrm{x}^{\mathtt{tgt}})}_{①} + \underbrace{\#\mathtt{occ}(c, \mathrm{y}^s) - \#\mathtt{occ}(c, \mathrm{x}^s)}_{②}$$

So, $\#\mathtt{occ}(c, y)$ can be computed fast, since ① depends only on the target problem and ② depends only on the source case and, thus, can be computed offline. Now, the number of occurrences of a character in a string has to be nonnegative, thus, if the value computed for $\#\mathtt{occ}(c, y)$ is negative, then $(\mathrm{x}^s, \mathrm{y}^s)$ is not adaptable to solve $\mathrm{x}^{\mathtt{tgt}}$ and can be filtered. It is noteworthy that only the characters c occurring in x^s, y^s and/or $\mathrm{x}^{\mathtt{tgt}}$ need to be taken into account.

A *sufficient condition* is related to $\mathcal{R}$, the subrelation of the analogical relation introduced in the preliminaries. Given a source case $(\mathrm{x}^s, \mathrm{y}^s)$, there exist ordered pairs of strings (S, T) such that y^s is obtained by substring replacement of S with T in $\mathrm{x}^{\mathtt{tgt}}$ (since $(S, T) = (\mathrm{x}^s, \mathrm{y}^s)$ is such a pair, the existence of such pairs is ensured). Now, a pair of strings (S, T) with S of minimal length is associated to $(\mathrm{x}^s, \mathrm{y}^s)$ in an offline process. The three cases $(\mathrm{x}^s, \mathrm{y}^s)$ $(s \in \{1, 2, 3\})$ introduced in the previous section are used below to illustrate the procedure. With the cases $(\mathrm{x}^s, \mathrm{y}^s)$ of the example developed in the previous section $(s \in \{1, 2, 3\})$:

$$\text{for } s = 1, (S, T) = (ve, s) \quad \text{for } s = 2, (S, T) = (s, ve) \quad \text{for } s = 3, (S, T) = (s, \epsilon)$$

Since $S = s$ is a substring of $\mathrm{x}^{\mathtt{tgt}}$, both $(\mathrm{x}^2, \mathrm{y}^2)$ and $(\mathrm{x}^3, \mathrm{y}^3)$ are adaptable to solve $\mathrm{x}^{\mathtt{tgt}}$. This does not hold for $(\mathrm{x}^1, \mathrm{y}^1)$: $S = ve$ is not a substring of $\mathrm{x}^{\mathtt{tgt}}$.

The Ranking Phase is based on a preference relation between two source cases that are adaptable in a candidate solution of $\mathrm{x}^{\mathtt{tgt}}$. Let $(\mathrm{x}^s, \mathrm{y}^s)$ be a source case that has not been filtered. This involves that the replacements on x^s to obtain y^s can be applied on $\mathrm{x}^{\mathtt{tgt}}$ (at one or several place(s)).

For the sake of simplicity of the explanations, let us assume that the transformation from x^s to y^s corresponds to a substring replacement of a string S by a string T (e.g., $(\mathrm{x}^s, \mathrm{y}^s)$ is an SR source case) and that S is also a substring of $\mathrm{x}^{\mathtt{tgt}}$ (that is $\mathcal{R}(\mathrm{x}^s, \mathrm{y}^s, \mathrm{x}^{\mathtt{tgt}}, y)$ is solvable). Now, let i^s be the position of the substring S in x^s such that the replacement S with T in x^s is made at position i^s and let $i^{\mathtt{tgt}}$ be a position of the substring S in $\mathrm{x}^{\mathtt{tgt}}$ (S may occur as a substring in several positions in $\mathrm{x}^{\mathtt{tgt}}$, so there are potentially several $i^{\mathtt{tgt}}$'s). Case ranking is based on a value $\mathtt{score}(S, \mathrm{x}^s, i^s, \mathrm{x}^{\mathtt{tgt}}, i^{\mathtt{tgt}}) \geq 0$, the higher this value is, the more preferred is the source case $(\mathrm{x}^s, \mathrm{y}^s)$ for adapting $\mathrm{x}^{\mathtt{tgt}}$ by substituting S with T at position i. The definition of this score is based on a general assumption using the notion of *context*.

In the following, this notion is explained, the assumption is presented, the way the score is computed based on this assumption and in the knowledge-light framework is presented and, finally, some future studies are discussed on how it can be defined using linguistic knowledge about French. But first, an example is introduced to illustrate these notions:

$$\begin{array}{ll} \mathrm{x}^s = \textit{You do not liked to eat beans.} & \mathrm{y}^s = \textit{You do not like to eat beans.} \\ \mathrm{x}^{\mathtt{tgt}} = \textit{We do wanted to go!} & \\ \text{thus } S = d, \quad T = \epsilon, \quad i^s = 15 & \text{and} \quad i^{\mathtt{tgt}} \in \{3, 11\} \end{array}$$

(a position i in a string x being represented by a value $i \in \{0, 1, \ldots, |\mathrm{x}| - 1\}$).

For a sentence $\mathbf{x}$ having a substring S at position i, the *context* of (S, i) in $\mathbf{x}$ gathers pieces of information (characters, words, etc.) "around" S ("the" S at position i). With this vague definition, the whole sentence $\mathbf{x}$ participates to the context of (S, i), but the idea is that pieces of information "close" to S have a greater importance in the context. Following this idea, $\texttt{score}(S, \mathbf{x}^s, i^s, \mathbf{x}^{\texttt{tgt}}, i^{\texttt{tgt}})$ measures the matching between the context of (S, i^s) in $\mathbf{x}^s$ and the context of $(S, i^{\texttt{tgt}})$ in $\mathbf{x}^{\texttt{tgt}}$, hence the following general assumption (the underlined terms are the ones that have to be instantiated in an implementation):

> The closer a linguistic entity of $\mathbf{x}^{\texttt{tgt}}$ is to the substring S at position i, the more its similarity to a matching linguistic entity of $\mathbf{x}^s$ contributes to $\texttt{score}(S, \mathbf{x}^s, i^s, \mathbf{x}^{\texttt{tgt}}, i^{\texttt{tgt}})$.

This assumption is applied as follows for our current knowledge-light approach to retrieval:

- The linguistic entities that are considered are words.
- The closeness between such entities is defined by the number of words that separate the word in which S occurs (0 for this word, 1 for its neighbors in the sentence, 2 for the neighbors of the neighbors, etc.). For example, for $\mathbf{x}^{\texttt{tgt}}$, the closest word is *wanted*, the second closest words are *do* and *to*, etc.
- The similarity between two linguistic entities is binary: if the two words are equal, their similarity measure is 1, otherwise, it is 0.

Only a short description of the score computing is given here. It is computed on the basis on a best match between the sentences $\mathbf{x}^s$ and $\mathbf{x}^{\texttt{tgt}}$. Assuming this best match is, for the example (with $i^{\texttt{tgt}} = 11$):

You *do* *not* *liked* *to* *eat* *beans* .

2ℓ 1ℓ 0 $1r$ $2r$ $3r$

We *do* *wanted* *to* *go* *!*

Then, $\texttt{score}(S, \mathbf{x}^s, i^s, \mathbf{x}^{\texttt{tgt}}, i^{\texttt{tgt}})$ is (with the matching lines indicated below):

$$\underbrace{0 \times \alpha^0}_{0} + \underbrace{1 \times \alpha^1 \times \beta}_{1\ell} + \underbrace{1 \times \alpha^1}_{1r} + \underbrace{0 \times \alpha^2 \times \beta}_{2\ell} + \underbrace{0 \times \alpha^2}_{2r} + \underbrace{0 \times \alpha^3 \times \beta}_{3r}$$

where α is a penalty for the distance to the word containing S and β is a mismatch penalty, when there is a need of words insertions, which corresponds to slanted lines in the matching (in the experiments, $\alpha = \beta = 0.5$). The score is computed for every position $i^{\texttt{tgt}}$ of S in $\mathbf{x}^{\texttt{tgt}}$ and its complexity in the worst case is in $\mathcal{O}(\#w(\mathbf{x}^s) \times \#w(\mathbf{x}^{\texttt{tgt}}))$ where $\#w(\mathbf{x}^s)(\mathbf{x})$ is the number of words in $\mathbf{x}$.

In future studies, the computing of the score may take into account linguistic knowledge:

- Various linguistic entities could be considered, such as word parts, words or groups of words.

- The closeness between such entities could be more accurately defined than the mere proximity in the string. Indeed, syntactical dependency shows that words that are distant in a sentence may have strong connections.
- The similarity between two linguistic entities could be gradual. The cosine similarity between word representations obtained from any pre-trained word embedding model will do it.

A Simple Modification of the Retrieval Procedure has been developed after some preliminary tests. It consists simply in extending the substring S to its two neighbor characters. For example, if $\mathtt{x}^s$ = *I does it.* and $\mathtt{y}^s$ = *I do it.*, then $S = oes\llcorner$ and $T = o\llcorner$ (for the filter and ranking phases). This modification has improved the result of the knowledge-light retrieval procedure presented above and has also highly increased the speed of retrieval, especially for cases for which the replay consists only in adding a substring (i.e., in the previous version, $S = \epsilon$).

7 Evaluation

TFC uses a knowledge-light approach, i.e. working only on strings and without language knowledge. This simple approach can be seen as a baseline for further more sophisticated knowledge-based systems. So, the goal of the evaluation is to establish the baseline.

The experiment consists in solving random problems using a case base. For that, we use an initial CB containing 300 cases to build the set of problems, called the test base and denoted by TB and smallest case bases, denoted by $\mathtt{CB}_n$, where n is the size of the case base. The number of problems to be solved has been fixed to 100 and the problems composing TB have been chosen randomly from CB. Four sizes of case base have been used, with $n \in \{50, 100, 150, 200\}$, to study the impact of the case base in the CBR system. The case bases $\mathtt{CB}_n$ are generated randomly from $\mathtt{CB} \setminus \mathtt{TB}$, with $\mathtt{CB}_{50} \subset \mathtt{CB}_{100} \subset \mathtt{CB}_{150} \subset \mathtt{CB}_{200}$.

TFC is evaluated according to three measures: the answer rate, the answer precision and the correct answer rate. Let ntp be the number of target problems posed to the system, na be the number of (correct or incorrect) answers and nca be the number of correct answers. Answer rate is defined as the average of the ratios na/ntp, the precision is defined as the average of the ratios nca/na, and the correct answer rate is defined as the average of the ratios nca/ntp. The averages of the three measures are computed on 100 runs, one run consisting in solving all the problems of TB using all $\mathtt{CB}_n$.

Table 1 presents the three measures for the different sizes of CB. The results show that, even if all measures increase wrt |CB|, the precision and the correct answer rate remain weak, e.g. a precision of 18.1% means that when the system returns an answer, this answer if false in more than four times out of five, which is not a surprising result. Another expected result is that the answer rate increases with the case base size. With a small case base, the system is only able to solve a few problems (59.2% of them for $\mathtt{CB}_{50}$). The reason is that no similar case can

Table 1. Answer rate, answer precision and correct answer rate for the different sizes of CB.

|CB|	50	100	150	200
Answer rate	59.2%	80.4%	89.7%	93.8%
Precision	15.9%	16.2%	17.2%	18.1%
Correct answer rate	9.4%	13.0%	15.4%	17.0%

be found because none of the case of $\mathtt{CB}_n$ addresses the error of $\mathtt{x}^{\mathtt{tgt}}$. By adding more source cases in $\mathtt{CB}_n$, the probability to have, in $\mathtt{CB}_n$, an error *similar* to the one of $\mathtt{x}^{\mathtt{tgt}}$ increases and the system is able to provide more answers.

However, studying the error causes shows that wrong substitutions are applied, coming from a source case (the most similar to $\mathtt{x}^{\mathtt{tgt}}$ from a string point of view) which is not a *good* case for solving $\mathtt{x}^{\mathtt{tgt}}$, i.e. the way the $\mathtt{x}^s$ is corrected into $\mathtt{y}^s$ is not suitable to solve $\mathtt{x}^{\mathtt{tgt}}$. So, the crucial issue is the retrieval process in order to retrieve a source case whose correction is suitable to the context of the target case.

8 Discussion

For many CBR systems, the retrieval phase design precedes the adaptation phase design. Then, this latter has to deal with the retrieved case to solve the target problem. This makes sense in many applications, for which the principle "similar problems have similar solutions" holds, where similarity between problems is defined by some similarity measure (or distance function) suited to the problem representation language and similarity between solutions reflects the easiness of adaptation. This is true in particular when adaptation by copy gives good results, or when adaptation consists in minor adjustments from $\mathtt{y}^s$ to $\mathtt{y}^{\mathtt{tgt}}$.

By contrast, for this first version of TFC, the reverse took place: the adaptation phase was designed before the retrieval phase. Indeed, an adaptation approach at the character level can be easily specified based on the idea of string replacement (which amounts to solve an equation $\mathcal{R}(\mathtt{x}^s, \mathtt{y}^s, \mathtt{x}^{\mathtt{tgt}}, x)$) and then improved thanks to the analogy on strings defined in [4] (which applies when several string replacements at non connected places of the target problem string are needed). Therefore, for TFC, the main issue is how retrieval has to deal with a given adaptation procedure. This can be considered at the light of two previous lines of studies in CBR.

The principle of adaptation-guided retrieval (AGR) already mentioned above is useful here. Indeed, AGR stands that a retrieved case has to be adaptable to solve $\mathtt{x}^{\mathtt{tgt}}$, which corresponds to the filter phase of the retrieval procedure presented in Sect. 6.

In early research on case-based planning (called *planning by analogy* at that time), the distinction between transformational and generative adaptations has been introduced [2] (actually, they were called "transformational and derivational analogies", but have been renamed in the wider scope of CBR [12]). Transformational adaptation aims at modifying $\mathtt{y}^s$ in $\mathtt{y}^{\mathtt{tgt}}$ on the basis of the differences between $\mathtt{x}^s$ and $\mathtt{x}^{\mathtt{tgt}}$. Generative adaptation consists in analyzing the transformation $\tau : \mathtt{x}^s \mapsto \mathtt{y}^s$ and then in *replaying* τ on $\mathtt{x}^{\mathtt{tgt}}$ (which may involve some modifications if τ is not applicable as such). TFC adaptation is a generative adaptation: τ is given by the string pair (S, T) such that $\mathtt{y}^s$ is obtained by substituting S with T in $\mathtt{x}^s$ and replay consists in making the same substitution on $\mathtt{x}^{\mathtt{tgt}}$.

This S can be linked to the notion of *footprint* of an initial state in a case-based planner such as Prodigy/analogy [11], i.e., the part of the initial state of the planning problem $\mathtt{x}^s$ that "plays" a role in the plan. Therefore, if S denotes also the footprint associated to a case $(\mathtt{x}^s, \mathtt{y}^s)$ in Prodigy/analogy then the condition "The target problem contains S" is, for both systems, a necessary and sufficient condition for the case $(\mathtt{x}^s, \mathtt{y}^s)$ be replayable as such on $\mathtt{x}^{\mathtt{tgt}}$ to get a solution $\mathtt{y}^{\mathtt{tgt}}$ (hence the filter phase of TFC's retrieval). A difference between these systems is that Prodigy/analogy has a complete knowledge for determining whether a solution $\mathtt{y}$ solves a problem $\mathtt{x}$ whereas TFC has not. Thus, in Prodigy/analogy, the above condition entails that $\mathtt{y}^{\mathtt{tgt}}$ is a correct plan whereas in TFC this condition is only a necessary condition for such a correctness, not a sufficient one. This justifies the use of the notion of the context of S in the source and target problems, with the idea that the more the contexts are similar, the more likely the replay gives a correct solution to $\mathtt{x}^{\mathtt{tgt}}$.

The idea of footprints has also been adapted for the system Resyn/CBR which aims at proposing synthesis plans in organic chemistry [6] and uses a hierarchical organization of state substructures (graphs in this application) to speed-up the process: such a hierarchical organization could also be used for TFC for the same purpose, but has not been implemented yet.

9 Conclusion

This paper has presented a challenge for the CBR community: how can correction of sentences be treated by CBR?

A first version of the *The French Correction* has been implemented in order to address this challenge for French sentences. A particularity of this application is that a first version of the adaptation process has appeared to be much simpler to design than the one of retrieval and also that designing adaptation before retrieval has appeared to be the right thing to do. Indeed, the design of retrieval without the knowledge of how the adaptation works has appeared to be a dead-end, hence the necessity of an adaptation-guided approach to retrieval.

Now, the knowledge-light approach to retrieval with a rather small case base that has been implemented gives weak results, which was not unexpected and provides a baseline for future versions. Therefore, two main directions of work for next versions of TFC can be envisaged. The first one consists in obtaining a large case base: this constitutes an ongoing work with the exploitation of the WiCoPaCo collection (cf. Sect. 4). The second one aims at designing more sophisticated inference engines. For this purpose, it is expected that the use of linguistic knowledge about French will improve the results with respect to the baseline defined in this first version (see Sect. 6.2). For this research directions, the question raised is what additional cases and additional pieces of linguistic knowledge will have a higher impact on the increase of TFC competence. For this purpose, the research presented in [10], that addresses a different type of case-based sentence modification and uses POS-tagging should be inspiring.

The first application of the analogy on strings defined in [4] is case-based machine translation: a case is a pair $(\mathtt{x}^s, \mathtt{y}^s)$, where $\mathtt{x}^s$ is a sentence in a natural language and $\mathtt{y}^s$ is a translation of $\mathtt{x}^s$ in another natural language. The approach proposed in [4] and studied in [5] at the light of the CBR methodology consists first in finding 3 source cases $(\mathtt{x}^a, \mathtt{y}^a)$, $(\mathtt{x}^b, \mathtt{y}^b)$ and $(\mathtt{x}^c, \mathtt{y}^c)$ such that $\mathtt{x}^a{:}\mathtt{x}^b::\mathtt{x}^c{:}\mathtt{x}^{\mathtt{tgt}}$ holds and then in solving the analogical equation $\mathtt{y}^a{:}\mathtt{y}^b::\mathtt{y}^c{:}y$: a solution y of this equation is a candidate solution $\mathtt{y}^{\mathtt{tgt}}$ of $\mathtt{x}^{\mathtt{tgt}}$. Now, this idea could be reused for TFC: this would mean that the problems would be sentences in an "incorrect French" language and the solutions would be sentences in a "correct French" language.

References

1. Aamodt, A., Plaza, E.: Case-based reasoning: foundational issues, methodological variations, and system approaches. AI Commun. **7**(1), 39–59 (1994)
2. Carbonell, J.G.: Derivational analogy: a theory of reconstructive problem solving and expertise acquisition. In: Learning, Machine (ed.) vol. 2, pp. 371–392. Inc, Morgan Kaufmann (1986)
3. Dutrey, C., Bouamor, H., Bernhard, D., Max, A.: Local modifications and paraphrases in Wikipedia's revision history. Procesamiento del Lenguaje Natural **46**, 51–58 (2010)
4. Lepage, Y., Denoual, É.: Purest ever example-based machine translation: detailed presentation and assessment. Mach. Transl. **19**, 251–282 (2005)
5. Lepage, Y., Lieber, J.: Case-based translation: first steps from a knowledge-light approach based on analogy to a knowledge-intensive one. In: Cox, M.T., Funk, P., Begum, S. (eds.) ICCBR 2018. LNCS (LNAI), vol. 11156, pp. 563–579. Springer, Cham (2018). https://doi.org/10.1007/978-3-030-01081-2_37
6. Lieber, J., Napoli, A.: Using classification in case-based planning. In Wahlster, W., (ed.) Proceedings of the 12th European Conference on Artificial Intelligence (ECAI 1996), 132–136. Budapest, Hungary, Wiley (1996)
7. Richter, M.M., Weber, R.O.: Case-based reasoning, a textbook. Springer, Heidelberg (2013). https://doi.org/10.1007/978-3-642-40167-1
8. Riesbeck, C.K., Schank, R.C.: Inside Case-Based Reasoning. Lawrence Erlbaum Associates Inc, Hillsdale (1989)
9. Smyth, B., Keane, M.T.: Using adaptation knowledge to retrieve and adapt design cases. Knowl.-Based Syst. **9**(2), 127–135 (1996)
10. Valls, J., Ontañón, S.: Natural language generation through case-based text modification. In: Agudo, B.D., Watson, I. (eds.) ICCBR 2012. LNCS (LNAI), vol. 7466, pp. 443–457. Springer, Heidelberg (2012). https://doi.org/10.1007/978-3-642-32986-9_33

11. Veloso, M.M. (ed.): Planning and Learning by Analogical Reasoning. LNCS, vol. 886. Springer, Heidelberg (1994). https://doi.org/10.1007/3-540-58811-6
12. Wilke, W., Bergmann, R.: Techniques and knowledge used for adaptation during case-based problem solving. In: Proceedings of the 11th International Conference on Industrial, Engineering and Other Applications of Applied Intelligent Systems. (1998)

Learning to Improve Efficiency for Adaptation Paths

David Leake(✉) and Xiaomeng Ye

Luddy School of Informatics, Computing, and Engineering, Indiana University, Bloomington, IN 47408, USA
{leake,xiaye}@iu.edu

Abstract. The ability of case-based reasoning systems to deal with new problems depends on the effectiveness of their case adaptation. One approach to increasing flexibility for novel problems is to perform adaptations by using adaptation paths—chains of adaptations—to address differences beyond those addressable by applying single adaptation rules. A recent approach to adaptation path generation, ROAD, proposes building adaptation paths using heuristic search guided by similarity, with a "reset" mechanism for recovering when similarity fails to predict adaptability. The ROAD approach is beneficial when similarity and adaptability are well aligned, but can make poor choices when similarity and adaptability diverge, increasing adaptation cost. This paper presents methods for increasing adaptation efficiency by maintenance exploiting information from adaptation path generation. The methods improve the similarity measure to better reflect adaptability and condense the adaptation rule set. Experimental evaluation supports the benefits for improving adaptation efficiency while preserving accuracy.

Keywords: Adaptation paths · Adaptation rule maintenance · Case adaptation · Case-based reasoning · Machine learning · Similarity maintenance

1 Introduction

Case-based Reasoning (CBR) solves new problems by adapting previous solutions to fit new circumstances (e.g., [16]). The case adaptation process is critical to the flexibility of CBR systems, enabling stored cases to cover a range of new problems. Case adaptation is often rule-guided, based on a set of adaptation rules designed to cover each possible class of difference between old and new problems in a single step (e.g., [6]). However, relying on one-step adaptations may require a large set of adaptation rules, and it may be hard to anticipate which rules will be needed. The knowledge acquisition problem for case adaptation is a classic problem for CBR (e.g., [7]). Covering problems with one-step adaptation may be especially problematic for sparse case bases and domains with highly novel problems. This has motivated research on path-based case adaptation using sequences of adaptation rules [2,4,14].

I. Watson and R. Weber (Eds.): ICCBR 2020, LNAI 12311, pp. 325–340, 2020.
https://doi.org/10.1007/978-3-030-58342-2_21

Making path-based adaptation effective depends on addressing two issues. The first is selecting the sequence of adaptation rules to apply, given that adaptation rules have varying reliability and that longer paths may be prone to quality degradation [13]. The second is controlling the computational cost of searching through sequences of adaptation rules. The RObust ADaptation (ROAD) [14] approach proposes addressing these problems by using heuristics to guide a greedy search process exploring alternative adaptation paths. As adaptation rules are applied, ROAD generates intermediate *ghost cases* [12], and extends the path from ghost cases closest to the target, based on similarity distance. This process aims to control adaptation path generation cost by finding short paths rapidly. To reduce the risk of solution quality degradation, ROAD uses a reset mechanism that is triggered when the expected reliability of a path falls below a threshold or when two paths are found to be developing divergent solutions. Previous experiments showed that ROAD can increase accuracy compared to relying on single-step adaptations. This paper presents methods aimed at increasing efficiency of the ROAD process.

The efficiency of similarity-based search with resetting depends on the similarity measure being a good proxy for adaptability. However, the correspondence between similarity and adaptability is not guaranteed [19]. When similarity distances diverge from true adaptation distances, a similarity-based adaptation path may proceed through ghost cases that are not easily adaptable, resulting in longer paths. This paper presents two maintenance methods that use information from the ROAD adaptation process to improve future performance. The first refines the system's similarity measure, bringing it closer to reflecting true adaptability. We call this *Reset-Induced Similarity Adjustment* (RISA). RISA uses knowledge of the final path to determine which prior cases should have been retrieved to minimize adaptation cost, and adjusts similarity criteria accordingly to improve future retrievals. This can be seen as ongoing CBR system maintenance [21] of similarity criteria, based on failures revealed by resetting. The RISA approach can be applied to any similarity measure that supports adjusting distances between pairs of cases (e.g., based on a ranking loss function).

The second maintenance method compacts the set of adaptation rules. Especially with the use of large-scale automatic rule generation methods, large sets of adaptation rules may be generated, making rule filtering potentially important to CBR system performance [9]. Also, in path-based adaptation using heuristic search, decreasing the number of rules to consider decreases the branching factor—and consequently, the computational cost—of the search. To compact the adaptation rule set, we propose *Compatibility-Based Adaptation Rule Selection* (CARS), which prioritizes adaptation rules for retention based on analysis of pairwise compatibility of adaptation rules in adaptation paths.

Experimental results in this study support that RISA, in conjunction with a local weighting scheme, can improve the similarity measure to produce shorter adaptation paths requiring fewer resets. They also show that trimming the adaptation rule set with CARS can decrease resets and result in shorter adaptation paths while maintaining comparable error rates.

The paper begins by reviewing the ROAD adaptation approach. It then presents the RISA algorithm and evaluation, followed by CARS and its evaluation. It closes by summarizing related work and discussing future directions.

2 The ROAD Adaptation Approach

Using adaptation paths is a promising way to increase adaptation flexibility, but depends on effective methods to guide path generation. ROAD [14] generates paths by similarity-guided greedy search and improves accuracy with a retrieval-based method for resetting the starting points of problematic paths.

2.1 Generating Adaptation Paths By Similarity-Guided Search

ROAD solves problems by retrieving the case most similar to the current problem and applying an adaptation path. It builds the path by greedy search, guided by similarity distance to the target, with the goal of generating short paths. When an adaptation rule is applied to a case, ROAD adapts both its solution and problem description to generate a hypothetical case, called a "ghost case" [12]. The next adaptation rule is selected in the context of that ghost case. After applications of adaptation rules to a case, the resulting ghost cases are compared to the target case, and the adaptation rule leading to the ghost case most similar to the target is used as the next adaptation step in the path. ROAD can pursue multiple paths simultaneously. Paths are prioritized based on their length where the shortest path (unless terminated) is developed first.

An adaptation path is a list containing the retrieved case, a sequence of ghost cases generated by adaptation, the adaptation rules applied, and the target case. The ROAD algorithm is described in detail in Leake and Ye [14].

To illustrate a use of path-based adaptation, we consider the problem of generating a recipe for making buttermilk pancakes from available ingredients, starting from a recipe for regular pancakes, when the agent has no buttermilk available. A first adaptation would be to substitute buttermilk for regular milk in the recipe, thus generating the ghost case of a recipe for buttermilk pancakes. That ghost case is more similar to the target, but still differs, because it does not satisfy the constraint to use available ingredients. However, it is possible to make buttermilk by mixing milk and vinegar. Consequently, a second adaptation could be applied to the ghost case, substituting milk and vinegar for the buttermilk. This two-step adaptation path would result in a recipe matching the target.

2.2 Improving Accuracy By Path Resetting

For a similarity measure that perfectly captures adaptation distance—*i.e*, that enables perfect adaptation-guided retrieval [19]—the initially retrieved source case would always have the smallest adaptation distance to the target of all cases in the case base. However, if the similarity measure does not perfectly capture adaptability, another case might be easier to adapt than the retrieved case. As the adaptation path generation process generates new ghost cases, the ghost cases may be near existing cases in the case base which are closer to the target than the retrieved case in terms of adaptation distance. To recover, ROAD "resets" the path to start from the nearby case by moving the head of the path to its nearby case. The rationale for such resets is to increase accuracy, by starting from a solution known to be correct, rather than relying on the solution of a ghost case generated from a sequence of adaptations. The accuracy benefit has been supported experimentally [14].

The resetting process is illustrated in Fig. 1. C_0 and C_1 are two cases in the case base. Given a query Q, for which the solution case would be T, the source case C_0 is retrieved. C_0 is closer to T than C_1 according to the similarity measure (indicated by the dashed arc indicating a radius of equal similarity values). As adaptation rules are applied successively, ghost cases G_1 and G_2 are generated. The ghost case G_2 is found to be more similar to C_1 than C_0. In this situation, ROAD resets the path to C_1. This is expected to increase reliability, because C_1's reliability is guaranteed (as it is a real case), while G_2 is a ghost case produced after adapting C_0 twice. At this point, the path continues from C_1 and yields the ghost case G_3, which is then adapted to T.

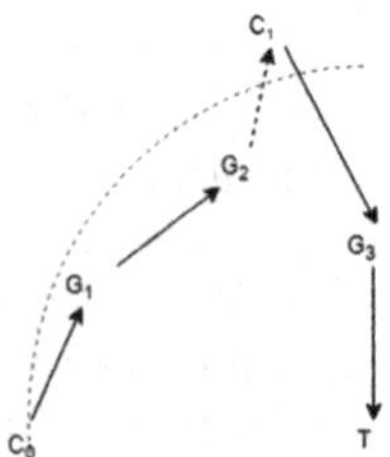

Fig. 1. Illustration of path resetting, from Leake and Ye [14]

3 Reset-Induced Similarity Adjustment

The quality of a CBR system's retrieval plays a critical role in system performance. Retrieval is generally based on similarity, which is used as a proxy for adaptability: the goal of retrieval is to retrieve the most adaptable cases [19]. With a perfect similarity measure, ROAD would never need to reset a path. Consequently, when resets are needed, it reveals deficiencies in the similarity measure. These are opportunities for similarity learning.

RISA uses generated adaptation paths to guide similarity learning. The goal of learning is to adjust the similarity measure so that the case to which the path was reset will become the initial retrieval in the future, enabling adaptation to be performed with fewer steps and decreasing the processing cost of future adaptations. The example in Fig. 1 illustrates the potential benefit of ROAD for adaptation path length. In the figure, ROAD would generate the same solution regardless of whether it retrieves C_1 or C_0 in its initial retrieval. However, if the system started by retrieving C_1, it would avoid the effort of building the path from C_0 to C_1.

3.1 The Reset-Induced Similarity Adjustment Algorithm

The RISA algorithm is shown in Algorithm 1. RISA takes as input (1) information recorded about resets during adaptation, and (2) a procedure to adjust feature weightings for similarity based on the stored information.

Information Recorded About Resets: To support RISA, the ROAD implementation was augmented with instrumentation to record its reset behaviors. Each time the system resets a path, it also stores a path segment record of the form $(C_{start}, C_{reset}, T)$ where C_{start} is the case most recently retrieved prior to the reset, C_{reset} is the case retrieved by adapting and resetting from C_{start}, and T is the target case. For the first reset record for a path, C_{start} is the case the CBR system retrieved for the original problem. In each subsequent path segment record that is generated during resetting, C_{start} is the case retrieved for the previous reset—from which the path is continuing—and C_{reset} is the case to which it is reset.

There are two situations in which a path segment record may not include a reset: When the path from the initially retrieved case can be pursued to the target without resetting, and when the path from a reset case can be pursued to the target without further resetting. In those cases the record uses *null* for C_{reset}. The presence of C_{reset} indicates a potential defect in the similarity measure. One strategy for addressing similarity defects, pursued in this paper and elsewhere [3], is to adjust feature weights. Other issues such as insufficient vocabulary knowledge and noisy cases might also lead to resets, but are beyond the scope of this paper.

Adjusting Feature Weights: For a record $(C_{start}, C_{reset}, T)$ produced by a path reset, RISA adjusts similarity criteria to increase the similarity of C_{reset} and T (pulling them closer), and to decrease the similarity of C_{start} and T (pushing them away from each other). As a result, the case retrieval process is more likely to retrieve C_{reset} directly for future problems similar to T.

A potential issue is that this adjustment may have ramifications for other retrievals, possibly affecting situations in which prior retrievals were correct. Consequently, for a $(C_{start}, null, T)$ record produced by a path not involving reset, RISA pulls C_{start} and T closer, to help preserve the current correct retrieval. The goal is to preserve the ability to generate high quality adaptation paths for similar starting and ending points in the updated similarity measure.

In general, there are many ways in which the push/pull effect could be achieved. For example, a feature weight updating policy can adjust the similarity distance between two cases. In our testbed RISA system for evaluation, we follow the approach of Bonzana, Cunningham and Smyth's ISAC [3]. To pull two

Algorithm 1. Reset-Induced Similarity Adjustment

Input:
Paths: records of paths $(C_{start}, C_{reset}, T)$. If the path is never reset $C_{reset} = null$
SM: similarity measure
Pull(SM,A,B): Updating procedure for SM that pulls A and B closer
Push(SM,A,B): Updating procedure for SM that pushes A and B away
Output:
SM: the modified similarity measure

```
for all (C_start, C_reset, T) in Paths do
    if C_reset = null then
        Pull(SM, C_start, T)
    else
        Push(SM, C_start, T)
        Pull(SM, C_reset, T)
return SM
```

cases closer, ISAC increases weightings of their matching features and decreases weightings of differing features. Similarity scores between the two cases are thus increased. Similarly, to push two cases away from each other, ISAC decreases weightings of matching features and increases weightings of unmatching features. ISAC adjusts feature weightings using the update formula:

$$w_i(t+1) = w_i(t) \pm \delta * \frac{F_c}{K_c}, \tag{1}$$

where $w_i(t)$ is the i-th feature weighting at time step t. δ is a fixed value. F_c is the number of times the case has been "falsely retrieved"—retrieved when another case would have been more suitable—and K_c is the number of times the case has been successfully retrieved. In the following evaluation, we apply this update procedure in ROAD, with failed retrievals corresponding to retrievals prompting a reset, and successful retrievals those for which no reset was needed.

3.2 Evaluation of RISA

The evaluation of RISA tested the effect of its similarity adjustment on adaptation efficiency and solution accuracy. Adaptation efficiency was measured by the ability to generate shorter adaptation paths and to decrease the number of resets required during adaptation. Solution accuracy was measured by relative error for a numerical prediction task.

The criteria for adaptation efficiency directly measure the ability of the system to retrieve adaptable cases; we expected RISA to increase the system's ability to do so. We did not expect a strong effect on accuracy, but sought to observe whether the decreased path length brought accuracy benefits. The experiments tested RISA for two alternative similarity schemes: Global weighting and local weighting. Because RISA's feature weight adjustments could have unexpected side-effects on retrievals of distant cases when the adjusted weights are global, we expected better performance for local weightings.

Experimental Design

Task Domain: The evaluation task was automobile price prediction, using the Kaggle automobile dataset [10]. The first two features were removed because they relate to insurance risk. Cases with missing features were removed as well, leaving 193 cases, each with 13 numeric and 10 nominal features in addition to price. Because the need for adaptation paths and difficulty of adaptation are affected by case-base sparsity, the experiments simulated varying levels of sparsity by removing the closest N cases to the target case before each trial, for varying N. For additional discussion of that process, see Leake and Ye [14].

Similarity Measure: The similarity between two cases is a weighted sum of feature similarity, with each feature weighted by either global or local weighting. Similarity of nominal features is 1 if they are identical and 0 otherwise; similarity between numerical features is their absolute difference normalized into $[0,1]$. All feature weights were initialized to the same value.

Global vs. Local Similarity: We test the effect of RISA for two feature weighting methods: (1) Global weighting relies on a single set of feature weights applied for all similarity comparisons; (2) Instance-specific weighting allows each case to have its own set of feature weightings, used for comparisons to that case [1,3,5].

Adaptation Rules: Adaptation rules were generated automatically from the case base using the case difference heuristic (CDH) approach [7]. This approach compares pairs of cases and generates rules that apply when a retrieved case and target case have similar problem differences, and adjusts the solution of the retrieved case according to the solution difference in the case pair from which the rule was learned. The process used here follows the algorithm in Leake and Schack [12]. The rule set generated depends on following parameters:

1. **Rule Count:** The number of rules to generate.
2. **Rule Specificity:** Rule specificity is determined by the number of feature differences to record in the rules. For example, $rspec = 0.1$ if 10% of all feature differences between two cases are included in the rule. Smaller $rspec$ values result in rules that are more generally applicable but less accurate, because their antecedents take into account fewer features.
3. **Rule Generating Distance**: The distance between pairs of cases generating rules. For example, if $ruleGenDist = 0.1$, rules are generated from cases whose difference is less than 10% of the maximum possible difference. A small $ruleGenDist$ value leads to rules covering only small inter-case differences.

A set of 300 rules is generated from pairs of random cases ($ruleGenDist = 1.0$), using half of the feature differences ($rspec = 0.5$). These configuration parameters were chosen based on a simple preliminary experiment to identify rule characteristics for which path lengths were high and increased efficiency would be most useful. In every run of the preliminary experiments, the closest 150 stored cases were removed around the query case to increase the need for longer paths. The average length of full paths and the average length of the paths after their last resets are recorded. The difference between the two measures shows the potential saving in efficiency: If the last reset case were retrieved directly, the system would avoid building the path from the original source case to the last reset case. The preliminary experiment used four rule sets of 300 rules. As shown in Table 1, rule set #1 has the longest average length and the biggest proportional benefit, so was chosen as the testbed rule set.

Table 1. Rule set configurations and corresponding path lengths

#	Rule specificity	Rule Gen Dist	Avg Path Len	Avg Path Len after Last Reset
1	0.5	1.0	6.523	2.208
2	1.0	1.0	2.476	1.079
3	1.0	0.2	1.992	0.830
4	0.8	0.2	2.111	0.974

ROAD Configuration for Experiments: All experiments are based on adaptation path generation by the ROAD system, described in Leake and Ye [14]. The performance of ROAD depends on multiple parameters. The test version of ROAD had the following configurations: (1) Multiple adaptation paths are generated simultaneously (at most 5 paths); (2) Maximum path length is 10; (3) Paths are reset when reliability decays below a threshold or when two paths disagree on the solutions.

Experimental Results

Effect of RISA with Global Weighting: Using every case in the case base as a target, by 10-fold cross validation, Tables 2 and 4 show that the effect of RISA with global weighting consistently decreases average path length and the number of resets. As shown, most differences are significant ($p < 0.05$).

Table 3 shows the effect of RISA with global weights on the average relative error. After RISA, the effect on error is mixed. The rates tend to become worse, but the differences are not significant. We hypothesize that this is due to the coarse-grained nature of updating weights for global weighting. Updating global weighting influences the similarities between all cases, which can have adverse effects on similarities for cases other than those prompting the updates. Thus with global weighting, RISA decreases path lengths as desired, but with possible degradation of accuracy.

Table 2. Effect of RISA on path length under global weighting

	Number of cases removed	150	125	100	75	50	25
Before RISA	Average path length	6.975	6.687	6.204	6.101	6.064	5.431
	Sd of path length	1.670	1.682	1.666	1.683	1.688	1.663
After RISA	Average path length	**6.581**	6.572	**5.850**	**5.548**	**5.651**	5.195
	Sd of path length	1.671	1.687	1.620	1.643	1.648	1.666
P value		**.021**	.505	**.035**	**.001**	**.015**	.17

Table 3. Effect of RISA on error under global weighting

	Number of cases removed	150	125	100	75	50	25
Before RISA	Average error	0.481	0.461	0.388	0.410	0.282	0.275
	Sd of error	0.816	0.814	0.724	0.890	0.544	0.527
After RISA	Average error	0.465	0.452	0.406	0.419	0.319	0.345
	Sd of error	0.734	0.799	0.848	0.868	0.672	0.747
P value		.83	.92	.82	.92	.55	.29

Effect of RISA with Instance-Specific Weighting: To address the issue of side-effects for adaptation, we tested RISA for local weighting. With local weighting, updating the feature weighting for a case only influences the similarities between this case and other cases, but not the similarities among other cases.

Tables 6 and 7 show the effects of RISA on efficiency in the instance-specific weighting configuration. In all runs, the number of resets and average path length consistently drop. Most path length results are significant, while the change in error is statistically insignificant, as shown in Table 5.

4 Compatibility-Based Adaptation Rule Selection

Commonly, adaptation rules are assumed to be independent, and selected without regard for interactions with other rules. However, it is well known that rules may not capture all aspects of a situation, resulting in uncertain outcomes, potentially resulting in degradation of adaptation results [13]. An adaptation path might further compound the cumulative error by applying multiple rules. In response, we propose a method for using information about the interactions of adaptation rules to learn which adaptation rules to favor.

Table 4. Effect of RISA on resets under global weighting

	Number of cases removed	150	125	100	75	50	25
Before RISA	Total number of resets	221	261	224	225	248	160
After RISA	Total number of resets	177	248	202	182	196	145

Table 5. Effect of RISA on the error under Instance-Specific Weighting

	Number of cases removed	150	125	100	75	50	25
Before RISA	Average error	0.438	0.381	0.430	0.410	0.340	0.293
	Sd of error	0.691	0.617	0.835	0.832	0.683	0.529
After RISA	Average error	0.451	0.393	0.372	0.410	0.321	0.265
	Sd of error	0.709	0.631	0.673	0.828	0.700	0.501
P Value		.85	.85	.45	.99	.78	.60

Table 6. Effect of RISA on resets under Instance-Specific Weighting

	Number of cases removed	150	125	100	75	50	25
Before RISA	Total number of resets	296	261	254	232	233	181
After RISA	Total number of resets	261	238	237	201	219	160

Given a case base and an adaptation rule set, it is possible to estimate reliability of adaptation rules by building paths with resetting disabled, and then comparing the final solution from the path with the actual solution of the nearest neighbor. The path's error can then be used to represent the reliability of the rules involved. This is the approach of CARS.

4.1 Compatibility-Based Adaptation Rule Selection Algorithm

Algorithm 2 shows the process that CARS uses to assess rule compatibility. It computes a rule compatibility matrix representing the compatibility between every pair of rules, calculated from a set of adaptation paths of length 2, generated based on test adaptations of a selected set of cases. This set of cases could be the entire case base or a subset (for efficiency).

Given *rcount* rules, the compatibility matrix has dimension $rcount \times rcount$. The entry (i, j) in the matrix records that $rule_i$ and $rule_j$ are compatible if $rule_i$ and $rule_j$ can be applied in sequence to a case. If adaptation rules are commutative (e.g., if each rule is multiplying a numerical solution value by a feature difference in a single dimension), entry (i, j) is equal to entry (j, i) and

Table 7. Effect of RISA on path length under Instance-Specific Weighting

	Number of cases removed	150	125	100	75	50	25
Before RISA	Average path length	7.154	6.712	6.502	6.218	6.003	5.794
	Sd of path length	1.706	1.649	1.654	1.698	1.689	1.718
After RISA	Average path length	**6.652**	**6.278**	6.205	**5.737**	**5.672**	5.494
	Sd of path length	1.645	1.585	1.618	1.631	1.607	1.673
P value		**.004**	**.009**	.08	**.005**	**.05**	.08

Algorithm 2. Assessing Rule Compatibility

Input:
CaseSet: Cases for testing
rules: List of adaptation rules
Output: Rule compatibility matrix

```
R = size(rules), N = size(CB)
Initialize matrix M of size R × R
for i ← 1 to R do
    for j ← 1 to R do
        M[i][j] ← undefined
for i ← 1 to R do
    for j ← 1 to R do
        totalError = 0
        errorCount = 0
        for all case in CaseSet do
            if rule[i].isApplicableTo(case) then
                ghost1 = rule[i].applies(case)
                if rule[j].isApplicableTo(ghost1) then
                    ghost2 = rule[j].applies(ghost1)
                    target = CaseSet.nearest(ghost2)
                    totalError+ = errorInSolution(ghost2, target)
                    totalCount+ = 1
                else
                    continue
            else
                continue
        if totalError ≠ 0.0 then
            M[i][j] = totalError/totalCount
return M
```

the matrix is symmetric. However, in many domains rules depend on each other and must be applied in a particular order (e.g., recipe generation).

CARS estimates compatibility between two rules based on an estimated error value after the two rules are successively applied to a case in a 2-step adaptation path. Error is estimated by retrieving the stored case closest to the ghost case generated by the adaptation path, and comparing the stored case and ghost case solutions. After computing the compatibility matrix, CARS uses the average value of each row as a proxy for the overall reliability of the corresponding rule.

CARS compresses the adaptation rule set by retaining only the most reliable rules. To do so, it sorts all rules based on reliability and trims the rule set by retaining only those falling above a selected percentile of the original rule set.

4.2 Evaluation of CARS

The evaluation of CARS addresses two questions:

- How does CARS rule deletion affect efficiency of adaptation path generation?
- How does CARS rule deletion affect solution accuracy?

Efficiency is measured in three ways: number of resets prompted by path reliability decay, number of resets prompted by disagreement between alternative paths being explored, and average adaptation path length. Tests assess the effect of CARS both on ROAD and on a baseline ablated version of ROAD that performs single-rule adaptation instead of using adaptation paths.

Experimental Design
As in the previous experiment, tests used the Kaggle automobile data set [10]. In all runs, after building the compatibility matrix based on the entire case base, 75 cases around the target query are removed to simulate situations where multiple adaptations are needed but the adaptation paths have moderate average length. The experiment uses the previous rule set configuration ($Rcount = 300$, $RuleGenDist = 1.0$, $Rspec = 0.5$), again with 10-fold cross validation. In the experiments, CARS is applied to assess compatibility and retain the top 80%, 60%, 40%, and 20% of rules; these conditions are compared to a baseline of 100% retention. We note that because of the case removals to simulate a sparse case base, as well as the rule retention and path building mechanisms in ROAD, the case bases and rules used to solve the test problems are different from those used when building the rule compatibility matrix.

Experimental Results
Table 8 shows the experimental results. We observe:

- The number of resets consistently decreases when fewer rules are used. With fewer rules the path searching algorithm explores fewer options, decreasing the number of prior cases near the path. In addition, we hypothesize that because the retained rules are more reliable, paths tend to agree with each other more often, decreasing resets due to path disagreement.
- The average path lengths become smaller as fewer rules are retained, because of fewer resets.
- The error improves markedly as the worst 20% of the rules are deleted (80% retention). Observed error is better than the initial rule set for 60% and 40% retention, with the benefit dropping compared to 80% retention, but the differences below 80% are not statistically significant.

Thus the results support the efficiency benefits of rule set compression, as well as improved accuracy at low compression rates. Effects for higher compression rates are an interesting question for future study. We expect a tradeoff between higher average rule quality and lower coverage with the compressed rule sets, resulting in decreasing accuracy when the rule set is too sparse. However, refining the reliability estimate process might help to delay serious accuracy loss.

Table 8. Performance by Rule retention level

Percent of rules retained	100%	80%	60%	40%	20%
Using single-rule reliability (baseline)					
Resets due to reliability decay	227	152	99	37	14
Resets due to path disagreement	137	81	72	42	22
Average eror	0.372	0.268	0.323	0.324	0.427
SD of error	0.407	0.229	0.321	0.281	0.365
P value (Comparing to no trimming)	N/A	.002	0.19	0.18	0.16
Average path length	6.126	4.689	3.841	2.662	1.932
SD of path length	3.011	2.575	2.366	1.630	1.200
P value (comparing to no trimming)	N/A	<.001	<.001	<.001	<.001
Using reliability from compatibility matrix (CARS)					
Resets due to reliability decay	227	49	17	1	0
Resets due to path disagreement	137	83	41	10	1
Average error	0.372	0.303	0.305	0.356	0.420
SD of error	0.407	0.267	0.244	0.281	0.316
P value (comparing to no trimming)	N/A	.049	.05	.65	.19
Average path length	6.126	3.322	2.346	1.548	1.231
SD of path length	3.011	2.053	1.366	0.719	0.468
P value (comparing to no trimming)	N/A	<.001	<.001	<.001	<.001

In summary, using CARS increases the efficiency of both the baseline and ROAD by reducing the number of resets and reducing path lengths, with a stronger effect on ROAD. Also, deletion of an initial set of the worst rules benefits accuracy for both. Beyond that deletion level there is weak or no significant effect on the accuracy until accuracy falls for very high deletion levels.

5 Related Work

RISA is a learning method for refining similarity criteria; CARS is a method for prioritizing adaptation rules for retention.

Learning to Refine Similarity Criteria: An extensive body of CBR research has addressed similarity learning (see, for example, Wettschereck et al. [20], and, for a recent overview, Mathisen et al. [18]). RISA differs in aiming to refine existing similarity criteria on the fly, rather than generating a similarity measure from scratch. RISA's failure-driven method for learning to refine similarity criteria is most closely related to Bonzano, Cunningham and Smyth's ISAC [3], which adjusts similarity weights in response to failed and successful retrievals, and whose updating strategy is applied by RISA. This work is also in the spirit of work on building similarity measures by Xiong and Funk [22], which adjusts local similarity to reflect the utility of pairs of cases.

Learning to Prioritize Adaptation Rules: Hanney and Keane's initial proposal for generating adaptation rules by the case difference heuristic also proposed selective retention, based on the frequency with which particular rules were generated from cases [8]. Adaptation rule maintenance to remove duplicates and resolve conflicts was proposed by Li et al. [15]. Additional work focuses on how to prioritize rule selection, without deleting rules from the rule set [11], and on combining systematic accuracy testing with retention of top-ranked rules [9]. The current work differs in addressing adaptation paths, rather than only individual rules, and in focusing on minimizing adaptation path length.

6 Conclusion and Future Directions

This paper presents an initial investigation of applying information from adaptation paths to improving efficiency of path-based adaptation. It proposes two knowledge-light approaches, focusing on similarity measures and adaptation rules. By learning from path generation failures, as shown by path resets in ROAD, RISA helps align the similarity measure with adaptability. Experimental results support its value for retrieving more adaptable cases. By favoring pairs of rules that have participated in successful adaptation paths, CARS compresses the adaptation rule set while retaining useful rules. Experimental results support its value for increasing adaptation efficiency and that deletion of least reliable rules can improve accuracy, subject to an efficiency/coverage tradeoff.

A next step is to test the methods for additional domains and to gather information on the domains for which the methods are most appropriate. For similarity maintenance, we also plan to compare the alternative strategy of learning only from the final reset rather than all intermediate resets. Learning from the final reset would focus on a more definitive retrieval, but would also reduce the amount of data available to the learning algorithm. For adaptation rule set compression, an interesting question is whether the criteria for assessing rule usefulness could be refined, for example, by considering compatibility and result accuracy separately, to prioritize rule retention based on a composite criterion. Another interesting question is the possible benefit of retaining rules with limited compatibility but adding constraints to avoid their use in combination.

A future opportunity is to apply information from adaptation paths for maintaining the case-base. Mathew and Chakraborti [17] show the value of taking potential adaptation chains into account when guiding case retention. In ROAD, parts of the problem space for which ghost cases are generated suggest gaps in the case base. Based on the CBR premise that similar problems are likely to recur in the future, those gaps are good candidates for case acquisition to increase efficiency by shortening commonly-used adaptation paths.

References

1. Aha, D.W., Goldstone, R.L.: Concept learning and flexible weighting. In: Proceedings of the 14th Annual Conference of the Cognitive Science Society, pp. 534–539. Erlbaum (1992)
2. Badra, F., Cordier, A., Lieber, J.: Opportunistic adaptation knowledge discovery. In: McGinty, L., Wilson, D.C. (eds.) ICCBR 2009. LNCS (LNAI), vol. 5650, pp. 60–74. Springer, Heidelberg (2009). https://doi.org/10.1007/978-3-642-02998-1_6
3. Bonzano, A., Cunningham, P., Smyth, B.: Using introspective learning to improve retrieval in CBR: a case study in air traffic control. In: Leake, D.B., Plaza, E. (eds.) ICCBR 1997. LNCS, vol. 1266, pp. 291–302. Springer, Heidelberg (1997). https://doi.org/10.1007/3-540-63233-6_500
4. D'Aquin, M., Lieber, J., Napoli, A.: Adaptation knowledge acquisition: a case study for case-based decision support in oncology. Comput. Intell. **22**(3/4), 161–176 (2006)
5. Friedman, J.H.: Flexible metric nearest neighbor classification. Technical report, Stanford University (1994)
6. Hammond, K.: Case-Based Planning: Viewing Planning as a Memory Task. Academic Press, San Diego (1989)
7. Hanney, K., Keane, M.T.: Learning adaptation rules from a case-base. In: Smith, I., Faltings, B. (eds.) EWCBR 1996. LNCS, vol. 1168, pp. 179–192. Springer, Heidelberg (1996). https://doi.org/10.1007/BFb0020610
8. Hanney, K., Keane, M., Smyth, B., Cunningham, P.: What kind of adaptation do CBR systems need? A review of current practice. In: Proceedings of the Fall Symposium on Adaptation of Knowledge for Reuse. AAAI (1995)
9. Jalali, V., Leake, D.: On retention of adaptation rules. In: Lamontagne, L., Plaza, E. (eds.) ICCBR 2014. LNCS (LNAI), vol. 8765, pp. 200–214. Springer, Cham (2014). https://doi.org/10.1007/978-3-319-11209-1_15
10. Kaggle: Automobile Dataset. Kaggle (2017). https://www.kaggle.com/toramky/automobile-dataset
11. Leake, D., Dial, S.A.: Using case provenance to propagate feedback to cases and adaptations. In: Althoff, K.-D., Bergmann, R., Minor, M., Hanft, A. (eds.) ECCBR 2008. LNCS (LNAI), vol. 5239, pp. 255–268. Springer, Heidelberg (2008). https://doi.org/10.1007/978-3-540-85502-6_17
12. Leake, D., Schack, B.: Exploration vs. exploitation in case-base maintenance: leveraging competence-based deletion with ghost cases. In: Cox, M.T., Funk, P., Begum, S. (eds.) ICCBR 2018. LNCS (LNAI), vol. 11156, pp. 202–218. Springer, Cham (2018). https://doi.org/10.1007/978-3-030-01081-2_14
13. Leake, D., Whitehead, M.: Case provenance: the value of remembering case sources. In: Weber, R.O., Richter, M.M. (eds.) ICCBR 2007. LNCS (LNAI), vol. 4626, pp. 194–208. Springer, Heidelberg (2007). https://doi.org/10.1007/978-3-540-74141-1_14
14. Leake, D., Ye, X.: On combining case adaptation rules. In: Bach, K., Marling, C. (eds.) ICCBR 2019. LNCS (LNAI), vol. 11680, pp. 204–218. Springer, Cham (2019). https://doi.org/10.1007/978-3-030-29249-2_14
15. Li, H., Hu, D., Hao, T., Wenyin, L., Chen, X.: Adaptation rule learning for case-based reasoning. In: 3rd International Conference on Semantics, Knowledge and Grid, pp. 44–49 (2007)
16. López de Mántaras, R., et al.: Retrieval, reuse, revision, and retention in CBR. Knowl. Eng. Rev. **20**(3), 215–240 (2005)

17. Mathew, D., Chakraborti, S.: Competence guided model for casebase maintenance. In: Proceedings of the 26th International Joint Conference on Artificial Intelligence, IJCAI, pp. 4904–4908 (2017)
18. Mathisen, B.M., Aamodt, A., Bach, K., Langseth, H.: Learning similarity measures from data. Prog. Artif. Intell. **9**, 129–143 (2019). https://doi.org/10.1007/s13748-019-00201-2
19. Smyth, B., Keane, M.: Adaptation-guided retrieval: questioning the similarity assumption in reasoning. Artif. Intell. **102**(2), 249–293 (1998)
20. Wettschereck, D., Aha, D., Mohri, T.: A review and empirical evaluation of feature-weighting methods for a class of lazy learning algorithms. Artif. Intell. Rev. **11**(1–5), 273–314 (1997). https://doi.org/10.1023/A:1006593614256
21. Wilson, D., Leake, D.: Maintaining case-based reasoners: dimensions and directions. Comput. Intell. **17**(2), 196–213 (2001)
22. Xiong, N., Funk, P.: Building similarity metrics reflecting utility in case-based reasoning. J. Intell. Fuzzy Syst. **17**(4), 407–416 (2006)

Special Track Challenges and Promises

On Bringing Case-Based Reasoning Methodology to Deep Learning

David Leake(✉) and David Crandall

Luddy School of Informatics, Computing, and Engineering, Indiana University, Bloomington, IN 47408, USA
{leake,djcran}@indiana.edu

Abstract. The case-based reasoning community is successfully pursuing multiple approaches for applying deep learning methods to advance case-based reasoning. This "Challenges and Promises" paper argues for a complementary endeavor: pursuing ways that the case-based reasoning methodology can advance deep learning. Starting from challenges in deep learning and proposed neural-symbolic integrations based on specific technologies, it proposes studying how CBR ideas can inform choices of components for a new reasoning pipeline.

Keywords: Automated machine learning · Case-based reasoning methodology · Challenge problems · Deep learning · Integrations · Pipelines

1 Introduction

Recent years have seen great accomplishments in deep learning. These have led to enthusiasm in the case-based reasoning (CBR) [9] community for studying how to apply deep learning methods in service of case-based reasoning. For example, the Call for Papers for the *2019 Workshop on Case-based Reasoning and Deep Learning* states that the "successes of DL call for novel methods and techniques that exploit DL for the benefit of CBR systems."[1] Research presented at that workshop and other venues supports the promise of this approach for advancing case-based reasoning. This "Challenges and Promises" paper proposes that the CBR community consider the reverse perspective: How application of case-based reasoning can shape the design of deep learning systems and help to address challenges for deep learning and machine learning as a whole.

As background to the challenges, the paper begins by highlighting two views on questions to address to advance deep learning and AI as a whole, presented in invited talks by Yann LeCun and Henry Kautz at the AAAI 2020 Conference on Artificial Intelligence in New York, NY. These focus, respectively, on challenges for deep learning and architectures for integrating neural and symbolic methods.

[1] https://iccbr2019.com/workshops/case-based-reasoning-and-deep-learning/.

I. Watson and R. Weber (Eds.): ICCBR 2020, LNAI 12311, pp. 343–348, 2020.
https://doi.org/10.1007/978-3-030-58342-2_22

The proposed integrations of neural and symbolic methods view each as a different technology, with particular strengths for particular types of tasks. We propose that the CBR community develop integrations shaped by a different perspective, that of Ian Watson's treatment of CBR as a *methodology* [16]. In that view, case-based reasoning is seen as a general high-level process that defines a set of tasks, but for which the needed functionality can be implemented using various technologies, both neurally inspired and symbolic.

This perspective suggests an opportunity for the CBR methodology to shape the high-level design of component-based deep learning systems, with collections of subparts corresponding to components of the CBR process—retrieve, reuse, revise, and retain [1]—and encoding the CBR knowledge containers—vocabulary, case knowledge, similarity knowledge, and adaptation knowledge [12]. It also raises questions of how such components can be implemented and integrated. Especially interesting is the addition of forms of *case adaptation* in deep learning frameworks, to enable the transformation of solutions for novel contexts. CBR can also play an important role in automated machine learning (AutoML), by helping to exploit experiences with AutoML systems. The paper closes by discussing the potential impact of the proposed initiatives.

2 Addressing Deep Learning Challenges Through Integrations

Challenges for Deep Learning: Deep learning has achieved remarkable success in many task domains. In fact, at least under some conditions, deep learning can match or exceed human-level performance in face recognition [15], language translation [4], and game playing [14]. However, important challenges remain. LeCun pointed to three key challenges for deep learning:[2]

1. Learning with fewer labeled samples and/or fewer trials
2. Learning to reason
3. Learning to plan complex action sequences.

Each of these is well-trodden ground for case-based reasoning. This suggests opportunities for integrations with case-based reasoning.

Models for Integrating Deep Learning with Symbolic Approaches: In his AAAI 2020 Engelmore lecture, Henry Kautz pointed to specific strengths of deep learning, such as learning hierarchically and that deep learning representations "directly support similarity." On the other hand, various other processes, such as combinatorial search, are natural for symbolic methods. In response to the divergent strengths, he advocated bringing together neural and symbolic traditions and proposed six possible combinations, including using the different technologies for specialized subroutines and a NeuroSymbolic approach in which symbolic

[2] Quoted from https://drive.google.com/file/d/1r-mDL4IX_hzZLDBKp8_e8VZqD7fOzBkF/view.

rules are used to structure a neural system.[3] This paper proposes integrations at a more abstract level, in which the design of deep learning architectures is structured by the high-level CBR methodology.

3 Implementing CBR with Deep Network Components

In the early days of case-based reasoning, CBR was often presented as an alternative technology to rule-based systems, associated with particular representation and implementation methods. In an influential paper, Ian Watson made a key observation: CBR can be implemented in many different ways using a range of methods. For example, CBR retrieval can be done using database technology [5]. Thus CBR is not a technology, but instead a *methodology:* a set of principles for a process of problem solving, interpretation, and learning that can be implemented using various technologies [16]. He frames the principles in terms of the classic four "REs" of the Aamodt and Plaza CBR cycle [1]:

Retrieve similar cases, Reuse a similar case, Revise the solution to fit if necessary, and learn by Retaining. Each of these steps can be applied using multiple technologies.

Following this view, we can see CBR as a set of principles that could guide, for example, integrating multiple deep learning approaches to provide a CBR process for an end-to-end solution to a deep learning challenge problem. This shares aspects with multiple items in Kautz's categorization, but differs in that the defining aspect is not the specific technology, but rather the need for a particular functional sequence of processing steps.

The challenge for the CBR community is then to define the requisite tasks and integration. Various steps have been taken to bring deep learning components into CBR systems (e.g., [3,8,10,13]). This challenge calls for an end-to-end effort to achieve CBR capabilities with a collection of deep learning-based components. This would have multiple benefits:

- **Providing CBR benefits while minimizing knowledge burdens:** CBR is no longer an alternative approach that loses the benefits of the knowledge-light processing of deep networks. When CBR is a unifying principle for guiding the design of deep learning systems, it can be implemented with the same technology.
- **Providing a framework for flexible technology integrations:** Even applying end-to-end CBR, the CBR process can still be implemented with whatever technology is most appropriate; the use of deep learning for some components does not preclude different technologies for others.
- **Providing increased flexibility through adaptation:** The *reasoning* part of CBR follows from case adaptation, the ability to transform solutions to new contexts. Explicitly integrating adaptation into deep learning systems could provide a new means for transfer.

[3] https://www.cs.rochester.edu/u/kautz/talks/Kautz%20Engelmore%20Lecture.pdf.

- **Providing a new basis for learning from few examples:** Implementing a "true" case-based reasoning process able to reason and learn from single cases could help address the challenge of learning from limited data.
- **Providing a model for generating structured solutions:** Similarly, implementing a "true" case-based reasoning process able to manipulate structured cases could enable processing structured data such as action plans.
- **Reducing storage requirements:** Cases can capture knowledge compactly, in contrast to the potentially enormous requirements of networks.

If it is not possible to fully develop such a process within a deep learning architecture, hybrid solutions can still provide powerful processing capabilities.

4 Questions for a CBR-Based Pipeline

As discussed, the CBR methodology is agnostic to technology. However, applying that methodology in a neural network context requires addressing several key questions:

- **Case representation:** How can the rich structured cases of CBR be represented in a network context?
- **The role of cases:** What are the tradeoffs of explicit case retrieval rather than direct solution generation, and what are their respective roles? We consider this further below.
- **Case adaptation:** How and where should adaptation be applied? Can case adaptation be learned and applied within other processes of the CBR cycle, such as via adaptation at interior points of the network, rather than only to the retrieved solution? This might be seen as related to the question transformation of early CBR [6] and efforts at supporting analogical reasoning directly with embedded representations [11]. Neural networks have previously been applied to case adaptation [2], and recent efforts have applied deep learning to case adaptation using the case difference heuristic [8].
- **The meaning of the Retain step:** A fundamental principle of CBR is that results are retained as new cases. However, when learning is achieved by gradient-based training methods, the cost of learning by retraining after every case is prohibitive. Consequently, a core question is how to achieve lazy learning in a neural network context, or whether the case store must necessarily be implemented with another technology.

Developing a CBR-based pipeline raises the question of the role of explicit case representation and manipulation. Deep learning systems are eager learners; they receive (large quantities of) training data and learn weights that encode generalizations from that data. Case-based reasoners are lazy learners, retaining raw cases (or cases with limited processing) to re-use them. When using CBR to shape a deep learning pipeline, a natural question is the role of cases. There are three possibilities: To include an explicit case retrieval phase for "pre-packaged" cases; to "assemble" or generate cases by a reconstructive process without literal case storage (cf. [7]), or to dispense with explicit case retrieval/generation, solely adding an adaptation phase after solution generation, in the absence of cases. Adding adaptation to deep learning pipelines is an interesting—and potentially highly impactful—challenge for the CBR community. However, the full benefits of CBR, such as single-example lazy learning and explainability, require the use of cases.

5 CBR for AutoML

CBR can also be brought to deep learning—and other machine learning methods—in the context of automated machine learning (AutoML). AutoML focuses on methods to take as input a dataset, a challenge problem, and a library of primitives including machine learning algorithms, to automatically develop an end-to-end machine learning pipeline. It is being pursued by the DARPA Data-Driven Discovery of Models (D3M) program.[4] Most D3M teams focus on algorithm selection and hyperparameter optimization. However, some apply a "meta-learning" approach exploiting a database of prior solutions generated by the former "first principles" methods. This can be seen as a case base, and the CBR methodology, and specific lessons and methods for indexing, similarity, and adaptation, could play an important role in exploiting it. However, to our knowledge, this opportunity for synergy has not yet been pursued.

6 Conclusion: Future Paths

This challenge paper has proposed that beyond focusing on applying deep learning methods for CBR, the CBR community should focus on how the CBR methodology can help address the next generation of deep learning challenges. This may be especially beneficial for a CBR perspective on how to view problems and design architectures.

Bringing CBR to deep learning has the potential for great impact on future AI systems and to increase the reach of CBR. As a coarse-grained measure of the degree of attention to deep learning, a search of the Semantic Scholar archive of scholarly articles on May 6, 2020 yielded 11,500 results for "case-based reasoning" in the last five years, versus approximately 284,000 for "deep learning." Bringing case-based reasoning methodology to deep learning could also provide components for a new generation of knowledge-light CBR applications. Bringing CBR to AutoML provides an opportunity to harness strengths of CBR for effective use of multiple machine learning methods.

Acknowledgment. This material is based upon work supported in part by the Department of the Navy, Office of Naval Research under award number N00014-19-1-2655. We thank the reviewers and Swaroop Vattam for helpful comments.

[4] https://www.darpa.mil/program/data-driven-discovery-of-models.

References

1. Aamodt, A., Plaza, E.: Case-based reasoning: foundational issues, methodological variations, and system approaches. AI Commun. **7**(1), 39–52 (1994)
2. Corchado, J.M., Lees, B.: Adaptation of cases for case based forecasting with neural network support. In: Pal, S.K., Dillon, T.S., Yeung, D.S. (eds.) Soft Computing in Case Based Reasoning. Springer, London (2001). https://doi.org/10.1007/978-1-4471-0687-6_13
3. Grace, K., Maher, M.L., Wilson, D.C., Najjar, N.A.: Combining CBR and deep learning to generate surprising recipe designs. In: Goel, A., Díaz-Agudo, M.B., Roth-Berghofer, T. (eds.) ICCBR 2016. LNCS (LNAI), vol. 9969, pp. 154–169. Springer, Cham (2016). https://doi.org/10.1007/978-3-319-47096-2_11
4. Hassan, H., et al.: Achieving human parity on automatic Chinese to English news translation (2018)
5. Kitano, H., Shimazu, H.: The experience sharing architecture: a case study in corporate-wide case-based software quality control. In: Leake, D. (ed.) Case-Based Reasoning: Experiences, Lessons, and Future Directions, pp. 235–268. AAAI Press, Menlo Park (1996)
6. Kolodner, J.: Retrieval and Organizational Strategies in Conceptual Memory. Lawrence Erlbaum, Hillsdale (1984)
7. Leake, D.: Assembling latent cases from the web: a challenge problem for cognitive CBR. In: Proceedings of the ICCBR-11 Workshop on Human-Centered and Cognitive Approaches to CBR (2011)
8. Liao, C., Liu, A., Chao, Y.: A machine learning approach to case adaptation. In: 2018 IEEE 1st International Conference on Artificial Intelligence and Knowledge Engineering (AIKE), pp. 106–109 (2018)
9. de Mántaras, R.L., et al.: Retrieval, reuse, revision, and retention in CBR. Knowl. Eng. Rev. **20**(3), 215–240 (2005)
10. Mathisen, B.M., Aamodt, A., Bach, K., Langseth̃, H.: Learning similarity measures from data. Prog. Artif. Intell. **9**, 129-143 (2019)
11. Mikolov, T., Chen, K., Corrado, G., Dean, J.: Efficient estimation of word representations in vector space. CoRR abs/1301.3781 (2013). http://arxiv.org/abs/1301.3781
12. Lenz, M., Burkhard, H.-D., Bartsch-Spörl, B., Wess, S. (eds.): Case-Based Reasoning Technology. LNCS (LNAI), vol. 1400. Springer, Heidelberg (1998). https://doi.org/10.1007/3-540-69351-3
13. Sani, S., Wiratunga, N., Massie, S.: Learning deep features for kNN-based human activity recognition. In: Proceedings of ICCBR 2017 Workshops (CAW, CBRDL, PO-CBR), Doctoral Consortium, and Competitions co-located with the 25th International Conference on Case-Based Reasoning (ICCBR 2017), Trondheim, Norway, June 26–28, 2017. CEUR Workshop Proceedings, vol. 2028, pp. 95–103. CEUR-WS.org (2017). http://ceur-ws.org/Vol-2028/paper9.pdf
14. Silver, D., et al.: Mastering the game of go without human knowledge. Nature **550**, 354–359 (2017)
15. Taigman, Y., Yang, M., Ranzato, M.A., Wolf, L.: Deepface: closing the gap to human-level performance in face verification. In: IEEE Conference on Computer Vision and Pattern Recognition (2014)
16. Watson, I.: Case-based reasoning is a methodology not a technology. Knowl. Based Syst. **12**, 303–308 (1996)

Opportunities for Case-Based Reasoning in Personal Flow and Productivity Management

Thomas C. Eskridge[1,2(✉)] and Troy R. Weekes[2]

[1] Department of Computer Science, L3 Harris Institute for Assured Information, Florida Institute of Technology, Melbourne, FL 32901, USA

[2] Department of Human-Centered Design, Florida Institute of Technology, Melbourne, FL 32901, USA

teskridge@fit.edu, tweekes1998@my.fit.edu

Abstract. Knowledge workers can benefit from tools to support them in performing deep, concentrated work. Research in biofeedback has shown success in training relaxation, but not in directly influencing task performance. One reason for this may be the difficulties users have in contextualizing biofeedback signals for different task situations. This presents an opportunity to leverage the strengths of case-based reasoning to select the feedback mechanism that will produce the best response. This paper describes initial research into the Adaptive Choice Case-Based Reasoning (ACCBR) system, that learns from and interacts with a user to assist them in achieving greater concentration and productivity.

Keywords: Neurofeedback · EEG · Flow · CBR

1 Introduction

By some estimates, there are currently more than 1 billion knowledge workers in the world [1]. Knowledge work includes "non-routine cognitive jobs" that require considerable amounts of concentration and creativity to perform. This work benefits from long stretches of uninterrupted work, resulting in feelings of "flow", where work is simultaneously challenging, engaging, and enjoyable [2].

There are numerous productivity enhancement tools available to assist knowledge workers in keeping track of tasks, appointments, and other necessities of their work life [3]. However, there is little work on developing tools to support workers in achieving and maintaining flow states for longer periods of time.

There have been numerous studies on neurofeedback therapies for a variety of conditions and diseases [4]. Specifically for the task of increasing the frequency and duration of deep, concentrated work, neurofeedback may provide the information necessary for the correct feedback signals to be delivered.

Figure 1a shows how standard neurofeedback is used by an operator performing a task. The operator must make choices based on task demands, and

I. Watson and R. Weber (Eds.): ICCBR 2020, LNAI 12311, pp. 349–354, 2020.
https://doi.org/10.1007/978-3-030-58342-2_23

then update their mental state based on the new task state and the rewards received. The operator then must integrate the neurofeedback signals with task feedback signals in order to improve task performance, which could end up being a divided attention task.

The Flow Choice Architecture (FCA) is being developed to integrate the mental state and task performance of a knowledge worker in order to suggest "nudges" that can help the knowledge worker enter and remain in flow. Nudges are external aids such as rituals, sounds, speech, or other "mental hacks" that subtly encourage behavior change [5]. If FCA classifies worker biosignals as distraction, it may "nudge" the user by showing task completion lists, highlighting the days work schedule, or verbalizing encouragement [6].

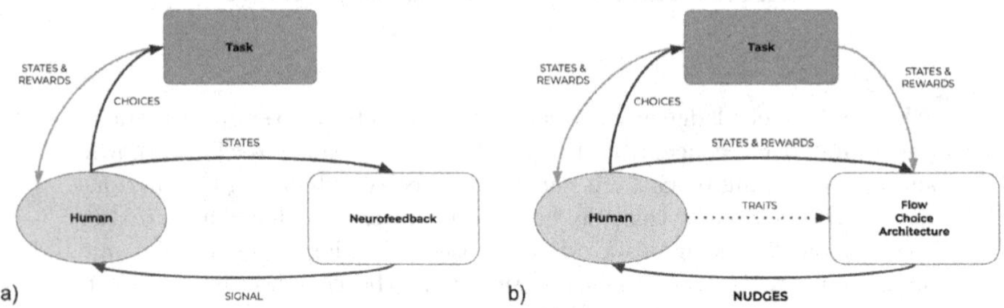

Fig. 1. (a) The user must integrate feedback from the task environment and neurofeedback. (b) The FCA observes the human and task states and reward signals to generate task-relevant nudges.

Figure 1b shows the interaction of the FCA with the knowledge worker as they perform their tasks. The mental and task states and rewards are used by the FCA to determine if a nudge is warranted. This information, including if there were previous nudges, is taken into account to determine the step most likely to influence the knowledge worker to enter flow. Nudges that have little effect on the operator's mental state will be selected less often than those that have a rapid and positive effect.

2 The Challenge Addressed

This domain features several difficult characteristics that CBR research can address with effective solutions. First, the domain requires *individualization.* The problem of motivating increased deep, concentrated work is inherently personal. The nudges that work for one person will not necessarily work for another, requiring personalization for each user. CBR case creation based on user experience provides a natural way to gather this personalized knowledge.

Second, the domain requires *context.* Although the structure of electroencephalogram (EEG) signals enables accurate tracking of user mental state, it does not contain enough information to determine the feedback signals needed to motivate increased performance. Contextual information such as time, task, and work history are also needed to determine a correct nudge. Cases provide a natural way to associate other information with the EEG signal, such as time of day, time spent working, task undertaken, operator traits, etc, to fine-tune the effectiveness of nudges. This may be an ideal representation for both storing and retrieving this contextual information.

Finally, solutions in the domain have *uncertain effects*. Nudges will be effective less than 100% of the time, meaning that even if the FCA makes the "correct" choice in nudges to suggest, the user may not give the desired response. By retrieving a set of cases similar to the current EEG, task, and context, the nudge suggestions made in FCA by the Adaptive Choice Case-based Reasoning (ACCBR) system can examine a range of alternatives and reason effectively about the exploration - exploitation tradeoff.

3 Background Research

3.1 Measuring Operator State

Evaluation of operator state was traditionally performed with subjective measures based on interviews or questionnaires, where participants assessed their state during or after a task [7]. These approaches depend on opinions of participants reported on subjective scales, and do not always assure reliable, comparable results. An alternative approach involves the monitoring of operator state using psychophysiological measures such as EEG, heart rate variability (HRV), electrodermal activity (EDA) and breathing rate.

Machine learning methods have been combined with feature selection techniques to measure a subject-independent operator workload or cognitive effort needed to perform a task [8]. Thejaswini et al. [9] used a channel-wise Support Vector Machine (SVM) classifier to detect emotional state, and achieved average classification accuracies of 79% (SEED dataset) and 76% (DEAP dataset).

3.2 CBR for Neurofeedback

Case-based reasoning has been successfully applied to the study of EEG signals in several studies. Cai et al. [10] investigated classification of depression using case representations containing four computed characteristics of EEG signals and seven other demographic features of the test subject. Using feature weighting and KNN as the retrieval mechanism, they were able to achieve a 91.25% accuracy in diagnosing depression in patients, significantly improving on 81.44% accuracy for EEG data alone and 88.97% from a previous study.

An integration of decision trees and CBR was used in [11] to classify patient EEGs into one of seven different psychological or physical disorders, including migraines and ADHD. Their work showed that even a very coarse discretization of EEG signals in conjunction with psychological and behavior features can produce accurate classification of different disorders.

Like these systems, ACCBR computes features from the raw EEG signals and combines them with other information to construct a case to be classified. However, ACCBR differs from these system in that the determination to make nudges is a continuous process, happening throughout the working day. This creates hundreds or thousands of case applications, allowing for continued learning and updating of the case base. In this sense, it is more similar to the continuous case-based reasoning work of [12].

4 ACCBR Description

ACCBR is one implementation of the "Nudge Controller" shown in Fig. 2. The purpose of ACCBR is to determine if the current mental and task state suggests that the operator would benefit from a nudge to achieve or remain in deep, concentrated work. To do this, it continually balances the stream of classifications of the EEG signals generated by the user with task and historical information to result in a decision to produce a nudge or to remain silent.

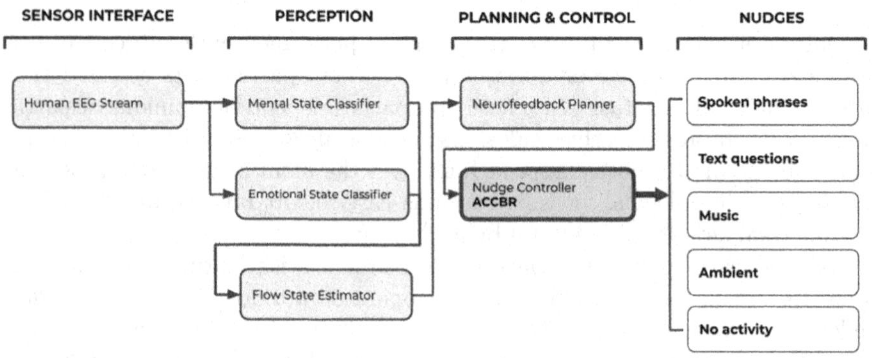

Fig. 2. Pipeline architecture of the neurofeedback-driven FCA where the modules process data on server and client threads in parallel.

4.1 ACCBR Cycle

The FCA begins with user demographic and trait information [13], knowledge of the task and task rewards and then begins on that task. FCA observes the operator and task state, and classifies the EEG signals being collected into on of the standard quadrants of the valence arousal scale, labeled: *neutral*, *sad*, *fear*, *happy*. When the classification has high confidence (i.e., when the same classification has been made several times in a row), it is combined with the task state and other contextual information to create a probe into case memory.

The probe will return one to five cases from case memory and a response based on the returned cases is generated. The response depends on the distribution of responses and the history of previous nudges. The nudge is executed, and FCA monitors operator state to determine the effectiveness of the nudge. The measurement of effectiveness comes from the transition of mental states to a more positive mental state and from the task completion status. This process continues until the end of work tasks or the operator is mentally fatigued.

5 Example of EEG Classification

Perhaps the most risky aspect of our approach is the belief that we can consistently and accurately classify EEG signals into one of the four bins indicating mental state (emotions). To alleviate this risk, we conducted an experiment to test the FCA EEG classification, which will directly affect our ability to collect high-quality cases.

In the experiment, we used the SEED-IV dataset, which contains EEG recordings from 15 participants that conducted 72 video clip trials that evoked one of four emotions: $neutral, sad, fear, happy$. Noise and artifacts such as blinks and jaw clenches were filtered from the raw EEG data and then segmented into 4-s epochs without overlap. A Fourier transform on each segment produced power spectral density (PSD) features in 5 frequency bands which were then reduced to three components using a Linear Discriminant Analysis (LDA) transformation that maximized the separability among the classes. These three components were classified using a densely-connected three-layer neural network. The dataset of 1,080 trials was randomly split 70:30 into training and test sets i.e. 756 and 354 trials respectively and run 10 times. Figure 3 shows the confusion matrix for the average of 10 runs of the experiment, which produced an average overall classification accuracy of 99% on the test trials.

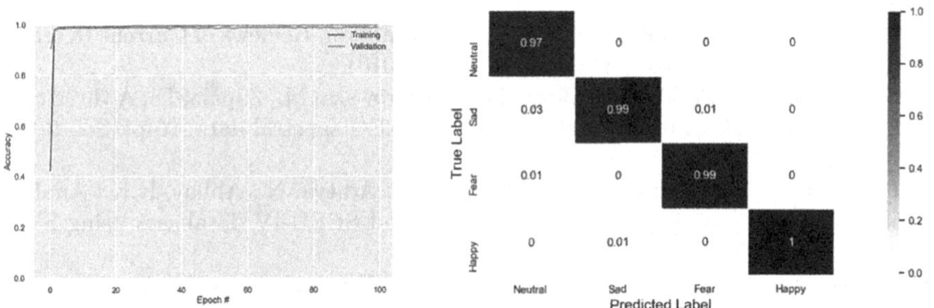

Fig. 3. Left: Training and validation set accuracy. Right: Confusion matrix.

6 Conclusions and Future Work

Our next steps in this research are to collect one- to three-hour sessions of users performing deep cognitive work tasks to determine the range of variability between users. We will use these sessions to develop individualized case bases and determine where additional efficiencies can be found.

While this is early-stage work, the EEG classification results already obtained and the methodology developed to contextualize the EEG signals shows promise for the development of a productivity tool that will support deep cognitive work.

We believe that many of the problems that are faced when working with neurofeedback and biofeedback systems in general can be addressed using the tools and techniques that are available in the case-based reasoning community. CBR systems have unique capabilities for knowledge acquisition and replay that are directly applicable to domains where there is significant uncertainty, where there are no general rules that will apply to all users, and where the signals collected on a continuous basis must be augmented with context in order to be effectively interpretable.

References

1. Craig Roth. 2019: When we exceeded 1 billion knowledge workers, December 11 2019. https://blogs.gartner.com/craig-roth/2019/12/11/2019-exceeded-1-billion-knowledge-workers/
2. Csikszentmihalyi, M., Larson, R.: Flow and The Foundations of Positive Psychology. Springer, Dordrecht (2014). https://doi.org/10.1007/978-94-017-9088-8
3. Allen, D.: Getting Things Done. Penguin, New York (2003)
4. Marzbani, H., Marateb, H.R., Mansourian, M.: Neurofeedback: a comprehensive review on system design, methodology and clinical applications. Basic Clin. Neurosci. **7**(2), 143–158 (2016)
5. Thaler, R.H., Sunstein, C.R.: Nudge: Improving Decisions About Health, Wealth, and Happiness. Penguin, New York (2009)
6. Weekes, T.R., Eskridge, T.C.: A neurofeedback-driven humanoid to support deep work. In: Proceedings of the 33rd Florida Conference on Recent Advances in Robotics, 14–16 May 2020
7. De Houwer, J., Hermans, D.: Cognition and Emotion: Reviews of Current Research and Theories. Psychology Press, New York (2010)
8. Plechawska-Wójcik, M., Tokovarov, M., Kaczorowska, M., Zapała, D.: A three-class classification of cognitive workload based on EEG spectral data. Appl. Sci. **9**(24), 5340 (2019)
9. Thejaswini, S., Ravikumar, K.M., Jhenkar, L., Aditya, N., Abhay, K.K.: Analysis of EEG based emotion detection of DEAP and SEED-IV databases using SVM. Int. J. Recent Technol. Eng **8**, 207–211 (2019)
10. Cai, H., Zhang, X., Zhang, Y., Wang, Z., Hu, B.: A case-based reasoning model for depression based on three-electrode EEG data. IEEE Trans. Affect. Comput. **11**(3), 383–392 (2020)
11. Pandey, B., Kundra, D.: Diagnosis of EEG-based diseases using data mining and case-based reasoning. Int. J. Intell. Syst. Des. Comput. **1**(1/2), 43 (2017)
12. Ram, A., Santamaría, J.C.: Continuous case-based reasoning. Artif. Intell. **90**(1–2), 25–77 (1997)
13. Weekes, T., Eskridge, T.C: Nudging into flow: optimizing productivity with a choice architecture. In: Cognitive Economics Workshop, London, UK, November 7–8 2019. Cognitive Economics Society (2019)

Author Index

Printed in the United States
By Bookmasters